ORIGINAL SIN

Two Major Trends in Contemporary Roman Catholic Reinterpretation

George Vandervelde

UNIVERSITY
PRESS OF
AMERICA

Copyright © 1981 by
University Press of America, Inc.
P.O. Box 19101, Washington, D.C. 20036

All rights reserved
Printed in the United States of America
ISBN: 0-8191-1850-8 (Perfect)
ISBN: 0-8191-1849-4 (Cloth)

Copyright © 1975 by
Rodopi of Amsterdam

Library of Congress Catalog Card Number: 81-40000

To Bea

ACKNOWLEDGEMENTS

The completion of my post-graduate studies at the Free University in Amsterdam provides a welcome occasion to thank all those who have played a special role in the preparation for and conclusion of this academic journey.

I thank the faculty of Calvin Seminary for laying the foundation for the post-graduate work that has culminated in this dissertation and the faculties of theology and philosophy of the Free University for building and enabling me to build on that basis.

To Professor G. C. Berkouwer I wish to express my sincere thanks for acting as my *promotor*. I am indebted to you far more deeply than footnotes in a study such as this could possibly indicate. That debt dates back to years before I came to Amsterdam, when I first began reading your books. And it accumulated rapidly by meeting you in person as teacher and as guide in the world of theology, particularly in the world of Roman Catholic theology. In the approach I came to take in this dissertation you left me full liberty; this testifies to the fact that in guiding your students you stimulate without dominating — that you take no pleasure in epigones. I feel greatly honored to be your forty-fifth *promovendus*.

I also wish to thank Professor J. Veenhof for being prepared to act as *coreferent*, which meant reading the entire manuscript at a relatively late stage. Your suggestions proved helpful and your enthusiasm was a source of encouragement.

A special word of thanks is due to drs. Jerald D. Gort and to drs. James E. Davison, who made room in their own busy schedules to read the manuscript. Their numerous suggestions for stylistic changes have made this a better book than it would otherwise have been.

I am grateful to the staff of the Free University Library for their services; and to Mr. W. A. Vastenhold of the library of the Katholieke Theologische Hogeschool in Amsterdam for his personal help, which greatly facilitated the research for this study.

It was the Board of Trustees of Calvin College and Seminary, Grand Rapids, Mich., who initially made it possible for me to undertake a course of graduate studies in Amsterdam by awarding me the Diamond Jubilee Scholarship. The Canada Council enabled me to continue and complete this study by awarding me a Doctoral Fellowship. To both of these bodies I express my sincere gratitude.

My thanks also goes to the staff of Rodopi for their excellent service and especially to Mr. P. Schippers for the personal interest with which he has guided and coordinated the production and publication of this book.

I am deeply grateful to my parents and parents-in-law for their prayers, their love and their interest that spanned even the gap of thousands of miles between us in the "old country" and them in the "new." Specifically, I wish to thank my Father: his dedication to the Gospel message regarding the integral meaning of Christ for all of life has had a lasting influence on me — an influence which, enriched and deepened by further study and reflection, can hopefully be felt in, through and beneath the analysis presented in this book.

Bea, how much you have meant for the completion of this project is inadequately expressed by dedicating this book to you. "To Bea or not to Bea" — that was no question.

TABLE OF CONTENTS

Abbreviations

Introduction: HISTORICAL BACKGROUND AND
                CONTEMPORARY PROBLEMS 1

A. HISTORICAL HIGHLIGHTS 2
    1. The Greek Fathers 3
    2. Latin Fathers before Augustine 7
    3. Pelagius 10
    4. Augustine 14
    5. The Councils of Carthage and Orange 21
    6. Anselm 26
    7. Thomas Aquinas 28
    8. The Council of Trent 32
    9. Post-Tridentine Development 41
B. THE CURRENT DISCUSSION 42
    1. Immediate Occasion 42
    2. Roman Catholic "Monopoly" 44
    3. Deeper Questions 49
    4. Testcase for Hermeneutics 51
C. NATURE, AIM, SCOPE AND STRUCTURE OF THIS STUDY 52

PART ONE: FRAMEWORK FOR A SOLUTION

Chapter I. MAN AS HISTORICAL BEING:
           FREEDOM AND SITUATEDNESS 57

A. PERSON AND SITUATION: SCHOONENBERG 61
    1. The Problematic Coexistence of Solidarity
       and Personal Responsibility in Scripture 61

  2. The Coexistence of Person and Nature 66
    a. Man as free person 66
    b. Man as embodied person and personalized body 68
  3. The Coexistence of Person and Situation 73
    a. Free decision with respect to determinative situation 75
    b. Capacity for free decision within determinative situation 77
    c. Free decision and inner situational determinant 80
B. TRANSCENDENTAL SUBJECT AND SPATIOTEMPORAL
  MEDIATION: RAHNER AND WEGER 84
  1. Human Nature: Necessary Transcendence
    and Spatiotemporal Mediation 86
  2. Human Person: Free Appropriation of Human Nature 90
    a. Appropriation of transcendental dynamic 91
    b. Appropriation of historically mediated transcendence 93
      i. History as medium of self-expression 95
      ii. History as medium of alien impressions 99
      iii. History as medium of self-realization and of self-alienation . . . 102

Chapter II. THE DUAL GOD-MAN RELATIONSHIP:
      GRACE AND NATURE 107

A. THE UNITY AND DUALITY OF NATURE
  AND GRACE AS GROUNDED IN GOD 109
  1. The Mutual Supposition of Nature and Grace 110
  2. The Distinction of Nature and Grace 111
  3. The Unity of Nature and Grace 114
  4. The Indispensable Duality of Nature and Grace 117
B. THE UNITY AND DUALITY OF NATURE
  AND GRACE AS MAN'S SITUATION 120
  1. The Unity of Nature and Grace 121
  2. The Duality Essential for Grace as Expressed in Human Freedom . . . 121
  3. The Supernatural *Existential* as Unifying Bond 124
C THE HISTORICAL GOD-MAN RELATIONSHIP: SALVATION HISTORY 127
  1. Evolutionary Background – Salvation History as Ascent 128
  2. Salvation History and Mediated Freedom 135
  3. Universal Scope and Particular Concentrations 138

PART TWO: ORIGINAL SIN AS HISTORICAL SITUATION

Chapter III. SITUATIONAL PRIVATION OF GRACE AS SIN . . . 147

A. PRELIMINARY DEFINITION AND QUALIFICATION
   OF ORIGINAL SIN AS SITUATION 147
B. HERMENEUTICAL PROBLEMS 150
   1. Choice of Starting Point and Traditional Options 150
   2. Encounter of Past and Present in the Question of Guilt 153
C. SITUATIONAL PRIVATION OF GRACE AS ANALOGICAL GUILT . . 155
   1. Original Sin as Sin by Attribution: Schoonenberg 155
      a. Analytical Dissociation 155
      b. Analogical Association 159
   2. Guilt as *Terminus a quo* or *ad quem*: Rahner and Weger 165
      a. From "Guilt" to "Original Sin" 166
      b. From "Divinizing Grace" via "Privation of Grace" to "Guilt" . . . 168
         i. Privation of grace as "unholiness" 172
         ii. Situational privation counter to God's will 174
         iii. Development from prepersonal privation to personal sin 176

Chapter IV. THE SITUATIONAL IMPACT OF ORIGINAL SIN
            UPON FREE ACTS 187

A. SITUATIONAL BONDAGE OF THE FREE WILL 187
B. ORIGINAL SIN AS SITUATIONAL DETERMINANT
   AND APPROPRIATION AS FREE SELF-DETERMINATION 196
   1. The Interaction between Being-situated and Self-situating 196
   2. Inevitable *Nachvollzug* and Free Appropriation 201
C. SITUATIONAL CONCUPISCENCE AND INTEGRATING FREE ACT . . 203
   1. Natural Lack of *Integritas* and Personal Integration 203
   2. Concupiscence in a Sinful Situation 206

Chapter V. PRIVATION OF GRACE—UNIVERSAL SITUATION? . 209

A. SOURCES OF THE PROBLEM 210
   1. Evolution, Polygenesis, Situational Nexus 210
   2. The Situational Presence of Grace 211
B. PROPOSED SOLUTIONS 214
   1. The Sin of the World and a "Second" Fall 215
      a. "The Fall"—a History of Falling 216

| i. The history of sin as descent 217
| ii. Contours of the history of sin 219
| iii. Sin-of-the-world, a *history* of *sin* 220
| b. The Second-fall Hypothesis 221
| i. Its intended function 224
| ii. Its intrinsic inadequacy and general incongruity 226
| iii. Its abandonment and the lingering problem 229
| 2. Definitive Fall within Polygenetic Origin 234
| a. Its Foundational Function 234
| b. Its Etiological Anchorage 238

Chapter VI. THE SACRAMENTAL CHURCH AS GROUND OF REINTERPRETATION 241

A. THE SACRAMENTAL BASIS 242
  1. Schoonenberg 242
  2. Weger 248
  3. Rahner 250
B. THE SACRAMENTAL MEDIUM AS PROBLEMATIC MESSAGE 254

PART THREE: ORIGINAL SIN AS PERSONAL SIN

Chapter VII. ORIGINAL SIN AS THE UNIVERSALITY OF ACTUAL SINS: A. VANNESTE 259

A. THE DYNAMICS OF RADICAL REINTERPRETATION 259
  1. Radical Reinterpretation 259
  2. The Anthropological Mainspring and the
     Soteriological Basis of Reinterpretation 260
B. THE REDUCTION OF ORIGINAL SIN TO
   THE UNIVERSALITY OF ACTUAL SINS 261
  1. The Demythologization of Original Sin
     as Condition (*Peccatum Originale Originatum*) 262
  2. Weakened Free Will contra Enslaved (Free) Will 267
C. THE CONTINGENCY AND THE ABSOLUTE
   UNIVERSALITY OF ACTUAL SINS 274
  1. The Problem 274
  2. Beyond the Self-Imposed Boundary of "History" 277
     a. Mythological Transcendence 278
     b. Theological Transcendence 280
     c. Implications for the Existential Meaning of the Doctrine 283

Chapter VIII. ORIGINAL SIN AS THE DEPTH DIMENSION
OF PERSONAL SIN: U. BAUMANN 289

A. DOMINANT MOTIFS: *SOLA GRATIA*
   AND PERSONAL RESPONSIBILITY 290
B. CONTEXT AND FUNCTION OF THE TRADITIONAL DOCTRINE . . 291
   1. Context: Moralism and Actualism 292
   2. Function 294
      a. Empirical Explanation 294
      b. Counterweight to Moralism 297
C. THE DEPTH DIMENSION OF SIN 300
   1. Biblical Foundation 300
   2. Threefold Expression 302
      a. Radicality 302
      b. Totality 304
      c. Universality 308

Epilogue: LINGERING PROBLEMS
AND POSSIBLE PERSPECTIVES 313

A. ORIGINAL SIN AS PRIVATION OF GRACE 313
B. SITUATION 318
C. FREEDOM, FATE AND HISTORY 322
D. HISTORY, SIN AND SALVATION 326

Selected Bibliography 335

ABBREVIATIONS

AAS	*Acta Apostolicae Sedis*
AER	*American Ecclesiastical Review*
ALG	*Aurelius Augustinus. Lehrer der Gnade* (text and trans.)
AvT	*Annalen van het Thijmgenootschap*
CT	*Concilium Tridentinum. Diariorum, Actorum, Epistularum, Tractatuum, nova collectio*
CollBG	*Collationes Brugenses et Gandavenses*
DO-C	*Documentatie Centrum Concilie*
DocVatII	*Documents of Vatican II*
DS	Denzinger-Schönmetzer, *Enchiridion Symbolorum*
DThC	*Dictionaire de Théologie Catholique*
EB	*Enchiridion Biblicum*
EphM	*Ephemerides Mariologicae*
EThL	*Ephemerides Theologicae Lovanienses*
HC	*Herders Correspondence*
IDO-C	*International Documentation on the Conciliar Church*
Jaarboek	*Jaarboek van het Werkgenootschap van Katholieke Theologen in Nederland*
JESt	*Journal of Ecumenical Studies*
JThSt	*Journal of Theological Studies*
LThK	*Lexikon für Theologie und Kirche.* 11 vols.
MS	*Mysterium Salutis* (German edition)
MThZ	*Münchner Theologische Zeitschrift*
NM	*De Nieuwe Mens*
NRTh	*Nouvelle Revue Théologique*
PL	*Patrologia Latina*, ed. J. P. Migne
RSPhTh	*Revue des Sciences Philosophiques et Théologiques*
RSR	*Revue des Sciences Religieuses*

SM	*Sacramentum Mundi* (German edition)
StZ	*Stimmen der Zeit*
ThD	*Theology Digest*
ThG	*Theologie der Gegenwart*
ThLZ	*Theologische Literaturzeitung*
ThuPh	*Theologie und Philosophie*
ThPQ	*Theologisch-praktische Quartalschrift*
ThQ	*Theologische Quartalschrift*
ThSt	*Theological Studies*
TThZ	*Trierer Theologische Zeitschrift*
TvTh	*Tijdschrift voor Theologie*
WuW	*Wort und Wahrheit*
ZKG	*Zeitschrift für Kirchengeschichte*
ZKTh	*Zeitschrift für katholische Theologie*

Note regarding translations:

An e, g, or d appended to an abbreviation has reference to, respectively, an English, German or Dutch translation of the original work.

Whenever practicable, English translations of publications in German, Dutch or French were used. When a more precise translation of a passage in the original was required, I have supplied my own; this is indicated in the footnote by listing the original work before the translation.

INTRODUCTION HISTORICAL BACKGROUND
AND CONTEMPORARY PROBLEMS

In the past two decades the doctrine of original sin has been the subject of a host of studies and reinterpretations by Roman Catholic theologians.[1] This flood of literature necessitates a choice between presenting either a complete survey of the great variety of reinterpretations or a thorough analysis of a few of its major streams. The present study[2] represents an attempt at the latter.[3] Two main currents of thought within contemporary Roman Catholic theology have been chosen, namely, the interpretation of original sin as historical situation, on the one hand, and as personal sin, on the other.[4] These two streams represent contrasting reinterpretations within Catholic thinking and bear significance as alternative approaches to a specific ecclesiastical doctrine.

The situationalists attempt a contemporary, *creative reinterpretation* of the fruits of a typically Roman Catholic theological *tradition*. The very core of their conception of original sin is a product of late (post-Tridentine) Roman Catholic theology. At the same time they attempt to integrate this

1 See sec. B, 1 below.
2 For a description of the delimitation and of the aim of this study, see sec. C below.
3 For *surveys* of the current discussion, see Urs Baumann, *Erbsünde? Ihr traditionelles Verständnis in der Krise heutiger Theologie* ("Ökumenische Forschungen"; Freiburg i. Br.: Herder, 1970), 91-108; J. L. Conner, "Original Sin: Contemporary Approaches," *ThSt* XXIX (1968), 215-40; Herbert Haag, "The Original sin Discussion, 1966-1971," *JESt*, X (1973), 259-89; idem, "Die hartnäckige Erbsünde: Überlegungen zu einigen Neuerscheinungen," *ThQ*, CL (1970), 358-66, 436-56; CLI (1971), 70-86; William Hamilton, "New Thinking on Original Sin," *HC*, IV (1967), 135-41; J. M. Reese, "Current Thinking on Original Sin," *AER*, CLVII (1967), 92-100; Karl Schmitz-Moorman, *Die Erbsünde: Überholte Vorstellung, bleibender Glaube* (Olten: Walter-Verlag, 1969), 59-75.
4 For the sake of convenience, the advocates of these alternative reinterpretations will frequently be referred to as situationalists and personalists, respectively. It must be kept in mind, however, that these designations have reference to contrasting *approaches to the doctrine of original sin,* not necessarily to contrasting philosophical positions. The general philosophical framework of these opposite interpretations of original sin may be quite similar (see ch. VII, sec. A,2; and ch. VIII, introductory paragraphs and sect. A).

traditional datum with a world view, with thought-forms and with a theological perspective each of which differs incisively from its counterparts in the traditional view. This creative confrontation of the present with a theological tradition is the source of the intriguing dynamics that energizes the situational reinterpretation of original sin. The personalists, by contrast, choose a much more radical approach to the reinterpretation of original sin, namely, a break with the dominant stream in their theological tradition. The personal reinterpretation derives its significance, therefore, not merely from its, often explicit, opposition to the situational *categories of reinterpretation* but, more deeply, from its, often implicit, opposition to the situationalists' understanding of the *essential meaning of the doctrine of original sin*. In fact, the opposition with respect to the categories of reinterpretation – "person" versus "situation" – reflects a prior divergence in the understanding of the nature of original sin.

Before considering the contemporary setting of the reinterpretation of original sin as historical situation and as personal sin, it is important to take cognizance of their larger historical setting. For each of these contemporary reinterpretations of original sin is – deliberately or inadvertently – a creative reconstitution of various facets of the history of this doctrine. Moreover, even this creative reconstitution has as its point of unity a basic assessment of man's historical condition vis-à-vis God – an assessment that has its antecedents in a limited range of historical options. In this twofold manner, the power of history, while not doing away with the originality of contemporary reinterpretations, makes itself felt.

A. HISTORICAL HIGHLIGHTS

The scope of this study precludes a full survey of the history of the doctrine of original sin, for the story of the development of this doctrine appears to contain a kaleidoscopic variety of conceptions,[5] some of them seemingly contradictory – even when propounded by a single person. In view

---

5 For the history of the doctrine of original sin, see: Julius Gross, *Geschichte des Erbsündendogmas: Ein Beitrag zur Geschichte des Problems vom Ursprung des Übels* (4 vols.; München: Ernst Reinhardt Verlag, 1960-72). A. Gaudel, "Péché originel," *DThC,* XII, 317-606; Henri Rondet, *Le Péché originel dans la tradition patristique et théologique* ("Le signe"; Paris: Fayard, 1967); G. M Lukken, *Original Sin in the Roman Liturgy* (Leiden: Brill, 1973); F. R. Tennant, *The Sources of the Doctrines of the Fall and Original Sin* (2d ed.; New York: Schocken Books, 1968); N. P. Williams, *The Ideas of the Fall and of Original Sin: A Historical and Critical Study* (London: Longmans, Green and Co. Ltd., 1927). For the period up to the Council of Orange, see also J. N. D. Kelly, *Early Christian Doctrines* (3d ed.; London: Adam and Charles Black, 1965).

of the imposing variety of material, this section represents an attempt to sketch the salient features of successive approaches to the doctrine of original sin and to discover the assessment of man's historical condition that underlies and unifies each of these approaches. This historical presentation is limited not only because it deals only with basic streams and patterns of thought but also because it highlights only those features in a specific historical conception that provide important background material for the contemporary reinterpretations to be dealt with in this study.

1. The Greek Fathers

The Greek Fathers view man as having been created immortal,[6] or neither mortal nor immortal but capable of both,[7] or naturally mortal but rendered immortal by a special divine gift.[8] In all cases man's present subjection to death as well as to suffering, sensual passions, ignorance and weakness is in some way ascribed to sin – whether primordial or personal.[9] This physical evil, accompanied by the resultant cultural corruption, that is unleashed by sin in turn has a detrimental effect upon morality in the present. The thrust of sensual passion, the pressure of cultural decadence and the prevalence of bad examples all combine to form a powerful negative force upon man's personal decisions.[10] In fact, this force of physical and cultural evil proves to be so powerful that sin becomes a general phenomenon.[11]

The crucial question that faced the Greek Fathers at this point was that concerning the *nature* of the power of evil. If physical and cultural evil is said to be the determining cause of the generality of personal sin, no one is responsible for the latter; in fact, properly speaking, personal sin does not exist, for no one sins culpably. Especially in view of the prevalence of Manichean and gnostic dualism of that time, it was of essential importance that the Fathers break the moral strangle hold of determinism. They succeeded in

---

6 Gross, I, 76-78 (Justin), 165 (Eusebius), 171 (Epiphanius), 182 (Chrysostom). Kelly, 168, 348-49.
7 Gross, I, 82 (Theophilus of Antioch), 165-66 (Eusebius). Kelly, 168.
8 Gross, I, 78 (Tatian), 126-27, 130-32 (Athanasius), 192-95, 203-204 (Theodore of Mopsuestia). Kelly, 346-47.
9 Gross, I, 85-86, 214-16.
10 Gross, I, 76 (Justin), 83 (Theophilus of Antioch), 85 (Melito of Sardes), 105-106 (Origen), 131 (Athanasius), 141-42 (Basil the Great), 147 (Gregory of Nazianzus), 154 (Gregory of Nyssa), 168-69 (Cyril of Jerusalem), 183 (Chrysostom), 196-98 (Theodore of Mopsuestia). Cf. Kelly, 167-68.
11 Gross, I, 76 (Justin), 79-80 (Tatian), 104 (Origen), 146 (Gregory of Nazianzus), 198 (Theodore of Mopsuestia).

doing so mainly by falling back upon a certain goodness that man, as the image of God, retains. Although some of the Fathers speak of man's likeness to God as being lost,[12] except perhaps for some sparks,[13] most hold that man's natural image, usually equated with the powers of intellect and free will, remains essentially intact.[14] This retention of the image is assured because it is usually conceived of in terms of an ontic continuity, similarity or affinity with God that constitutes the very essence of man and thus cannot be lost.[15]

Although the image of God in man is thought of as being essentially retained, it is by no means viewed as being unaffected by physical evil and cultural decadence. These negative forces are thought to soil the image as dirt on a mirror,[16] corrode it as rust on iron [17] obscure it as a cloud before the sun.[18] Nevertheless, beneath this accumulation of evil, the image remains as an ontic given constituting man's nature. Therefore, in their thinking, neither physical evil, nor carnal passions, nor bad examples can coerce man to sin. Man remains free and is capable of moral virtue.[19] On that basis he can be challenged to cleanse his mirror-image and to let it shine forth in its original

---

12 The distinction between a natural lower image and a higher gratuitous image — though not always designated as, respectively, image and likeness — was prevalent in Greek theology. See Gross, I, 87 (Irenaeus), 106-107 (Origen), 126-27 (Athanasius), 151-52 (Gregory of Nyssa), 168 (Cyril of Jerusalem), 182 (Chrysostom). See also Leo Scheffczyk, "Die Frage nach der Gottebenbildlichkeit in der Modernen Theologie: Eine Einführung, "*Der Mensch als Bild Gottes,* ed. Leo Scheffczyk (Darmstadt: Wissenschaftliche Buchgesellschaft, 1969), xxxiv-xxxvi.

13 Gross, I, 79 (Tatian).

14 Gross, I, 76 (Justin), 78-80 (Tatian), 80-81 (Athenagoras), 85-87 (Irenaeus), 126, 129, 132 (Athanasius), 143 (Basil the Great), 151-52 (Gregory of Nyssa), 165, 166-67 (Eusebius), 168-69 (Cyril of Jerusalem), 171 (Epiphanius), 183-86, 190 (Chrysostom).

15 Gross, I, 78-80 (Tatian), 80-81 (Athenagoras), 96-98 (Clemens of Alexandria), 129 (Athanasius), 151-52 (Gregory of Nyssa), 157 (Evagrius), 166-67 (Eusebius). Cf. Kelly, 352.

Some notable exceptions to the trend of localizing the image of God in man ontically: Epiphanius expressly refused to localize the image of God in any part of man and confessed ignorance as to the precise nature of this image (Gross, I, 171); Chrysostom conceived of the image in terms of man's task and activity of ruling (Gross, I, 182); Theodore of Mopsuestia saw man's position as center and goal of the cosmos, his creativity and his powers of comprehension as constituting the image and likeness of God in man (Gross, I, 194-95).

16 Gross, I, 128 (Athanasius). Cf. Kelly, 347.

17 Gross, I, 152-54 (Gregory of Nyssa).

18 Gross, I, 146 (Gregory of Nazianzus).

19 In addition to the references in n. 14 above, see also Gross, I, 83 (Theophilus of Antioch), 97 (Clement of Alexandria), 114 (Origen), 142 (Basil the Great), 146 (Gregory of Nazianzus), 178-79 (Titus of Bostra).

luster.[20] This moral power retained by man does not, in their view, constitute a sovereign human power, but one that is created and sustained by God and is, moreover, aided and directed by God's special pedagogic nurture ("paideia") culminating in the life and teaching of Jesus Christ.[21]

This rough sketch of the mainstream of the thought of the Greek Fathers indicates that it left little room for an idea of original sin conceived of as a culpable reality in Adam's posterity, a reality that incisively qualifies man's will and moral capacities. Rather than original sin, the central idea is that of inherited evil and inherited (physical) corruption compounded by the legacy of social decadence.[22] Accordingly, the Greek Fathers interpreted what was to become the *locus classicus* of the doctrine of original sin, Ro 5: 12-21, mainly in terms of the death to which man became subject, whereas the sin mentioned for example in 5:12d is understood as referring to man's *personal* sins.[23]

Although the teaching of original sin appears to be foreign to the main stream of Greek theology, some patristic currents of thought adumbrate this doctrine. An awareness that man's involvement in sin lies deeper than his individual, voluntary participation in the generality of personal sins finds articulation in the theology of Irenaeus. As a counterpart of his theory of man's recapitulation in Christ, Irenaeus views all men as being seminally present in Adam, the original head of the human race.[24] By virtue of this mystical

---

20 Gross, I, 154 (Gregory of Nyssa).

21 Gross, I, 146 (Gregory of Nazianzus), 160-61 (Evagrius), 165 (Eusebius), 188-89 (Chrysostom), 198 (Theodore of Mopsuestia). Cf. Kelly, 352. For a summary of the powerful influence of the notion *paideia* (nurture) upon the Greek Church Fathers, see Gisbert Greshake, *Gnade als konkrete Freiheit: Eine Untersuchung zur Gnadenlehre Pelagius* (Mainz: Matthias-Grünewald-Verlag, 1972), 173-84.

22 Gross uses the terms *Erbübel* and *Erbverderbnis* to characterize the conception prevalent in Greek theology of man's involvement in evil; he uses the term *Erbsünde* to characterize a conception which he holds was introduced by Augustine (Gross, I, 85, 94, 180-81, 215; see also no. 35 and 98 below). In an extensive review of the first two volumes of *Geschichte des Erbsündendogmas*, Alois Stenzel severely criticizes Gross for imposing the Augustinian doctrine of original sin as a "corset" upon the preceding historical period ("Zur Geschichte des Erbsündendogmas," *Scholastik*, XXXIX (1964), 410-11).

23 See Joseph Freundorfer, *Erbsünde und Erbtod beim Apostel Paulus: Eine religionsgeschichtliche und exegetische Untersuchung über Römerbrief 5:12-21* ("Neutestamentliche Abhandlungen"; Münster i. W.: Aschendorffschen Verlagsbuchhandlung, 1927), 111-29. See also St. Lyonnet, "Le sens de *eph hoi* en Rom 5:12 et l'exégèse des Pères grecs," *Biblica*, 36 (1955), 436-56; Karl Hermann Schelke, *Paulus Lehrer der Väter: Die altkirchliche Auslegung von Römer 1-11* (Düsseldorf: Patmos-Verlag, 1956), 162-78. See also P. Schoonenberg, *Man and Sin: A Theological View*, trans. Joseph Donceel (London: Sheed and Ward, 1965), 142-45.

24 Gross, I, 90-94. Kelly, 170-74.

realism,[25] all men are conceived of as existing in Adam and hence as being personally involved in Adam's sin[26] and sharing in his guilt.[27] Though less central – and outflanked by the idea of a pre-cosmic fall – a certain sense of real solidarity of all men with Adam is also found in the writings of Origen. Transposing what is said in the letter to the Hebrews of the relation Levi-Abraham, Origen speaks of our presence in Adam's loins.[28] In addition to the idea of solidarity, Origen at times points also to a sinful stain or a body-of-sin inherited by the children from their parents.[29] Similarly, the Cappadocians entertain thoughts about man's inclusion in Adam and about "inherited sin." Without developing an elaborate theory regarding human solidarity, they speak rather unproblematically, seemingly as a matter of course, of Adam's sin as if it were our own.[30] Moreover, Basil of Caesarea urges the rich to give food to the poor in order to wipe out the sin which Adam transmitted.[31] And Gregory of Nyssa concludes from the fact that like produces like that a sinner is born from a sinner.[32]

Although these strands of thought indicate an awareness of a deeper, communal involvement of man in sin, they are definitely subordinate to a central thread of moral optimism that runs through the anthropology of the Greek Fathers. Kelly's conclusion, therefore, that some elements of the thought of the Greek Fathers contain "the outline of a real theory of original sin"[33] is qualified by his description of other elements that reflect a dominant moral optimism.[34] It is this dominant stream, as it comes to expression

25 Gross, I, 92. Gross distinguishes this mystical-religious realism from the typically philosophical realism as found in the thought of Athanasius (*ibid.*). Cf. Kelly, 172: "mystical solidarity, or rather identity." See also Freundorfer, 109.
26 Interestingly, in support of this inclusion in Adam, Irenaeus does not appeal to Ro 5:12 but to Ro 5:19 (Freundorfer, 108-10).
27 Gross, I, 92-93; Freundorfer, 109; Kelly, 172. Because Irenaeus also says that man is guilty only by his free will and because he denies that infants share in Adam's guilt, Gross contends that Irenaeus' conception of man's involvement in Adam's sin in no way includes the notion of participation in guilt (Gross, I, 94-95).
28 Gross, I, 102-104. Freundorfer, 113.
29 Gross, I, 104-106.
30 Kelly, 350.
31 Kelly, 351. To deny that this statement affirms the notion of "inherited-guilt" (*Erbschuld*), Gross uses the anachronistic argument that whatever is wiped out cannot possibly be *Erbschuld* because the inherited first sin – i.e., original sin in the sense of the dogma of Trent – can in no way be removed by almsgiving (Gross, I, 141). As a second argument in support of his interpretation, Gross points out that Basil is here addressing people whose inherited first sin has already been removed by baptism (*ibid.*) – an argument that presupposes what it intends to refute.
32 Kelly, 351.
33 *Ibid.*
34 Kelly, 352; cf. 183, 344, 349.

in the treatment of sin and evil by the Greek Fathers, that leads Gross to conclude that their thought is inimical to the idea of original sin.[35]

2. Latin Fathers before Augustin

In the writings of Tertullian certain motifs and expressions occur that appear to pave the way for later conceptions of man's deep involvement in sin. Not only does he at times use terminology suggesting the participation of all men in Adam's sin;[36] he also introduces the idea of inherited sin. This notion becomes understandable against the background of his traducianism.[37] All individual souls were in some way contained in Adam from whom they ultimately derive.[38] In this way, a notion of our presence in Adam's sin is combined with that of inherited sin. Each person, therefore, incurs a "corrupt nature" which has become his "second nature" (*alia natura*).[39] Significantly, Tertullian speaks of this corrupt nature as a reality "derived from the fault of our origin (*ex originis vitio*)."[40] By his sin Adam is said to have "infected the entire human race with his seed, making it the channel (*traducem*) of damnation."[41]

As such these statements regarding "inherited" and "original sin" appear to stand close to Augustine's notion of original sin. However, these statements are counterbalanced by a strong emphasis upon man's remaining free will and goodness. Despite the corruption of man's nature, some natural good continues to dwell in the soul. Since this goodness comes from God, it is dimmed rather than extinguished by the power of sin. Or rather, this goodness is a light that is covered by evil and thus invisible, but nevertheless present. Upon the removal of that covering through the second birth by water and the power from above, the soul sees its own full light once more.[42] This original, inextinguishable light of the soul comprises immortality, reason and the free will.[43] Not only is Tertullian a "firm believer in free-will";[44] in the

---

35 Gross speaks of an unbridgeable chasm separating the Greek *Schöpfungsoptimismus* that is reflected in the *Erbübellehre* of the Greek Fathers from the *Erbsündenpessimismus* of the Augustinian-ecclesiastical tradition (Gross, I, 112, 205; see also I, 82, 95, 162, 163, 179, 208; cf. n. 21 above).
36 Kelly, 175. Cf. Gross, I, 118.
37 Kelly, 175, 345. Cf. Gross, I, 118, n. 35.
38 Kelly, 175.
39 See Gross, I, 116. Kelly, 175-76.
40 See Kelly 176. Gross, I, 116, n. 25.
41 See Kelly, 176. Cf. Gross, I, 118.
42 See Gross, I, 119.
43 *Ibid.*
44 Kelly, 175.

course of his rejection of infant baptism, he also expressly dissociates the inherited corruption from the notion of guilt.[45] Nevertheless, despite this clear distinction between Tertullian's view of sin and evil and later developments, by his description of the legacy of evil as *tradux* and of man's corrupt nature as *originis vitium,* a seed was planted for the Augustinian doctrine of original sin.[46]

In this context, Cyprian is important, not so much for his doctrine of "original sin," but for his statements linking the necessity of infant baptism to the legacy of evil. Interestingly, however, he does not advocate the sacrament of baptism for the remission of the child's own guilt. The child is said to be afflicted with the wounds of Adam, specifically, death and evil desire. The child must be baptized unto the remission of sins, but "not his own but someone else's."[47] An extremely significant dimension of this defense of infant baptism is the dominant place that is assigned to the official church and its sacraments as exclusive medium of grace.[48] That ecclesiastical motif comes to play a crucial role in the later development of the doctrine of original sin.

Moving closer to the matrix of the classic doctrine of original sin, Ambrose and his anonymous contemporary, later designated as "Ambrosiaster," had a significant influence upon Augustine's elaboration of this doctrine. Ambrosiaster introduced an exegesis based on a Latin translation of Ro 5:12 that was to become "the pivot of the doctrine of original sin."[49] In the Latin translation available to Ambrosiaster, the crucial clause in Ro 5:12, ". . so death spread to all men *because* (or, inasmuch as [*eph hoi*]) *all men sinned,*" is rendered "in whom (*in quo*) all sinned."[50] In itself the Latin phrase *in quo* need not have caused misunderstanding of the original meaning, for, as elsewhere (Php 3:12), it could have been understood as a causal conjunction.[51] Ambrosiaster, however, may well have been the first to understand the *in quo* of Ro 5:12 as a relative conjunction with as its antecedent Adam.[52] Possibly even more significant for the development of the doctrine

---

45 Gross, I, 118-20. Kelly, 176.
46 Gross, I, 121.
47 "illi remittuntur non propria sed aliena peccata." See Gross, I, 121-23. Kelly, 176.
48 Gross, I, 123. Regarding Cyprian's addage, "extra ecclesiam nulla salus" and its subsequent history see G. C. Berkouwer, *De Kerk I: Eenheid en Katholiciteit* (Kampen: Kok, 1970), 171-202; and Karl Rahner, "Die Gliedschaft in der Kirche nach der Lehre der Enzyklika Pius' XII. 'Mystici Corporis Christi,' " *Schriften zur Theologie* (Zürich: Benziger Verlag, 1954-73), II, 7-94; hereafter this work will be cited as *Schriften.*
49 Kelly, 353-54.
50 Freundorfer, 132-37. Kelly, 354.
51 Freundorfer, 130.
52 Freundorfer, 132-34. Cf. Kelly, 354.

of original sin is Ambrosiaster's further commentary on this passage:

> It is therefore plain that all men sinned in Adam as in a lump (*quasi in massa*). For Adam himself was corrupted by sin and all whom he begat were born under sin. Thus we are all sinners from him, since we all derive from him."[53]

Especially the idea of sinning *in massa* provides fruitful soil for Augustine's reflection upon the reality of original sin.

In the writings of Ambrose, one finds an even stronger emphasis upon the idea of man's solidarity in sin by virtue of the participation of all in Adam's transgression:

> In Adam I fell, in Adam I was cast out of Paradise, in Adam I died. How should God restore me, unless He find in me Adam, justified in Christ, exactly as in that first Adam I was subject to guilt (*culpae obnoxium*) and destined to death? [54]

In view of the subsequent development of the doctrine of original sin, the realistic language with which Ambrosiaster and Ambrose describe the participation of all in Adam's transgression occasions an intriguing question: is such inclusion conceived of as entailing a sharing of all men in Adam's guilt? Whereas the descriptions of this solidarity themselves suggest an affirmative answer, many other statements display a great hesitancy on this score. The sin that we contract from Adam appears to be understood as a "tyrannical power,"[55] or as a "corrupting force."[56] Although that power in some way forces everyone into sin in its proper sense, namely, as culpable act, in itself this inclination does not involve guilt.[57] Accordingly, in contrast to Augustine, who drew a different conclusion from similar thought patterns, neither Ambrose nor Ambrosiaster consider this inherited sin in itself to be worthy of punishment.[58] Ambrose argues this point, moreover, by explicitly distinguishing our inherited, alien unrighteousness for which we shall *not* be punished from our personal sins for which we *shall* be punished.[59]

Despite their realistic language concerning man's solidarity in sin, Ambrosiaster and Ambrose stop short not only of the idea of guilt by inheritance and participation but also of the idea of moral impotence due to willful aversion from God. On the contrary, both hold a rather optimistic view of man's present condition. According to Ambrosiaster, human nature retains the capacity to know and to choose the good, leading man effectively to righteousness and faith.[60] And although Ambrose recognizes that the serpent's

---

53 See Kelly, 354; Freundorfer, 134; Gross, I, 231-32.
54 See Kelly, 354; Gross, I, 239.
55 Gross, I, 234 (with reference to Ambrosiaster), 242 (with reference to Ambrose).
56 Kelly, 354 (with reference to Ambrose).
57 Gross, I, 234. Kelly, 354-55. Freundorfer, 135.
58 Gross, I, 236, 241-42. Kelly, 355. Freundorfer, 135.
59 Kelly, 355. Gross, I, 241-42.
60 Gross, I, 236.

poison has weakened man's moral powers, causing him to limp, he does not consider man to have been morally paralyzed.[61] This positive view of man's present condition is also reflected by the fact that Ambrosiaster's exegesis of Ro 5:12 does not become an integral part of his conception of the influence of Adam's sin. In his interpretation of the rest of Ro 5:12-21, for example, he attributes the death of all men to their imitation of Adam's sin.[62] In line with the exegesis of the Greek Fathers, Ambrosiaster's interpretation of Ro 5:12-21 ascribes the dominant role, not to original, but to personal sin.[63]

3. Pelagius

Appalled by the moral indifference and defeatism of the hosts of nominal Christians that were flooding the Church of his time, Pelagius began a counter-offensive, teaching and preaching Christianity as a new way of life.[64] It was in service of this mobilization campaign that Pelagius held before his listeners a picture of man's historical condition that was to bring him in direct conflict with Augustine. This confrontation is significant, not merely for its historical repercussions, but also in terms of its historical antecedents, namely the rootage of Pelagius' optimistic assessment of man in specific Greek traditions.[65]

The core of Pelagius' view of man's present condition is found in the conviction that human nature is and remains basically good.[66] Hence, by the power of his nature, specifically his free will, man is capable of the good and even of attaining unto the perfection of sinlessness (*impeccantia*).[67] Augus-

61 Gross, I, 241-43.
62 Ambrosiaster's exegesis of Ro 5:12, says Freundorfer, represents a *Fremdkörper* within the rest of his commentary on Ro 5 (Freundorfer, 136).
63 Freundorfer, 136-37.
64 See Greshake, 27-30. Gross, I, 275-76. Peter Brown, "Pelagius and his Supporters: Aims and Environment," *JThSt,* XIX (1968), 275-76. Bernhard Lohse, *Epochen der Dogmengeschichte* (Stuttgart: Kreuz-Verlag, 1963), 112-13.
65 Gross calls the *Schöpfungsoptimismus* of the Greek tradition the principal root of Pelagianism (Gross, I, 205; cf. 279) and points to the Stoic origin of Pelagius' central thesis concerning human nature (Gross, I, 276). Greshake, too, traces the Greek origin of many facets of Pelagius' thought (Greshake, 158-92). He concludes that there is not a theological motif in Pelagius' theology that has not, in one way or another, emerged in Greek theology (Greshake, 184).
66 A. Vanneste, *Het dogma van de erfzonde: Zinloze mythe of openbaring van een grondstructuur van het menselijk bestaan?* ("Woord en Beleving"; Tielt: Lannoo, 1969), 50-53, 67. Gross, I, 279.
67 Gross, I, 276, 279. Kelly, 358-60. Greshake, 66-67. Greshake contends that for Pelagius *impeccantia* was merely a limiting concept, held before the Christian as a stimulus to virtuous acts, rather than a concretely realizable goal (Greshake, 67). In the same vein, Pelagius argues that even if it were true that man cannot help but sin, it would be ruinously demoralizing to inform him of such inability (Greshake, 87).

tine's prayer, "Give what Thou commandest and command what Thou wilt," by virtue of its pessimistic view of the capabilities of human nature, Pelagius finds impalatable. Instead, he proceeds from the assumption that God does not command anything of which man as creature is not himself capable.[68]

This positive evaluation of man's present condition does not mean that Pelagius is oblivious to the power of sin. Despite his contention that some men had lived sinlessly in the old covenant, he acknowledges that, strangely enough, since the coming of Christ sin had become general.[69] Pelagius explained this grip of sin upon the lives of men by Adam's bad example and its imitation by his offspring. It is important to note that this imitation theory is not a superficial attempt to explain the universal spread of sin as a conscious copying process: man, confronted with an external example, consciously chooses to "do the same thing." The example of sin is, in Pelagius' conception doubtlessly followed willingly, but it has greater power over man than an incidental external example does. This power becomes understandable from a consideration of Pelagius' view of the contrast between the *imago Dei* and the *imago Adae* and in terms of his emphasis upon the force of habit or custom (*consuetudo*).

Adam was created in the image of God. This image is a dynamic gift that enables and directs man to reflect God in his acts.[70] Since God is reflected especially in righteousness, the image of God is increasingly realized as man lives (up)rightly in all his tasks and activities.[71] To the extent that man progresses towards the goal of ever greater likeness unto God, he increasingly manifests God's marvellous gifts and thus becomes as it were an ever clearer "transparency" of *God's* glory.[72] When Adam sinned, it was this image of God, man's God-given nature, task and law, that was obscured and in a certain sense corrupted.[73] Due to the fall, the *imago Adae* eclipsed, as it were, the *imago Dei*. The law inhering in man's nature that enables man to discern between right and wrong has fallen into almost total oblivion and is fragmented.[74] It is this detrimental force of the *imago Adae* that gains historical power by changing the concrete situation for posterity.[75] Man does not simply confront this situation as an external reality that he comes upon in his

---

68 Gross, I, 277. Kelly, 357. Greshake, 52.
69 Greshake, 99.
70 Greshake, 54-56.
71 Greshake, 56-57.
72 Greshake, 57, 69.
73 Greshake, 81-82.
74 Greshake, 81.
75 Greshake, 83.

free decisions; rather, this situation confronts man as a magnitude that precedes and qualifies his free decisions, a present dynamic that leads him to sin.[76] Within this dynamic of the *imago Adae,* sin attains the power of custom, a power so great, says Pelagius, that man appears to be born unto perdition and begins to sin *quasi naturaliter.*[77] By force of habit, sin attains a power akin to that of nature — sin becomes as it were "second nature."[78] As his thoughts concerning the image of Adam and concerning the force of habit indicate, it is an oversimplification to say that Pelagius thought lightly of the power of sin.

That Pelagius became the object of Augustine's severe criticism in spite of Pelagius' recognition of the power of sin can best be understood by considering his conception of its remedy, God's grace. In Pelagius' thought, the most fundamental meaning of grace is God's gift of man's good nature (*bonum naturae*) which consists primarily of the capability of freely choosing and doing the good.[79] All other forms of grace are subservient to the re-activation of the grace of this creation-dynamic.[80] Besides this foundational grace, Pelagius points to various concretizations of grace. In the first place, he speaks of the specifically redemptive grace of the forgiveness of personal sins.[81] Since all adults have in fact committed personal sins, everyone of them is in need of this new start that is given without any merit and appropriated only by faith.[82] In addition to redemptive grace, Pelagius recognizes basically two other concretizations of grace, more directly linked to the foundational grace of human nature, namely, the law or teaching and the person and life of Jesus Christ.

The law finds its articulation in the Old Testament commandments, centrally in the command to love God and one's neighbor.[83] It is only in this *explicit articulation* that the law represents a special form or concretization of grace. *Originally* the law is simply identical with the (good) human nature in its directedness to God.[84] Since this natural law is covered, obscured,

76 Greshake, 84, 88.
77 Greshake, 88.
78 Greshake, 89-91, Gross, I, 278.
79 Gross, I, 276, 279. Greshake, 121, 143. Cf. Kelly, 358.
80 Greshake, 121, 143.
81 Greshake, 101-11, 145. Kelly, 359-60.
82 Greshake, 101-107. Infants have, of course, not committed any sins, so that they are not baptized, according to Pelagius, "in the remission of sins" (see Greshake, 108-109; Gross, 278; Kelly, 359-60).
83 Greshake, 95.
84 Greshake, 76, 81, 94, 100. This identification of human nature and law is a remnant of Stoicism, which becomes evident in Pelagius' adoption of the Stoic imperative, *vivere secundum naturam* (see Greshake, 204, n. 45).

fragmented and even corrupted by sin, God graciously grants positivizations of this inner law. Thus, that which nature possesses intrinsically becomes externally audible and visible in order to impinge anew upon man's inner conscience.[85] In an extremely apt analogy, Pelagius compares the function of the external law to the mould that has been used to make a statue. After the original "image" (of God) has become damaged or defaced, a replica can be made by means of this mould.[86] The inner mould of human nature is graciously externalized so that man can conform to his original image once more. In the external law, therefore, man encounters his proper self.[87] The law is a mirror in which man can see his own true image.[88] This encounter of man and law is captured in more dynamic terms by Greshake's designation "Resonanzgeschehen": the divine directive articulated in the external law strikes the good nature that in some form remains in man and effects or makes possible an appropriate response.[89]

The second major specific form of grace is Jesus Christ. He is the fullest concretization of the original grace of nature.[90] In His teaching and personal example, Christ is the most concrete form (mould) of the original gracious creation dynamic of man's free nature.[91] As the *direct*[92] image of God, Christ is a mirror of what man is and ought to be.[93] Confronted with God's grace-in-person, man's *memoria* — the noetic-ontological link with his original nature — is actualized and man is unveiled once more as the image of God.[94] In this way, Christ's "example" does not simply abandon man to his "own" powers of imitation. Rather, imitation of Christ is made possible by participation in Christ, i.e., in His grace, in His nature.[95] Even more powerfully than the form of the law, the image of God embodied in Christ's example effects a resonating response in man's deepest being.[96]

The crux of Pelagius' understanding of the efficacy of special grace lies, of course, in the presupposition that despite the defacement and corruption

85 Greshake, 96.
86 Greshake, 94.
87 Greshake, 95.
88 Greshake, 86.
89 Greshake, 97.
90 Greshake, 113.
91 Greshake, 114-17.
92 In distinction from man who is an image of an image, namely, of the arch-image, Jesus Christ (see Greshake, 54-55).
93 Greshake, 121.
94 *Ibid.* For the role which the notion of *memoria* plays in Pelagius' ontology of grace, see Greshake, 96, 121, 123.
95 See Greshake, 113-15, 123, 131-33; cf. 75.
96 Greshake, 121; cf. 117.

caused by sin, man remains *essentially* good. Precisely as foundational form of grace the goodness of human nature provides an ontological substratum for the special forms of grace.[97] It is basic presupposition concerning man's retention of a certain natural goodness — however minimal — that explains Augustine's frontal attack upon Pelagius' position.

4. Augustine

It is rather disconcerting to learn that the "Father" of the doctrine of original sin, as Gross calls Augustine,[98] did not draw a single and clear picture of his "offspring" but instead left us with a collage of various conceptions.[99] Fortunately, this collage does have a unifying center. From that focal point it becomes clear that the collage is meant to depict man as being so deeply enmeshed in sin that his only hope of salvation is the forgiving and redeeming grace that appeared in Jesus Christ.[100] It is this basic conviction concerning man's condition as revealed by the grace bestowed in Jesus Christ that leads Augustine to identify Pelagius as a foe of the heart of the gospel.[101]

Stated in these rather general terms, Augustine's entire polemic against Pelagius appears to rest upon a massive misunderstanding, for in many ways Pelagius himself may be seen as an apostle of grace, a man whose moral

---

97 Greshake, 97. The idea of an ontological continuum between man in his present condition and God's grace in Jesus Christ is implicit not only in the idea of resonance-effect and *memoria*, but also in Pelagius' conception of man as the image of God (see Greshake, 59-60, 69) and in his conception of human nature (see Greshake, 75, 123).

98 Gross, I, 375; cf. 186, 294, 348, 349, 353, 368; see also Gross, II, 572 where Gross speaks of "die von Augustinus ... ersonnene Lehre von der Vererbung der Adamssünde als solcher mittels der Zeugung..." (emphasis added). This view of the origin of the doctrine of original sin is reflected in the volume titles of his *Geschichte des Erbsündendogmas*. Whereas each of the last three volumes are entitled *Entwicklungsgeschichte des Erbsündendogmas*, the first volume, which concludes with an extensive treatment of Augustine's view, is entitled *Entstehungsgeschichte des Erbsündendogmas*. See Stenzel's criticism of this view of the origin and development of the doctrine of original sin (*Scholastik*, XXXIX (1964), 408-11; see n. 22 above).

99 Gross, I, 319. Cf. Baumann, 33-34; A. Vanneste, "Saint Paul et la doctrine augustienne du péché originel," *Studiorum Paulinorum Congressus Internationalis Catholicus 1961* ("Analecta Biblica, 17-18"; Rome: Biblical Institute Press, 1963), II, 516.

100 See Gross, I, 273-74; Vanneste, *Studiorum*, II, 518-22. See also W. Köhler, *Dogmengeschichte als Geschichte des christlichen Selbstbewusstseins: Von den Anfängen bis zur Reformation* (2d ed. rev.; Zürich, Niehans, 1943), 123: "So ist die Gnadenlehre die Voraussetzung für Augustins Sündenlehre gewesen, nicht umgekehrt. Die Sündenlehre ist die Wiederspiegelung der Gnadenlehre."

101 Vanneste, *Het Dogma*, 52. Idem, "L'histoire du dogme du péché originel," [review of Gross, *Geschichte* I], *EThL*, XXXVIII (1962), 902.

imperatives are buttressed by an embracive "ontology of grace."[102] But although misunderstandings undoubtedly marr it, at heart the polemic involves a real and basic divergence of positions.[103] It is precisely Pelagius' embracive "ontology of grace" with its fundamental identification of grace with the good of human nature that is the factual bone of contention. From Augustine's viewpoint any identification of grace with human nature could not but appear as a fundamental illusion that obscures the radicality of man's enslavement to sin and deprecates the radicality of the remedy provided in Jesus Christ.[104] This basic divergence regarding the meaning of redeeming grace in Christ is clearly reflected in a corresponding divergence regarding the meaning of "nature." The latter divergence is a direct consequence of Augustine's rejection of a basic identification of grace with human nature. Between bondage and freedom, between sin and grace there is, in Augustine's view, no middle ground, i.e., no natural dynamic of "grace" inclining man to the good.[105] Greshake paraphrases Augustine's most incisive criticism by stating that if a middle ground between Adam and Christ were real, Christ would have died in vain,[106] for then, indeed, Christ's *life* as teacher and example would have sufficed, namely, as aid facilitating the salvation of nature.[107] Whereas Pelagius viewed nature as an abiding good root of human acts, Augustine viewed nature as being taken up in a deeper root, namely, either that of love for God or that of self-love.[108] To these "totally different" conceptions of human nature[109] correspond two divergent conceptions of the grace that appeared in Jesus Christ. These conceptions, in turn, represent articulations of two different fundamental experiences of reality, more specifically, of man's position vis-à-vis God's revelation in Jesus Christ.[110]

---

102 H. H. Esser, *Das Paulusverständnis des Pelagius nach seinem Pauluskommentar* (Bonn: Unpublished Dissertation, 1961), 54. See also Gross I, 277; Greshake, 195.

103 See Greshake, 68, 72-75, 195-97, 200 (n. 18), 230-52.

104 Greshake, 196-97, 230-52.

105 Greshake, 200, 203.

106 Greshake, 200-201. Accordingly, Augustine frequently quotes I Cor 1:17 ("ne evacuetur crux Christi") in opposition to Pelagius' view (see Vanneste, *Studiorum*, II, 521).

107 Gross, I, 277.

108 Greshake, 203. Cf. Vanneste, *Het Dogma*, 67. In *Gratia Christi*, I, XVIII, 19 (*PL* XLIV, 369-70; *ALG*, II, 346-47) Augustine explicitly rejects Pelagius' assertion that the root of good and evil is one and the same, namely, man's free will. Augustine then proceeds by positing *caritas* and *cupiditas* as opposite roots of good and evil, of virtue and vice (*ibid.*, XX, 21 [*PL*, XLIV, 370; *ALG*, II, 348-49]).

109 Greshake, 203.

110 Greshake, 197. Greshake frequently points to this basic difference in *Grundhaltung* or *Grunderfahrung* (Greshake, 196-97, 231-32, 250-51). Unfortunately, in his

Subservient to his understanding of man's condition as unveiled by Christ's life and death, Augustine's doctrine of original sin is essentially an attempt to articulate the concrete nexus within which the deep-seated root of sin thrives. One of the prevalent conceptions by means of which he attempts to express this nexus is the familiar idea of man's inclusion in Adam.[111] Supported by his understanding of *"in quo omnes peccaverunt"* (Ro 5:12) as a relative clause, with as its antecedent, Adam,[112] Augustine depicted our involvement in Adam's transgression more vividly than any theologian before him.[113] By means of this conception, Augustine attempts to maintain both that sin, also original sin in us, is a matter of the will, and that this will is basically misdirected from the beginning of our individual existence.[114] The seed of our common human nature was present in Adam and thus we in him.[115] By birth all men belong to Adam and his sin, just as all who are reborn belong to Christ.[116]

Besides conceiving of original sin in terms of inclusion in Adam, Augustine also views Adam's sin as being perpetuated in and by concupiscence, which is in some way identified with original sin. The difficulty in understanding Augustine's idea of concupiscence lies in the fact that this idea too compromises several seemingly contradictory elements.[117] It is viewed as punishment for Adam's sin and at the same time as the cause and as the essence of original sin as condition.[118] It is equated with *lex peccati, cupiditas* and *libido.*[119]

critical analysis of the divergences between the positions of Pelagius and Augustine (Greshake, 193-274), Greshake allows differences regarding the *operation* of grace (the question concerning the interior and exterior operation of grace, for example) to dominate and obscure the more basic and decisive difference concerning the *nature* of grace (in addition to the references in nn. 102-109, consider the following clear statement of this decisive difference: "Deswegen auch ist für Augustin nicht – wie bei Pelagius – die menschliche Natur die Grundgestalt der Gnade, sondern die Versöhnung des Sünders am Kreuz" [Greshake, 226]).

111 See Gross, I, 319-22.
112 Freundorfer, 139-46. Eearlier, Augustine had held that *peccatum,* rather than the rather remote *homo,* represented the antecedent of the relative pronoun *quo* (see Freundorfer, 142-43; Gross, I, 304-306).
113 Kelly, 364.
114 *Ibid.*
115 Gross, I, 320, 336-37. The conception of man's seminal inclusion in Adam is complicated by Augustine's life-long vacillation between traducianism and creationism (see Gross, I, 266-67, 338-45). Considering this question concerning the *transmission* of original sin secondary to the *fact* of original sin, Augustine left the question as to the origin of the soul undecided (Gross, I, 345).
116 See Gross, I, 320.
117 Gross, I, 324.
118 Gross, I, 324, 326-31.
119 Gross, I, 324.

The decisive issue in connection with Augustine's identification or close association of concupiscence and the essence of original sin is whether sin is thereby reduced to a natural given, to man's sensual drives, more specifically, to his sexual drive, or whether, conversely, the notion of concupiscence is augmented, "enlarged," to compromise the notion of sin as a stance of the *whole* man.

In Augustine's thought, both the reductionistic and the expansionistic tendencies are in evidence. Frequently, the sin inherited from Adam appears as nothing other than man's (natural) sexual desire.[120] In Adam this carnal passion was wholly absent. Procreation was a rather staid and tranquil affair, devoid of passion or lust and governed solely by reason and by will — just as in sowing a field the farmer's hand is moved, not by unruly passion, but by rational-voluntary purpose.[121] Through Adam's transgression, however, human nature was corrupted so that procreation was no longer possible without carnal concupiscence, the rebellion of man's sensual against his spiritual powers.[122] Because all men are born out of this procreation mixed with passion, no one escapes contamination.[123] When original sin is reduced to carnal desire in this way and is held accountable for subsequent personal sins,[124] it appears difficult to maintain even the latter as being truly culpable. Although the tendency of reducing concupiscence to *libido* is extremely prevalent, Augustine also expands concupiscence, as it were, by equating it with *cupiditas*, which is then understood as man's total rebellion against God.[125] This rebellion of the *entire* man is in effect a continuation of the first sin of Adam. For, just as Adam's sin did not consist primarily of carnal passion but of spiritual rebellion (pride, envy, distrust, avarice),[126] so Adam's descendants are involved in rebellion against God, in proud self-love.[127] Although this comprehensive meaning of the term concupiscence is relatively rare in Augustine's thought, the reality thus connoted is nonetheless central.[128] It comes to expression, for example, in the idea of the bondage of

---

120 Gross, 322-325. Kelly, 365. Friedrich Loofs, *Leitfaden zum Studium der Dogmengeschichte.* Ed. Kurt Aland (6th ed.; Tübingen: Max Niemeyer, 1959), 307.
121 Gross, I, 323.
122 Gross, I, 324.
123 Kelly, 365. Gross, 335-36.
124 Gross, I, 327.
125 Gross, I, 324; cf. 332, 338. Kelly, 364-65. Baumann, 34. For Augustine's definition of *cupiditas*, see *De Doctrina Christiana*, III, 10, 16 (*PL*, XXXIV, 72).
126 Kelly, 362-63. Gross, I, 300, 321.
127 Baumann, 34.
128 See Loofs, 307.

man's free will or the loss of freedom and the concomitant necessity of sinning.

Augustine usually distinguishes between true freedom, *libertas*, which consists of man's whole-hearted directedness to his true goal, love of God, and freedom of choice, *liberum arbitrium,* which has reference to the voluntary character of this directedness.[129] Due to Adam's sin, man lost his liberty, i.e., he is no longer free to love and serve God.[130] Nevertheless, in this apostate directedness of man's whole being in self-love, he retains his freedom of choice.[131] Within this perversion of his true direction, man remains free in the sense that he sins willingly, "with a passion," so to speak.[132] Or to capture both the freedom that is lost and that which is retained, one can say that man's free choice is qualified by the bondage to sin. Accordingly, Augustine can speak of the *bondage* of the *free* will.[133] In this condition of original sin, man is actively involved in a necessity of sinning (*necessitas peccandi*): he is not able not to sin.[134] The reality that is intended by these seemingly paradoxical statements can also be described in terms of the two opposite roots of human activity mentioned earlier. Although man sins voluntarily and in that sense freely, this free will does not provide a base *outside* the sinful direction of man's being but is taken up *within* this directedness.[135] Hence, this active, misdirected free will provides no platform from which to redirect man's life, no neutral, let alone positive, Archimedean point on which to place either the fulcrum of man's free choice or the lever of God's liberating grace.[136] Within the dynamics of the *massa*

129 See Kelly, 365-66, cf. 368; Gross, I, 350-54; Greshake, 198-99.
130 Kelly, 365. Gross, I, 351-52. Greshake, 198-99.
131 Gross points out that Augustine sometimes speaks of man's free choice as being lost (Gross, I, 351). Generally, however, Augustine proceeds axiomatically from the thesis that – *within* a specific life-direction – free choice remains (see Loofs, 329; Greshake, 198).
132 Greshake, 199. Gross, I, 353.
133 Gross, I, 352.
134 Greshake, 199, Kelly, 365-66. Gross, 352-53.
135 With reference to Augustine's insight into the basic directedness of man's existence, Lohse credits him with an "extraordinary deepening of the doctrine of sin" that was handed down to him: "Sünde ist ihm nicht nur diese oder jene verkehrte Tat. Sünde ist daher auch nicht etwas, was durch einen blossen Appell an das Bessere im Menschen, durch Belehrung, beseitigt werden könnte. Vielmehr ist Sünde seit Adams Fall die *verkehrte Grundrichtung der gesamten menschlichen Existenz,* aus der sich keiner befreien kann; sie ist die *Existenzform,* in der wir uns immer schon vorfinden. Damit hat Augustin den vor ihm herrschenden Moralismus im Sündenbegriff überwunden" (*Epochen,* 118, emphasis added).
136 See Greshake, 204-205: "Weil es bei Augustin im Menschen zwischen Gnade und Sünde kein *qualifizierendes* Mittleres gibt (so wie bei Pelagius das grundsätzliche 'posse'

peccati the "good" that man performs is sterile, Augustine holds, because it is directed to the wrong goal.[137] During his polemic with Pelagianism, Augustine applied this criterion of man's ultimate goal even more rigorously by asserting that "of himself man has nothing but deceit and sin." Conversely, if man does have something of truth and righteousness, it stems from God's redeeming grace.[138]

Before summing up the positive intention of Augustine's bleak depiction of man's subjection to original sin, it may be well to look briefly at a crystallization point of his doctrine of original sin in which the negative thrust of his conception is painfully felt: the destiny of infants who die without having been baptized. As proof of the culpable subjection of infants to original sin, Augustine adduces the practise of baptizing them in the remission of sins and the exorcism of the devil. From this liturgical practise Augustine concludes that, since he has not yet committed any personal sin, the infant is cleansed of original sin and thus liberated from the power of satan.[139] Moreover, Augustine did not shrink back from affirming the corollary of this function of baptism: an infant dying without baptism suffers the punishment of hell.[140] On the basis of Jn 3:5 Augustine concludes that due to original sin infants too must be baptized to enjoy the eternal bliss of heaven.[141] In harmony with his rejection of a *bonum naturae* as middle ground in this life, Augustine rejects the Pelagian expedient of a median realm in the afterlife as an abode between heaven and hell for unbaptized infants.[142]

Heartless as Augustine's ideas about the destiny of unbaptized infants appear to be,[143] any assessment of this theme must take into account that,

---

der Natur), ist vollends klar, dass der einmal in Sünde gefallene Mensch nicht von sich aus umkehren kann, da es in ihm sozusagen keinen 'Punkt' ausserhalb der Sünde gibt, von dem her die Sünde in Frage gestellt, korrigiert und überwunden werden könnte. Der Mensch hat keinen Frei-Raum der Entscheidung angesichts der beiden Grundmöglich keiten, sondern er ist immer schon der so oder so Entschiedene. Darum kann ach nur Gott, der den Menschen gut, d.h. mit der Gabe der caritas geschaffen hat, ihn so wiederherstellen, dass er die Liebe neu geschenkt erhält." See also Greshake, 221.

137 See Gross, 354-55.
138 Augustine, *In Evangelium Ioannis Tractatus,* V, 1 (*PL*, XXXV, 1414).
139 Gross, I, 313-14. A second argument for the reality of original sin takes the form of a theodicy: assuming the righteousness of God, the suffering and death of infants can be explained only if they are truly involved in Adam's sin and guilt (see Gross, I, 303, 314-15).
140 Gross, I, 364-65.
141 Gross, I, 306-307.
142 Gross, I, 307-308.
143 In the context of his discussion of Augustine's view concerning the destiny of

strange as it may seem, this too was taught by Augustine as *doctor gratiae*. Overwhelmed by the sovereignty and efficacy of God's grace for undeserving sinners, Augustine concludes that without the divinely instituted means of grace, man is irrevocably lost. To deny that an infant is involved in sin and therefore in need of forgiveness and cleansing is to deny that Christ died for all as a Savior of sinful man.[144] Unfortunately, the near-identification of the official Church and its sacraments as the exclusive gateway to the eternal bliss of God's kingdom appears to leave Augustine no other option than to consign unbaptized infants to the punishment of hell.[145]

Despite the somber tones of many elements of Augustine's doctrine of original sin, tones in which some discern an echo of his Manichean past,[146] this "pessimism" regarding man in sin is misunderstood if it is isolated from Augustine's conviction regarding the light and power of God's redeeming grace.[147] It is from within this positive perspective that Augustine articulates the idea that man constitutes a *massa damnata*, culpably involved in original sin.[148] Not the demolition of human nature, but its redirection by the effica-

unbaptized infants, Gross, failing to repress a note of caustic sarcasm, refers to Augustine as "unser Menschenfreund" (Gross, I, 365). Cf. n. 146 below.

144 See Vanneste, *Studiorum*, II, 521. Cf. Rondet, *Le Péché originel dans la tradition patristique et théologique*, 144.

145 Walter Simonis argues that Augustine's entire doctrine of original sin is simply a logical deduction from an ecclesiological axiom that has *a priori* validity: *extra ecclesiam salus non est* ("Heilsnotwendigkeit der Kirche und Erbsünde bei Augustinus: Ein dogmengeschichtlicher Beitrag zur Klärung zweier Fragen der gegenwärtigen theologischen Diskussion," *ThuPh*, XLIII [1968], 481-482). Though taking cognizance of Simonis' article (Greshake, 223-24, n. 146), Greshake, conversely, considers Augustine's accentuation of the necessity of baptism to be rooted in his doctrine of original sin: "Wenn Augustin im pelagianischen Streit das Heil der Neugeborenen an die Taufe necessitate medii bindet, so geschieht dies nicht so sehr aus einer vertieften Einsicht in die ekklesiale oder sakramentale Struktur des Heils, sondern im Zuge der 'Logik' der Erbsündenlehre, deren Zuspitzung sich gerade in der Frage nach der Situation der Neugeborenen ergab. Die absolut notwendige Bindung des Heils an die Taufe war nun das eindeutigste Argument für die absolute Gratuität der Gnade" (Greshake, 225, n. 150). Similarly, Rudolf Lorenz finds Simonis' thesis unconvincing ("Zwölf Jahre Augustinusforschung," *Theologische Rundschau*, XL [1975], 16-17).

146 Gross, 372. Concerning the question as to remnants of Augustine's Manichean past in his later period, see Alfred Adam, "Das Fortwirken des Manichäismus bei Augustin," *ZKG*, LXIX (1958), 1-25; *idem*, "Der manichäische Ursprung der Lehre von der zwei Reichen bei Augustin," *ThLZ*, LXXVII (1952), 385-90; W. Geerlings, "Zur Frage des Nachwirkens des Manichäismus in der Theologie Augustins," ZKTh, XCIII (1971), 45-60.

147 When Augustine says, for example, that man has nothing but lies and deceit (see sec. A, 4 above), the qualification "of himself" as well as the acknowledgement that by virtue of God's grace truth and righteousness *does* exist is evidence of the inadequacy of the term "pessimism" as a description of Augustine's position.

148 See Gross, I, 273-74, 293-94 (here Gross attributes Augustine's emphasis upon

cious power of God's redeeming love is the ultimate goal of Augustine's life and teaching.[149] Pessimism regarding sinful man is Augustine's penultimate word. His last word is optimism — but then, an "optimism of grace."[150]

5. The Councils of Carthage (418) and Orange (529)

Pelagian tenets, especially as propagated by Pelagius' ardent follower, Celestius, were condemned by several synods and councils, the most important of which is the Council of Carthage held in 418. Its first canon condemns the thesis that Adam was created mortal, meaning that he would have died a physical death even if he had not sinned.[151] The second canon deals directly with original sin:

> Whoever denies that newly born infants are to be baptized, or says that they are indeed baptized for the remission of sins but that they do not derive [*trahere*] anything of the original sin from Adam which is expiated in the bath of regeneration; and consequently, that for them the form of baptism — "for the remission of sins" — is to be understood, not in a true, but in a false sense: let him be anathema. Because the words of the Apostle: "By one man sin entered into the world (and through sin death), and so passed into all men; in whom all have sinned" (cf. Ro 5:12), cannot be understood in any other way than as the Catholic Church everywhere has always understood them. Because of this rule of faith even infants, who have not yet been able to commit any personal sins, are truly baptized for the remission of sins that in them *that* may be washed away by regeneration which they have contracted by generation [*ut in eis regeneratione mundetur, quod generatione traxerunt*].[152]

The central role that the subject of infant baptism had attained in the controversy regarding original sin is strikingly reflected in this canon. Notable too

---

redeeming grace to a deep religious feeling which *erroneously* leads him to attribute everything to Christ's redemption and almost nothing to human nature), 354 (here the doctrine of the *massa peccati* is said to play the role of dark backdrop to Augustine's theology of grace).

149 Thus Gross, I, 374. Gross himself is of the opinion that this high and noble goal of Augustine's view of man in sin does not extenuate the pernicious consequences of that view. Augustine, according to Gross, erected his monument to divine grace on the wreckage of the moral freedom of man. In its ultimate conclusion, Gross continues, Augustine's system excludes morality and leads to ethical nihilism (Gross, I, 374). In Gross' view, therefore, Augustin's victory over Pelagius is a Pyrrhic one: Augustine was victorious, not only over Pelagius, but also over "Vernunft und Menschlichkeit" (Gross, I, 375). Gross concludes his first volume, however, by asserting that this victory cannot possibly last, but *must* sooner or later turn into defeat (Gross, I, 376).

150 See Gross, I, 373. Cf. Henri Rondet, *Gratia Christi: Essai d'histoire du dogme et de théologie dogmatique* ("Verbum Salutis"; Paris: Beauchesne, 1958), 137-39; and *idem, Essais sur la théologie de la grâce* (Paris: Beauchesne, 1964), 264-66.

151 *DS*, 222.

152 *DS*, 223.

is the fact that although the nature of original sin is not defined, that which is removed by baptism is indirectly said to be sin in a true sense. Of special historical significance is the emphatic appeal to the *in quo omnes peccaverunt* of Ro 5:12 as ground for the doctrine of original sin.[153]

The remaining canons condemn various Pelagian notions closely related to the subject of original sin. The idea of a third realm (*medius locus*) in which unbaptized infants enjoy eternal bliss is rejected.[154] Those who view grace merely as illumination or as an aid facilitating a righteous life, rather than as a power *enabling* man to live in accordance with God's commands are condemned.[155] Finally, a series of canons is directed against those who teach sinlessness as a real possibility.[156] Significantly, however, the Council of Carthage makes no direct pronouncements regarding a key question in the Augustinian-Pelagian polemic, namely, that of the condition of man's will.[157]

In contrast to the Council of Carthage, the Council of Orange addresses itself directly to the question of free will.[158] This shift of focus is due to the fact that the teachings of this council are directed against a position that came to be designated as Semi-Pelagianism.[159] Its representatives do not deny the reality of original sin but deny that it entails the destruction of the powers of free will. In their view, man's will is weakened and ill, but not lost or dead.[160] In this context, the first two canons deal with original sin.

> Canon 1: If anyone says that it was not the whole man, that is, both body and soul, that was "changed for the worse" through the offense of Adam's sin, but believes that the freedom of the soul remained untouched and that only the body was made subject to corruption, he is deceived by the error of Pelagius and contradicts the words of Scripture: "The soul that sinneth, the same shall die" (Eze 18:20); and: "Do you not know that to whom you offer yourselves as slaves for

---

[153] Concerning the use of this *locus classicus*, see secs. A, 2 and 4 above and sec. A, 8, d below.

[154] *DS*, 224.

[155] *DS*, 226-27.

[156] *DS*, 228-30.

[157] Loofs calls attention to the fact that Carthage makes no mention of characteristic features of Augustine's doctrine of grace, such as the total moral inability of natural man to choose the good, irresistible grace and unconditional predestination (*Leitfaden*, 348; similarly, Gross, I, 375).

[158] In the preface, grace and free will is said to be the subject to which the Council addresses itself (*DS*, 370).

[159] This term was first employed towards the end of the sixteenth century. See M. Jacquin, "A quelle date apparait le terme 'Semipélagien'? " *RSPhTh*, I (1907), 506-508.

[160] Kelly, 370-71. Loofs, 350-54. For the Semi-Pelagian view on the doctrine of original sin, see Gross, II, 26-95.

obedience, to him whom you obey you are slaves?" (Ro 6:16); and: "By whatever a man is overcome, of that he also becomes the slave" (cf. II Pe 2:19).[161]

> Canon 2: If anyone asserts that Adam's sin was injurious only to Adam and not to his descendants, or if he declares that it was only the death of the body which is punishment for sin, and not sin which is the death of the soul, that passed from one man to all the human race, he attributes an injustice to God and contradicts the words of the Apostle: "Through one man sin entered into the world and through sin death, and thus death has passed into all men; in whom all have sinned" (cf. Ro 5:12).[162]

The first canon goes beyond that of Carthage on this subject in that the effect of original sin upon man's will is specified. This is done, positively, by teaching that the whole man, body and soul, has changed for the worse (a phrase frequently used by Augustine),[163] and, negatively, by opposing anyone who believes that the freedom of the soul remains uninjured (*animae liberate illaesa durante*). The second canon also marks a further development in comparison to the teachings of the Council of Carthage. Whereas Carthage states in effect that "something" of original sin is contracted from Adam,[164] this canon specifies that it is sin itself that is passed on and, moreover, that this sin constitutes the "death of the soul."[165]

The moot point concerning the teachings of the Council of Orange concerns the question whether they reflect the Augustinian conception of man as enslaved in sin, incapable of doing any good, except by virtue of God's redeeming and renewing grace. An affirmative answer to that question is suggested by a certain progression that is present within the two canons on original sin. It is clear that the first canon focusses upon the condition of the *soul*, more specifically, upon the condition of man's will. When it is affirmed that the soul has changed for the worse[166] and that the freedom of the soul does not remain uninjured, these statements in themselves could be interpreted in a Semi-Pelagian manner as meaning that man's will is merely *weakened*.[167] However, two of the Scripture passages adduced in support of this deteriora-

---

161 *DS*, 371.
162 *DS*, 372.
163 See the relevant note in *DS*, 371 and Vanneste's discussion of several parallel passages from Augustine's works ("Le Décret du Concile de Trente sur le péché originel: Les trois premiers canons," *NRTh*, LXXXVII [1965], 702-705.
164 See sec. A, 5 above.
165 This phrase is frequently used by Augustine to describe (original) sin. See *In Evangelium Ioannis Tractatus*, XLIX, 3 (*PL*, XXXV, 1748); *De Civitate Dei*, XIII, 15 (*PL*, XLI, 387); *De Natura et Gratia*, XXIII, 25 (*PL*, XLIV, 259; *ALG*, I, 472).
166 See also *DS*, 385.
167 E.g., Vanneste, as explained below.

tion speak of man's *enslavement* to sin. Moreover, it is striking that the second canon speaks of the *death* of man's *soul.* In light of the close association between the soul and freedom that is expressed in the first canon, it seems entirely plausible to interpret the phrase "death of the soul" as an explication of the *way in which* the soul and its freedom is changed for the worse.[168]

This "Augustinian" interpretation finds support in many of the remaining canons that teach the radical necessity of grace and the drastic effect of sin. Grace is said to be necessary to instill in man the very desire for being cleansed from sin[169] and the desire for and beginning of faith.[170] Further, it is taught that interior grace is necessary to direct us to God and make us obedient[171] and that prevenient grace is necessary to enable us to do that which is good before God.[172] The corollaries of this teaching regarding the necessity of grace are found in numerous descriptions of the grave condition of man in sin. Due to Adam's sin, man's free will is said to be, not only weakened,[173] but also vitiated[174] and inclined (to evil).[175] Some statements even suggest that man's free will is lost.[176] Accordingly, it is said that without the illumination of the Holy Spirit man is incapable of doing any good pertaining to salvation.[177] The "Augustinian" interpretation of these pronouncements and, by inference, of the first two canons becomes even more plausible in view of the fact that most of the positive canons[178] consist of quotations deriving – via the *Sententiae* of Prosper of Aquitaine – from Augustine himself. Most strikingly, Augustine's view of sinful man's capacity for virtue is affirmed in two canons. In canon seventeen the courage of the heathen is ascribed to worldly desire (*cupiditas*), while the courage of Christians is ascribed to love of God (*caritas Dei*).[179] Moreover, canon twenty-two adopts Augustine's thesis that of himself man has nothing but deceit and sin.[180]

---

168 See A. D. R. Polman, *Onze Nederlandsche Geloofsbelijdenis* (Franeker: Wever, n.d.), II, 120.
169 *DS*, 374.
170 *DS*, 375.
171 *DS*, 376.
172 *DS*, 396.
173 *DS*, 378, 383, cf. 396.
174 *DS*, 378.
175 *DS*, 396.
176 *DS*, 383, cf. 391.
177 *DS*, 377.
178 Canons 9-25 (*DS*, 379-95).
179 *DS*, 387.
180 *DS*, 392; cf. sec. A, 4 above. Loofs calls canon 22 "eine wahre crux der römische Theologen" (*Leitfaden,* 357, n. 5. See also the relevant note in *DS*).

Although some consider the cumulative evidence sufficient to conclude that the Council of Orange rejects Semi-Pelagianism unambiguously,[181] others are more hesistant.[182] Vanneste, however, argues that the Council of Orange expressly sanctions a basic tenet of Semi-Pelagianism. He calls attention to the significant divergence between canon thirteen and the quotation of Augustine as found in Prosper's *Sententiae* upon which this canon is based.[183]

> Prosper: The free will (*arbitrium voluntatis*) is truly free only when it does not serve vice and sin. Such freedom, which was given by God but is lost, can be returned only by Him who was able to grant it. Accordingly the [divine] truth says: "If the Son shall set you free, you shall be free indeed."

> Orange: *De reparatione liberi arbitrii.* The free will (*arbitrium voluntatis*) which is weakened (*infirmatum*) in the first man can be restored (reparari) only by the grace of baptism; "that which is lost can be returned only by him who was able to grant it. Accordingly, the Truth itself says: 'If the Son shall set you free, you shall be free indeed.' "[184]

As Vanneste points out, the focus of the original quotation is slavery in sin so that it can be appropriately said that man's freedom is *lost* until it is *returned* by God. Canon thirteen strikingly substitutes the idea of *weakening* for that of losing, and, correspondingly, the idea of *repairing* for that of returning. When, after this amended section, the canon continues with a direct quotation of the original source which speaks of something being lost and returned, these notions (as well as the Scripture passage regarding liberation by Christ) hang in midair.[185] Because of the significant alteration involved in this canon and because of the general predominance of the themes of weakness, injury and deterioration over those of slavery and loss in the teachings of the Council of Orange, Vanneste concludes that in the first canon regarding original sin the Semi-Pelagian thesis regarding man's free will is expressly sanctioned.[186]

181 E.g., Gross, II, 93: "Unbestreitbar ist demnach in Orange die augustinische These von der Vernichtung der Freiheit zum sittlich Guten durch die Erbsünde vom kirchlichen Lehramt erstmals formell sanktioniert worden." Cf. Polman, II, 120; G. E. Meuleman, "Natuur en genade," *Protestantse Verkenningen na Vaticanum II*, H. Berkhof et al. ('s-Gravenhage: Boekencentrum, 1967), 75-76.

182 Berkouwer, e.g., expresses his misgivings concerning the Council of Orange because it approaches the question as to the relationship of God's sovereign grace and man's weakened will in terms of a relationship of *powers* and *effects* — without dealing with grace as God's *mercy* and as *justification* (*Conflict met Rome* [3d ed.; Kampen: Kok, 1955], 108, cf. 106).

183 *NRTh*, LXXXVII, 700. *Het Dogma*, 93.

184 *DS*, 383.

185 *NRTh*, LXXXVII, 700. *Het Dogma*, 93. Cf. Berkouwer, *Conflict met Rome*, 108-109.

186 *NRTh*, LXXXVII, 701-706; 702: "Le premier canon d'Orange consacre donc la

Perhaps these divergent interpretations indicate that the teachings of the Council of Orange themselves are ambiguous.[187] In that case, certain teachings of this Council clearly reject important elements of Semi-Pelagianism, while at the same time some of the teachings of this Council themselves contain elements that are indicative of a development towards Semi-Pelagianism.[188] Whatever the authentic direction of the Council of Orange may be, it represents a remarkable culmination point of the preceding developments. Upon the subsequent developments that will be treated presently, however, this Council had no direct impact, for its teachings appear to be unknown to the theologians of the twelfth to the sixteenth century.[189] That is precisely the period in which, due to a new theological framework, a decisive shift in the understanding of the doctrine of original sin takes place. The repercussions of that shift extend as far as the contemporary reinterpretation of original sin.

6. Anselm

The profundity of Augustine's thought and the weight of his authority, increased by ecclesiastical approbation of significant elements of his thought, combined to ensure a rather general acceptance of his conception of original sin until the beginning of the twelfth century — despite the continuous presence of currents of thought that tended to undermine its core.[190] The first major change in the very definition of original sin was introduced by Anselm. For that reason we will leap across six centuries and briefly delineate the basic features of Anselm's conception of original sin.

Although Anselm wishes to be, and in many ways was, an advocate of Augustine's thought, his definition of original sin contains the seeds of a

---

doctrine de Fauste de Riez au sujet du libre arbitre." Cf. *Het Dogma*, 92-94, 97. In this context, Vanneste contrasts Augustine's approach to the question of man's freedom to the approach of the Council of Orange: although Augustine frequently applies the theme of corruption (weakness, injury, illness, deterioration) to the domain of human *nature* generally, he carefully avoids applying the theme of corruption to the domain of *freedom*; Augustine prefers to speak of freedom in terms of the *slavery* caused by sin and the genuine liberty bestowed by Christ (*NRTh*, LXXXVII, 706). This indeed points to a decisive difference in orientation.

187 It is telling that Vanneste not so much as mentions canons 17 and 22.
188 Loofs, 357.
189 Gross, II, 94.
190 Gross, II, 13, 133-34, 437, 506-507, 572-73; III, 9. Gross points out that although the doctrine of original sin was commonly understood in an Augustinian sense, many of the concomitant teachings, such as the loss of freedom and the irresistable efficacy of grace, were being challenged and attenuated (Gross, II, 13, 437, 572).

significant turning point in the history of this doctrine.[191] Whereas Augustine had understood original sin positively, i.e., as a culpable active inclination of man's will against God (*amor sui, cupiditas*), Anselm defined original sin negatively as the privation or absence of "owed" justice (*carentia/ absentia debitae iustitiae*).[192] The justice of which we are deprived is constituted by the voluntary conformity of man's will with God's will, i.e., the rectitude of man's will.[193] Although this rectitude or justice is a special gift of God, it consists, not of a special supernatural quality bestowed upon human nature, but of the right directedness of this nature, specifically the will, itself.[194] It is significant to note that, despite his negative definition of original sin, Anselm derives this definition not so much by speculation regarding "paradise lost," as by reflection upon the notion of *sin*.[195] Because all sin is injustice, Anselm argues, and original sin is strictly sin (*originale peccatum est absolute peccatum*), the latter is nothing other than *iniustitia*, which is condemnable before God.[196] From this notion of sin as injustice, Anselm proceeds to specify the unique nature of original sin as the absence of the justice that we *ought to* (*debere→debitum*) have,[197] namely, by way of Adam.[198]

In what sense is this privation of justice truly and properly sin? On the one hand, the notion of sin with which Anselm begins appears to be literally a point of *departure,* for the privation of justice involves no *personal* guilt (*culpa*), which Anselm holds to be strictly a matter of the will, but merely a destitution of human *nature.*[199] This natural destitution appears to obtain the character of a debt (*debitum*) only by virtue of God's plan of salvation according to which justice, the rectitude of will, ought to have been passed on via nature.[200] On the other hand, however, Anselm appears to be able to be true to his starting point, the notion of sin, by virtue of his realism. The idea

---

191 Gross considers the difference between Augustine's and Anselm's conception of the essence of original sin to be of "epochaler Bedeutung" (Gross, III, 23).
192 *Liber de Conceptu Virginali et Originali Peccato,* ch. XXVII (*PL,* CLVIII, 461); ch. III (*PL,* CLVIII, 435-36). See Gross, III, 21; Vanneste, *NRTh,* LXXXVII, 708.
193 Gross, III, 15-16.
194 Gross, III, 16. See also J. B. Kors, *La justice primitive et le péché originel d'après S. Thomas* (Bibliothèque Thomiste," II; Kain: Le Saulchoir, 1922), 27-29; A. M. Landgraf, *Dogmengeschichte der Frühscholastik* (Regensburg: Friedrich Pustet, 1952-56), I/1, 42.
195 Vanneste, *NRTh,* LXXXVII, 708. Cf. Kors, 31-32.
196 *Liber de Conceptu Virginali et Originali Peccato,* ch. III (*PL,* CLVIII, 435-36).
197 *Ibid.*
198 Gross, III, 19-22.
199 Gross, III, 17, 19-20. Kors, 31-33.
200 Gross, III, 17, 20-22. Kors, 25.

of all men's inclusion in Adam and his sin, corroborated by the *in quo* reading of Ro 5:12, enables him to maintain both the voluntary and the "natural" character of the wrongly directed will in those subject to original sin.[201] Despite the difficulties entailed in this realism, it introduces an active element in Anselm's negative definition of original sin. Accordingly, this privative condition includes a willful necessity of sinning that is curbed only by the efficaciousness of God's grace.[202] In this way, Anselm remained an exponent of the Augustinian view of mankind as a *massa peccatrix* worthy of damnation.[203] Infants who died without being baptized are, therefore, destined for hell, though again subject to the lightest damnation.[204]

Although fed by the mainstream of the Augustinian conception of man in sin and undergirded by philosophic realism, Anselm's definition of original sin marks the point of transition towards a purely negative understanding of original sin. This transition is facilitated by the increasingly clearer distinction that is made between the reality of nature and that of grace.

7. Thomas Aquinas

Thomas Aquinas expressly combines the Augustinian identification of original sin with concupiscence and the Anselmian negative definition of original sin as the absence of justice. The former becomes the material element and the latter the formal element of his own definition of original sin as the privation of original justice.[205] However, Augustine's positive understanding of original sin as concupiscence in the comprehensive religious sense of *amor sui* or *cupiditas* is neutralized. This is due to several factors. First, the focal point of the doctrine of original sin has shifted from man's enslavement in sin and God's redeeming mercy, to the reality of supernatural grace and the (disastrous) effect of its loss upon human nature. Secondly, due to this shift, the notion of concupiscence that is retained as an element of this loss is divested of moral qualification and understood as a disorder of (human) *nature*. Finally, as element of original sin, this concupiscence is itself understood wholly negatively, as is reflected by its *subsumption* under the *negative* definition of original sin. To understand the significance of this theological development, Thomas' conception of the original justice that is lost due to

---

201 See Gross, III, 17, 19, 24. Kors, 29-31, 33-34.
202 See Gross, III, 19, 24-26.
203 Gross, III, 24. Cf. Kors, 34, esp. n. 6.
204 Gross, III, 24-25.
205 *Summa Theologiae,* I-II, 82, 3 resp. See Gross, III, 250-51.

Adam's sin must first be considered.[206]

Original justice is constituted by a hierarchical three-fold submission, the first of which concerns the relationship of man to God, while the second and third submissions concern the relationships between various constituents of man. The first submission is that of reason and especially of the will to God; this submission is therefore also referred to as the rectitude of the will. The second submission is that of the lower powers in man to reason, and the third, the submission of the body to the soul.[207] The first submission is the cause of the second and third. This intra-human harmony (the second and third submission), Thomas argues, is not a natural condition, else it would not have been lost due to sin. If such harmony does obtain, therefore, the first submission must in turn be caused by a supernatural gift of grace.[208] Existing by virtue of sanctifying grace (*gratia gratum faciens*), the first submission is described as a *supernatural* subjection which is the root of original justice.[209] Accordingly, original justice is viewed as including sanctifying grace.[210] In Adam original justice was conferred upon human nature and was to be passed on by propagation.[211]

When Adam rebelled against God, the supernatural gift of grace was withdrawn and the interior harmony of his nature was lost.[212] Consequently, the nature that he passes on lacks its original internal harmony as well as its supernatural submission to God.[213] This is the condition of original sin in which all men are born. Within this privation of original justice, then, Thomas

---

206 Thomas' conception of original justice has been a subject of considerable controversy. The question in dispute is whether Thomas teaches that an adequate or that an inadequate distinction exists between original justice and sanctifying grace. An adequate distinction (*distinctio realis adequata*) is one between two entities that are *not* related as part-whole, e.g., arm-leg. An inadequate distinction (*distinctio realis inadequata*) is one between two entities that *are* related as part-whole, e.g., arm-body. For a brief resumé of this controversy and references to the relevant literature, see William A. Van Roo, *Grace and Original Justice According to St. Thomas* ("Analecta Gregoriana," LXXV; Rome: Apud Aedes Universitatis Gregorianae, 1955), 7-9.
207 *Summa Theologiae*, I, 95, 1 resp. For the central place which Thomas accords to the will in original justice, see *ibid.*, I-II, 82, 3 resp.
208 *Ibid.*, I, 95, 1 resp.
209 *Ibid.*, I, 100, 1 *ad* 2.
210 *De Malo*, 4, 2 *ad* 1 in contr. (third series of objections); *ibid.*, 5, 1 *ad* 13. See Van Roo, 147-48.
211 *Summa Theologiae*, I, 100, 1 resp. and *ad* 2. Cf. Van Roo, 111-12; Gross, III, 257. Cf. *Summa Theologiae*, I, 100 *ad* 2, where Thomas says that grace would not have been conferred *by the power of* the seed, but (by a special act) at the moment that the soul is infused.
212 *Summa Theologiae*, I-II, 82, 1 resp., 3 resp.
213 *Ibid.*, I, 100, 1 resp. and *ad* 2.

distinguishes between a formal and a material element. The formal element consists of the loss of the rectitude of the will, its submission to God. The material element consists of the loss of interior harmony within man, i.e., the loss of the second and the third submission, causing natural powers of the soul to turn inordinately to a changeable good. This material element is also called concupiscence.[214] This meaning of concupiscence is evidence of the extent to which the negative conception of original sin predominates. As part of original sin, concupiscence is not a positive evil inclination of the will, but a negative dis-order, the unleashing of natural drives due to the loss of the bond of original justice.[215]

This negative, privational conception of original sin is reflected in Thomas' view of the destiny of infants who die without having been baptized. Whereas Augustine and, despite his negative definition of original sin, even Anselm, had relegated such infants to the punishment of hell in its mildest form, Aquinas holds that these infants live in a state of relative deprivation, namely, the deprivation of the *visio Dei*. Moreover, since they are ignorant of the supernatural gift that they lack, they do not even experience the pain of loss, but live in a state of natural bliss.[216]

If anywhere, the privative notion of original sin might be offset at the point where Thomas reflects upon the way in which the privation of original justice may be called guilt, for he holds that one can speak of guilt only as a voluntary reality.[217] To provide a ground for the guilt of original sin, Thomas has recourse to the notion that humanity constitutes a single body, appealing to the fact that a civic community can be spoken of as one body and one man.[218] In applying the body-analogy to the reality of original sin,

---

214 *Ibid.,* I-II, 82, 3 resp. Cf. Gross, III, 252, 260, 263.

215 Kors, 169: "Saint Thomas commence par établir le caractère purement privatif du péché originel. Non seulement la partie formelle de ce péché, c'est-à-dire la privation de la justice originelle dans la volonté, a un caractère négatif, mais encore la partie matérielle, la concupiscence est dans la même condition." In a presentation of Thomas' view, Labourdette too warns emphatically against viewing the concupiscence that is part of original sin as anything other than a *privative* condition: "Gardons-nous ici encore de sortir d'un sens tout privatif... La concupiscence désigne purement et simplement la puissance même (ou les diverses puissances) *comme privées* de la rectitude gratuite du premier état; il y a certes là toute la positivité de ces puissances; mais le péché est dans la privation qui les affecte" (M. M. Labourdette, *Le péché originel et les origines de l'homme* [Paris: Alsatia, 1953], 84).

216 Gross, III, 243-44, 253-54. Cf. Kors, 169 (in the same paragraph as is cited in the previous footnote): "De là procède logiquement que les peines dues au péché originel sont elles-mêmes d'ordre privatif."

217 *Summa Theologiae,* I-II, 81, 1 resp.

218 *Ibid.*

however, he elaborates the image in a very specific direction. Just as murder is not solely an act of the will but also an act of the hand, so the disorder which exists in man is due to the will of the first parents who by motion of generation moves all who derive their origin from him.[219] Although Thomas begins by viewing mankind as an organic moral unity, the image shifs towards the idea of a "first mover" who causes a *disorder* in (human) nature. Accordingly, Thomas calls original sin a sin of *nature* — i.e., of that nature which a *person* receives.[220] This elaboration of the body-analogy indicates that the unity of mankind is seen, not in terms of our involvement in Adam's sin, but in terms of the derivation of our defective, disordered nature from Adam.[221] Even the reflection upon the guilt of original sin, therefore, fails to offset the negative conception of that sin.

What are the effects of original sin? Thomas distinguishes a threefold good of nature (*bonum naturae*) of which each aspect is variously affected by sin: 1) the principles that constitute nature together with the properties and capacities that proceed from these principles, 2) the natural inclination to virtue that is rooted in man's rational nature, 3) original justice.[222] Since the first *bonum naturae* constitutes the essential nature of a specific being, it cannot be destroyed nor even diminished by sin. The third good of nature, original justice, being the effect of a special gift, is wholly lost due to Adam's sin. The second good, the natural inclination to virtue, is diminished but not destroyed by sin.[223]

The specific effect of original sin can readily be derived from what Thomas has said about the effect of sin generally upon the threefold natural good. The damage caused by original sin — the loss of the third natural good — is precisely delimited by the characteristics of the first and second natural goods, i.e., by the total invulnerability of the principles and capacities of nature, on the one hand, and by the limited vulnerability of the natural inclination to virtue, on the other. Thomas points out that the inclination to virtue is a kind of intermediate magnitude, for it lies between its *soil*, man's rational nature, and its *goal*, virtue.[224] With respect to its base, the inclination to virtue is in no way diminished by sin because this inclination is rooted in man's rational (metaphysical) *nature*.[225] The inclination to virtue, there-

219 *Ibid.*
220 *Ibid.*
221 See Kors, 165-66 for a sketch contrasting Thomas' and Augustine's conception of the unity of mankind. See also Loofs, 455.
222 *Summa Theologiae*, I-II, 85, 1 and 2.
223 *Ibid.*
224 *Ibid.*, 2 resp.
225 *Ibid.*

fore, can be diminished only with respect to the attainment of its goal. The actual attainment of virtue is frustrated positively by personal sin and negatively by original sin. Personal sin *counteracts* the inclination to virtue and thus places an impediment between the inclination to and the goal of virtue.[226] Original sin *deprives* the inclination to virtue of its proper orientation and thus renders the goal elusive.[227] Accordingly Thomas speaks of four wounds of nature each of which consists of the deprivation of a specific power of the soul of its proper orientation to a specific virtue: the *wound of ignorance* (reason insofar as it is deprived of its order to the true); the *wound of malice* (the will insofar as it is deprived of its order to the good); the *wound of weakness* (the irascible insofar as it is deprived of its order to the arduous); the *wound of concupiscence* (the concupiscible insofar as it is deprived of its order to the delectable).[228] Considering the cumulative effect of these wounds, it is not surprising to discover that Thomas speaks of original sin itself as a "sickness of nature" (*languor naturae*).[229]

It is obvious that in Thomas' view the detrimental effect of original sin is considerable. So serious is the illness it entails that before sanctifying grace can elevate, it must *heal* human nature.[230] Yet, it is equally obvious that within Thomas' conception the detrimental effect of original sin is limited due to its *privative* character and due to the inviolable boundaries of deprivation, namely, the inalienable principles and properties of (human) *"nature."*

After Thomas, the negative conception of original sin vies with the various Augustinian conceptions that continue to be advocated.[231] Nevertheless, the privative understanding of original sin becomes predominant, undergoing an interesting modification that is to become dominant in Roman Catholic theology after the Council of Trent. In that modified form, the privative understanding of original sin makes itself felt even in the current reinterpretations.

8. The Council of Trent

For the Roman Catholic Church, the decree promulgated on June 17, 1546 at the fifth session of the Council of Trent is the single most important document on the subject of original sin. Reaffirming major sections of earlier

---

226 *Ibid.*
227 *Ibid.,* 3 resp.
228 *Ibid.*
229 *Ibid.,* 82, 1 resp.
230 Thus Labourdette, 91, 95. See *Summa Theologiae,* I-II, 109, 3 resp.
231 See Gross, III, 172-213, 269-302, 367-77.

teachings on this subject (Carthage and Orange), modifying and supplementing these to ward off contemporary errors, the decree of the Council of Trent represents the most comprehensive and definitive statement on original sin issued by the extraordinary teaching authority of the Church.[232] Unfortunately, the scope, finality and authority of this decree is not always matched by an equal measure of clarity. This is largely due to the fact that, although the participants of the Council were generally agreed on the errors to be combatted,[233] they were far from agreed upon the nature of the reality to be defended. Augustinian, Anselmian and Thomistic conceptions of the nature of original sin divided the ranks. To prevent this internal discord from interfering with the proceedings of the Council, the papal legates instructed the conciliar theologians to determine the nature of original sin, not by definition, but by describing its effects.[234] Although this directive could hardly banish the competing notions regarding the nature of original sin from the discussions that preceded the acceptance of the final form of the decree,[235] this decree itself succeeds amazingly well in avoiding an explicit sanction of either the Augustinian, the Anselmian or the Thomistic conception regarding the nature of original sin. This success, however, was attained at the cost of considerable ambiguity on crucial issues. Some of this ambiguity will be pointed out in the following presentation of the first five canons of the decree on original sin.[236]

a. *Canon One*

If anyone does not profess that the first man Adam immediately lost the justice and holiness in which he was constituted when he disobeyed the command of God in paradise; and that, through the offense of this sin, he incurred the wrath and the indignation of God, and consequently incurred the death with which God had previously threatened him and, together with death, bondage in the power who from that time "had the empire of death" (He 2:14), that is, of the devil; "and that it is the whole Adam, both body and soul, who was changed for the worse through the offense of this sin" [cf. *DS*, 371]: let him be anathema.[237]

---

232 Vanneste, "La préhistoire du décret du Concile de Trente sur le péché originel," *NRTh*, LXXXVI, 355.

233 *Concilium Tridentinum. Diariorum, Actorum, Epistularum, Tractatuum Nova Collectio*, ed. Societas Goerresiana (Freiburg i. Br.: Herder, 1901-63), 212-13 (list of 13 errors). Hereafter this series will be cited as *CT*.

234 *CT*, V, 163-64. See also Hubert Jedin, *Geschichte des Konzils von Trient* (Freiburg i. Br.: Herder, 1949-70), II, 112.

235 Gross, IV, 106-108.

236 Canon 6 (*DS*, 1516), which declares that the virgin Mary is not included in this decree on original sin, will not be dealt with.

237 *DS*, 1511.

This canon is largely a reaffirmation of the first canon of the Council of Orange.[238] There are some important differences, however. The canon as a whole is marked by a difference of approach. Whereas the first canon of the Council of Orange speaks of Adam within the perspective of the present condition of "man," the above canon speaks exclusively of Adam, "the first man." This shift of emphasis reflects the increasingly independent attention that is paid by scholastic thought to Adam's original state.[239]

A striking difference in comparison to previous magisterial pronouncements is the description of the effect of the fall as involving the loss of "justice and holiness." Although in itself this description could represent simply an inference from scriptural passages describing man's salvation in Christ,[240] it has as its immediate background the discussions among the schoolmen concerning the nature of Adam's original state.[241] Due to the lack of unanimity among the conciliar theologians on this score, the phrase *"sanctitatem et iustitiam, in qua creatus fuit, amisse"* was the subject of considerable discussion. One delegate, for example, wished to qualify the justice which Adam lost as being "original."[242] Another wished to change or omit the word holiness because it might suggest the idea that Adam was created *in grace.*[243] In diametrical opposition to this suggestion, one preliminary text for the present canon explicitly stated that Adam was created in grace.[244] In order to circumvent these nettlesome questions that divided the schoolmen, some suggested that the entire phrase, "holiness and justice," be replaced by the term "innocence" or "rectitude," or, simpler still, by the statement that Adam truly erred in original sin.[245] In the final text of this canon, the phrase "holiness and justice" remains, but, interestingly, the term "created" has deliberately been replaced by the term "constituted." This was done in order to avoid taking a position with respect to the dispute among the theological schools regarding the moment at which Adam received grace.[246]

The concluding phrase of this canon is extremely significant in that it is

---

238 See sec. A, 5 above.
239 Vanneste, *NRTh*, LXXXVII, 707-10. Labourdette considers this *separate* treatment of Adam by the Council of Trent to be an indication that the historicity of Adam is not merely presupposed, but is part and parcel of the intended teaching (*Le péché originel*, 33-34).
240 See, e.g., Eph 4:23; I Cor 1:30 (cited in canon 3).
241 Vanneste, *NRTh*, LXXXVII, 708-12.
242 *Ibid.*, 710.
243 *CT*, V, 203.
244 *Ibid.*, 198, cf. 203. See Vanneste, *NRTh*, LXXXVII, 710.
245 *CT*, V, 199, 200-201, 205.
246 See Gross, IV, 110; Vanneste, *NRTh*, LXXXVII, 711.

a literal citation of a *part* of the first canon of the Council of Orange. Only the statement regarding the deterioration of man's body and soul has been retained. However, the immediately following teaching of the Council of Orange to the effect that the freedom of the soul does not remain uninjured[247] has been deleted. This omission is all the more intriguing in view of the fact that the preliminary text of the present canon did contain a weakened version of the phrase used by the Council of Orange,[248] and in view of the fact that Trent's decree on justification – precisely in the canon that recapitulates the teaching of original sin – explicitly teaches that the free will, "though attenuated in its powers and inclined [to evil] was by no means extinguished."[249] The full significance of the omission in the first canon of the decree on original sin cannot be determined on the basis of this canon itself but only in terms of the function that is ascribed to the free will in the process of justification.[250]

b. *Canon Two*

> If anyone asserts that Adam's sin was injurious only to Adam and not to his descendants," and that it was for himself alone that he lost the holiness and justice which he had received from God, and not for us also; or that after his defilement by the sin of disobedience, he "transmitted to the whole human race only death" and punishment "of the body but not sin also, which is the death of the soul": let him be anathema. "For he contradicts the words of the Apostle: 'Through one man sin entered into the world, and through sin death, and so death passed upon all men; in whom all have sinned' " (Ro 5:12; *DS*, 372).[251]

Because the major part of this canon is a literal reiteration of the second canon of the Council of Orange,[252] a brief comment on the central modification introduced by the Council of Trent suffices. The affirmation of the idea that Adam lost holiness and justice for all men, inserted as it is within the quotation of the second canon of the Council of Orange, functions as a specification or elaboration of the way in which Adam's sin injures all men. The nature and the repercussion of that elaboration is difficult to determine. As was noted, the description of original sin as involving the loss of holiness and justice is meant to avoid sanctioning any one of the current definitions of original sin. In view of the nature of the discussion that preceded the acceptance of this phrase in the final version of canon one, however, and in view of the insertion of this new element in the midst of an

---

247 See sec. A, 5 above.
248 *CT*, V, 196.
249 *DS*, 1521, cf. 1555.
250 Vanneste, *NRTh*, LXXXVII, 706-707.
251 *DS*, 1512.
252 See sec. A, 5 above.

ancient text, this amendment is plausibly explained as a vague approbation of a privative notion of original sin.[253] In that case, the question arises as to the relative weight of that privative notion within an original text to which that notion is foreign. Does that foreign element become dominant by the very fact of its *deliberate* insertion? Or is that foreign element *absorbed* by the original text so that its positive description of original sin ("sin [itself]," "the death of the soul") remains dominant? At this point the Council's hesitancy to determine the nature of original sin by definition has resulted in a vague description of its effects.[254]

c. *Canon Three*

> If anyone asserts that this sin of Adam, which is one by origin, and which is communicated to all men by propagation not by imitation (*propagatione, non imitatione transfusum*), and which is in all men and proper to each, is taken away either through the powers of human nature or through a remedy other than the merit of the one mediator, our Lord Jesus Christ who reconciled us to God in his blood, "being made unto us justice, santification and redemption" (I Cor 1:30); or denies that, through the sacrament of baptism rightly conferred in the form of the Church, this merit of Jesus Christ is applied both to adults and to infants: let him be anathema. Because "there is no other name under heaven given to men by which we must saved" (Ac 4:12). Hence that voice: "Behold the lamb of God, behold him who takes away the sins of the world" (cf. Jn 1:29). And: "All you who have been baptized into Christ, have put on Christ" (Ga 3:27).[255]

Although the principal purpose of this and the following canons is to indicate the remedy for original sin,[256] they also provide, implicitly and explicitly, a further specification of the reality of original sin itself. The third canon, for example, specifies the way in which original sin is transmitted. Rejecting the Pelagian imitation theory, it teaches that original sin is transfused by propagation — a description closely akin to the formulation found in the second canon of the Council of Carthage, *generatione traxerunt*.[257] Moreover, this canon specifies that Adam's sin is one in its origin (*origine unum*) and, transmitted by propagation, is in each human being as his own sin (*omnibus inest unicuique proprium*). This statement is directed primarily

---

253 See Vanneste's conclusion regarding canon 1 (*NRTh*, LXXXVII, 711-12).

254 Cf. Josef Weismayer, " 'Erbsünde' und Sündenverflochtenheit in der theologischen Tradition und in den lehramtlichen Aussagen," *Ist Adam an allem schuld? Erbsünde oder Sündenverflochtenheit?* Ferdinand Dexinger, Ferdinand Staudinger, Hedwig Wahle and Josef Weismayer (Innsbruck: Tyrolia-Verlag, 1971), 349, n. 81: "Der Begriff des 'peccatum' in diesem Zusammenhang wurde nicht geklärt, obwohl Kardinal de Nobilibus dies wiederholt urgiert hatte: vgl. *Concilium Tridentinum* V 200, 205."

255 *DS*, 1513.

256 As is reflected in the preamble to this decree (*DS*, 1510), some of the canons (1 and 2) deal with original sin itself, while others (3, 4 and 5) deal with its remedy.

257 See sec. A, 5 above.

against the teaching of Pighius who held that original sin is numerically one, consisting in the sin of Adam. Adam's posterity is affected by his sin, not in its reality, but only by virtue of the imputation of this single original sin to all men.[258] Trent grants that original sin is one, but only *in its origin*; via propagation it inheres *in each* human being.

This explication of the reality of original sin in all men is subservient to the central thrust of this canon, namely, the presentation of the only remedy for original sin, the reconciling and redeeming work of Jesus Christ conferred upon both infants and adults through the sacrament of baptism. The concentration upon this sacramental remedy obtains a somewhat exclusive ring when one observes that the preliminary text of this canon stated that the merit of Jesus Christ is applied by faith and the sacrament,[259] and that, against the express wishes of the Augustinian theologian Seripando, this reference to faith was deleted.[260]

d. *Canon Four*

"If anyone denies that newly born infants are to be baptized," *even though they may have been born of baptized parents,* "or says that they are indeed baptized for the remission of sins but that they do not derive anything of the original sin from Adam that *must be* expiated in the bath of regeneration" *to obtain eternal life*; "and, consequently, that for them the form of baptism – 'for the remission of sins' – is to be understood, not in a true, but in a false sense: let him be anathema. Because the words of the Apostle:'Through one man sin entered into the world, and through sin death, and so *death* passed upon all men; in whom all have sinned' (Ro 5:12), cannot be understood in any other way than as the Catholic Church everywhere has always understood them. Because of this rule of faith," *from a tradition of the apostles* "even infants, who have not yet been able to commit any personal sins, are truly baptized for the remission of sins, that in them that which they have *c*ontracted [*contraxerunt*] by generation may be washed away by regeneration" (*DS*, 223). *"For unless a man be born again of water and the Holy Spirit, he cannot enter into the kingdom of God"* (Jn 3:5).[261]

This canon is largely a literal quotation of the second canon of the Council of Carthage.[262] Only the *underlined* phrases – most of which underscore the necessity of baptism as remedy for original sin – are added by the Council of Trent. The first insertion represents an articulation of the strict universality of original sin. Already in the Pelagian controversy the objection

---

258 Vanneste, *NRTh*, LXXXVII, 720-25. Gross, IV, 113-14. Schoonenberg, *Man and Sin*, 175.

259 *CT*, V, 197.

260 Regarding this significant modification, see Jedin, 123, 129-30; Eduard Stakemeier, *Der Kampf um Augustin auf dem Tridentinum* (Paderborn: Bonifacius-Druckerei, 1937), 80-81.

261 *DS*, 1514.

262 See sec. A, 5 above.

had been raised that parents cannot possibly pass on something which they themselves lack. Hence, if original sin is taken away by baptism, it was argued, the children of baptized parents should be born without original sin.[263] This seemingly logical argument appears to have been revived by some at the time of the Council of Trent.[264] Rejecting that argument, Trent simply affirms that even the children of baptized parents are to be baptized. The necessity of baptism is again underscored by the following alteration. Whereas the second canon of the Council of Carthage could have been interpreted as merely commending the sacrament of baptism as a *factual* remedy for original sin (*quod lavacro regenerationis expietur*), the Council of Trent presents baptism unequivocally as a *necessary* remedy for original sin (*quod regenerationis lavacro necesse sit expiari*). Moreover, this sacrament is said to be necessary for obtaining eternal life — a reaffirmation of the third canon of the Council of Carthage.[265] To substantiate this affirmation of the strict and universal necessity of baptism the Council of Trent makes an explicit appeal to the apostolic tradition and, in conclusion, adduces Jn 3:5.

A final note is in order regarding an element in this canon that becomes problematical precisely because it is adopted without change from the second canon of the Council of Carthage. The fact that, unlike canon two, this canon does not merely cite Ro 5:12,[266] but also reaffirms a specific interpretation of that passage that was sanctioned a century earlier gains new significance in view of the fact that Erasmus' demonstration of the exegetical untenability of this traditional interpretation was known to the fathers of Trent.[267] Not only the alteration, but also the mere repetition of an ancient tradition by the magisterium can prove to be a problematical procedure.[268]

e. *Canon Five*
>If anyone denies that through the grace of our Lord Jesus Christ conferred in baptism the guilt of original sin is remitted, or even asserts that everything having the true and proper nature of sin is not taken away but is only brushed over or not imputed: let him be anathema. For God hates nothing in the regenerated because "there is no condemnation for those who are truly buried with Christ by means of

---

263 Gross, I, 337.
264 *CT*, V, 212 (error no. 3).
265 *DS*, 224 (cf. sec. A, 5 above).
266 Interestingly, due to the use of the Vulgate, the term "death" which does not appear in the Scripture passage as cited by the Council of Carthage (see sec. A, 5 above) does appear in the present text. Regarding this *correction* Baumann comments: "Aber man scheint in Trient nicht bemerkt zu haben, dass der Vulgatatext ohne exegetischen Salto mortale nicht mehr als eine 'Erbtodlehre' hergibt" (Baumann, 76).
267 Gross, IV, 112. *CT*, V, 212.
268 See Schoonenberg's comments in *Man and Sin*, 170-71.

baptism into death" (Ro 6:4), who "do not walk according to the flesh" (Ro 8:1),[269] but putting off the old man and putting on the new man "which was created according to God" (cf. Eph 4:22ff.; Col 3:9f.), are made innocent, without stain, pure, no longer hateful, but beloved sons of God, "heirs indeed of God and joint heirs with Christ" (Ro 8:17), so that absolutely nothing delays their entrance into heaven. It is the mind of this council and it professes that concupiscence or the tinder [of sin] remains in the baptized; but since it is left to provide a trial, it has no power to injure those who do not consent and who, by the grace of Jesus Christ, manfully resist. Moreover, those "who compete according to the rules will be crowned" (II Tm 2:5). As for this concupiscence which the Apostle sometimes calls "sin" (Ro 6:12ff.), this holy council declares that the Catholic Church has never understood it to be called sin as being truly and properly sin in those born again, but because it is from sin and inclines to sin. If anyone thinks the contrary: let him be anathema.[270]

This is the only canon thus far that does not represent a reaffirmation and elaboration of previous ecclesiastical pronouncements concerning original sin. It is aimed directly at the teaching of the Reformers, especially of Luther. Luther held that concupiscence, understood as man's culpable bias to evil, remains in the Christian and constitutes sin in a true and proper sense because, due to this concupiscence, the fulfillment of the command, "Thou shalt not covet," is impossible.[271] For that reason the Christian can be described as *simul iustus et peccator: "just*, because in faith he shares in Christ's redemption and, in the power of that faith, fights against the evil within; *sinner*, because precisely this evil, 'invincible concupiscence,' continues to dwell in him."[272] Because it deals with this central question as to man's position vis-à-vis God's grace, this canon lays the foundation for the subsequent decree on justification.[273]

In the bull *Exsurge Domine*, Pope Leo X had condemned Luther's thesis, "To deny that sin remains in a child after baptism is to despise both Paul and Christ alike."[274] In keeping with this papal pronouncement, the fifth canon condemns those who assert that everything having the true and

---

269 As it appears in *DS*, this part of canon five consists of a remarkable conflation and erroneous identification of scripture passages. Accurate indication of the citation and correct identification of the sources demands the following reading: For God hates nothing in the regenerated because "there is no condemnation for those who are" (Ro 8:1) truly "buried with Christ by means of baptism into death" (Ro 6:4), who "do not walk according to the flesh" (Ro 8:4) . . . .

270 *DS*, 1515.

271 Jedin, 121. Vanneste, *NRTh*, LXXXVI, 359-61; *Het Dogma*, 143-46.

272 Jedin, 121.

273 Jedin, 137; cf. 121, 123.

274 *DS*, 1452. See also the next error (concerning the *fomes peccati*) condemned by this bull (*DS*, 1453). Luther's identification of original sin and concupiscence and his valuation of the latter in the baptized are found also among the list of errors compiled for the fifth session of the Council (see errors five and six, *CT*, V, 212).

proper nature of sin is not taken away (*tolli*) but merely "smoothed over" (*radi*) or not imputed. Although concupiscence or the tinder of sin (*fomes [peccati]*) remains after baptism, it is not regarded as sin in the true and proper sense, but only in an analogical sense, i.e., by virtue of the fact that the *origin* and the (possible) *effect* of concupiscence is sin.[275]

Though directed against the reformers, the central thrust of this canon met with considerable resistance at the Council of Trent itself. The leader of this opposition was Seripando. As an Augustinian, he closely associated original sin with concupiscence, which he viewed as the *actus* of original sin that, in the unbaptized, constitutes guilt.[276] In the baptized, concupiscence is sin, not in a strict, but nevertheless in a certain (true) sense (*aliqua ratione*) of the word.[277] If God hates sin, Seripando argued, he must also hate concupiscence, the source of sin,[278] Although he was willing to differentiate between God's attitude toward the regenerated and that toward the unregenerated,[279] he consistently opposed the prevalent tendency to reduce concupiscence from a morally qualified inclination to evil to a morally neutral human drive.[280] In the justified, the guilt of original sin is removed but its *actus*, concupiscence, remains.[281]

The definitive text of canon five in no way accommodates Seripando's views. All the phrases to which he objected were retained. Moreover, those phrases in the preliminary text that were even slightly favorable to Seripando's views were deleted. Thus the descriptions of that which remains in the baptized as a "weakness and illness of nature" and as "remnants of sin" that appeared in the preliminary text,[282] do not appear in the final text of canon five.[283] Although the rejection of the positive conception of original sin

---

275 In the same way that the term "health" is used analogically to describe an apple or someone's complexion. For a discussion of this type of analogy, see ch. III, sec. C, 1, b below.

276 Jedin, 122. Stakemeier, 80.

277 Jedin, 122. Stakemeier, 89.

278 Stakemeier, 82, cf. 89.

279 Seripando formulated his position as follows: "In the regenerated no evil remains which God hates, but a great weakness which is displeasing to God and must be healed all through life, until God heals all our diseases and redeems us from corruption. (see Stakemeier, 82; Jedin, 130-31).

280 See Stakemeier, 81, 83, 89, 97, 98.

281 See Stakemeier, 88, 98. See also Stakemeier's helpful delineation of the difference between Luther's and Seripando's understanding of concupiscence (Stakemeier, 118-21).

282 *CT*, V, 197.

283 Despite appearances to the contrary, Stakemeier concludes that Seripando's views were not repudiated by this canon: "Das Konzil hat die Auffassungen Seripandos korri-

entailed in Seripando's, and *a fortiori* Luther's, view of concupiscence formally concerned an assessment only of the baptized, this decision could not fail to have repercussions upon the entire assessment of man's condition as unveiled by God's grace.[284] Nevertheless, concerning the precise nature of original sin, the fifth canon, too, remains vague. This vagueness, combined with the exclusive concentration on the *sacramental* remedy for original sin, provides the soil for the unambiguous specification of the nature of original sin that becomes dominant in post-Tridentine theology.

9. Post-Tridentine Development

Not emulating the reticence displayed by the magisterium at the Council of Trent, the various theological schools continue to espouse and elaborate their definitions of original sin.[285] One of these becomes predominant. It has the advantage of being derived — at least formally — from those teachings of the Council of Trent that display a greater degree of clarity than the teaching regarding original sin itself. Not only does the decree on original sin present grace exclusively in its *sacramental* mediation, the decree on justification presents that which is bestowed in the sacrament of baptism as infused grace.[286] That sets the stage for Bellarmine (1542-1621) and others to determine the precise nature of original sin, at least in its formal element, in the following manner: since the remedy for original sin is the sacrament of baptism, and since by this sacrament sanctifying grace is infused, original sin must entail the privation of sanctifying grace.[287] Thus, by one ingeneous stroke, the laborious procedure of determining the nature of original sin that had become prevalent in scholastic theology is obviated. That of which man is deprived in the condition of original sin need no longer be derived by tenuous speculation regard-

---

giert und sie festgelegt in einem Sinne, der von Seripando selbst schon aufgezeigt war" (Stakemeier, 129).

284 See Jedin's comment regarding the intrinsic relationship between the conception of concupiscence and the assessment of man's stance vis-à-vis God (n. 273 above).

285 For the various interpretations of original sin in the 16th to the 18th century, see Gross, IV, 119-93.

286 *DS,* 1528, 1529, 1530, 1561.

287 See Gross, IV, 132-33 (Bellarmine), 136-37 (Suarez). The definition of original sin as the privation of grace has its roots in Thomas' definition of original sin as a privation of original justice, since sanctifying grace is indispensible to original justice (see sec. A, 7 above). It is not surprizing, therefore, that the explicit definition of original sin in terms of sanctifying grace emerges within the Thomistic tradition: Petrus de Palude (1280-1342), Jacques de Lausanne (-1322), Nicholaus Cusanus (1401-1464), Dionysius Carthusanius (1402-71); see Gross, IV, 320-31, 326, 328; 380-81; 385. The definition of original sin as the absence of sanctifying grace is first mentioned by William of Auvergne (-1249), who rejects it as erroneous (Gross, III, 326).

ing that which man possessed in his *original* state, but can be derived from the ecclesiastical teaching regarding that which man possesses in his *present* (sanctified) state.

The sheer simplicity of this procedure, its unassailable formal point of departure and the general prevalence of the negative conception of original sin combine to assure the further specification of original sin as the privation of sanctifying grace a dominant role in post-Tridentine Roman Catholic theology.[288] So powerful is this tradition that even in contemporary theology this specific understanding of the nature of original sin constitutes the unquestioned *primum datum* of the situational reinterpretation of original sin.

B. THE CURRENT DISCUSSION

1. Immediate Occasion

Since the early fifties, Roman Catholic publications on the subject of original sin have been issued in a constant stream,[289] and as yet the discussion shows no signs of abating.[290] An adequate explanation for this veritable "flood"[291] of literature is difficult to find because it is not unleashed, as in the fifth century, by a frontal attack on what is considered to be the heart of the gospel. The immediate occassion, however, of this rather sudden proliferation of literature on a seemingly obscure subject lies more readily at hand. The intensity of the current discussion has been occasioned by the gradual erosion of the framework that seems indispensable for the traditional doctrine of original sin, a framework that was never at issue until modern times. This framework consists essentially of a static view of man and his world: the world and man proceed ready-made from God's hands; all men originate from

---

[288] See Gross' comments regarding the 16th, 17th and 18th centuries (Gross, IV, 127-28, 151) and regarding the 19th and 20th century (Gross, IV, 212-13, 242, 283).

Michael Schmaus is an interesting exponent of this powerful tradition (*Katholische Dogmatik*, II/1 5th ed.; [München: Max Hueber Verlag, 1954], 372-77 regarding the essence of original sin). He describes the privation of original sin as involving primarily man's loss of the "divine, triune life," "sanctifying grace," "supernatural relatedness" to God, "supernatural divine life" (pp. 373-74). This conception of the essence of original sin, says Schmaus, is held by the majority of theologians (p. 373: *opinio communior*). He ascribes this development to the post-Tridentine elaboration of Tridentine teachings regarding justification (pp. 373-74). He then adds that this convergence of theological opinion can also appeal to the Greek Fathers: "Denn diese betonen vor allem den Verlust des Heiligen Geistes und der vergöttlichenden Gnade" (p. 374).

[289] In the last decade alone, one can count at least seventy titles dealing with the subject of original sin (see Baumann, 92).

[290] Haag, *ThQ*, CL, 238.

[291] Baumann, 92.

a single human pair; historical development is orientated to and bound by its beginning; a primordial fall has catastrophic and historically irreversible consequences for all men. For centuries this world view provided a stable frame of reference, nay more, the existential habitat *within* which discussions regarding the nature of original sin took place. Even significant divergences regarding the nature of original sin unquestioningly presupposed this common framework. By contrast, the contemporary discussion of the doctrine of original sin presupposes that this stable framework has been eroded and finally washed away by a dynamic, evolutionary world view.[292] The world is no longer viewed as a stable stage upon which God has placed accomplished human actors, but as an accelerating stream within which at various points rudimentary forms of human life appear. The "good creation" lies not at the beginning, but at the end of history. Within this view there is hardly room for a pristine paradise, much less for a primordial fall with catastrophic consequences for all men. Thus the mainstays of the traditional doctrine of original sin have crumbled.

This altered view of man and his world gains added effect via its repercussions upon one's view of revelation. In the traditional doctrine of original sin, Adam, paradise, monogenesis, the fall were assumed to be part and parcel of revealed truth. The devotion of a separate canon by the Council of Trent to the first man Adam and his fall[293] rests on the presupposition that the Bible provides historical information regarding primeval times. The information provided by the science of paleontology, however, neccesitates a basic reassessment of the nature of biblical revelation, specifically of that which was assumed to be the scriptural basis for the traditional doctrine of original sin.[294] Stimulated by the encyclical *Divino Afflante Spiritu* (1943), which displayed a more positive attitude to contemporary biblical studies in general and encouraged the study of the literary genres of biblical writings in particular,[295] Roman Catholic theology increasingly proceeded from the conviction that the early chapters of Genesis do not intend to provide information

---

292 See, e.g., the new Dutch Catechism which describes the antiquated and the contemporary world view, respectively, as static and dynamic (*A New Catechism: Catholic Faith for Adults,* trans. Kevin Smyth [London: Burns and Oates, 1967], 263; *De Nieuwe katechismus: Geloofsvérkondiging voor volwassenen* [Hilversum: Paul Brand, 1966], 309). Karl Schmitz-Moormann contrasts the traditional to the contemporary world view as a "Seins-Welt" to a "Werde-Welt" (Schmitz-Moorman, 9-10; see also the introductory chapter, Schmitz-Moorman, 13-26).

293 See sec. A, 8, a above.

294 See Berkouwer's discussion of the influence of scientific information upon one's understanding of Scripture, *De Heilige Schrift,* II (Kampen: Kok, 1967), 299-305.

295 See n. 301 below.

regarding hoary antiquity but to illuminate the historical-religious situation confronting the biblical writer.[296]

2. Roman Catholic "Monopoly"

The combined effect of the modern world view and the new approaches to the biblical material may explain the explosion of literature on the doctrine of original sin in the past two decades; it does not explain why we are confronted by an almost exlusively *Roman Catholic* explosion. In an ecumenical age such a "monopoly" appears to be an anomaly. Hypothetically, some factors can be adduced that may elucidate this curious phenomenon.

One factor concerns a significant difference of emphasis that marks the Roman Catholic and the Protestant approach to the doctrine of original sin. In line with certain elements of Augustine's doctrine of original sin, the mainstream of contemporary Protestant theology distilled from the traditional doctrine the notion that in his deepest being man stands in conflict with God. Accordingly, original sin is viewed, not so much as a distinct reality that can be regarded as being morally neutralized in baptism, but as the essence, core and root of sin, as man's common *Ursünde*. [297] This concentration on man's central religious directedness has a twofold effect: the doctrine of original sin becomes less amenable to separate treatment and appears to be sheltered from the storm unleashed by the shifting view of human origins. An explosion of Protestant literature devoted specifically to the doctrine of original sin triggered by an altered world view is therefore unlikely.

In Roman Catholic theology, original sin can more readily be treated separately, for it is a reality that *as sin* is taken away by baptism and that remains absent even in the presence of personal sins. Moreover, as the separate Tridentine canon devoted to Adam and the theological preoccupation with a privative understanding of original sin indicate, this doctrine is viewed as being intricately related to the Adamic framework. Even when the *nature* of original sin comes to be determined without reverting to speculation regarding man's original state,[298] the *reality* of original sin continues to depend

---

296 See, e.g., Herbert Haag, *Biblische Schöpfungslehre und kirchliche Erbsündenlehre* ("Stuttgarter Bibelstudien," 10, 4th ed.; Stuttgart: Katholisches Bibelwerk, 1968), 57; *Is Original Sin in Scripture?* trans. Dorothy Thompson (New York: Sheed and Ward, 1969), 92.

297 See Baumann's extensive survey of the interpretation of original sin in contemporary Protestant theology (Baumann, 109-81, cf. 186-90). Significantly, in the title above this survey, Baumann uses the term "Ursünde" (Baumann, 109), whereas the term "Erbsünde" (though in quotation marks) appears above the equivalent survey of Roman Catholic theology (Baumann, 91).

298 See sec. A, 9 above.

on the Adamic framework. A protracted Roman Catholic discussion of the doctrine of original sin is therefore likely to be triggered by a changed view of human origins.

The somewhat belated and rather sudden, (concentrated) eruption of Roman Catholic literature on the doctrine of original sin, however, may be rendered plausible by a complex of more general factors. An eruption may be imagined to take place after a gradual build-up of pressure within a solid enclosure. The solid enclosure is given with the idea of the Church as infallible teacher of dogma which assigns to theology the subservient role of demonstrating that a particular dogma — in the sense in which it has been defined by the Church — is contained in the sources.[299] A gradual build-up of pressure is ensured by the inevitable influx of the modern world view and of new approaches to "the sources," on the one hand, and the initially negative and defensive stance with respect to these issues by the magisterium, on the other.[300] When the encyclicals *Divino Afflante Spiritu* (1943), mentioned earlier, as well as *Humani Generis* (1950) officially opened, or in some respects merely unlocked, the door to new approaches to the biblical writings and to modern theories concerning the origin of man and his world,[301] the question as to what remains of the infallible dogma after its mainstays collapse could not but burst into the open.

299 See *Humani Generis* (1950), *DS*, 3886, *Ecclesia Docens*, 27.

300 See the encyclical *Providentissimus Deus* (1893) which reflects an extremely defensive position with respect to contemporary approaches to Scripture (*EB*, 100-27; *Ecclesia Docens*, pp. 32-60). See also the decisions of the Pontifical Biblical Commission (founded in 1902) regarding the early chapters of Genesis (*DS*, 3512-14; see Berkouwer's analysis in *Vatikaans Concilie en nieuwe theologie* [Kampen: Kok, 1964], 135-39; *The Second Vatican Council and the New Catholicism,* trans. Lewis B. Smedes [Grand Rapids: Eerdman, 1965], 113-16). W. Grossouw says that until approximately 1920 this Commission defended overly conservative positions which retarded the progress of scholarship ("Korte voorgeschiedenis van de hedendaagse katholieke bijbelwetenschap," *DO-C*, no. 20 [Nov. 8, 1962], 2). Another manifestation of the negative position of the Church is the censure under which Teilhard de Chardin was placed in 1924; he was ordered not to speak nor to write in opposition to the traditional position of the Church regarding the question of original sin (see Schmitz-Moormann, 122).

301 *Divino Afflante Spiritu* is of importance because it takes a far less negative stance with respect to new developments in biblical studies. It strongly encourages the study of the cultural environment of the biblical writers, the sources which they used and the historically conditioned type of writing which they adopted (*DS*, 3829-31; *Ecclesia Docens*, 40-45). This openness to a comprehensive study of the cultural-historical setting of the biblical writings finds even more emphatic expression in a letter of the Pontifical Biblical Commission written in 1948 to kardinal Suhard (see *DS*, 3862-64). Grossouw considers this letter to represent a tacit retraction of some earlier decrees of the same commission (W. Grossouw, "Enkele gegevens omtrent de tegenwoordige situatie van de katholieke bijbelwetenschap," *DO-C*, no. 21 [Nov. 8, 1962], 1). *Humani Generis* declares

The increasing pressure for theological change and flexibility was wholly released by the advent of the Second Vatican Council. For the reinterpretation of the doctrine of original sin, this Council was of inestimable significance, less by virtue of specific pronouncements than by virtue of the climate it created. The Council created an air of expectancy and renewal that persisted even when some of its decisions were less renovating than had been hoped.[302] At the outset a climate conducive to theological-doctrinal renewal was officially fostered by a remarkable statement by Pope John XXIII on the opening day of the Council:

> What is needed is that this certain and immutable doctrine, to which the faithful owe obedience, be studied afresh and reformulated in contemporary terms. For this deposit of faith, or truths which are contained in our time-honored teaching, is one thing; the manner in which these truths are set forth (with their meaning preserved intact) is something else.[303]

Although it has as its context a strong emphasis upon the certainty and the immutability of ecclesiastical doctrine, this official sanction of the distinction between the substance and the formulation of dogma, coming at so critical a point in the history of the Catholic Church, helped to clear away the institutional obstacles that hampered the theological currents of reinterpretation.

Even more important for the reinterpretation of the doctrine of original sin, the Second Vatican Council refrained from providing a *material delimitation and fixation of the latitude* of the Pope's substance-formulation distinction. The significance of this conciliar restraint is illustrated by the fact that a rather reactionary and conservative chapter on original sin contained in a *schema* written by one of the preparatory committees[304] did not find its

---

the theory of man's evolution to be an open question insofar as it concerns the evolution of the body; man's soul is immediately created by God (*DS*, 3896; *Ecclesia Docens*, 38). Polygenism, by contrast, is declared to be not an open question because its reconcilability with the doctrine of original sin is in no way apparent (*DS*, 3898; *Ecclesia Docens*, 39). Despite such cautious strictures (for Teilhard de Chardin's extremely critical reaction to *Humani Generis*, see Schmitz-Moormann, 163-64), these encyclicals did officially open the door to current approaches to Scripture and theories regarding the origin of man (see Berkouwer, *Vatikaans Concilie*, 134-49; *The Second Vatican Council*, 112-23).

302 See, e.g., Karl Rahner's critical assessment of the decisions of the Council (*Karl Rahner antwortet Eberhard Simons. Zur Lage der Theologie: Probleme nach dem Konzil* ["Das theologische Interview" no. 1; Düsseldorf: Patmos-Verlag, 1969], 17-25).

303 *Gaudet Mater Ecclesia*, *AAS*, LIV (1962), 792; *Ecclesia Docens*, 39; cf. *The Documents of Vatican II*, ed. Walter M. Abbott (London: Geoffrey Chapman, 1967), 715; hereafter this work will be cited as *DocVatII*. For an assessment of the significance of this statement, see G. C. Berkouwer, *Vatikaans Concilie*, 18-22; *The Second Vatican Council*, 22-26.

304 "Schema Constitutionis dogmaticae de deposito Fidei pure custodiendo," ch.

way into the definitive documents of the Council. In this chapter that which in the classic ecclesiastical teaching of original sin functions as *unquestioned framework* is elevated to the status of *unquestionable constituent* of the doctrine: original sin is declared to have its ground not in the fact that the individual by birth becomes a member of a corrupt society but in the fact that he is generated in a nature infected by the sin of Adam inasmuch as he is the foundation, head and source of the whole of human nature.[305] Moreover, in the concluding paragraphs of this chapter monogenism is directly taught.[306] Had the substance of this chapter been incorporated in a decree or constitution of the Council, all of the reinterpretations of original sin dealt with in the present study would have stood officially condemned. In its official pronouncements, however, the Second Vatican Council did not deal with original sin as such but merely alluded to the traditional doctrine.[307] Thus the Council in effect granted the Catholic theologians the elbowroom that is required for a flexible and creative application of the substance-formulation distinction to the doctrine of original sin.[308]

Subsequent attempts by Pope Paul VI,[309] by a Committee of Cardi-

VIII: "De peccato originali in filiis Adae," *Schemata Constitutionum et Decretorum de quibus disceptabitur in Concilii sessionibus,* Series Prima (Rome: Typis Polyglottis Vaticanis, 1962), 54-60. See Schoonenberg's vehement opposition to this chapter ("Erfzonde, II," *DO-C,* no. 45 [March 29, 1963], 9-10).

305 "De deposito Fidei pure custodiendo," ch. VIII, par. 45; cf. par. 44.

306 See *ibid.,* pars. 48 and 49.

307 See esp. *Dogmatic Constitution on the Church (Lumen Gentium),* ch. I, par. 2 *(DocVatII, 15)* and *Patoral Constitution on the Church in the Modern World (Gaudium et Spes),* Introductory statement, par. 10 *(DocVatII,* 207-208), ch. I, par. 13 *(DocVatII,* 211), par. 18 *(DocVatII,* 215), par. 22 *(DocVatII,* 220); ch. III, par. 37 *(DocVatII,* 235). See also *Decree on the Instruments of Social Communication (Inter Mirifica),* ch. I, par. 7 *(DocVatII,* 323) and *Decree on the Apostolate of the Laity (Apostolicam Actuositatem),* ch. II, par. VII *(DocVatII,* 497).

308 Joseph Ratzinger expresses his assessment of the fact that the Council refrained from making a more detailed pronouncement on original sin in an intriguing and highly paradoxical statement: "Ebenso vermied man es angesichts der neuen Debatten im Fragenkreis von Urstand und Ursünde, dieses Thema ausdrücklich zu behandeln. Auch hier war man sich einig, dass der *wesentliche Gehalt der Aussagen von Trient unaufgebbar* ist, dass aber der Theologie die Möglichkeit gelassen werden muss, *neu danach zu fragen, was eigentlich dieser wesentliche Gehalt sei"* (*Lexikon für Theologie und Kirche. Das Zweite Vatikanische Konzil: Konstitutionen, Dekrete und Erklärungen,* ed. Herbert Vorgrimler [Freiburg: Herder, 1966-68], III, 321, emphasis added).

For a description of the liberating impact of the Council on theology generally, see the last two chapters of (T.) Mark Schoof, *Aggiornamento: De doorbraak van een nieuwe katholieke theologie* (Baarn: Wereldvenster, 1968), 273-81; *Breakthrough: The Beginnings of the New Catholic Theology,* trans. N. D. Smith (Dublin: Gill and MacMillan, 1970), 228-75.

309 See his "Address to Conference of Theologians Discussing Original Sin" (July 11,

nals[310] and by the Congregation of Faith[311] to constrict the latitude of reinterpretation with respect to the doctrine of original sin had little or no effect on the theological currents that were allowed to run their course by the Second Vatican Council. These currents, long pent up, hesitantly allowed to run a restricted course in the 1950's, and positively stimulated in the early sixties, had become too strong and too wide to be officially curbed or even redirected in the late sixties.[312]

Thus a complex of typically Roman Catholic factors combined to store up and intensify the pressure for reinterpretation in such a way that even an initially hesitant release of pressure is sufficient to trigger the torrent of literature that constitutes the seemingly anomalous and anachronistic Roman Catholic monopoly on the discussion of original sin. Although the problems surrounding this doctrine confront both the Catholic and the Protestant the-

1966), *AAS*, LVIII (1966), 649-55; English translation in *The Pope Speaks*, XI (1966), 229-35. In this address, Pope Paul explicitly speaks of limits within which the reinterpretation of original sin must take place and refers, in this context, to his encyclical *Mysterium Fidei* in which the limits within which the doctrine of transsubstantiation must be (re)interpreted are delineated. See also the section on original sin in Pope Paul VI's "Credo" (*Sollemnis Professio Fidei*), *AAS*, LX (1968), 439-40; *The Pope Speaks*, XIII (1968), 278-79. In his "Address," Pope Paul circumscribes the limits of reinterpreting original sin by positing that Adam is the first man and the progenitor of all men; that his sin is passed on to all men by propagation and inheres in each as his own sin; and that original sin is properly called sin, the death of the soul (*AAS*, LVIII, 654; *The Pope Speaks*, XI, 234). Furthermore, in his "Credo," the Pope strongly emphasizes that human *nature* is the seat and the medium of original sin, and he describes original sin in terms of the privation of supernatural grace (*AAS*, LX, 439-40; *The Pope Speaks*, XIII, 278-79).

310 See the *Supplement to A New Catechism*, Edouard Dhanis and Jan Visser on behalf of the Commission of Cardinals appointed to examine *A New Catechism*, trans. Kevin Smyth (London: Burns and Oates, 1969); a translation of *Aanvulling bij De Nieuwe Katechismus* (2d ed.; Hilversum: Paul Brand, 1969). This document (the most extensive section of which is the one devoted to original sin) is the meagre result of a concerted attempt by Rome to correct the *New Catechism* by thoroughly revising it — hence Haag's gloss on the title: ". . . the Supplement (really 'Correction') to the Dutch Catechism . . ." (*JESt*, X, 262).

311 See the reaction of this body to Haag's book on original sin as documented by Haag, "Ein Verfahren der Glaubenskongregation," *ThQ*, CLII (1973), 184-92.

312 That Pope Paul's and the Congregation for Faith's efforts were to no avail is attested to by the fact that of the subsequent publications on original sin by *Roman Catholic theologians* few remain within and some move far beyond the boundaries delineated by the ecclesiastical authorities in Rome. The appearance of a mere *Supplement* rather than a revised and corrected *New Catechism* (see n. 310 above) is the clearest and most significant witness to the failure of Rome to impose its boundaries of reinterpretation upon its theologians and even upon its church provinces (the Dutch Bishops commissioned the writing of the *New Dutch Catechism* and subsequently supported its authors' opposition to the incorporation of the corrections demanded by Rome). For

ologian, these problems attain a crisis-level more readily in a Roman Catholic context. If an *infallible* dogma is discovered to have *"clay* feet,"[313] the frequent appearance of the word "crisis" in the Catholic discussions of original sin[314] appears to be warranted. Fiolet is not indulging in metaphoric hyperbole, therefore, when he evokes the image of an electrical storm that unleashes its fury in the original sin discussion:

> The threatening thunder heads which the rapid developments in exegesis, the renewal of theological thought, and the provocative data of modern science have driven together above the Christian view of origins are discharged in the storm center of problems surrounding original sin.[315]

Caught in the middle of this storm by virtue of their profession and their faith, Roman Catholic theologians have not scurried for shelter but have attempted to channel — if not tame — the storm by creative reinterpretation. The "climatic" conditions created by the common factors mentioned by Fiolet and the typical constellation of elements that constitutes the Roman Catholic "topography" combined to yield the current stream of literature.

3. Deeper Questions

In this restless theological activity, questions more basic than those concerning the date, number and location of our primeval progenitors assert themselves. Indeed, many of the authors writing about original sin recognize that the impulse proceeding from the natural sciences constitutes the occasion or the catalyst, but not the sole reason for reinterpreting and renovating that doctrine.[316] In the unlikely event, for example, that monogenism were to become the accepted hypothesis among natural scientists once more, it would by no means occasion the theologians to reverse the process of reinter-

---

the story of this conflict, see W. Bless (ed.), *Witboek over de Nieuwe Katechismus* (Utrecht: Ambo, 1969). See Gross' assessment of the historical significance of the publication of the *Supplement*: "Welch ein Unterschied zwischen der lahmen Reaktion Roms auf den Holländischen Katechismus und Roms Vorgehen gegen den Modernismus! Wie tief müssen seither Autorität und Macht des Heiligen Stuhles selbst im katholischen Bereich gesunken sein! " (Gross, IV, 323).

313 Baumann, 81.

314 See H. A. M. Fiolet, "De erfzonde als verbondsmysterie," *Jaarboek, 1963-64*, 61, 62 ("serious crisis"); Schoonenberg, "Zonde der wereld en erfzonde," *Bijdragen*, XXIV (1963), 349; Baumann, 237 (the word also appears in the subtitle of his book).

315 Fiolet, *Jaarboek 1963-64*, 53.

316 Schoonenberg, "Theologie und Lehramt: Die Hermeneutik am Beispiel der Erbsünden-Diskussion," *WuW*, XXII (1967), 738; *idem*, "Tweegesprek over het ontstaan der zondigheid," *TvTh*, IV (1964), 69. See also Baumann, 92. Cf. Karl-Heinz Weger, *Theologie der Erbsünde ("Quaestiones Disputatae,"* 44; Freiburg: Herder, 1970), 48.

pretation and to repristinate the traditional conception of original sin.[317] Moreover, the relationship between natural science and the reinterpretation of original sin is not constituted by the simple procedure of adopting scientific data and, in turn, adapting Church doctrine. Schoonenberg, for example, is driven by the constant concern to *counteract* the tendency of reducing original sin to a necessary phase in the process of evolution.[318]

The shaking of the foundations of the doctrine of original sin has led to a deeper reflection on the problems and possible perspectives that inhere in the doctrine itself. Anyone dealing with the subject of original sin is confronted, willy nilly, with questions as basic as those concerning the condition and status of man before God, man's relationship to fellow man of the past, present and future. What word plumbs the depth of man's position in this world? Is the decisive and definitive word "tragedy," or is the most incisive- — be it penultimate — word "guilt"? These are the essential questions with which the doctrine of original sin deals.[319] Yet, as answer to such questions, this doctrine appears to take on Delphic qualities. Whereas the word "sin" points to man's responsibility, the word "original" appears to destroy such responsibility.[320] This dreadful irony that plagues the doctrine of original sin comes to poignant expression in the fact that for some the doctrine of original sin contains the seeds of "the revolutionary power of Christianity,"[321] while for others it entails "the paralyzing conception of being entangled in alien guilt and punishment and abandoned to a universal and irresistable moral decline."[322]

317 Schoonenberg, *ThTh*, IV, 69. Similarly Weger, 48-49, n. 88.
318 Schoonenberg, *Bijdragen*, XXIV, 349, 371.
319 Baumann, 17. Fiolet, *Jaarboek 1963-64*, 65. Weger, 28. Cf. Haag, *Biblische Schöpfungslehre*, 38-39.
320 Schoonenberg, "Gesprek over de erfzonde," *Ex Auditu Verbi: Theologische opstellen aangeboden aan Prof. Dr. G. C. Berkouwer*, ed. J. T. Bakker, H. M. Kuitert, G. E. Meuleman, R. Schippers (Kampen: Kok, 1965), 258. It must be kept in mind that Schoonenberg expresses this problem, of course, in terms of the Dutch word "erfzonde," literally "inherited-sin." That Schoonenberg should call attention to the problem of original sin and guilt in a volume of essays dedicated to Prof. Berkouwer is highly appropriate. In the latter's volumes dealing with hamartiology, the question formulated by Schoonenberg plays a central role (see Berkouwer, *De zonde*, I [Kampen: Kok, 1958], 5-19; *De zonde*, II [Kampen: Kok, 1960], esp. 207-18, the introductory chapter of the section dealing with original sin; this chapter entitled "The Problem (alien guilt?)" introduces the theme of the entire section on original sin; in the English translation, *Sin*, trans. Philip C. Holtrop [Grand Rapids: Eerdmans, 1971], 11-26 and 425-35; the fact that Berkouwer considers the question of alien guilt to be *the* problem of original sin is somewhat lost in the translation of the chapter title: "The Problem of Alien Guilt").
321 Baumann, 16.
322 Gross, I, 13.

4. Testcase for Hermeneutics

In its current discussion by Roman Catholic theologians, the doctrine of original sin clearly represents a testcase for hermeneutics.[323] No other dogma is so directly affected by the incisive divergence between the horizon under which it is first articulated and elaborated and the horizon under which it is presently being reinterpreted. For that reason the dynamics, problems and consequences of the hermeneutical process can be observed at close range in the reinterpretation of original sin.

In and through the struggle with the teachings of Scripture and magisterium regarding original sin, the hermeneutical question becomes especially urgent when a divergence is discerned between the modern view of man and the teaching of the Church[324] or a biblical motif.[325] Such a divergence may concern merely a difference of non-essential presuppositions, formulations or thought-forms, but it may also concern a confrontation of inimical central views of man. The question as to which type of divergence one is dealing with in a particular instance is not easily decided. For although the facile juxtapositioning of "the modern view of man" and "the teaching of Scripture and magisterium" suggests that these counterparts are objectifiable magnitudes, susceptible to disinterested scholarly analysis, such objectivity is an illusion. In all discussions regarding original sin, an inextricable subjective element plays a central role – even in a historical work in which reason is said to be the only guide.[326] Whenever the content of a certain passage conflicts with the interpreter's self-understanding, the question as to whether one is dealing with an "antiquated representation" or with the "abiding faith"[327] can be answered only if a critical analysis of the text is conjoined with an equally critical analysis of one's understanding of man.

---

323 Schoonenberg, "Testcase erfzonde," *NM,* XIX (1967), 194-205. See also a recent article by M. Michel, "Le péché originel, question herméneutique," *RSR,* XLVIII (1974), 113-35.

324 Fiolet, *Jaarboek, 1963-64*, 65.

325 Schoonenberg, *Het geloof van ons doopsel* ('s-Hertogenbosch: Malmberg, 1955-62), IV, 82, 88. Hereafter this work will be cited as *Geloof.*

326 Although in his *magnum opus*, Gross, e.g., wishes to give "Vernunft die führende Rolle des Sichtens, Prufens und Ordnens . . ." (*Geschichte, I,* 11) Ilse Bertinetti says of his work, "Der von Gross angestrebte bezw. auch in die Entwicklungsgeschichte der Erbsündenlehre hineingedeutete Humanisierungsprozess ist letztlich nicht anderes als eine erneute Aufnahme semipelagianischer Gedanken" (*Krisis des Erbsündendogmas: Eine Untersuchung zur theologischen Gegenwartsproblematik von Gesamtschuld und ethischer Verantwortung* [unpublished *Habilitationsschrift,* Theologische Fakultät der Humboldt-Universität, Berlin, 1970], 74).

327 Cf. the subtitle of Schmitz-Moormann's book.

Although every interpreter knows that hermeneutics is not the art of eisegesis nor the art of excision,[328] the danger of both lies always at hand. Signalling that danger may be no more than a facile warning from the sidelines. It may also describe a personal struggle:

> The person who wishes to mutilate the message of salvation is always present; he lives in the first place in our own self. To remain with our testcase: the dispute with Pelagianism continues because "boasting" of our own achievement and overlooking our inner need of salvation died with Pelagius as little as it came into the world with Pelagius.[329]

At this level, the hermeneutical question does not merely touch upon shifting horizons of reinterpretation but zeroes in on the central position of the reinterpreter within those horizons. That position entails a basic view of man and of salvation in Christ, a view which constitutes the anchorage point of reinterpretation. Although, or perhaps because, this anchorage point is more often tacitly assumed than explicitly reflected upon and accounted for, it is of extraordinary significance in shaping the limits, problems and results of reinterpretation. Thus the doctrine of original sin becomes a testcase not only for the process, but also for the starting point of reinterpretation.

C. NATURE, AIM, SCOPE AND STRUCTURE OF THIS STUDY

As to its nature, this study represents an in depth analysis, in distinction from a descriptive survey,[330] of a segment of *material* (as opposed to formal) hermeneutics. The *process* of reinterpretation will be considered in subservience to the peculiar *subject matter* of this reinterpretation.

The aim of this study is to investigate the degree and manner in which the *product* of reinterpretation is affected by the reinterpreter's initial understanding of the kernel meaning of original sin, by his choice of the central categories of reinterpretation and by his view of the origin, history and destiny of man and his world. This study is intended, in other words, as an exploration of the effect that the religious-theological starting point, the philosophical-anthropological "atmosphere" and the cosmic horizon of reinterpretation have upon the outcome of reinterpretation.

Although the above circumscription of the nature and aim of this study entails an *automatic* delimitation of its scope, the attempt to achieve the

---

328 Schoonenberg, "Theologie als kritische Prophetie," *Die Funktion der Theologie in Kirche und Gesellschaft: Beiträge zu einer notwendigen Diskussion*, ed. Paul Neuenzeit (München: Kösel-Verlag, 1969), 381.
329 Schoonenberg, *NM*, XIX, 204. Cf. Vanneste, *Het Dogma*, 176-77.
330 See the opening paragraphs of this chapter and n. 3 above.

described aim, while remaining true to the nature of this study, is in danger of foundering in the flood of material that remains. To keep the described aim within the reach of an in depth analysis, therefore, a further, *deliberate* delimitation of the subject matter is mandatory. This has been achieved by giving predominance to one of the two traditional foci of the doctrine of original sin and by selecting from the gamut of contemporary reinterpretations two dominant and opposite currents.

With the aid of the traditional foci, we have delimited the scope of this study by focussing on original sin not as a designation of the primordial fall (*peccatum originale originans*) but as a designation of a present reality (*peccatum originale originatum*). In accordance with that focus, a specific view of human origins, Adam or the fall will not be analyzed for its own sake but will be treated as the *new horizon* within which original sin *as present reality* is being reinterpreted. In other words, any view pertaining to the "originating sin" will be considered exclusively in terms of its repercussions upon the corresponding assessment of "originated sin."

With respect to the contemporary discussion, we have delimited the scope of this study further by concentrating on two dominant alternatives: the reinterpretation of original sin in terms of man's situatedness, on the one hand, and in terms of personal sin, on the other.

The situational reinterpretation of original sin provides an ideal subject for studying the dynamics and effects of shifting horizons, new categories and a specific point of departure upon the doctrine of original sin because the advocates of this approach attempt to do full justice to the basic elements that characterize the Roman Catholic ecclesiastical and theological tradition, while integrating this legacy with a new or expanded cosmic, philosophical and theological framework. This dynamic confrontation of old and new brings the ground, horizon, possibilities and limitations of this creative endeavor clearly to light.

The reinterpretation of original sin in terms of personal sin provides stark contrast to the situational reinterpretation. The advocates of the personal reinterpretation of original sin that will be considered have weighed the situational reinterpretation and have found it wanting. They proceed in a direction that is not only diametrically opposite to that of the situationalists but also represents a bold departure from the dominant stream in the Roman Catholic theological tradition. The question will be raised, therefore, whether this novel alternative within Roman Catholic theology is capable of solving the serious problems that attend the situational reinterpretation of original sin.

Because of its complexity, the framework within which the situationalists reinterpret the doctrine of original sin will be set forth (part I) before turning to the actual reinterpretation itself (part II). This seeming detour frees the presentation and analysis of the situational reinterpretation of original sin from the burden of extensive background explanations. Moreover, this arrangement has the added advantage that the reader who is fairly well acquainted with this theological and philosophical framework can proceed directly to part II, consulting part I only where necessary.

For the presentation and analysis of the personal reinterpretation of original sin a separate treatment of the framework of this reinterpretation is superfluous for three interrelated reasons: 1) in comparison to the situational approach, the personal reinterpretation is far less complex; 2) the philosophical motifs that play a part in this reinterpretation are also present in the philosophical framework of the situationalists; 3) in the personal reinterpretation a cosmic-historical horizon of the magnitude of that set forth in part I is lost from view. In part III, therefore, we can proceed directly to a consideration of two distinct interpretations of original sin in terms of personal sin.

Finally, in the Epilogue we will summarize the key problems encountered in the situational and in the personal reinterpretation of original sin and search for possible perspectives within and beyond these alternative reinterpretations.

PART I

FRAMEWORK FOR A SOLUTION

CHAPTER I MAN AS HISTORICAL BEING: FREEDOM AND SITUATEDNESS

Despite the divergent interpretation of original sin by the situationalists, on the one hand, and by the personalists,[1] on the other, both parties are stimulated to their endeavor by a basic dissatisfaction with the understanding of human solidarity as reflected in the traditional doctrine. Moreover, agreement is present also in the basis for this dissatisfaction, namely, a concern to safeguard the personal responsibility that appears to be jeopardized by the traditional doctrine. The situationalists and personalists part ways, however, when it comes to proposing a solution.

The situationalists set out on a much more difficult course, for, in distinction from the personalists, they refuse to abandon tangible solidarity and concrete history. They consider both to be essential to a proper understanding of the doctrine of original sin. This concern for history necessitates reflection on several facets that the personalists consider to be largely irrelevant or of lesser importance for the question of original sin. The situationalists cannot simply discard, for example, the classic concepts used to express solidarity without introducing more adequate concepts. Thus, Schoonenberg expressly defines and delimits the concept situation to replace that of heredity [2] and Weger introduces the historical thought-form in place of the naturalistic thought-form in which the traditional doctrine of original sin is cast.[3] Furthermore, beyond this structural analysis of man as historical being, the broader scope of the situational interpretation of original sin necessitates a consideration and evaluation of history as a spatiotemporal process, specifically as *Heilsgeschichte* and, in the case of original sin, as *Unheilsgeschichte*.

Due to its inclusiveness, the situational reinterpretation of original sin

---

1 Concerning the designations "situationalists" and "personalists," see Introduction, n. 4 above.
2 P. Schoonenberg, *Geloof,* IV, 183-91; *Man and Sin,* 185-87.
3 Weger, *Theologie der Erbsünde,* 36-42.

cannot be fully appreciated as to its import and ramifications without an understanding of the underlying view of history as the content and context of man. Accordingly, attention will first be paid to man as historical being: as personal freedom in relation to situation, in Schoonenberg's terms; as transcendental subject in relation to categorical mediation or manifestation, in Rahner's and Weger's terms. This exposition of the constituents of history as conceived of by the situationalists will yield a cross section of that history. Thereupon, a longitudinal view will be presented by considering history as a spatiotemporal process. That can be obtained only by introducing the dynamic of grace which, as basic, driving force, qualifies this process as *Heilsgeschichte*. *Unheilsgeschichte,* the situational equivalent of original sin, can then be understood in the next chapter as largely a converse of *Heilsgeschichte.*

Before turning to the constituents of history as construed by the situationalists, some provisional comments concerning their mutual relationship are in order. The interrelationship of Schoonenberg, Rahner and Weger can best be specified as one of complex interdependence. That interdependence is complex, not merely because of the interaction itself, but especially because it takes place at different levels.

In the elaboration of a comprehensive situational interpretation of original sin, Schoonenberg has played a pioneering role. For almost a decade, he has devoted himself to exploring, elaborating and refining this conception.[4] Due to the creativeness of his early innovations, the extensiveness of his subsequent publications, and the breadth of his mature conception, most contemporary reinterpretations of original sin come to terms, explicitly or implicitly, with his views. Certainly none of the theologians being considered in this study, not even the personalists, have wholly by-passed Schoonenberg's conception. Whether Schoonenberg's conception is surpassed by the refinements introduced by the other situationalists, or even obviated by the alternative presented by the personalists, are questions to be considered at a later point.

Although Schoonenberg may be regarded as the pioneer of the situation theory of original sin, for the situation theory itself he is dependent on existentialistic thought-forms.[5] Moreover, many building blocks basic to the

---

[4] One of Schoonenberg's first articles dealing with original sin appeared in 1960: "Zonde en Verlossing als Grondsituaties van het Mensdom," *AvT,* XLVIII (1960), 136-51. One of his last articles on the subject was published in 1969: "Altes Testament, Neues Testament und Erbsündenlehre," *ThPQ,* CXVII (1969), 115-24.

[5] Schoonenberg himself considers the concept situation to be an indispensable category of existential, personalistic thought (*Geloof,* IV, 145). In the preface of the

situation theory are adopted from the theology of Karl Rahner.⁶ Frequently such elements are not merely adopted, but also adapted to serve the specific purpose of reinterpreting the doctrine of original sin.

This rather functional or practical approach to the concepts and categories employed distinguishes Schoonenberg's treatment of the doctrine of original sin from that of Rahner. Schoonenberg selects and hones the required concepts in the course of and for the specific purpose of reinterpreting original sin in such a way that it can be experienced as a reality by contemporary man.⁷ Schoonenberg adjusts and refines the situation theory in the process of

previous volume, Schoonenberg says that he draws from Scripture and from the phenomenology and philosophy of interpersonal relationships (*Geloof*, III, 10). According to L. Bakker, Schoonenberg is indebted philosophically especially to D. M. DePetter and to Gabriel Marcel (L. Bakker, "Schoonenberg's theologie: spiegel van onze eigen ontwikkeling?" *TvTh* XI (1971), 357, 371. Christa Campbell Betty contends that Schoonenberg is indebted for his notion of situation to the "existentialist notions of Heidegger and Jaspers," but adds that Schoonenberg does not explicate the concept situation in terms of the philosophy of either (Christa Campbell Betty, "Piet Schoonenberg's Theory of Original Sin," *Thought*, XLV [1970], 97). Although Schoonenberg's dependence on these philosophers is undoubtedly real, it is likely of an indirect nature. For an analysis of the central role that the idea of situation plays in Heidegger's thought, see S.U. Zuidema, "Kontemporain situationisme," *Philosophia Reformata*, XXIII (1958), 28-30, 85-94; translation: "Contemporary Situationism in John Dewey and Martin Heidegger: A Comparison," *Communication and Confrontation: A Philosophical Appraisal and Critique of Modern Society and Contemporary Thought* (Toronto: Wedge, 1972), 198-214.

6 For example, Schoonenberg's conception of the relation between person and nature is developed in direct discussion with Rahner (See *Geloof*, IV, 58, *Man and Sin*, 184n.). The difficulty of tracing the precise relationship of Schoonenberg's thought to that of other theologians or philosophers is illustrated by this reference, for here, in the fourth volume of his dogmatics (1962), he acknowledgess his indebtedness to Rahner for an exposition found in the first volume (1955) of that work. Similarly with respect to the theme of nature and grace, developed in that first volume, Schoonenberg does not acknowledge his indebtedness to H. DeLubac until years later in an epilogue to an English translation of sections of *Geloof*, I and II (*Covenant and Creation*, trans. Peter Tomlinson [London: Sheed and Ward, 1968], 189-90). In the latter instance, Schoonenberg explains this delay by alluding to the fact that it was not propitious to acknowledge this indebtedness initially due to the uncertain ecclesiastical situation of that time (*ibid*, 190). At that time Schoonenberg was suspect due to his affinity with the "théologie nouvelle," which he dealt with in his doctoral dissertation, *Theologie als geloofsvertolking: Een kritische samenvatting van de leerstellige inhoud der hedendaagse katholieke franse literatuur over de verhouding der speculatieve theologie tot het geloof* (Maastricht, 1948). Schoonenberg wished to revise this dissertation to meet the objections that had been raised, "but when this had been completed, the encyclical *Humani Generis* [1950] appeared, which provided the new censors with fresh material for misgivings" ("Ten geleide [introduction], Schoonenberg zestig jaar," *TvTh*, XI (1971), 351). For a discussion of the content of this dissertation, see L. Bakker's article (*ibid.*, 353-63). See also n. 12 below.

7 *Geloof*, IV, 144. This practical concern is more prominent in the theology of

that reinterpretation. Rahner, by contrast, addressing himself directly to the doctrine of original sin in his later writings,[8] draws on a rather well-defined, complex framework that he had developed in his previous philosophical and theological writings.[9] To contrast the approaches somewhat crudely: in reading especially the earlier publications on original sin by Schoonenberg, one has the feeling of having entered a relatively self-contained theological workshop where even the required tools are adjusted and sharpened;[10] in reading Rahner's discussion of the subject, one has the sensation of having entered the *assembly* area and, noticing the sophisticated tools employed, feels compelled to look for the toolmaking area.

Another distinctive feature of Schoonenberg's approach to original sin is his intensive and extensive treatment of the relevant biblical material.[11] In the genesis and development of his situational interpretation of original sin, the data of Scripture are given a prominent place. In fact, they are meant to constitute the epicenter of reinterpretation.[12] Specifically, Schoonenberg expressly develops his situation theory to capture the biblical theme basic to the doctrine of original sin — while, as we shall see, at the same time divesting

---

Schoonenberg than in that of Rahner. Though this concern is by no means absent from Rahner's work, it is frequently less apparent due to the rigors of his transcendental-theology (see n. 164 below). For reflections on the practical bent of Schoonenberg's theology, see T. M. Schoof, *Aggiornamento*, 146-48; *Breakthrough*, 133-35; Bakker, *TvTh*, XI, 373, 380-81, and Fr. Haarsma, "Op het raakvlak tussen dogmatiek en pastoraat," *TvTh*, XI (1971), 423-38 (title of English summary, "Where dogmatics and pastorate meet," p. 437).

8 Karl Rahner, "Erbsünde," *SM*, I, 1104-17; *SMe*, IV, 328-34; *idem*, "Die Sünde Adams," *Schriften, IX, 259-75*. Previously, Rahner had dealt with the subject of original sin indirectly, namely, in relationship to the problems of monogenism and of concupiscence: "Theologisches zum Monogenismus," *Schriften*, I, 252-322; "Zum theologischen Begriff der Konkupiszenz," *ibid.*, 377-414. Also later, Rahner deals with original sin in its relationship to problems such as the above: "Erbsünde und Evolution," *Concilium*, III (1967), 458-65; "Exkurs: Erbsünde und Monogenismus," in Weger, *Theologie der Erbsünde*, 176-223. Cited hereafter as *Exkurs.*

9 See n. 164 below.

10 The concept situation, for example, is carefully delimited *within* the context and for the specific purpose of reinterpreting the doctrine of original sin (see sec. A, 3 below). Schoonenberg himself says that he began training his theological muscles in the process of reinterpreting the doctrine of original sin (*Die Antwort der Theologen* [Düsseldorf: Patmos], 1965), p. 36.

11 *Geloof,* IV, 75-97. This material is found in summary form in later publications and translations (cf. e.g., *Man and Sin,* 98-103).

12 Schoonenberg, "Gesprek over de erfzonde," *Ex Auditu Verbi,* 268. This centrality expressly assigned to Scripture is wholly in accord with the theological method which Schoonenberg advocated already in his dissertation. There he opposes a conclusionistic, deductionistic theology which takes as its point of departure a specific, historical conceptualization of the content of faith and, via conclusions, moves increasingly farther

that theme of an attendant difficulty.¹³ Because of Schoonenberg's serious grappling with Scripture, his treatment of the biblical material is most instructive with respect to the general hermeneutical problem involved – interpreting documents of the past with the aid of, and in terms of, categories and concepts of the present.

Weger, the third situationalist to be considered, represents a unique instance of dependence. Writing on the subject of original sin after most of Schoonenberg's and Rahner's essays had been published, he explicitly draws on the conceptions of both.¹⁴ With respect to many of his basic categories, however, he displays greater affinity with the thought of Karl Rahner. Thus, when he wishes to guard himself against a central criticism levelled at Schoonenberg's conception of original sin by providing a more adequate anthropological basis,¹⁵ this basis is laid with the aid, primarily, of Rahner's transcendental framework. Put paradoxically, Weger's reinterpretation of original sin is more Rahnerian than Rahner's own. This "paradox" is explained by the fact that Weger uses themes derived from Rahner more explicitly and more comprehensively *in application to the doctrine of original sin* than Rahner himself has done.

In view of the complex interdependence sketched above, the conceptions of the situationalists are treated separately where necessary, in combination where possible. As for the following section, in order to do justice to Schoonenberg's distinct approach in introducing and adapting the central categories for his reinterpretation of original sin, his conception of man and his situation is given separate treatment. On the other hand, in view of his considerable dependence on Rahner, Weger's conception of man's freedom and historical situation is largely subordinated to that of Rahner.

A. PERSON AND SITUATION: SCHOONENBERG

1. The Problematic Coexistence of Solidarity and Personal Responsibility in Scripture

Schoonenberg considers the doctrine of original sin to have roots that go deeper and spread beyond its *locus classicus,* Ro 5:12-21.¹⁶ This more

from the concrete center of faith. Instead of this centrifugal, Schoonenberg advocates a centripetal mode of thought which continually draws from the wellspring of faith, namely, the concrete faith-experience and the earliest expressions of that experience found in Scripture, especially in the Old Testament. (See L. Bakker, *TvTh*, XI, 355-63).

13 See sec. A, 1 below.
14 Weger, *Theologie der Erbsünde,* 7.
15 *Ibid.,* 145.
16 A passage in which personal sin plays a greater role than traditionally assumed,

extensive root system finds its soil in the biblical notion of human solidarity in sin.[17] Since it is beyond the scope of this study to present the biblical material itself, we will focus primarily on Schoonenberg's reflections on this material.

In the first place, Schoonenberg is struck by the very fact of this solidarity, for it is a notion that is, as he says, foreign to our Western conceptions.[18] Yet, in Scripture, the idea that sin has power over man *collectively* is so dominant that Schoonenberg considers the treatment of this theme before that of individual sin to be more appropriate than the reverse procedure.[19] Secondly, concerning the nature of that solidarity, Schoonenberg points out that in Scripture this collectivity does not consist merely of the fact that "next to us there are also others who are sinners."[20] The Bible attests not merely to a universality of individual *sins*, he observes, but also to a "communal bondage to sin; we participate in each other's sinful existence...."[21] Moreover, in the Old Testament *this* solidarity is not restricted to a band of contemporaries, but encompasses successive generations, even the entire history of Israel.[22] With a view to his own reinterpretation of original sin,[23] it is interesting to note that Schoonenberg calls attention to the fact that in the Old Testament this solidarity is not exhausted by the idea of a fateful nexus that joins culprit and victim, father and son,[24] but also includes the notion of solidarity in sin itself, solidarity in guilt.[25] Though *foreign* to our way of thinking, says Schoonenberg, a confession of communal guilt that includes the sins of the fathers, was entirely *natural* to the Israelite.[26] In the New

---

according to Schoonenberg. See *Man and Sin*, 133-39 and "Der Mensch in der Sünde," *Mysterium Salutis: Grundriss heilsgeschichtlicher Dogmatik*, ed. Johannes Feiner and Magnus Löhrer (Einsiedeln: Benziger Verlag, 1965 –), II, 133-39; cited hereafter as *MS*.

17 *Man and Sin*, 98; *MS*, II, 886; *Geloof*, IV, 142. Reflecting on the development of his reinterpretation of original sin, Schoonenberg says that his view did not arise in the first place out of philosophical speculation concerning human solidarity, but "out of the impressive fact that 'Scripture has placed *all* under sin' (Ga 3:22), out of the solidarity in salvation and sin in both testaments, and notably out of the Johannine concept 'the world' " (*Ex Auditu Verbi*, 268).

18 *Geloof*, IV, 88, cf. 76.

19 *Man and Sin*, ix; *Geloof*, IV, 76.

20 *Geloof*, IV, 76.

21 *Ibid.*

22 *Geloof*, IV, 80-83, 79, 75; *MS*, II, 887.

23 See esp. ch. III, sec. C, 1.

24 *Geloof*, IV, 92-93; *Man and Sin*, 103-104; *MS*, II, 889-90.

25 *Geloof*, IV, 82-83, with reference to Lv 25:39ff., 45; Esd 9:7; Ne 9:34; Tob 3:3; Jr 14:20; Dn 8:6, 9, 16.

26 *Geloof* IV, 82-83.

Testament, Schoonenberg finds a similar — possibly even greater — accentuation of man's solidarity in sin, coming to poignant expression in the prevalence of the singular form *hamartia,* and in John's phrase "the sin of the world."[27]

Schoonenberg considers it too facile a procedure to relegate the solidarity motif to the realm of primitive and antiquated conceptions, partly because it carries over into the New Testament, but especially because in the whole of Scripture the idea of solidarity in sin is not as one might expect supplanted but complemented by the idea of personal responsibility: "These two lines of thought run a parallel course throughout Scripture, which makes it at least probable that the solidarity, too, is real."[28] Whether Schoonenberg consistently views these two notions as coexisting peacefully is not entirely clear. Often, he speaks of the two lines of thought as being simply contiguous,[29] complementary[30] or equally basic.[31] Yet, at one point, Schoonenberg says that "the texts of the Old, as well as those of the New Testament, are charged with a continuous tension between the collective and individual aspects of man's act and being: the spark continually leaps across."[32]

However Schoonenberg conceives of the specific relationship between the two motifs in Scripture, he does detect a gradual development, within and even beyond the Scriptures, towards an ever-clearer insight into man's personal responsibility.[33] He considers the beginning of this insight to have

---

27 *Man and Sin,* 101; *MS,* II, 887-88; *Geloof,* IV, 86.
28 *Man and Sin,* 103; *MS,* II, 889; cf. *Geloof,* IV, 90-91, 76, 78.
29 *Man and Sin,* 102; *MS,* II, 889; *Geloof,* IV, 90.
30 *Geloof,* IV, 76.
31 *Man and Sin,* 99; *MS,* II, 887; *Geloof,* IV, 77; "equally original."
32 *Geloof* IV, 77. Cf. *ibid.,* 76, where Schoonenberg says that a kind of collectivism had to *make room for* a continually clearer insight into man's personal responsibility, and p. 89, where he speaks of a restriction of collective responsibility (with reference to instances in which punishment was limited to a small group, rather than extending to all of Israel: the sons of Korah [Nu 16], the family of Achan [Jos 7]). When Schoonenberg speaks of "collectivism" in these and other instances, it is not clear whether the term is used as an equivalent for true solidarity, or as a term denoting an aberration of genuine solidarity. The former seems more likely since Schoonenberg does not consider complete absorption of the individual into the group to be represented in Scripture (*Geloof,* IV, 77, 79, 87; *Man and Sin,* 99; *MS,* II, 887). Yet elsewhere, the latter is suggested when he says that "the primitive idea of 'corporate personality' and thus with it the idea of guilt leaping over from the King to his people, from the patriarch to his posterity and from Adam to humanity is *restricted* by the growing insight that God judges each according to his works" (*Geloof,* IV, 168 emphasis added). Cf. n. 37 below.
33 *Man and Sin,* 101; *MS,* II, 888; *Geloof,* IV, 44, 88. Schoonenberg contends that although freedom in Scripture is understood primarily in the religious sense, so that a

emerged very early. In the story of Joseph's "stolen" vessel, for example, Schoonenberg finds evidence of a "sense of justice that is on the way towards separating personal responsibility from collective solidarity."[34] And already in the book of Deuteronomy, a "clear separation is made between personal guilt and kinship."[35] As further evidence of this development, Schoonenberg adduces the fact that the idea that God punishes the sins of ancestors in their posterity is later rejected with unequivocal and polemic pointedness by Ezekiel and Jeremiah.[36]

Schoonenberg detects a similar emphasis in the New Testament where "it is even more evident, if that be possible, than it was in Israel (since the time of the prophets) that God rewards everyone according to his own works."[37] According to Schoonenberg, personal sin plays a prominent role even within the *locus classicus* of the doctrine of original sin, Ro 5: 12-21.[38] And yet, this accentuation of personal sin in no way means that Paul attenuates the element of solidarity. Remarkably, the *contrary* is true: "In contrast with the communion which, as redeemed, we have with the Redeemer, the communion in sin comes strongly to the fore, more strongly perhaps than in the Old Testament."[39]

Despite the growing insight into personal responsibility that is reflected in Scripture, its authors, Schoonenberg contends, failed to attain to complete clarity concerning the distinction between personal and communal sin.[40] Insofar as it became clear that God ultimately punishes only personal guilt, the distinction did dawn in the writer's consciousness, but an *analysis* of that

proper concept of "freedom of the will" was not developed, the idea of the free will is implicit in the biblical idea of "heart" as "the inner center of the person, the seat, not only of feelings but also, and mainly, of the free will as the seat of good and evil" (*Man and Sin*, 16-17; *MS*, II, 853).

34 *Geloof*, IV, 88.
35 *Ibid.*, 89 with reference to Dt 24:16; cf. *MS*, II, 888 and *Man and Sin*, 101.
36 *Geloof*, IV, 90 (with reference to Eze 18 and Jr 31:29-30; *Man and Sin*, 102; *MS*, II, 888-89.
37 *Man and Sin*, 103; *MS*, II, 889 with reference to Mt 16:27; Jn 5:29; Ro 2:6; 14:12; I Cor 3:8; II Cor 5:10; 11:15; Ga 6:5; Eph 6:8; I Pe 1:17; Re 20:12ff.; 22:12. Because most of these texts have some references to the last judgment, Schoonenberg places the relationship of solidarity and personal responsibility in eschatological perspective: "In the final analysis, in the life to come, therefore, no one will any longer be punished for or participate in the guilt of others (which in no way implies that in the life hereafter there will be no communion – the Bible says quite the contrary – only that the wicked will be removed from the midst of the righteous). Presently the wheat and the weeds are intertwined until the time of harvest" (*Geloof*, IV, 92).
38 *Man and Sin*, 133-39; *MS*, II, 902-905; *Geloof*, IV, 110-16.
39 *Man and Sin*, 140; *Geloof*, IV, 116.
40 *Geloof*, IV, 92.

distinction is lacking.[41] One might say that in Schoonenberg's view this distinction was present in Scripture but remained implicit in the practical prophetic accentuation of personal responsibility. The distinction was intuitively felt, not analytically clarified. Even though Paul, for example, gives personal sin a prominent place within his discussion of "original sin," the latter does not, in Schoonenberg's opinion, appear in its distinctness but is interwoven with personal sin,[42] "expressed in personal sin."[43] Schoonenberg suggests an interesting reason for this lack of clarity when he says that the authors of the Bible "did not yet have at their disposal a refined conceptual apparatus with which to distinguish personal guilt from the other solidarity in evil."[44]

In order to clearly distinguish these two essential strands contained in Scripture and especially in order to give the strand of solidarity in sin a more conscious place — as reality — in our existence, Schoonenberg proposes the concept "situation" as the central category of reinterpretation.[45] At times Schoonenberg goes beyond merely presenting this concept as being worthy of consideration and suggests that a concept such as situation is inherently required by the dual motifs found intermingled in Scripture, solidarity in sin and personal responsibility. The fact that both must be maintained simultaneously, yet clearly distinguished, makes a concept such as situation mandatory. For, on the one hand, the "principle of personal responsibility" would be violated if human solidarity were such that it entailed the transfer of guilt from one person to another; on the other hand, the "reality of solidarity" would be dissolved if it were simply the "sum total of individual sins without inner connection."[46] Therefore, a connecting link is required that unites the sins of one person to those of another without the transfer of guilt. In other words, a highly sophisticated coupling device is needed that, capacitor-like, screens and connects at the same time. That link is "situation."[47]

41 *Ibid.*, 116.
42 *Ibid.*, 111, 115, 116, 131, 157, 158.
43 *Man and Sin,* 139; *MS,* II, 906; cf. *Man and Sin,* 134: "Paul speaks here of a bond which the first sin has with the sins of all men, and he says that this bond is established, that this domination is undergone, only when one sins personally."
44 *Geloof,* IV, 92. The breakthrough to clarity concerning the distinction of personal guilt from solidarity in sin was hindered, according to Schoonenberg, by the fact that in Scripture sin is seen first of all in its religious dimension rather than in its psychological constitution. Aside from this general fact, Schoonenberg mentions other specific causes for the lack of clarity in Scripture, such as the view that God caused evil, and the remnants of dynamistic thought as reflected in II Sm 6:6ff.; I Sm 13:7-14; II Kgs 13:18ff. (*Geloof,* IV, 44-45; cf. *Man and Sin,* 16-17 and *MS,* II, 852-53.
45 *Geloof,* IV, 144.
46 Schoonenberg, "Zonde der wereld en erfzonde," *Bijdragen,* XXIV (1963), 353; *Man and Sin,* 103-104; *MS,* II, 889.
47 *Ibid.*

2. The Coexistence of Person and Nature

a. *Man as Free Person*

In Schoonenberg's reinterpretation of original sin, his central concern is to safeguard personal responsibility while maintaining human solidarity. In that endeavor, his conception of person is of fundamental significance. It serves as the controlling idea that specifies, not only the meaning of responsibility, but also – by negation – the meaning of the counterpart of person, nature and, by extension, situation.

As an equivalent of *hypostasis* and *suppositum,* the term "person" as such, Schoonenberg points out, has reference simply to an independent being, something that "does not belong as part or modality to another being, but constitutes its own totality."[48] As such, the term "person" could therefore be predicated of any independent reality, whether human or subhuman.[49] The uniqueness of the *human* person (and thus the specific meaning of "person" in its usual sense) consists, according to Schoonenberg, of consciousness and freedom or self-determination:[50] "Only [human] persons are fully *hypostases* and realize this in their activity by self-consciousness and self-determination or freedom."[51] Although in relation to the situation theory the idea of self-consciousness is less prominent than that of freedom, Schoonenberg frequently treats the two in close conjunction. For that reason the idea of self-consciousness can serve as an avenue to the more crucial idea of freedom.

Whereas the term "being-in-itself" is used to designate the subsistance that is common to every independent entity, the term "presence-to-itself" is used to designate the self-consciousness that is unique to man.[52] Man is aware of his own being; he is *self*-conscious, transparent to himself.[53] This is a specifically human mode of being: "Being-in-itself attains such a depth and magnitude in a person that it is also a knowingly-being-with-itself, a consciousness. Personal being is therefore a being-in-oneself-even-unto-consciousness."[54] This consciousness is so closely related to man's being that it is not

---

48 *Geloof,* III, 112.
49 *Ibid.*
50 Cf. T. Van Bavel, "God absorbeert niet: de christologie van Schoonenberg," *TvTh,* XI, 394, 404. Van Bavel places Schoonenberg's conception of person within the context of the modern concept of person, dating from the time of Descartes (pp. 403-406).
51 *Geloof,* III, 113, cf. 130-31.
52 *God's World in the Making,* trans. Walter Van de Putte (2d ed.; Dublin: Gill and Son, 1968 [first ed., 1965]), 24-29; *Gods wordende wereld: Vijf theologische essays* ("Woord en Beleving"; Tielt: Lannoo, 1962), 21-24; *Geloof,* III, 112-13.
53 *God's World in the Making,* 25; *Gods wordende wereld,* 21.
54 *Ibid.*

merely something he *has* — he *is* self-consciousness.[55]

Freedom, in turn, adds to the reality of self-consciousness that of self-determination: "Freedom is a person's power to be the origin of changes, of meaning, of one's own attitude — origin, therefore, also for oneself."[56] Then, in a cumulation of parallel sentences and clauses, Schoonenberg gives expression to the idea of freedom in correlation with that of consciousness: "The being-in-oneself of person is not only knowing, but also original; not only being-present-with-oneself, but also being-out-of-oneself; besides being conscious, it is also free."[57] Compressing both ideas, Schoonenberg concludes by saying that person is "being-in-oneself-even-unto-consciousness-and-freedom."[58]

In view of this "origin-ality" proper to the idea of freedom, Schoonenberg's conception of freedom is not simply to be equated with the notion of the free choice of a particular object. Schoonenberg sees the latter as a frequent (though not necessary) *surface* manifestation of freedom in its deeper sense.[59] Choosing between alternative objects involves merely a change in the external relationship between the choosing subject and the chosen object.[60] Freedom in its deeper sense, personal freedom, involves an act in which our will determines "the relationship of our person to the whole of reality: to God and fellowman and world."[61] Whereas the choice of a particular object may affect only the external relationship between the subject and an object, this deeper choice centrally and incisively affects the subject himself.[62] In

---

55 *Ibid.*
56 *Gods wordende wereld*, 21-22; *God's World in the Making*, 25.
57 *Ibid.*, 22 and 26 respectively.
58 *Ibid.* It must be kept in mind that the autonomy entailed in Schoonenberg's conception of freedom is considered to be a creational given and thus not an autonomy vis-à-vis God. Creation is interpreted as participation in God's being or, more accurately, in God's *activity*, so that God's activity and man's can be said to vary in direct, rather than in inverse, proportion. See *Geloof*, I, 96-97 where Schoonenberg introduces an idea that is to become the basic theme of his theology, namely, the rejection of the dilemma 'God *or* man." Later this becomes the title of his inaugural address: *God of mens: een vals dilemma* ('s-Hertogenbosch: L.C.G. Malmberg, 1965); this essay is found in expanded and translated form in *The Christ: A Study of the God-Man Relationship in the Whole of Creation and in Jesus Christ*, trans. Della Couling (New York: Herder and Herder, 1971), 13-49. For the idea of man's activity as participation in God's creativity, see especially *Covenant and Creation*, 196 and 198; *The Christ*, 21 and 30. For a discussion of Schoonenberg's God-*and*-man principle, see L. Bakker, *TvTh*, XI, 372-79.
59 *Geloof*, III, 147.
60 *Ibid.*
61 *Ibid.*
62 *Geloof*, IV, 61-62. Both aspects of freedom may be subsumed under the concept *liberum arbitrium*, which Schoonenberg describes as the freedom common to all men

this depth-dimension of freedom, man does not merely stand "on his own feet"[63] – he holds his very being in his hands.[64] His self is at his disposal.[65]

Schoonenberg's conception of freedom in its radical sense finds its most explicit expression in the term "self-determination."[66] When this profound sense of freedom is not explicitly stated, its meaning is, nonetheless, usually present – frequently compressed in the prevalent term "person," for, as Schoonenberg says, "person is the subject itself of freedom,"[67] "the center of free decision."[68] What was said of self-consciousness holds true also for freedom, "a person not merely has freedom: the person *is* freedom."[69]

b. *Man as Embodied Person and Personalized Body*

In Schoonenberg's conception, man cannot be defined, however, simply in terms of freedom and self-determination.[70] Man is also nature. It is Schoonenberg's conception of nature, in its relationship to the idea of person,[71] that finds its extension in his conception of situation. That conception of nature, therefore, serves as an excellent key to an understanding of the specific quality of situation which Schoonenberg delineates for the purpose of reinterpreting original sin.

Although Schoonenberg conceives of nature in basically two opposite ways, either including or excluding the idea of person,[72] the latter is more

---

(*Geloof*, IV, 222; *Man and Sin*, 85) in contrast to specifically Christian freedom, *libertas*, the "concrete" and "complete" freedom constituted by a positive relationship to God in Christ (*Geloof*, IV, 242-43; *Geloof*, III, 150-51).

63 *God's World in the Making*, 27; *Gods wordende wereld*, 22.
64 *Geloof*, IV, 61, 63, 260; cf. *Man and Sin*, 33.
65 *Geloof*, IV, 62.
66 See *Geloof*, III, 147; *Man and Sin*, 105.
67 *Man and Sin*, 69; *MS*, II, 873.
68 *Geloof*, IV, 61; *Man and Sin*, 33.
69 *Gods wordende wereld*, 22; *God's World in the Making*, 25-26. See also *Geloof*, IV, 61-62; *Man and Sin*, 19, 33; *MS*, II, 853.
70 *God's World in the Making*, 29, 58-59; *Gods wordende wereld*, 24, 46.
71 As mentioned, Schoonenberg registers his indebtedness for his conception of person-nature to Rahner (n. 6 above). Rahner elaborates upon this theme especially in *Schriften*, I, 392-400. There he indicates that the dualism of person and nature has a dual rootage. It roots, on the one hand, in man's *finitude* and the concomitant distinction of existence and essence: in his concrete existence (freedom, person), man can never wholly realize his essence (nature). On the other hand, the duality of person and nature roots in the *materiality* of man and thus in the distinction of form and matter.
72 See *Geloof*, III, 113-14, 190; *Man and Sin*, 33, 69, 76. Nature and person are viewed as being distinct when the term nature is used generically ("man") and the term person is used to designate the concrete individual ("I"); see *Man and Sin*, 33, 69, and *Geloof*, III, 113). Person and nature are equated when the individual existence is viewed

prevalent and provides a direct link to the concept situation. The concept nature excludes the idea of person, not in the sense that in reality nature and person have nothing to do with one another, but because the concept nature is filled with a content precisely opposite to that of the concept person. The concept nature in this sense is carefully delimited from the concept person: nature is precisely that which is presupposed by person, available for and at the disposal of free choice, capable of being ruled and moulded by personal decision.[73]

This preliminary description of nature could create the impression that Schoonenberg conceives of nature simply as pliable material totally at the disposal of freedom, of person. Nature proves to be less subservient, however. It is more than pure passivity. Its very facticity and fixity, or as Schoonenberg speaks of it, its "givenness" and "Vorhandenheit"[74] represents a *counter*-reality, in some sense even a *counter-force,* to personal freedom; for nature, displaying a certain sluggishness and intractability, offers resistance to freedom.[75] Although such counter-"activity" by a phenomenon that appears, at first glance, to represent pure potentiality seems somewhat surprising, it becomes plausible in view of the fact that human nature embodies a principle distinct from that of person, namely, the principle of materiality. This principle makes itself felt in man via his body, for the opposition of the givenness of nature to the freedom of person, says Schoonenberg, stems from or at least derives its human form from the opposition between material body and spiritual soul.[76] To understand the significance of nature as the opposite of person, therefore, it is necessary to understand Schoonenberg's conception of man as a bipolar unity of being, a conception which involves a significant correction upon the traditional view of man as being composed of two substances.

Schoonenberg takes issue with that traditional view because it con-

---

as *being* man's concrete essence and thus as man's nature; see *Geloof,* III, 114. Even generically, however, person and nature can be equated when person is seen as being the essence *of man* (universal), subsumed under the concept human nature; see *Man and Sin,* 76.

73 *Man and Sin,* 69, 76; cf. *Geloof,* IV, 216-19.
74 *MS,* II, 859; *Geloof,* IV, 58, 61, 62; *Man and Sin,* 33. Similarly, Rahner, *Schriften,* I, 393.
75 *Geloof,* I, 160; IV, 62-63; *Man and Sin,* 33-34. Similarly Rahner, *Schriften,* I, 396, 399, 400, 401, 403. Nature is viewed as counter-*reality* simply by virtue of the fact that it precedes and limits freedom (see *Man and Sin,* 33; *Geloof,* III, 114; IV, 61-62, 259-60; see also the material presented in terms of freedom and situation, sec. A, 3 below). Nature as counter-*force* is not thereby explained. Cf. n. 90 below.
76 *Geloof,* IV, 59n.

strues man as being a combination of two parts. Schoonenberg does not object to the duality so much as to the inaccurate conception of that duality, the conception that this duality is constituted by two substances, soul and body.[77] Soul and body do not constitute commensurate counterparts, in Schoonenberg's view. They are mismatched. He demonstrates this lack of correspondence by carefully distinguishing principles or poles of being from concretely existent being.

The soul, Schoonenberg holds, is not itself a *concrete* reality, but a principle or pole of being. It is a " 'being by means of which' [*ens quo*] within the concrete reality or 'being which ' [*ens quod*] man is."[78] Correspondingly, its counterpart must also be a principle of being. Since body is a concrete reality, it does not correspond to soul. Rather, the counterpart of soul is the principle of materiality, the materiality of the body.[79] Materiality (*materia prima*) is also purely a (real) principle of being, "as intangible, invisible and incapable of being imagined as the soul itself . . . ."[80] Moreover, these two principles are each other's exact opposites: "Just as the soul is the principle of being-in-oneself, of immanence or life, of self-consciousness and freedom, so materiality or prime matter is the principle of extension and division, of being dependent and subjected, of passivity."[81]

The *concrete* reality within which the principles of soul and materiality come to expression is man as person and as body. Person and body both have reference to the concrete reality of the whole man.[82] They are distinguished by Schoonenberg as "two ways in which the whole man exists."[83] Man *is* person and *is* body. He is person insofar as he exists by virtue of the soul principle, exists, i.e., as freedom, as self-determination. He is body insofar as he exists by virtue of the materiality principle, exists, i.e., as subject to and at the mercy of, for example, natural processes.[84]

77 *God's World in the Making*, 55; *Gods wordende wereld*, 42.
78 *Ibid.*
79 Similarly, Rahner, *Schriften*, IV, 422n, cf. 305.
80 *God's World in the Making*, 55-56; *Gods wordende wereld*, 42-43.
81 *Gods wordende wereld*, 43; *God's World in the Making*, 56. The term "immanence" should probably be understood in the sense of interiority in view of the connotation of its opposite term, "uitgeleverd zijn" which literally means "being extradited" and figuratively "being at the mercy of." In the English translation the term has been rendered "being involved," which can be construed both actively and passively and is, therefore, too ambiguous to convey the decidedly passive meaning of the original. We have settled for "being subjected."
82 *God's World in the Making*, 55; *Gods wordende wereld*, 42.
83 *Ibid.*, 56 and 43 respectively.
84 *Ibid.*, 56-59 and 43-47 respectively.

What is the effect of this correction of the view of man as a combination of body and soul? In the first place, Schoonenberg has replaced the higher-lower picture of body and soul with an inner-outer picture of person and body.[85] Closely related to this change in perspective, Schoonenberg has, in the second place, replaced the substantialistic conception of soul by the actualistic conception of person, which, especially as self-determination, is viewed as acting, not *upon a body*, but within a relatively fluid corporeality. By his free decisions, a person makes the body increasingly *his* body[86] by imparting himself to and penetrating corporeality.[87] In this sense, man is a unity — he *is* his (personalized) body.[88]

At the same time, duality remains — as is evident from Schoonenberg's description of man as a *bipolar* unity of being.[89] That duality remains because the corporeality of man's body represents a principle within his own concrete being that, as we have seen, is opposite to that of freedom, self-determination, person. It is man's *bodily* nature, therefore, that offers resistance to freedom.[90] Although man's bodily nature is seen as raw material for the free act, materiality is not, as it were, *burned up* in that act. As a result, the resistance of corporeality is never totally abolished.[91] In *personalizing* corporeality, it remains *corporeality* that is personalized. Person becomes

---

85 He does so with the aid of the Teilhardian concepts the "Within" and the "Without"; see *God's World in the Making,* 24-26, 35, 57; *Gods wordende wereld,* 20-22, 29, 45.
86 *God's World in the Making,* 25; *Gods wordende wereld,* 21.
87 *Ibid.,* 34 and 28 respectively.
88 *Ibid.,* 57 and 42 respectively.
89 *Gods wordende wereld,* 28; *God's World in the Making,* 34.
90 See *Man and Sin,* 33 where both the idea of nature as counter-reality and the idea of material nature as counter-force come to the fore: "... our person ... realizes itself in our own nature and also in our world. On the other hand, there are resistances to this realization not only — obviously — in our world, which remains something alien to ourselves, but even in our own individual human nature. For, despite its union with our person, nature is previous to it as an inescapable datum, as something 'at hand' that must be taken into account, as raw materials with which it must construct itself, as a creature of which it is not the creator, as both a field of operation and a resistance." *Geloof,* IV, 62. Cf. *Man and Sin,* 34, where Schoonenberg speaks of the "resistance of our bodily nature." For strikingly similar expressions by Rahner, see esp. n. 256 below.
91 See "Sünde und Schuld," *SM,* IV, 770, where Schoonenberg explicates the fact that man stands "leiblich in der Welt" as follows: "Der Mensch drückt die Entscheidungen seines Personzentrums auf die eine oder andere Weise aus, und durch diese Verleiblichung wächst seine innere Haltung. Anderseits jedoch gehört die Leiblichkeit des Menschen zusammen mit dem Nicht-Ich zu der Welt, die er zu *seiner* Welt macht, *ohne je ihren Widerstand aufzuheben"* (emphasis, other than that of *seiner,* added). See also the quotation in the previous footnote in which the world is said to *remain alien* to us.

imbrued in materiality[92] so that man is not merely *"personalized* body,"[93] but at the same time *"embodied* person."[94] Accordingly, in man "spirituality" takes on some of the characteristics intrinsic to materiality. Man is "drawn out," extended through space and time, subject to multiplicity, what is more, subject to biotic, natural processes (whether beneficent or baneful) and to historical situations beyond the control of person, man's inner being.[95]

The older body-soul view of man, of course, was not oblivious to this subjection to alien forces (at least to natural forces and processes). But because these forces could be relegated to the lower realm of the body, both the depth of positive and the sting of negative forces were depreciated. Within Schoonenberg's view such depreciation is ruled out, for body is coextensive with person. Although as person man can place himself in opposition to, for example, his illness, its impact is massive and total, for it is not simply (his) body that is ill. *He* is ill.[96] Natural processes do not take place in a lower realm, but cut right through man's being. Consequently, such processes, in their impersonality, mean self-estrangement.[97] A fissure runs through the center of man's being: "Das menschliche Sein, so wie wir es jetzt antreffen, weisst eine gewisse Spaltung und einen Gegensatz in sich selbst auf . . . ."[98]

Schoonenberg's correction of the traditional view of man elucidates two characteristics of "nature": its sluggishness (resistance to person) and its massivity. The *inertia* of nature in its human form derives from man's participation in materiality; by virtue of that fact, nature entails a principle, a law of its own opposite to that of person. The *total impact* of nature also becomes clear. Because corporeality is drawn "upwards" into "spirituality," nature confronts a person in a "personified" (in the sense of hypostatized) way and thus confronts person at its level — as equal in stature but opposite in essence.[99] That encounter represents the embracive and incisive confron-

---

92 *God's World in the Making,* 34; *Gods wordende wereld,* 28.
93 *Gods wordende wereld,* 28, cf. 42-43; *God's World in the Making,* 34, cf. 55-56.
94 *Man and Sin,* 36; *Geloof,* IV, 66.
95 *God's World in the Making,* 24-25, 26, 29, 56. *Gods wordende wereld,* 21, 22, 24, 43, 46.
96 *Ibid.,* 55 and 42 respectively.
97 *Ibid.,* 26 and 22 respectively.
98 *MS,* II, 857. See also *Geloof,* IV, 58 and *Man and Sin,* 30 ("ontological split"). Cf. Rahner, *Schriften,* I, 384: "der Mensch ist mit sich selbst entzweit"; cf. *ibid.,* 394, 405.
99 See *Geloof,* I, 184; III, 113-14; IV, 58-59n, 61, 63, 179, 182, 235-36, 239; *Man and Sin,* 33, 184. To the extent that this conception of the opposition between person and nature involves the idea of concupiscence, it must be kept in mind that concupiscence is seen as being primarily a structural given entailed in man's spiritual-bodily nature. Sin aggravates, but does not create, that opposition (see ch. IV, sec. C below).

tation of person and nature, opposites that are nevertheless enclosed within one being. It is that intricate relationship that finds its (modified) extension in the relation of person and *situation*.

3. The Coexistence of Person and Situation

In light of the discussion of person and nature and their rootage in the principles of spirituality and materiality, the relationship between person and situation can be readily understood; for situation, as Schoonenberg himself puts it, represents "the modification of being bodily in the world, the modification through which and in which persons meet as persons."[100] The modification consists of the fact that the somewhat abstract way of considering the individual person in relation to his body and nature is abandoned in favor of viewing persons in relation to their common *social-historical body,* so to speak. Whereas the expression of the materiality principle in man's individual body can be viewed as being "natural" in a restricted sense insofar as body is closely related to natural-biological processes (as in the case of illness, for example); in man's common body, situation, that principle receives its *historical* expression. Schoonenberg considers situation to be a typically "historical concept."[101] In fact, he describes history itself as "the interaction of decisions and situations,"[102] or, more specifically, as "the continual interaction of personal decisions which create a situation for others, who in turn respond to that situation."[103]

Although situation, as *historical* reality, transcends "nature" as physical-biological reality, it does not transcend the materiality principle. On the contrary, that principle has been *extended*. This extension becomes evident from the specific feature of situation which, as we shall see, Schoonenberg consistently and adamantly maintains: its givenness, its determinate and even determinative character.[104]

---

100 *Geloof,* IV, 151; Schoonenberg speaks of corporeal existence in the world as being man's fundamental situation of which other situations are variants (*ibid.;* cf. *ibid.,* 146, where Schoonenberg speaks of corporeality as man's fundamental situation). This intrinsic relationship between situation and "bodily-situation" also emerges when Schoonenberg mentions being-situated incidentally within the context of his discussion of the relation person-body (see *God's World in the Making,* 24, 58; *Gods wordende wereld,* 21, 46).
101 *Geloof,* IV, 151.
102 *Man and Sin,* 104; *MS,* II, 890.
103 *Geloof,* IV, 151; cf. *Geloof,* I, 37.
104 *Geloof,* IV, 146; *Man and Sin,* 105-106; *MS,* II, 890. The interaction of freedom and situation that constitutes history is, therefore, described as an interaction between freedom and necessity (*Geloof,* I, 37); cf. *Covenant and Creation,* 202.

Schoonenberg's constant focus on situation in its givenness does not mean that the idea of person is negated. That fundamental idea remains present in more ways than one but, due to the relentless concentration on the givenness of situation, the idea of person *appears* to recede to the background. Therefore, it is not surprising that, soon after introducing the situational view of original sin, Schoonenberg was criticised for seeing situation too extrinsically.[105] Especially because the idea of situation is meant to clarify the reality of original sin, such criticism could not readily be ignored. It provided Schoonenberg with an occasion for elucidating an element that had been fundamentally present in the situation theory from its inception. Admitting that, terminologically, he had left himself open to the charge of extrinsicality, Schoonenberg goes on to make unmistakably clear that, in speaking of situation, he intended to speak of the *subject* as situated:

> I have ... overlooked the fact that situation is a complex of circumstances, a determination of the "Um-Welt," of the milieu and not of the subject which finds itself in that milieu. One's original sin, however, is not a determination of his milieu but of himself .... For that reason it is better to change the term and no longer to speak of "situation," but of "being-situated."[106]

Elsewhere, Schoonenberg explains the change in terminology more clearly when he says, "We are interested, after all, in the subject himself in the situation, in his subjection to the situation as an inner determination of that subject."[107] He makes the same point even more forcefully by putting the matter exclusively: "We are interested, not in the situation, but in the fact that the person is situated."[108]

In the delimitation and application of the concept "situation," the idea of person is present — even decisively — in two related ways. In the first place, the idea of person is present as *"object* of investigation." As Schoonenberg points out, his whole concern focusses in person: he investigates situation only as it affects person; his object of study is the person-being-situated.

---

105 M. Bruna, "Tweegesprek over het ontstaan der zondigheid," *TvTh*, IV (1964), 59. Also Peter Lengsfeld, *Adam und Christus: die Adam-Christus Typologie im Neuen Testament und ihre Verwendung bei M. Scheeben und Karl Barth* ("Koinonia," IX; Essen: Ludgerus-Verlag, 1965), 229, n. 499; and Michael Seybold, "Erbsünde und Sünde der Welt," *MThZ*, XXVIII (1967), 58.

106 Schoonenberg, "Tweegesprek over het ontstaan der zondigheid," *TvTh*, IV (1964), 74.

107 Schoonenberg in a report of a discussion appended to the essay by Fiolet, "De erfzonde als verbondsmysterie," *Jaarboek, 1963/64*, 85.

108 *Man and Sin*, 105; *MS*, II, 891. That this emphasis on *person*-in-situation does not represent the introduction of a *new* element is evidenced by the fact that already in *Geloof*, IV, Schoonenberg states that in considering the situation he is concerned about "the person as such" (p. 146).

In the second place, person is present as *"principle* of investigation." As in the case of the relation person-nature, the idea of person functions as implicit criterion for determining – by negation – the specific meaning of situation. As will become evident, whatever the idea of person entails, the idea of situation lacks.

The constant coexistence of person and situation, more accurately, of freedom and being-situated, will be discussed in three stages. In each section the specific relationship between personal freedom and situation will be explored. These three stages do not represent different ideas of situation, but each stage explicates a dimension of situation that in the other stages remains implicit.

a. *Free Decision With Respect To Determinative Situation*

As is evident from his concentration on the *person* in the situation, Schoonenberg's stress on the objective givenness of situation in no way entails an attenuation of man's freedom. The uniqueness of the human, interpersonal situation consists of the fact that it does not coerce a specific response from a person:

> ... it is no contradiction to speak of a situated liberty. For we do not mean here that our freedom is determined by the situation so that it is forced from without to perform certain actions. That would indeed constitute a contradiction, since freedom means precisely not to be determined from without, but to determine oneself from within.[109]

The person subject to a situation is not rendered a passive *object*, but remains a free subject vis-à-vis the one who created the situation.[110]

Yet, the converse is equally true: Schoonenberg's accentuation of the free person in no way entails an attenuation of the objective givenness of the situation. The situation is, in fact, in some way determinative for man.[111] Schoonenberg illustrates this determinative influence by means of the situation that is created when someone reveals his innermost being by giving himself in love.[112] This act of love does not determine the specific

---

109 *Man and Sin*, 105. Cf. *ibid.* 104 and *MS*, II, 890.

110 *Geloof*, IV, 147.

111 The phrase "determinative for" and the term "determinant" will frequently be utilized to capture the meaning of the Dutch term "bepalen" and the German term "bestimmen" (see *MS*, II, 891: "innere Bestimmtheit der Person durch die Situation," and "Bestimmt-Sein dieses Menschen selbst"). The difficulty of translating these terms is reflected in the various renderings that are found in *Man and Sin*: "affect" (105-106), "restrict" (106, 111, 112), and "determine" (104, 105, 196).

112 *Geloof,* IV, 147.

response, the re-action of the person who is loved.[113] The situation does not program the response. The one subject to this situation can accept or reject the proffered love. Nevertheless, he *is* placed in an inescapable situation: it is *this* love that he must accept or reject. He has been placed in a situation which becomes the content of his freely given response.[114]

This last formulation implicitly expresses the relationship that obtains between free decision and determinative situation. Schoonenberg makes that relationship explicit in terms of content and direction:

> Interpersonal relationships consist of the continual creation of situations for the other, situations that leave his freedom intact as to the *direction* of the response, but which are determinative for this freedom as to its *content:* it is precisely *this* situation that he must accept or reject.[115]

Schoonenberg formulates this coexistence of situation and freedom by speaking of the latter as being determined or limited in its "field of action" or "operation"[116] namely, "in its possible objects, in the insights and the motives presented to it."[117] To summarize, the situation is *determinative* for *freedom*: although the situation determines the content of a free decision, it in no way obliterates, but qualifies freedom — namely, as "situated freedom."[118]

The concept situation as described to this point is hardly equal to its ultimate task. As mentioned earlier, for Schoonenberg the anti-Pelagian thrust is the inherent and essential point of the doctrine of original sin and is therefore crucial for all reinterpretation. The concept situation as explicated thus far, however, could be seen as a mere variation on a Pelagian theme, for despite his emphasis on the determinative impact of the situation, Schoonenberg has spoken largely in terms of a person capable of "reacting to," by "entering into or withdrawing from," the given situation.[119] Such terminology suggests that the situation is inescapable only in that the person involved *must* react to *it*. The situation is clearly escapable, however, in that the person concerned can react to it by leaving it.

Schoonenberg recognizes that the situation as portrayed thus far is inadequate for his purposes. He faults Pelagius for having considered only the

---

113 *Ibid.*
114 *Ibid.*
115 *Ibid.* Cf. *Man and Sin,* 104; *MS,* II, 890.
116 *Man and Sin,* 105, 106, 111, 112; *MS,* II, 891 ("das Bestimmt-Sein im Spielraum der eigenen Freiheit"); cf. *MS,* II, 894.
117 *Man and Sin,* 106.
118 *Ibid.*
119 *Geloof,* IV, 147.

influence that an example has on adults.[120] In opposition to this somewhat superficial view of the phenomenon of interpersonal relationships, Schoonenberg points out, the Church teaches that we are affected by Adam's sin in another, deeper way than by the influence of an example that is consciously imitated.[121] Although Schoonenberg acknowledges that a Pelagian example theory also views original sin as a situation and that his own use of the concept situation is an extension of the idea of example,[122] he contends that his conception of situation is capable of indicating precisely that deeper, more incisive influence pointed to by the magisterium.[123]

b. *Capacity For Free Decision Within Determinative Situation*

In order to disclose the depth dimension of his situation theory, Schoonenberg introduces a situation which he considers to be qualitatively different from that obtaining between adults.[124] It is the situation of a child who is still totally dependent on moral nurture, but for whom positive moral nurture is lacking.[125] This situation functions so pivotally in Schoonenberg's situational view of original sin that it is more accurately described as a model than as an illustration.[126]

To function as model for original sin, the situation of the child must, of course, be negatively qualified. Schoonenberg uses the example "of a child born in a family whose livelihood is theft or prostitution, in which the norms of honesty or chastity are not observed, in which these values are not operative."[127] Schoonenberg is fully aware of the fact that a situation totally

120 *Ibid.*, 159.
121 *Ibid.*, 188-90.
122 Schoonenberg, "Mysterium Iniquitatis: ein Versuch über die Erbsünde," *WuW*, XXI (1966), 584. Here Schoonenberg acknowledges that a Pelagian strain may be present in the development of his theory, but adds, "wobei ich aber meine, die pelagianische Lehre vom schlechten Beispiel weitergeführt zu haben als Pelagius selbst und dadurch zur Orthodoxie zurückgebogen zu haben" (*ibid.*). Cf. *Man and Sin*, 112-16 where Schoonenberg describes the degrees of sinful influence and points out that even at its lowest degree of influence the example of others has a greater impact than that of a merely external audio-visual aid. This discussion is found in shortened form in *MS*, II, 894-95.
123 *Geloof,* IV, 159, 190.
124 *Ibid.*, 149.
125 *Man and Sin,* 116; *MS,* II, 894-95; cf. *Geloof,* IV, 149.
126 The term model is more appropriate than the term example because the situation of the child about to be described is not an arbitrary example but is intrinsic to Schoonenberg's description of original sin as situation. Cf. the description of model by F. J. A. De Grijs, "De erfzonde," *Bijdragen,* XXXI (1970), 125-26: "The model is a sign, a representation created by man in the closest conceivable connection with the reality represented."
127 *Bijdragen,* XXIV, 362; *Man and Sin,* 116; *MS,* II, 894.

devoid of a particular value is "a boundary case, an asymptotic case which the concrete situation approximates."[128] Nevertheless, as model the case of the child born in a family of thieves is pushed to the extreme limit,[131] i.e., the situation is either assumed to be wholly devoid of a particular moral value,[130] or is utilised only insofar as it is negatively qualified.[131]

Under the conditions of this model, says Schoonenberg, the child born in a family of thieves "cannot develop honesty; and that inability is meant absolutely."[132] An absolute inability results because for the formation of moral values the child is wholly dependent on the nurture of those in its immediate vicinity; in that sense a child is, as Schoonenberg says, a *tabula rasa*.[133] If a moral value "does not, in one way or another, impinge upon us from without, neither the concept of that value, nor its appeal, nor, consequently, the possibility of its realization will be present."[134]

One might conclude that the coexistence of freedom and situation so carefully maintained earlier has been fundamentally destroyed in the model of the child, and has been supplanted by a monolithically dominant, determinant situation. In view of the resulting absolute moral inability, this conclusion seems inescapable. Nevertheless, that conclusion is unwarranted to the extent that Schoonenberg – even in the case of the model – is still dealing with a *person* in a basic sense. In the model, the idea of person is retained – incognito, as it were – in the form of the capacity for free decisions that remains present.

Schoonenberg insists that the absolute inability of the child is not due to the absence of freedom or of the capacity for a particular value:

> Such a person has, like everyone else, the capacity for every virtue, but this capacity cannot come to expression in certain areas; the road to its development remains closed; the capacity remains imprisoned when the moral value is not brought to mind and when its summons does not resound.[135]

To clarify this conjunction of moral inability and moral capacity,[136] Schoo-

---

128 *Bijdragen*, XXIV, 362; *Man and Sin*, 116.
129 *Man and Sin*, 116; *Bijdragen*, XXIV, 363 ("absoluut stellen").
130 *Man and Sin*, 116; *MS*, II, 894 ("absolut fehlt").
131 *Man and Sin*, 116.
132 *Ibid.*; MS, II, 895.
133 *Geloof*, IV, 149; Schoonenberg, "Sünde der Welt," *ThG*, V (1962), 161
134 *Geloof*, IV, 150.
135 *Ibid.*
136 For the sake of convenience the term ability (and variants) is used to designate that which is concretely possible, whereas the term capacity (and variants) is used to designate that which is in principle possible but not concretely practicable. Concerning the problem to which this terminology points, see n. 142 below.

nenberg compares it to the conjunction of an intellectual inability and intellectual capacity. "Someone who has never in any way had knowledge of polar bears cannot develop a concept of them; yet this does not detract in any way from his intellectual capacity."[137] Our free will is both the subject of a similar capacity, and subject to similar limitations:

> Through it, too, our person stands open to the whole of reality to embrace and to mould it in love, open to all values to practice them (by virtue of the will, too, the center of our person is *quodomodo omnia*). But also in this case, the will affirms as a value only that which is presented to it, both through the cognitive capacities and through the spontaneous drives of our bodily and spiritual (or rather, our total human) appetitive powers. If a value is not presented in that way, the will can neither realize nor embrace it.[138]

The salvaged capacity for moral activity seems paltry beside the sheer massivity of the absolute moral inability which Schoonenberg defends with equal insistence. Nevertheless, that capacity, though problematic,[139] remains of fundamental significance, so much so that it appears to threaten the posited absolute inability. In the case of the model, it is that capacity that allows Schoonenberg to maintain that even here "freedom in no way ceases to exist."[140] Surprising as such a statement may seem in view of the inability posited, it is wholly in line with the idea of man as person. As Schoonenberg says elsewhere, man is person from the very beginning, even from his first coming-to-be.[141] That means that a beginning of free self-determination is assumed to be present even in an infant.[142]

---

137 *Bijdragen*, XXIV, 363; *Man and Sin*, 116; *MS*, II, 895.
138 *Bijdragen*, XXIV, 363; *Man and Sin*, 116-17.
139 See n. 142 below.
140 *Bijdragen*, XXIV, 363; *Man and Sin*, 116.
141 *God's World in the Making*, 34; *Gods wordende wereld*, 28.
142 *Bijdragen*, XXIV, 378: "a very first beginning" of personal decision (cf. *Man and Sin*, 181). Cf. *Ex Auditu Verbi*, 263: man is "Stellungnahme" and "Selbstbestimmung" from the moment that he is man; (the German terms are exact equivalents for the Dutch terms in the text). It is evident that Schoonenberg views the free act of an infant as being of a lower degree than that of the adult. He speaks, for example, of the infant as a dormant, though not wholly unconcious, person (*Gods wordende wereld*, 49; *God's World in the Making*, 62). At first glance, a problematic ambivalence appears to mark Schoonenberg's view of the child. At one point, he contends that the basic constituent of person, free decision, is lacking in the case of an infant: "Ein Kind kann noch nicht die zentrale Entscheidung vollziehen, die zu einer Todsünde nötig ist" ("Sünde-Sakrament-Jugendalter: einige theologische Bemerkungen," *Einübung des Glaubens*, ed. Günter Stachel and Alois Zenner [Würzburg: Echter-Verlag, 1965], 106). In other instances, however, Schoonenberg attributes precisely such a central personal act to the infant: "... every human being, also the smallest child and also the most primitive primordial being of the human race, enters his good or evil eternity by his own conscious personal choice" (*Gods wordende wereld*, 80; cf. *Geloof*, IV, 163). A possible explana-

c. *Free Decision and Inner Situational Determinant*

At whatever point freedom, as total act, is thought to begin, it is clear that by means of the model, Schoonenberg wishes to uncover a depth dimension of situation that is a reality also *within the adult*. The model of the child is designed to pinpoint a dimension of being-situated that is more incisive – even for the adult – than the situation that a person happens to walk into at a particular time and place. That the incisiveness of being-situated uncovered by means of the model is retained in the case of the adult can be demonstrated in two (converging) ways, by considering, first, Schoonenberg's use of the term *Existential* to apply to the situation of both child and adult,[143] and, second, his analysis and correction of the Pelagian theory of inter-human relationships.

Not occurring in Schoonenberg's earlier publications,[144] the term *Existential* comes to play an important role in indicating that the qualitatively different, deeper situation introduced by way of the model extends into the life of the adult. Schoonenberg distinguishes the situation of the child by speaking of it as an *existentiale*, in contrast to an *existentielle* situation. An *existentielle* situation is one that *we* come upon, give meaning and shape.[145] An *existentiale* situation, on the other hand, is one that literally

---

tion for the possibility of the free act in the latter case lies in Schoonenberg's view that such a total act ultimately takes place only (and perhaps also for the infant) at the transition point marked by death (see *Man and Sin,* 32, 34; *Geloof,* IV, 60, 63). In any case, the fact remains that Schoonenberg wishes to speak only of the situatedness of *persons.* Accordingly, to the extent that the child in the model, for example, cannot be said to exist as a person (*Man and Sin,* 113; *Bijdragen,* XXIV, 364), that model becomes irrelevant for the reinterpretation of original sin – a conclusion diametrically opposed to the intended function of that model.

143 This Heideggerian term will generally be left untranslated in the text and, insofar as is possible, used only in this noun form. At all times, the term *Existential* must be sharply distinguished as designating a basis *structure of* existence (see the more precise description in n. 163 below; also ch. II, sec.B, 3 below) from the *English* term "existential" (German: *existenziell*) which designates concrete, unique *existence itself.* The translations suggested by others have not been adopted because they are either cumbersome or confusing. Robinson and Cobb have translated *Existential* as "existentialist," and *existenziell* as "existential." Macquarrie and Robinson have translated *Existential* as "existentiale," and *existenziell* as "existentiell." See James M. Robinson and John B. Cobb, Jr., (eds.), *New Frontiers in Theology, Discussions among German and American Theologians,* Vol. I: *The Later Heidegger and Theology* (New York: Harper and Row, 1963), ix-x; and Martin Heidegger, *Being and Time,* trans. John Macquarrie and Edward Robinson (New York: Harper and Row, 1962), 33, n. 2: "There seems to be little reason for resorting to the more elaborate neologisms proposed by other writers."

144 The term becomes prevalent in the publications subsequent to Schoonenberg's first extensive treatment of original sin in *Geloof,* IV (1962).

145 *MS,* II, 894; *Man and Sin,* 116n, where the translator points out that two dif-

precedes our active existing, our free decisions.[146] Situation in this sense has simply been determined by others. Our decisions have in no way affected its shape. On the contrary, as Schoonenberg says repeatedly, that situation *encompasses* our existence.[147]

When Schoonenberg speaks of the *existentiale* situation of the adult, he, in effect, directs that adult back to his own inchoate emptiness as person, the point at which he arrives in a world and in a situation that he has neither created nor moulded. It is that mode of being-situated that remains present in his active existence as a constitutive, determinate element in every concrete decision, as a determinant within man. By momentarily removing the element of personal decision[148] from the line of sight, Schoonenberg clears the way for a full view of the awesome massivity and fixity of being-situated that enters the very being of man as an interior determination of the subject.[149]

There is a second way in which it can be shown that the structural depth of the situation illuminated by Schoonenberg's model of the child extends into the very fiber of the adult. That can be demonstrated by Schoonenberg's analysis and correction of a structural deficiency adhering to the Pelagian conception of human interrelatedness. In that confrontation with Pelagianism, it becomes evident that the case of the dependent child does not function as a mere pedagogic aid – superfluous after the reality it illustrates has been clarified – but as a model that is inherently related to the reality which it uncovers.

The Church rejected Pelagianism by teaching that original sin is passed on, not by imitation, but by propagation.[150] Rejected by this *non imitatione,* says Schoonenberg, is

> die Auffassung, dass die Sünde Adams nur durch Nachahmung auf andere Menschen übergehe und dass folglich bei den neugeborenen Kindern, die doch einer solchen Nachahmung nicht fähig sind, keineswegs von Sünde gesprochen

---

ferent German terms are employed in the original. Subsequently in this English translation, the term *Existential* is either circumscribed in terms of "preceding and encompassing" (116, 120, 186), rendered as "initially" (181), or translated by means of the English term "existential" (118, 120, 187) without indicating that it stands for a Dutch or German term *with the opposite meaning.*

146 *MS,* II, 894, 930.
147 *MS,* II, 894, 896, 930; *Ex Auditu Verbi,* 264.
148 An element which Schoonenberg admits is never absent in reality (*Man and Sin,* 181; *MS,* II, 890; *Ex Auditu Verbi,* 263).
149 *MS,* II, 928: "Ein das Subjekt innerlich bestimmendes Moment."
150 *DS,* 1513: "propagatione, non imitatione transfusum." *DS,* 1514: "generatione contraxerunt." The latter expression is taken over directly from a canon promulgated at the Council of Carthage (*DS,* 223).

> werden könne und diese Kinder deshalb auch nicht "zur Vergebung der Sünde" getauft werden sollten.[151]

The substance of this formulation anticipates the discussion of the specific content of original sin conceived of as situation. Of interest at this point is the fact that, with the aid of the situation theory, Schoonenberg considers it possible – even structurally – to pinpoint a basic deficiency of the Pelagian imitation theory and, by extending and deepening Pelagius' approach,[152] to suggest a corrective. He does both with an implicit appeal to the model of the dependent child:

> Beispiele und Werturteile üben nicht nur dann ihren Einfluss aus, wenn man mit eigener personaler Entscheidung sich ihnen konfrontiert. Sie bilden auch eine *Situation, in der ein Mensch empfangen und geboren wird*....[153]

In other words, Schoonenberg finds the Pelagian theory deficient because it abstracts man-standing-over-against from man-born-into a given world, a given history, a given situation. The explanation of human interrelatedness as an example-imitation syndrome breaks the structural continuity between man as adult and as child, and thus between personal existence and situational *Existential*. In opposition to a superficial example theory, Schoonenberg advocates the idea of situation as an *Existential* that is, as it were, osmotically present in man's existence. Opposing an individualistic isolation of man, he posits the general thesis that, in personal self-determination, being-determined constitutes a unique element.[154] In this way, Schoonenberg preserves the depth dimension of being-situated, without for a moment negating the idea of personal freedom.

Schoonenberg's conception of being-situated both in its determinancy and in its interiority can best be clarified by briefly drawing together several strands of his thought that were discussed previously.

Because, as we have seen, existing-in-the-world-*bodily* represents man's fundamental situation of which other modes of being situated are variants, the *interiority* of being situated historically is given with the interiority of man's body. In the discussion of person and body,[155] the latter was considered to be man's own primarily in the measure that he has personally

---

151 Schoonenberg, "Theologie und Lehramt: Hermeneutik am Beispiel der Erbsünde-Diskussion," *WuW*, XXII (1967), 744; (translation of) "Testcase Erfzonde," *NM*, XIX (1967-68), 202-203.
152 See n. 122 above.
153 *WuW*, XXII, 746, emphasis added; *NM*. XIX, 204.
154 *Ex Auditu Verbi*, 263 where he suggests that the discovery of this unique element is of prime importance in extricating the theology of original sin out of its impasse.
155 Sec. A, 2, b above.

appropriated it, has *made* it his. Nevertheless, the body was recognized to be man's own also *prior* to such personalization.[156] That is evidenced by the fact that the principle of materiality, of passivity, was said to be present *within* man, as well as by the fact that its corresponding concrete reality, body, was said to be *man's mode of existence.*[157] Body, even in its opposition to person was seen, therefore, to be *man's* body. In view of the intrinsic relationship between the foundational bodily situatedness and its historical variant, it is not surprizing that the interiority of both types of situations is the same. As is indicated by the very term, being-situated, too, is a *passive* "mode of existence"[158] and as such it represents the diametrical opposite of the active mode of existence that is peculiar to person. Nevertheless, as in the case of *bodily* existence, being-situated historically is predicated of *man*; it is truly *his* (passive) *mode of existence.* The term "being-situated" is preferred precisely because it gives expression to the fact that it is the *subject* that is being-situated.[159] Accordingly, Schoonenberg insists that this situatedness is a "Bestimmt-Sein dieses Menschen selbst" and a "Wirklichkeit im Menschen selbst."[160]

In what sense can the interior reality of being-situated be construed as a *determinant*? It is a determinant in three senses in accordance with the dual rootage and the specific quality of the idea of situation. Being-situated is rooted in nature (as man's generic essence and individual characteristics) and in corporeality. Situatedness is both an expression and a modification of corporeality and nature. It is an expression of nature in its formal givenness and of materiality in its massive fixity. The modification introduced by situatedness consists of the fact that its *content* is specified, not by the givenness of one's generic and individual characteristics as in the case of nature, nor by natural-biological processes as (normally) in the case of corporeality, but by the free decisions of fellow human beings. Being-situated acquires its specific determinant quality by assimilating the characteristics of nature and corporeality and raising them to a higher level. Situatedness is a determinant purely formally, i.e., in its givenness as a mode of being proper to man, as his nature. Situatedness is simply there, a *factum.* Further, being-situated is a determinant in its tangible fixity as a corporeal, physical reality. By finding its expression in a concrete *Umwelt* as a specific configuration of

---

156 The priority in view is not temporal but ontological.
157 Sec. A, 2, b above.
158 "Daseinsweise", *MS*, II, 929, 930.
159 See the statements annotated as nn. 106-108 above.
160 *MS*, II, 891.

corporeal realities — physical objects, books, people, institutions — being-situated displays a certain solidity and rigidity that is opposed to the fluidity and flexibility of free decisions. The "natural" and corporeal aspects of determinativeness inhering in being-situated acquire their *situational* quality by virtue of the fact that the specific content of this mode of existence has been determined by the free decisions of other human beings. Because that content, in turn, constitutes the content of subsequent free decisions,[161] being-situated may be said to be determinative for free decisions. This is the specific sense in which Schoonenberg speaks of situation as determinative. It must be kept in mind, however, that, were it not for its rootage in nature and corporeality, situation would not have a determinative quality at all. It is precisely the determinative qualities of corporeality and nature, however, that find their highest manifestation in being-situated as an interior determinant of man.

B. TRANSCENDENTAL SUBJECT AND SPATIOTEMPORAL MEDIATION: RAHNER AND WEGER

As is to be expected in view of their interdependence,[162] Rahner's and Weger's view of man as historical being has a great deal in common with that of Schoonenberg. The basic framework of person and nature, which Schoonenberg developed with the aid of and in discussion with Rahner's view, remains central. Furthermore, the specific qualification of human nature as historical situatedness, so crucial for Schoonenberg's reinterpretation of original sin, is shared by Rahner and Weger. Similarly, the concept *Existential*, used by Schoonenberg to indicate the depth dimension of situation, is prevalent in both Rahner's and Weger's expositions, though with wider application.[163] Apart from direct influence, these and other similarities may be due to commonly shared thought-forms.

New in the thought of Rahner and Weger is the explicit and con-

---

161 Explicitly stated in sec. A, 3, a above; implicit throughout the discussion of situation and freedom.

162 See the introductory paragraphs of this chapter.

163 In Rahner's thought an *Existential* is any inextricable relational structuration of man's existence. The concept applies, therefore, to man's corporeality, as well as to his social, cultural and historical situatedness (*Schriften*, II, 253); also man's natural (*ibid.*) and supernatural (*ibid.,* 252-53) relationship to God constitute *Existentialia* (see also ch. II, sec. B, 3 below). For an analysis of Rahner's conception of *Existential* see Peter Eicher, *Die anthropologische Wende: Karl Rahners philosophischer Weg vom Wesen des Menschen zur personalen Existenz* ("Dokimion," Band I; Freiburg (Switzerland): Universitätsverlag, 1970), 151, n. 2 and 356-58.

centrated attention devoted to man's transcendental dimension. Although that dimension is by no means absent nor of little importance in Schoonenberg's thought, in developing the idea of situation, it remains largely implicit. As part of his transcendental theology,[164] Rahner, by contrast, methodically explicates and elaborates man's transcendental drive.[165] Accordingly, man's freedom receives more direct attention and attains explicit preponderance. To avoid misunderstanding, it bears repeating that the idea of freedom is equally central for Schoonenberg, but in developing the idea of situation the idea of freedom is frequently kept in methodological abeyance, suppressed momentarily in order to focus *directly* on the givenness and the depth

164 For Rahner's elaboration of the method and purpose of transcendental theology, see especially, "Theology und Anthropologie," *Schriften,* VIII, 43-65 (much of this material is found also in "Grundsätzliche Uberlegungen zur Anthropologie und Protologie im Rahmen der Theologie," *MS,* II, 406-420), and "Uberlegungen zur Methode der Theologie," *Schriften,* IX, 79-126. This method of theologizing has its philosophical roots in the transcendental Thomism of J. Maréchal but is significantly influenced by the philosophy of Heidegger; see O. Muck, *Die transcendentale Methode in der scholastischen Philosophie der Gegenwart* (Innsbruck: Felizian Rauch, 1964), 197-211 (Muck here classifies Rahner with J. B. Lotz and W. Brugger as those elaborating the Maréchalian philosophy "in Auseinandersetzung mit Heidegger," pp. 179-228). In addition to Muck's analysis and the comprehensive treatment of Rahner's philosophy by Eicher (see n. 163 above), who makes extensive use of Rahner's *theological* writings, see: Karl Lehmann, "Theologische Portraits: Karl Rahner," *Bilanz der Theologie im 20. Jahrhundert,* Vol. IV: *Bahnbrechende Theologen,* ed. Herbert Vorgrimler and Robert Van der Gucht (Freiburg: Herder, 1970) 143-81; H. Vorgrimler, *Karl Rahner* (Tielt, Lannoo, 1962); Gerald A. McCool, "The Philosophy of the Human Person in Karl Rahner's Theology," *ThSt,* XXII (1961), 537-62. McCool considers Rahner's transcendental anthropology to constitute "one of the most obvious threads of unity running through the disparate series of occasional essays which make up the three volumes of *Schriften zur Theologie"* (p. 538; cf. 539; see also Vorgrimler, 61, Lehmann, 158-70, Schoofs, *Aggiornamento,* 141-42; *Breakthrough,* 129). The groundwork of this transcendental approach is found in Rahner's philosophical works, *Geist in Welt: zur Metaphysik der endlichen Erkenntnis bei Thomas von Aquin* überarbeitet und ergänzt von J. B. Metz; (München: Kösel-Verlag, 1957 [first published in 1939] and *Hörer des Wortes: zur Grundlegung einer Religionsphilosophie* (neu bearbeitet von J. B. Metz; München: Kösel-Verlag, 1963 [first published in 1941]). That these philosophical works do not represent a stage superseded by Rahner's theological writings is evidenced, aside from their republication, by the fact that a philosophical essay summarizing the basic tenets of Rahner's philosophy which was written in 1938 is published for the first time in the last volume of *Schriften:* "Die Wahrheit bei Thomas von Aquin" (*Schriften,* X, 21-40; in a footnote on p. 21 the two philosophical works mentioned above are called "grundlegende(n) Werke," and this essay is said to have "besondere Wert für das Grundanliegen im Denken des Vfs. . . .").

165 Despite the formidable rigor of this method, its application in theology serves primarily a practical purpose: uncovering the core of the Christian faith and explicating its relevance for man and his world; see *Schriften* VIII, 43-65; IX, 79-126; Vorgrimler, pp. 79-82; Lehmann, pp. 147-49, 158-59, 164-69, 172-73.

dimension of situation.¹⁶⁶ In Rahner's and, in dependence on him, in Weger's thought, freedom is explicitly given its central place. At the same time, the specific meaning of situation which Schoonenberg was determined to conceptualize is fully retained by Rahner and Weger but, subsumed under the concept "spatiotemporal mediation,"¹⁶⁷ it is gathered up in a comprehensive synthesis with man's transcendental freedom. That synthesis makes it possible to explore aspects of man's situatedness that remain somewhat obscure in Schoonenberg's expositions and to evaluate more accurately the possibilities and the limitations of a situational interpretation of original sin.

1. Human Nature: Necessary Transcendence and Spatiotemporal Mediation

Rahner expresses the essence of man's nature most frequently by means of the concept "transcendence." Man can therefore be defined as "absolut unbegrenzte Transzendentalität"¹⁶⁸ or as "absolute Offenheit."¹⁶⁹ The very essence of man is transcendence.¹⁷⁰ As "Geist" he *is* transcendental subject.¹⁷¹ As the term indicates, transcendence involves "going-beyond," in this case going beyond that which is experienced, seen and felt immediately towards "another" encompassing reality. Thus, to include the terminus¹⁷² of

---

166 See the introductory paragraphs of sec. A, 3 above; see also sec. A, 3, c above.

167 The term "spatiotemporal" will be used as an equivalent of "kategorial," the more prevalent term in Rahner's and Weger's writings. The term "spatiotemporal" is less confusing than the term "categorical" and indicates that the categories to which the term "kategorial" refers are primarily those of space and time.

168 *Schriften*, IX, 105.

169 *Schriften*, IV, 22.

170 *Ibid.*, 74, 231.

171 *Ibid.*, 58. Cf. *Hörer des Wortes*, 71, 86. This openness of the human spirit for being as such is the *anthropological* correlate of the *metaphysical* principle of the original unity of being and knowing: "das Sein des Seienden ist – 'Erkennbarkeit' " (*Hörer des Wortes*, 56). As is implicit in this citation, the unity of being and knowing is ultimately grounded in an original identity: "Sein der Seienden und Erkennen sind also deshalb korrelat, weil sie ursprünglich in ihrem Grunde *dasselbe* sind" (*Hörer des Wortes*, 56-57; similarly, *Schriften*, X, 38). This unity and correlation finds expression in the title of chapter III of *Hörer des Wortes*, "Die Gelichtetheit von Sein." Rahner attempts to ward off an idealistic understanding of this unity by pointing to the starting point of philosophy, namely, the *question* concerning being. The fact that man must *ask* concerning being entails that he is not simply identical with being, for such identity would render the question superfluous, even impossible. Man has being analogously (see chapter IV, "Die Analogie der 'Seinshabe' " *Hörer des Wortes*, 63-70).

172 The term "terminus" is used as a translation for Rahner's prevalent term "Woraufhin" (used frequently in combination with "Wovonher"; see, e.g., *Schriften*, IV, 69-70, 72-73; VI, 216-17, 220, 292-93; VIII, 183).

transcendence, man is defined in his essential nature as absolute transcendence to being-as-such, to absolute being, to God.[173]

This transcendence is of a peculiar kind, however. To understand the nature of "going-beyond," it must be seen in connection with the other dimension of man, his spatiotemporal dimension. Whereas man is transcendence by virtue of being spirit (*Geist*), he is bound to the categories of space and time by virtue of being *embodied* spirit and spiritualized *body*.[174] Correspondingly, man knows and grasps *directly* only the realities appearing in the categories of space and time. This is his "world,"[175] man's original situation.[176] If man is immediately present only to himself and to the objects opposite him, however, the infinite and absolute transcendence that was said to constitute man's very essence seems to be precluded. Man appears to be characterized not by openness, disclosure, but by enclosure. He appears to be encapsulated within the world of subject and object.

It is precisely at this point of seeming enclosure that the specific mode of man's transcendence emerges. In fact, in Rahner's view, the relation of man to his world presupposes — as the condition of its possibility — transcendence. Without entering in detail into the complex argumentation with which Rahner supports that thesis,[177] the mode of transcendence can be pictured, somewhat crudely, with the aid of key concepts employed in that

---

173 The terminus of man's transcendence is variously designated as "das absolute Sein" (*Schriften*, IV, 68, 71; VI, 208), "das Absolute" (*Schriften*, IV, 58; at one point corrected as "der Absolute," IV, 148), "unendliche und notwendige Sein" (*Schriften*, VI, 188), "das reine Sein und das reine Erkennen" in identity (*Schriften*, X, 38), "tragende Grund" (="Wovonher") and "letzte Woraufhin" (*Schriften*, VI, 217; X, 557-59), "bewegende Ursache" (*Schriften*, VI, 233), "das Sein schlechthin" *Schriften*, IV, 231), "das Sein überhaupt" (*Schriften*, II, 286-87; IV, 22, 231; VI, 216-17), "das Ganze" *Schriften*, II, 286-87). Although many of these names are often found juxtaposed (*Schriften*, II, 286-87; IV, 22, 69; VI, 208; sometimes including the phrase "which we call God" [*Schriften*, IV, 69; VI, 188, 208, 217]), these designations are not all of the same order (see, e.g., Rahner, "Die Hominisation als theologische Frage," Paul Overhage and Karl Rahner, *Das Problem der Hominisation: über den biologischen Ursprung des Menschen* ["Questiones Disputatae," 12/13; Freiburg: Herder 1961], 71. Cited hereafter as *Hominisation*). Moreover, it must be kept in mind that, although God is the ground *of* all beings, as such He also tran*scends* all beings (*Hominisation*, 58, 80-81) and is therefore frequently designated as "das Geheimnis" and "das Namenlose" (see, e.g., *Schriften*, IV, 70).

174 *Schriften*, II, 287; see also II, 221; III. 313; IV, 478; V, 184-90; and chapters 5, 10, 11, and 12 of *Hörer des Wortes*). Cf. Weger, *Theologie der Erbsünde*, 112, 117.

175 That world is not simply creation as such, but the world as object of man as subject (*Schriften*, VI, 197).

176 See *Schriften*, VI, 197, 199; *Hominisation*, 46-48; Ficher, 121-25, 298-302.

177 The argumentation is tersely described in *Schriften*, IV, 70-71, elaborated in *Schriften*, X, 21-38 and especially in *Hörer des Wortes*, 47-88.

argumentation, especially the concept "horizon." One must picture a horizon behind which the sun has just disappeared. The sun's rays still illumine the horizon and, indirectly, everything between it and the observer.[178] The horizon, though real, has something ethereal, elusive about it. It is not seen in and by itself, nor grasped directly, but is apprehended only *as* boundary, *as* limiting, contextual reality. Similarly, man knows particular entities directly, but only by virtue of the definition and outline provided by the luminous horizon that is not directly grasped: these entities *are*, i.e., they participate in being (this *is* a tree); they represent a certain mode of being (this is a *tree*); they represent a particular instance of that being (*this* is a tree). The "simple" knowledge of an object entails an implicit recognition of its limitation, its finitude, particularity and specific generic quality. The recognition of that limitation has as its positive corollary an implicit affirmation of "something" beyond that boundary; otherwise the notion of boundary becomes meaningless. But that "something-beyond" itself is not seen; only the particular spatiotemporal entities are seen directly. That "something-beyond" presents itself as luminous horizon *implicitly*, as the condition of possibility for the knowledge of objects. That horizon is, therefore, frequently referred to as *a priori* horizon.[179] The act that corresponds to this specific nature of horizon is man's transcendence, which, when designated in its peculiar mode of implicit reaching-beyond, is referred to as *prolepsis*.[180] Proleptic transcendence, one might say, involves not the com-prehension of a particular reality, but the ap-prehension of an infinite, enveloping reality. Any attempt to comprehend the horizon as a finite reality presupposes another horizon that gives meaning to the comprehended "horizon." Thus, the true horizon is always *present* as an ever *receding* reality.[181]

178 This image is inappropriate in several ways. The objects are, of course, not merely opaque obstructions between observing subject and illuminating source. The very reality of these objects is dependent on that light; these objects represent particular embodiments of that light (see especially *Hörer des Wortes*, 47-62). Furthermore, the light does not illumine the objects as such but illumines via the *intellectus agens* which is the (*a priori*) *lumen*, according to Rahner (*Hörer des Wortes*, 84-85, 98; *Schriften*, X, 28-37). The inappropriateness of the horizon-imagery represents not merely a difficulty of illustration, but a difficulty that is inherent to the combination of the idea of horizon with the idea of an *a priori* (condition of possibility) *within* the human subject, *an* a priori derived from an analysis of man as (theoretically) knowing subject.

179 See, e.g., *Schriften*, IV, 37-38, 225; V, 502-503; X, 539, 540.

180 The term usually employed by Rahner is "Vorgriff" (see *Hörer des Wortes,* 71-88, *Schriften,* IV, 69-72). Weger prefers the term "Ausgriff" (*Theologie der Erbsünde,* 112, 113).

181 See especially *Schriften,* IV, 70-73; e.g.: "Dieses Woraufhin unserer Transzendenz west darum an in einem nur ihm eigenen Modus des Abweisens und der Abwesenheit. Es gibt sich uns im Modus des Sichversagens, des Schweigens, der Ferne" (72).

It has become evident that man's implicit transcendence and his explicit grasp of particular objects do not represent independent, but interdependent modes of knowledge. That inextricable and specific interrelatedness finds expression in the term mediation. Particular objects can be known only by transcending them. But the converse is equally true: human transcendence is possible only *in-and-through* the medium of space and time. Hence, man's transcendence is said to be spatiotemporally mediated.[182]

The idea of necessary transcendence and spatiotemporal mediation applies not only to man as cognitive being but – due to the original unity of the true and the good, and of knowing and willing – also to man as volitional being.[183] As volitional being, man is transcendentally directed to the absolute as absolute value or absolute good.[184] The spatiotemporal reality mediating this transcendence is finite reality as it represents particular values.[185] The relationship that obtains between volitional transcendence and its categorical mediation is essentially the same as in the case of cognition.[186] The affirmation of a particular value requires as the a priori condition of its possibility the volitional affirmation of absolute value.

Before turning to the idea of man's free appropriation of his natural being, it may be well to call attention to one point: with respect to the transcendence described, man is by no means free – not even in his *volitional* transcendence. As part of man's *nature,* this transcendental drive entails an ineluctable volitional affirmation of absolute value. That affirmation is inescapable because it is the very condition of possibility for man's daily dealing with reality. Man may be free to choose between particular objects embodying particular values, but whatever his choice, the terminus of his transcendental drive is volitionally, but necessarily affirmed.[187] Within this

---

182 See *Schriften,* IV, 84; VI, 288; IX, 99; *Hörer des Wortes,* 67-68, 147.

183 Although cognition and volition are sometimes viewed as two faculties of man (*Schriften,* IV, 54-55), they frequently appear conjointly as two fundamental modes of being (see, e.g., *Schriften* IV, 59-60; *Hörer des Wortes,* 125-26). The unity of knowing and willing is rooted in the ultimate identity of *ens-bonum-verum,* which, in turn, is identical with the series *ens-intellectus-voluntas* (Hörer des Wortes, 118-19, 182; *Schriften,* VI, 287; see Eicher, 180-84).

184 *Schriften,* V, 502-503; cf. I, 391: das "Gut schlechthin" and God as "das absolute Gut." Cf. Weger, *Theologie der Erbsünde,* 110-11.

185 *Ibid.*

186 The difference between a cognitive and a volitional act lies in their relationship to spatiotemporal reality. In cognitive acts man is related to the impressions of particular objects passively. In volitional acts man is directed to value objects by a spontaneous drive which constitutes the condition of possibility for a free decision (*Schriften,* I, 389-90).

187 Regarding the combination of volitional and necessary affirmation, see especially

framework, then, the only room left for freedom is that of choosing between this or that value-object, a notion of freedom that both Rahner and Weger deprecate as falling far short of true freedom.[188] Although freedom of choice with respect to objects is possible by virtue of man's natural transcendental dynamic,[189] one is not free with respect to that dynamic itself.[190]

2. Human Person: Free Appropriation of Human Nature

In contrast to freedom of choice with respect to particular, finite entities, Rahner and Weger speak of man's deeper freedom as transcendental freedom,[191] or as "Seinsfreiheit."[192] This freedom is possible because as subject man is defined as a relational being. He stands in relation not only to God and the world but also to himself:[193]

Hörer des Wortes, chapters 7 and 8 (e.g., p. 129: "Die Liebe zu Gott, die im Grunde des menschlichen Daseins notwendig geschieht ..."). Rahner's thought on this subject is so complex that Eicher, for example, concludes a discussion of this matter by saying, "Wir befinden uns hier an der Grenze des – schon sprachlich – noch Verständlichen" (p. 184). Elsewhere he notes regarding the same subject, "Selbst E. Simons, dessen eigene Ausführungen der spekulativen Höhe Rahners keineswegs nachstehen, beurteilt dieses Kapitel [chapter 7 of *Hörer des Wortes*] als kaum verständlich" (p. 346 with reference to Eberhard Simons, *Philosophie der Offenbarung: Auseinandersetzung mit Karl Rahner* [Stuttgart: Kohlhammer, 1966], 46-50).

188 The freedom that is possible *within* the transcendental framework of a necessary affirmation of absolute value is the freedom of choice with respect to particular values (see *Hörer des Wortes,* 128, as well as the note by Metz on that and the following page). For the evaluation and subordination of this notion of freedom of choice see Rahner, *Schriften,* I, 392-93; II, 96-100, 259-62; VI, 216-25; Weger, *Theologie der Erbsünde,* 110-11.

189 Cf. *Hörer des Wortes,* 73: "Menschliches Handeln ist frei. Freiheit ist aber von vornherein nur dort denkbar, wo der Handelnde einen Stand hat, der von dem Stand dessen, mit dem er handelt, unabhängig ist. Dadurch nun, dass der Mensch in seiner urteilenden Erkenntnis seine vollkommene Rückkehr zu sich selbst vollzieht und so einen Stand gegen und unabhängig vom erkannten Gegenstand gewinnt, kann er als von diesem freier frei mit ihm handeln."

190 The deeper freedom, to be discussed momentarily, is possible only *in relation to* this framework, whereby man appears to assume a position outside the framework itself (see, e.g., *Hörer des Wortes,* 129-30). In so far as freedom is considered to be the fundamental, original act of man, the source of his own being, that free act must, of course, also be seen as the *source* of the transcendental framework (see *Hörer des Wortes,* 122). In a different context, Eicher poses the critical question that is pertinent to the entire transcendental approach: "Wer ist dieser primär fragende Mensch? Ein fragender Punkt ausserhalb der Welt? " (154; see also 259, n. 2 and 386 n. 1).

191 Rahner, *Schriften,* V, 116; VIII, 272. Weger, 110-11.

192 Rahner, *Schriften,* VI, 222-23, 243-44; *LThK,* IV, 333-34.

193 For an analysis of the idea of man as free self-relationship see Eicher (343-56), who traces this conception to Kierkegaard (343, n. 1).

> Der Mensch ist jenes Seiende, dem es in seinem Sein um dieses selber geht, das immer schon ein Verhältnis zu sich selbst hat, Subjektivität und nie einfach Natur, immer schon Person, nie einfach "vorfindlich," sondern schon immer "fur sich," "befindlich" ist.[194]

Man exists in self-relation as knowledge and as free act (again, in orignal and ultimate unity) as "*Selbst*-besitz und *Selbst*-tat."[195] Within this self-relation, Rahner speaks of man's freedom — in possibly even stronger terms than Schoonenberg does — as radical "Selbstverfügung"[196] and hence of man as "*sui ipsius faber.*"[197] In spite of his creatureliness, or rather, as Rahner would say, *because of* his creatureliness and as the apex of creaturely reality[198] (prescinding from angels), man is in a significant sense his own creation:

> Der Mensch ist der seiner Freiheit Überbürdete und Aufgegebene; diese Freiheit ist schöpferisch und ihr Geschöpf ist der Mensch in Endgültigkeit selbst, so dass der gottgesetzte Anfang dieser Freiheitsgeschichte — sein Wesen, wie wir sagen — nicht das Fixfertige und dauernd in seiner Wesenheit Intangible ist, sondern die Ermächtigung zur Freiheit, in der der Freie sich selbst in Endgültigkeit hinein unableitbar setzt.[199]

It is this original, inner free act that constitutes man as *person.*[200]

a. *Appropriation of Transcendental Dynamic*

The relationship between man's necessary transcendence (nature) and his free self-relationship (person) can best be described in terms of "appropriation,"[201] a concept that plays a crucial role in the situational reinterpre-

---

194 Cf. *Schriften,* III, 395.
195 *Schriften,* VI, 288, emphasis added.
196 *Schriften,* VIII, 169-70; IV, 433; VI, 250-51.
197 *Schriften,* VIII, 270, cf. 271 ("autopraxis"); see also II, 98.
198 One of Rahner's central theses is that man's independence and autonomy do not vary inversely, but directly as his dependence on God (see *Schriften,* I, 183; IV, 151; VI, 223, 242).
199 *Schriften,* VIII, 270; cf. *ibid.*: man is "das radikal offene, unfertige Wesen, und wenn sein Wesen fertig ist, ist es das durch ihn selbst in Freiheit geschaffene."
200 *Schriften,* III, 86: "Wo person ist, da ist Freiheit, d.h. aber Selbstverfügung über ihre eigene Wirklichkeit, die Gestaltung ihres Seins und ihres Lebens aus inneren Entscheidung heraus." See also *Schriften,* I, 392-400; II, 86-88; 251-52; III, 90, 138, 395; VI, 183; as well as the reference to person in quotation 194 above. For Rahner's varied usage of the concept person, see Eicher, 358-60. Eicher contends that "Personalität" must be understood as man's most fundamental *Existential* (357-58). This is quite plausible in view of the fact that the term person can designate the "Selbst*verhältnis*" that man *is,* an inextricable relational structure of existence, but also problematical since person again refers to both nature and to that which is opposed to nature, viz., freedom (see n. 71 above).
201 The term appropriation is used to capture the connotation of terms such as

tation of original sin. Appropriation aptly describes the act of man's personal decision with respect to his given being, for it captures both the creatureliness and the creativeness of man's freedom. The idea of creatureliness is retained because appropriation presupposes that a specific reality is already *given*, i.e., a reality whose origin and structure cannot be ascribed to man's free act.[202] The idea of creativity is retained because appropriation entails a *free act* (with respect to given reality), an act that in Rahner's view, as we have seen, is creative in a profound sense. When Rahner wishes to point out man's creatureliness, he does so by stating that in his freedom man is not absolute creativity. In relation to man's free act, his given, finite nature is ontically prior, namely, as the condition of the possibility and as the limiting norm of that free act.[203] Rahner is equally adamant, however, in defending the idea that man's deepest act is authentically creative; man is in some sense his own origin, maker, creator.[204] This creative creatureliness converges in appropriation because that act involves, at one and the same time, the *free* re-*constitution* of one's given nature and the free *re*-constitution of one's *given nature*.[205]

Free appropriation involves, most centrally, a positive decision with respect to one's "transzendentale Grundbewegung."[206] Because that transcendental dynamic has meaning only in relation to its goal and ground, a decision with respect to one's transcendental directedness involves at the same time a decision with respect to God.[207] Love for God is the acceptance of one's transcendental drive with all that it entails.[208]

Man is not pure transcendence, however, but, as we have seen,

---

"Übernahme" (Rahner, *Hörer des Wortes,* 108, 119; *Schriften,* I, 396; IV, 238; Weger, *Theologie der Erbsünde,* 112, 120, 121, 149, 170), "Annahme" (Rahner, *Schriften,* V, 503; VIII, 310-11), and "Aneignung" (Rahner, *Schriften,* II, 261; Weger, *Theologie der Erbsünde,* 120, 141, 142, 171, 172). Weger displays a certain predilection for the term "Nachvollzug" (*Theologie der Erbsünde,* 119, 121, 129, 141-44, 149-50, 164-66, 172).

202 *Schriften,* II, 86.
203 *Schriften,* II, 86, 260; III, 86; VIII, 289; cf. V, 165.
204 See the quotation annotated as n. 196 above.
205 See *Hörer des Wortes,* 130, where Rahner speaks in terms of appropriation but qualifies that act by saying that man "*setzt* von sich aus aufs neue frei die richtigen [Strukturgesetze], die er immer schon notwendig bejaht . . . ." (see also *ibid.,* 108, 119, 126, 127). Eicher compares Rahner's idea of "Setzung" to Fichte's central thesis (Eicher, 205-208, 210, 307, n. 5). To do justice to man's creatureliness, Rahner works with the idea that in his (self)-*Setzung* (person) man experiences his *Gesetztheit* (nature); see, *Hörer des Wortes,* 110-11.
206 *Schriften,* V, 503.
207 *Schriften,* I, 391-92; II, 260; V, 496-503.
208 *Schriften,* V, 503, cf. 496-99.

mediated transcendence. Accordingly, the acceptance of one's nature is impossible without accepting one's transcendental being in its concreteness, i.e., immersed in space and time, in history. Personal appropriation of one's nature is the appropriation of historically mediated transcendence.

b. *Appropriation of Historically Mediated Transcendence*

Like Schoonenberg,[209] Rahner uses the term "history" for two related concepts. In its broad sense, "history" designates the phenomenon of freedom and person described above. In this sense, the term "history" serves to demarcate the uniquely human realm from, for example, the realm of purely natural-biological processes.[210] In his freedom, a person cannot be regarded as a particular instance of a general process, nor subsumed as a specific case under a universal law. He can neither be derived nor calculated from a prior ground.[211] As free event, man is unique, irrepeatable, unpredictable[212] – his own ground. Free event, however, constitutes the *sine qua non*,[213] not the substance, of human history. More narrowly, the term "history" serves to designate the specific feature of *human* history, namely, the extension of free decisions into space and time.[214] In his freedom, man is not pure spirit; he is "als *geschichtliches* Wesen Geist."[215]

It is the nature of the relationship between the *sine qua non* and the substance of history that is crucial for our purposes. Several terms are used to express the relationship of free act to spatiotemporal reality, such as "manifestation," "objectification" and "mediation."[216] Of these, the term "mediation" is most comprehensive and pivotal. It will serve as the key, therefore, to an understanding of the dynamics entailed in the personal appropriation of historically mediated transcendence.

The idea of historical mediation involves a complex dual dynamics. Put

---

209 See the introductory paragraphs of sec. A, 3 above.
210 *Hörer des Wortes*, 144.
211 *Ibid.*, 143; *Schriften*, III, 395.
212 *Hörer des Wortes*, 143-44, 166. Cf. *Das Dynamische in der Kirche* ("Quaestiones Disputatae," 5; Freiburg: Herder, 1958), 10.
213 *Hörer des Wortes*, 165.
214 *Ibid.*, 165; cf. 143-44, 194, 197.
215 *Ibid.*, 143; cf. *Schriften*, IV, 37; VI, 70-71.
216 For the term "objectification" see, e.g., *Schriften*, II, 287-90, and for the term "manifestation," *Schriften*, IV, 478. Both terms will be encountered also in the following discussion of mediation. The terms "objectification" and "manifestation" predominate in Weger's thought (*Theologie der Erbsünde*, 117-21, 123, 125-37). He reserves the term "Vermittlung" for the interpersonal communication of grace (*ibid.*, 122-23, 127-37), though he uses the two terms also in this context.

simply and rather mechanically, it involves the dual motion of free output and non-free, necessary input — through one and the same medium. On the one hand, spatiotemporal history is the medium for self-*ex*pression. Here the motion originates from the center of man (person) and is directed outward. Thus history functions as output, or transmission medium. On the other hand, history is the medium for outside-*im*pression. Here the motion originates outside of the individual man and is directed inward towards his center, towards person. Thus history functions also as output, or transmission medium.

Because the idea of mediation captures both directions (free act and being-situated) in, as it were, a *single* test tube, the resultant interaction can be examined much more closely than was possible within the scope of Schoonenberg's approach. Principally concerned to point out the impact of being-situated, Schoonenberg concentrates his attention on its interiority as *Existential* within every free decision. As a result the quality of that free decision is either attenuated to a dormant capacity or left unspecified as to its depth and scope. Within the context of Schoonenberg's discussion of being-situated, freedom is not explicitly considered as the radical and encompassing act which Schoonenberg has affirmed it to be. On the contrary, that fundamental idea of freedom tends to be overshadowed (not abolished) due to his concentration on the encompassing scope and deep impact of *being-situated*. More significantly, the crucial issue as to the effect of being-situated *upon that deepest human act* is not considered structurally.[217] Rahner, by contrast, does precisely that. By considering history in terms of spatio-temporal mediation, he, in effect, turns the embracive free act in upon a similarly embracive, yet interior, *Existential* and forges a dynamic synthesis.

If the full impact of that synthesis is to be appreciated, an analysis of its interacting elements is necessary. For that reason the two directions of mediation will be somewhat artificially separated. First the idea of mediation will be examined from the viewpoint of freedom as active agency; history will, therefore, come into view largely as output medium. Next, the idea of mediation will be examined from the viewpoint of the medium as "active" agency, i.e. history will come into view as input medium, in its effect on freedom. After this analysis, the synthesis of both directions will be presented by enquiring what the total appropriation of one's nature as mediated transcendence entails.

---

217 Schoonenberg does consider this question in terms of the impact of original sin upon man's acts (see ch. IV, sec. A below).

i. *History as medium of self-expression*

At its simplest level, the idea of output medium conveys the notion that a free act expresses itself, embodies itself in material reality.[218] The self becomes manifest or objectified in spatial dimensions.[219] A free act is never an absolutely private, interior occurrence within the recesses of man's being but, due to man's corporeality, extends outward to form a concrete, palpable reality.[220] Moreover, that extension into materiality is not to be deprecated as an incidental, secondary product of man's deepest self. Man's self-expression in material reality is the only way he truly is, has and knows himself.[221] Man recognizes himself in his objectification as in a mirror, knows himself as in a symbol,[222] and thus possesses himself. In other words, the self-relationship that constitutes man is not an ethereal spiritual communion, but *materially mediated* communication.[223] Besides concreteness, material mediation introduces the idea of dynamic process into self-relationship. Whereas in itself the idea of self-relation could be construed as having reference to a purely static self-possession, mediation sets man in motion. He *is* not simply his self-*possession*. He is what he *becomes* by self-*realization*,[224] i.e., by way of the continual mediation of his free acts.[225] Man comes to himself, finds himself only by re-alizing himself in his material medium.[226]

If *material* mediation gives the idea of self-relation body and dynamic process, *temporal* mediation gives it the momentum of linear progression. Without the element of time, the process introduced with material mediation would originate from and return to one and the same point, having a dynamics akin to marching on the spot. The idea of mediation receives its typically historical character when it is considered not merely as *spatial* objectification but as objectification that takes place successively through time — as spatio*temporal* mediation.

The linearity introduced with the idea of temporal mediation appears to be so obvious that it approaches triviality. Nevertheless, the idea of temporal succession is problematic in view of the unity and embraciveness that has been

---

218 *Schriften*, II, 206.
219 *Schriften*, II, 287-91; IV, 474; VI, 234.
220 *Schriften*, I, 313; II, 127, 252; cf. IV, 304-308, "Der Leib als Symbol des Menschen," against the background of pp. 281-91.
221 *Schriften*, IV, 284-86; cf. I, 313.
222 See *Schriften*, IV, 284-86, 474.
223 *Schriften*, II, 284; VI, 228, 288.
224 See *Schriften*, IV, 278, 282-86.
225 See *Schriften*, II, 284.
226 *Schriften*, II, 284; IV, 475; IX, 99, 121-22.

ascribed to man's fundamental act of self-determination. That act is singular and all-encompassing; yet, time appears to disperse man along the fragmented line of countless incidents and decisions. Total decision and temporal extension seem incompatible.

Sometimes Rahner explicates the relationship between free act and temporal extention in terms of an *option fondamentale* that as such is rather formal and empty but that gathers its content in the dispersion of time.[227] Elsewhere, Rahner emphasizes that man's comprehensive self-appropriation is not accomplished at once, in the twinkling of an eye (as in the case of angels), but that it has its *history*.[228]

The relationship between man's fundamental freedom and his spatio-temporal mediation is further explicated when Rahner introduces the distinction within man of original, medial and definitive person.[229] Although these designations include a temporal aspect in the sense that original person has a specific relation to the beginning, definitive person to the end, and medial person to the interim, they are not to be understood as strictly successive phases *within* time.[230] Rather, they are primarily aspects of every free decision as it relates to the total decision of self-appropriation.

Original person is the most fundamental aspect of man, his transcendence and his freedom. That other terms are needed to describe man is due to his corporeality. Hence, medial person has reference to original person realizing himself in and through a medium other than himself, "in einem Mittleren, das gebildet wird in einer Einheit von seiner beseelten Leiblichkeit und leiblichen Seelenhaftigkeit, von deren gegenständlichen, sach- und satzhaften Objektivationen, von der Umwelt von ebenso leibhaftigen Personen und Dingen, von den darin vollzogenen Objektivationen durch die 'äusseren' Handlungen."[231]

The remarkable feature of this conception of medial person is that the medium from which freedom as personified in original person is distinct is

227 *Schriften,* II, 241; V, 197, 505; VI, 224, 225, 245; *Exkurs,* 204, 218.
228 *Schriften,* V, 497. Cf. V, 197-98 where man's free, total summation of spatiotemporal dispersion is also compared to the free decision of angelic beings. This retarding effect of materiality on the realization of *human* decisions explains, in Rahner's view, why penitence is possible for man but not for angels: an evil decision by man goes counter to the "momentum" innate to, or conferred upon man's nature, so that such a decision cannot transform man totally. Hence a remnant of the original momentum of nature remains, providing a possible springboard for a subsequent change of heart, penitence (see *Schriften,* I, 397, n. 2, and 403-404).
229 *Schriften,* II, 280-90.
230 See, e.g., *Schriften,* II, 288.
231 *Schriften,* II, 287.

not merely the "dead" material to be used *for* self-expression (*Vorhandenheit*), but also the "living," personalized material *of* self-expression. Original person is seen as being distinct even from *embodied* free decisions, from the *unity* of medium and message, so to speak. In other words, a distinction is introduced, not simply *within* mediated person, but *that totality* is distinguished from original person. Original person transcends the concretized person.[232]

Despite this transcendence, however, original person is unseparated from medial person so that it is impossible to draw fixed boundaries. A continuous process of osmosis takes place between these two spheres of man: man continually transforms himself into his objectifications without being absorbed by them, continually gives himself in them without abandoning himself in them; indeed, while objectivizing himself, man is continually referred back to himself (subjectivity) and to God.[233]

Definitive person comes into view when one realizes that this continuous osmotic process is not an *endless* back and forth movement, an eternal recurrence of the same.[234] On the contrary, freedom is the root which, via the stem (medial person), yields a final, definitive fruit. In the notion of definitive person, a direct connection with linear time is manifest. Man is not merely original person *transcending* time, nor merely original person *immersed* in time, but original person attaining fullness *through* time. Although man enters this definitive stage, *as stage*, at death, its quality is anticipated by every embracive free decision;[235] for freedom, as Rahner says, is the capacity for the eternal:[236] in his free act, the subject "setzt sich als end-gültiges."[237] Conversely, eternity is said to be a mode of freedom

---

232 See *Schriften*, II, 87 where in support of the non-identity of original free act and its embodiments Rahner appeals to the scholastic distinction of *anima intellectualis* from its "function" as *forma corporis*. Cf. IV, 287-88 where Rahner further explicates the distinctness of the form and its "aktuellen Formalursächlichkeit" and adds that this distinction cannot be simply a "bloss gedachter." See also *Schriften*, I, 395; *Hominisation*, 52-53, 79-88; Rahner, "Die Frage nach dem Erscheinungsbild des Menschen als Quaestio disputata der Theologie," in Paul Overhage, *Um das Erscheinungsbild der ersten Menschen* ("Quaestiones Disputatae," 7; Freiburg: Herder, 1959), 13. Cited hereafter as *Erscheinungsbild*.

233 *Schriften*, II, 287.

234 Cf. *Schriften*, V, 166-67; VII, 275-76; IX, 334; *Zur Theologie des Todes* ("Quaestiones Disputatae," 2; Freiburg: Herder, 1958), 27.

235 For Rahner's view of death, see, in addition to *Zur Theologie des Todes, Schriften*, III, 91-104; IV, 429-37; VIII, 273-80; X, 181-99. For an excellent summary of Rahner's view, see Eicher, 364-72.

236 *Schriften*, III, 224-25; IX, 312-17.

237 *Schriften*, IV, 432; cf. 433: "Freiheit nämlich ist immer absolut, ist das Ja, das

fulfilled in time.[238] In its radicality, freedom embraces and permeates man's entire existence and brings it to its definitive fruition.

The question remains whether the relation between original freedom and the temporality of history is more than tangential. If the free act actually spans time, it appears to be placed *above* time, itself unmediated by time. To be true to Rahner's intentions, however, it must be noted that even the spanning of time that takes place in a radical free act is seen as occurring in the *midst* of time. Man embraces time only indirectly, i.e., mediated by history. That becomes evident from Rahner's reflections on individual and collective "beginnings." He proceeds from the necessity of picturing a first, pristine moment in which freedom was as yet unfilled, in the former case due to the absence of an individual decision, in the latter case due to the absence of every decision, thus the absence also of a historical situation.[239] Such "virginal" or "neutral" freedom,[240] says Rahner, must have existed if freedom is rightly burdened with itself.[241] Although necessarily pictured as such,[242] that beginning is not the first moment of a homo-geneous series, but *sui generis*: the unique ground of the whole of history, unique as posited by God and as experienced by man in his irrepeatable free act.[243] Deriving directly from God, that freedom is pure originality, i.e., not yet obscured by any situation, whether caused by one's own decision or those of others.[244] That beginning is, therefore, totally transparent.[245]

In this conception of beginnings, the *ground* of historical freedom, reduced to its inchoate originality, is paradoxically stripped of all history (both as free decision and as situation), emptied of all content. That ground, however, is never experienced as such. It is not present in its purity, but hidden in history.[246] Man always experiences himself as freedom that has already chosen[247] and, furthermore, as freedom that is already situated by the decisions of others.[248] Thus one's individual and collective beginnings are

um sich weiss und alles wagt und für immer gültig sein will"; see also *Schriften*, II, 261 regarding the absolute value inhering in freedom and person.
  238 *Schriften*, IV, 430; cf. V, 171; VIII, 594-96. For Rahner's view of time see especially *Schriften*, IX, 302-33, as well as the works listed in n. 235 above.
  239 *Exkurs*, 193; *Schriften*, IX, 265.
  240 *Exkurs*, 193-94, cf. 215.
  241 *Schriften*, IX, 265; cf. *Exkurs*, 217.
  242 *Schriften*, X, 199, cf. 183-85.
  243 *Schriften*, IX, 266; *Exkurs*, 193; *Schriften*, X, 199.
  244 *Schriften*, IX, 265-66; *Exkurs*, 193-94; *Hominisation*, 86-87.
  245 *Schriften*, IX, 266.
  246 *Exkurs*, 194.
  247 *Schriften*, IX, 265-66; *Exkurs*, 193.
  248 *Ibid.*

rendered remote by the intervening situation, concealed by history.[249] Our free act, therefore, is not simply transparant origin. But neither is it totally opaque. *Within* history, the free act is indirectly open to its "beginning," its origin, its ground. Thereby man's situation, though not transparent, remains transluscent.[250] In fact, this origin becomes increasingly manifest only by man's onward movement *through* history into the future, reaching proleptically towards the end.[251] For, in Rahner's view, the origin is increasingly disclosed in history as its ground and law[252] and will be fully manifest in the end. The *proton* is to be sought in the *eschaton*.[253]

ii. *History as medium of alien impressions*

Thus far we have looked at history as output medium, that is, mainly from the viewpoint of man's freedom which uses history as the material for his *self*-expression and *self*-realization. So closely are input and output medium related, however, that even in that presentation it proved impossible to wholly suppress the former. In the following exposition, we will attempt to observe freedom explicitly from the viewpoint of history as input medium. The effect of that medium, the impact of mediation upon freedom, will be examined.

The process of objectification and mediation not only has an effect on the material employed in that it is *rendered medium,* but that material has an effect on person in that he becomes a person mediated by *this* material. In expressing itself, materially, freedom materializes itself; thereby it becomes united with something other than itself. Man's objectifications, says Rahner, are his *self*-expressions, yet not fully because they represent himself-in-other-

---

249 *Schriften,* IX, 266.
250 Elsewhere, Rahner speaks of a "hell-dunkle Situation, die durchzuhalten der Kreatur aufgetragen ist, weil sie in dem Nicht-über-sich-zur-restlosen-Klarheit-kommen, in dem Nicht-mit-sich-definitiv-fertig werden nicht nur ein bedauerliches Faktum realisiert, sondern eine Grundsituation der Kreatur, die ihr wesentlich ist, weil sie sich darin gerade bedingungslos Gott ausliefert" (*Schriften,* II, 291; cf. V, 190 and I, 399).
251 *Exkurs,* 209; cf. *Schriften,* IV, 410.
252 *Schriften,* IX, 265-66; *Exkurs,* 209-10.
253 In a single Rahnerian sentence: "Der entzogene Anfang – man könnte ihn auch Urgeschichte nennen – als jetzt waltender ist konstituiert durch jene Ursprünglichkeit, die unserer Freiheit verborgen vorausliegt, *und* durch das Ereignis der ersten Freiheit, das per definitionem anderer Art ist als die uns jetzt zugängliche Freiheit, die immer schon aus einer durch kreatürliche Freiheit, der eigenen oder anderen, mitbestimmten Situation handelt, die jenes Ursprüngliche uns entzogen gemacht hat, so dass wir nicht mehr aus seinem lichten Wesen heraus handeln können, sondern es suchen in der Zukunft, Protologie in Eschatologie treiben müssen" (*Schriften,* IX, 265-66). For the formulation of a similar thesis in terms of *anamnesis* and *prognosis,* see *Schriften,* IV, 410-11).

reality. Expressed *in* the otherness of his medium, man's objectifications cannot be *simply* himself as himself (original person).[254]

The material for human mediation is other and alien to freedom because it is given for freedom and thus prior to freedom, not produced by freedom. Although the ontic priority of nature (essence) to freedom (existence) itself constitutes the otherness of man's medium, it is not finitude as such, but *material* finitude that constitutes his medium as alien and even resistant to the free act.[255] The mediating material, says Rahner, brings with it "personfremde Strukturen" to which the person must subject himself to a variable degree if he is to realize himself through his medium.[256] Contrary to pure existentialism, man's free act is not absolutely creative, but always entails a submission to "die Gesetzlichkeit der Materie des freien Handelns (der 'Natur' des Menschen, seiner 'Leiblichkeit' in einem metaphysischen Sinn, der 'Welt')."[257] As we have seen, time similarly has a quality that is alien to the genius of original freedom: dispersion and fragmentation in contrast to unity and wholeness.

The forces to which man is subject due to his spatiotemporal mediation

---

254 *Schriften*, II, 287.

255 See *Schriften*, II, 86-87; I, 392-405 (On p. 396, n. 1, e.g., Rahner points out that part of the tendency of man's free decision "steckenbleibt in der trägen Masse ihres naturhaften Materials im Menschen....") For other instances in which materiality is spoken of in terms of alien otherness, see *Schriften*, III, 87; V, 189-90, 214; *Erscheinungsbild*, 15. It is striking that, whereas in terms of man materiality is frequently qualified as both alien and otherness, only the term "otherness" is frequently used to describe God's *adoption* of materiality in the incarnation (see, e.g., *Schriften*, V, 205; VI, 205-206; VIII, 605; *Hominisation*, 54). One might explain this difference by the fact that God, despite the "absolute difference" between Himself and the world (*Schriften*, V, 219), cannot create something "was ihm und seinem Wesen in absolut disparater Fremdheit gegenübersteht" (*Schriften*, VIII, 607). This thesis, however, is here used as an argument for the commensurability of spirit and matter and would, therefore, also seem to rule out the idea of matter as alien-other with respect to man's freedom, a preeminently spiritual reality (see, e.g., *Schriften*, IV, 495; VI, 203, 207; VIII, 605). That materiality is nevertheless spoken of as alien may be due to the fact that, although Rahner posits that matter and spirit are related to God with equal immediacy (*Schriften*, VI, 188-89), so that matter is not alien to spirit (*Ibid.*, 204), this equality is in fact not consistently maintained. That which is open to God is "Geist," not matter (see sec. B, 1 above), and true being is "Geist" (*Hörer des Wortes*, 144; cf. *Hominisation*, 51-52; *Schriften*, IV, 74; V, 189-90). Accordingly, man's spirituality is called (from man's point of view) the *higher* reality which itself includes the transcendental relationship to God (*Schriften*, VI, 189. Cf. IV, 74, 495; VI, 200-201). Eicher sums up Rahner's view as follows: "So ist für Rahner das primäre Moment der ontologischen Konstitution und der ursprünglichen Erfahrung die Geistigkeit, woran die Körperlichkeit und die sinnlich erfahrene Welt nur mehr ein Moment darstellt" (Eicher, 317).

256 *Schriften*, II, 287, cf. 289.

257 *Schriften*, II, 87.

range from the simple phenomenon of extension and dispersion, to the more complex natural-biological processes such as death,[258] as well to the intricate constellation that constitutes historical situatedness. By virtue of his corporeality, man is open to outside influences without prior, free consent.[259] He does not "personally" select the situations to which he will, in turn, "personally" address himself. The situations have already been selected; they are simple there, encountering man and impinging upon him interiorly.[260] Especially this historical dimension of man's input medium is significant for the situational reinterpretation of original sin. It is therefore not surprising to find that Weger, like Schoonenberg, is concerned to explicate this aspect of historical mediation. Although Weger's position on historical situatedness is very similar to that of Schoonenberg, it may be well to briefly examine his view for the following reason: Weger rightly considers the question as to the interiority of historical situatedness crucial for the situational reinterpretation of original sin[261] and expressly wishes to preclude the charge levelled against Schoonenberg's view, namely, that a lack of such interiority is inherent to the situational view.[262]

Intercommunication is a fundamental given of man, says Weger.[263] The sense in which intercommunication is basic to the reinterpretation of original sin is not that of conscious encounter between subjects, but that of unconscious, inner presence of other subjects as they have objectivized themselves.[264] By virtue of the recipient's corporeality, those objectifications permeate — osmotically, as it were — other human beings.[265] Fellowman is not merely existentially encountered; he is given as a spatiotemporal *Existential,* prior and interior to free decisions.[266] That *Existential* is qualified historically because our fellowman brings with him the history of his family and his people.[267] That history is similarly present, not only as consciously experienced, but especially as common context, or rather,

---

258 See n. 235 above.
259 *Schriften,* I, 395n; III, 86, 88, 90.
260 See *Schriften,* I, 395n; II, 98; VIII, 310.
261 Weger, *Theologie der Erbsünde,* 109.
262 *Ibid.,* 145. In this context Weger does not indicate whether he considers this to be a valid criticism. In view of his defense of Schoonenberg (*ibid.,* 146-47) it is safe to conclude that Weger considers this criticism to be basically unfounded; he merely wishes to preclude such criticism by providing a better anthropological basis (*ibid.,* 145).
263 *Ibid.,* 113, 114.
264 Due to his corporeality, man of necessity expresses himself in spatiotemporal objectifications (*ibid.,* 117, cf. 112).
265 *Ibid.,* 115, 116, 120, 149.
266 *Ibid.,* 115-16.
267 *Ibid.,* 117.

as ubiquitous atmosphere — inescapably penetrating, unquestioningly breathed.[268] Interior to man and ontically prior to his free decisions,[269] history has its impact upon those decisions: "Wichtig ist für uns vor allem die Einsicht, dass der Mensch im Vollzug seiner Freiheit nie nur einer geschichtlich geprägten, personalen Mitwelt *gegenübersteht,* sondern vorpersonal von dieser Fremdgeschichte innerlich bestimmt ist und als der von ihr Bestimmte handelt."[270] Man not merely makes his own history, but *is* — inescapably — the history others have made.[271]

iii. *History as medium of self-realization and of self-alienation*

Having set forth the idea of history separately as output and as input medium — medium of expression and of impression — the dual dynamics must now be considered simultaneously. Before doing so, however, the two forces involved will be simply juxtaposed so that their diametrical opposition may become manifest. Against that background, one can appreciate the awesome tensions that are generated as these opposite forces coalesce in the idea of appropriation.[272]

Whereas man as personal, free being entails radical "Selbstverfügung,"[273] in history he experiences his "unauflösliche Verfügtheit."[274] Though as subject man is *faber sui ipsius,*[275] as finite, corporeal being he is a *product* of his environment.[276] The apex of creaturely "Selbstbestimmung"[277] finds his freedom continuously and profoundly exposed to the uncontrollable situation.[278] The free act is irreducible, unique and indivisible,[279] yet taken up into a larger whole and dispersed by time.[280] A radical

---

268 *Ibid.*, 117-19 with recourse to the idea of an "objektive Geist," and "der geschichtlich gewordene Geist" (*ibid.*, 119, cf. 150).
269 *Ibid.*, 145, 149.
270 *Ibid.*, 120.
271 *Ibid.*, 149.
272 In Weger's presentation of the situational framework, the opposition between situation and freedom remains largely implicit in the prevalent idea of "Fremdgeschichte" (see the quotation above and also Weger, *ibid.*, 112, 118, 121). Within the context of his reinterpretation of original sin, that opposition emerges forcefully in the form of "fremdverursachte, dem Menschen aber trotzdem innere und eigene Schuld vor Gott . . ." (Weger, *ibid.*, 152; see ch. III, sec. C, 2, b, iii below).
273 See the introductory paragraphs of sec. B, 2 above.
274 *Schriften*, IV, 475.
275 See the introductory paragraphs of sec. B, 2 above.
276 *Schriften*, IV, 474.
277 *Ibid.*,; cf. the introductory paragraphs of sec. B, 2 above.
278 *Schriften*, VIII, 269, 310; cf. IV, 495.
279 *Schriften*, IV, 474; VI, 250; *Exkurs*, 221.
280 *Schriften*, IV, 474; V, 197-98, 497. See also sec. B, 2, a, i above.

free act is definitive,[281] yet history is essentially finite and ambiguous, each of its moments relativized by the next.[282]

Considered in themselves, the diametrical opposites appear to be susceptible of no treatment beyond their careful compartmentalization — self-evident testimony to the ontic dualism in man that is given with the dualism of spirit and materiality.[283] To stop there, however, is to contradict everything that Rahner has said about the unity of man as materially mediated transcendence. The nature and repercussions of that unity will come into full view from the perspective of man's self-appropriation.

Though mutually exclusive conceptually, the opposite forces entailed in man's spatiotemporal, historical mediation do not in fact exist side by side, in splendid isolation. Rather, without for a moment attenuating their distinctness and opposition, they are viewed as interpenetrating forces. In itself that interpenetration is, of course, simply given with man's *nature*. One does not sense the incisive effect of that natural phenomenon, however, until one realizes that the impact of a force such as historical situatedness varies, not in inverse, but in direct proportion with the radicality and scope of self-appropriation — man's *free* act.

Formally, the direct proportionality between free self-appropriation and the impact of historical situatedness can be demonstrated in terms of the natural-material substratum of the latter. In his free act, says Rahner, man "gathers up" his nature within himself, within person. In doing so, he, on the one hand, places all that which is not "gathered up" in opposition to himself as being the exterior "without." On the other hand, because by that same free act he has "gathered up" *material* nature *within* himself, he experiences the impact from "without" acutely within his free act.[284] The very *self-ex*pression of freedom entails the appropriation of an imposed *alien-im*pression.[285] Not only are these opposites coextensive and simultaneous; they become, in some sense, identical.[286]

---

281 See sec. B, 2, b, i above.
282 See *Schriften*, V, 115, 130-31.
283 Rahner speaks of the ontic dualism in man "von Geist und Materialität, von Freiheit und Gebundenheit an die Vorgegebenheiten dieser Freiheit im Notwendigen, von Einzelheit und im Materiellen verwurzelter Vergesellschaftung der Menschen" (*Schriften*, IV, 495). See also *Schriften* III, 86 ("metaphysische Dualismus von Natur und Person"); I, 394-405; IV, 260, 422n.
284 See *Schriften*, III, 87 and the entire article on "Passion und Aszese," pp. 73-104.
285 *Schriften*, II, 87.
286 *Schriften*, II, 288, 291; III, 88. Accordingly, Rahner describes human freedom in the paradoxical statement, "Die Freiheit, die sich in Leiblichkeit vollzieht, ist ja wesentlich die Freiheit, die sich dem Eingriff von aussen, der Verfügung durch anderes und

In his free self-appropriation, man is *not* free to select only the physical-biological givenness of his being as material for appropriation. His self-appropriation includes inescapably the acceptance of his *historical* givenness. He must freely accept himself, says Rahner, as being "immer schon auch das Verfügte."[287] He enters a world that he has neither created nor selected as "Gegenstand" and "Widerstand" of his free choice. Rather, he is "thrown" into a determinate world. And even in his free act, that world retains its character of being "fremdbestimmt."[288] As historically mediate transcendence, man exercises his original freedom towards himself only in passing through and accepting the history that is simply given and inescapably imposed upon him.[289] Thus man experiences his creatureliness in a free yes or no to necessity.[290] Moreover, as in the relationship with his physical-biological nature, man's growth in possessing himself as subject is said to be proportional to an increasingly intensified experience of his inextricable subjectedness.[291]

In Rahner's view, alien impressions penetrate man so deeply that they permeate – and thereby jeopardize – his self-expressions: Freedom occurs amidst the "Selbstverfügung der Fremdverfügung;"[292] the very act of self-realization entails self-alienation;[293] to find himself, man must lose himself, give himself to alien forces.[294] That amidst these awesome forces it is possi-

---

andere aussetzt; Leiblichkeit ist der Raum der Begegnung zwischen der Tat von innen und dem Erleiden von aussen. *Freiheit in Leibhaftigkeit überantwortet sich darum immer mitten in der Selbstverfügung der Fremdverfügung*" (*Schriften*, VII, 277 emphasis added).

287 *Schriften*, VIII, 310.
288 *Schriften*, VIII, 310: "Der Mensch soll sein Wesen, immer schon auch der Verfügte zu sein, in Freiheit annehmen. Er ist ja nicht der durch sich ins Dasein *Gerufene*. Er ist der in eine bestimmte Welt Geworfene, die ihm zwar als 'Gegenstand' seines freien Ja und Nein zugemutet ist, die er aber nicht selbst zum 'Gegenstand' und Widerstand seiner Freiheit ausgewählt hat; diese Welt tritt ihm vielmehr als die fremdbestimmte entgegen, wenn er in seiner Freiheitsgeschichte beginnt, und sie kann nie so 'aufgearbeitet' werden, dass er einmal nur noch mit *dem* 'Material' seiner Freiheit arbeitet, das er sich selbst ausgesucht hat." The quotation marks enclosing "Gegenstand" are most likely intended to preclude the notion that man's situation is to be regarded as an *external object*. The term "Widerstand," not in quotation marks, should then be taken as an explication of the intended connotation of "Gegenstand," namely, literally *Gegen*stand, resistance.
289 *Schriften*, VI, 233.
290 *Ibid.*
291 *Schriften*, IV, 475.
292 *Schriften*, VII, 277.
293 *Schriften*, II, 288; V, 190; VI, 194; cf. I, 384, 394, 405 regarding the (vertical) "Entzweiung des Menschen *in sich selbst*' (emphasis added).
294 *Schriften*, VI, 234; cf. VII, 277.

ble for man to ultimately find himself rather than to totally lose himself, to attain self-realization rather than to fall to self-destruction is due only to the undisputed position consistently ascribed to freedom: it remains the root and origin of man's fundamental and ultimate being.[295] In fact, the hegemony of freedom is such that its explicit articulation appears to shatter the entire synthesis of freedom and historical mediation so painstakingly achieved. For Rahner maintains that nothing ultimately significant can impinge upon man except via his free self-appropriation.[296] Thus by a turn of his free decision, it appears, man is capable of closing the door to the world and its history behind him, thereby locking himself into stoic *autarkeia*. That key, however, is beyond the reach of freedom due to the combination of two factors: 1) Man's free act is inclusive and total; it embraces all "external" and "alien" forces so that these affect man totally. 2) As person, man *is* free to chose for or against his own being; he is *not* free not to choose.[297]

In retrospect, the conceptions of man as historical being, his freedom and situatedness, as articulated by Schoonenberg, Rahner and Weger do not manifest basic divergences. Despite terminological differences, the fundamental categories are essentially the same. The significant difference is one of approach. One could distinguish Schoonenberg's approach as being more strictly analytical and that of Weger, and especially that of Rahner, as being more analytical-synthetical. Schoonenberg is particularly and almost exclusively concerned to analyse and demonstrate the phenomenon of being-

---

295 That decisive hegemony of freedom as origin and essence of man's being is maintained throughout Rahner's development. In the course of that development, freedom comes to be seen as more and more deeply embedded in history and interhuman relationships, but when Rahner explicitly addresses the question as to the relation of freedom and spatiotemporal history, the priority of freedom appears once more: "Es soll natürlich hier nicht bestritten werden, dass der leibhaftige, sich selbst durch das fremde Andere von Raum und Zeit suchen müssende Mensch auch ein Wesen von Raumzeitlichkeit ist. Aber von daher darf seine freie Subjekthaftigkeit nicht ursprünglich gedacht werden . . . . Ursprünglicher als seine Raumzeitlichkeit und Zeiträumlichkeit ist er das Wesen der sich vollziehen müssenden Freiheit" (*Schriften*, X, 198, here in rejection of the dilemma posed by an infinite extension of time into the future [eternity], yet a "beginning" of time in the past [creation]). For the idea of the "originality" of freedom, see also the introductory paragraphs of sec. B, 2 above and *Schriften*, II, 86-87; VIII, 272; IX, 238.

296 *Schriften*, VI, 223.

297 To this extent man's nature embraces even his free decision, not merely in the sense that person can be understood as an *Existential* that is simply given with human nature (see n. 200 above), but especially in the sense that this *Existential* entails a (categorical) imperative: man must make a radical choice. See, e.g., *Schriften*, IV, 475; VI, 224; VIII, 289 ("Freiheit ist die *notwendigkeit* der Selbstbestimmung . . .," (emphasis added).

situated as a passive element within every free decision, as an *Existential*. Within the presentation of the situational framework, it is especially Rahner[298] who, in terms of appropriation and mediation, moves beyond an analysis of that *Existential* as an element within free decisions to set forth explicitly the relationship of the comprehensive, free act of self-determination to one's inner *Existential* of situatedness. Thereby he achieves the highest possible synthesis of freedom and historical situatedness. That incisive analysis and synthesis facilitate a probe of the ultimate depth to which the situation of original sin penetrates man.

---

298 As to Weger see n. 273 above.

CHAPTER II THE DUAL GOD-MAN RELATIONSHIP: GRACE AND NATURE

The anthropological-historical themes — freedom, person, situatedness, mediation — examined to this point, though of fundamental significance, do not as such constitute a framework that is adequate for the reinterpretation of the doctrine of original sin. These themes represent only the *natural* constituents of that framework.[1] The reality of original sin, however, has its effect within the *super*natural dimension of grace. For that reason the interrelationship of nature[2] and grace forms a crucial part of the framework for reinterpreting original sin.

In many ways the scope and significance of the entire project of reinterpreting original sin hinges upon the possibility of indicating an intimate interrelationship between nature and grace. If grace is merely a gratuitous superstructure which, indeed, enriches, elevates and perfects nature, but to which nature itself has only the negative relationship of non-contradiction,[3] man can be conceived of as living his daily life within the substructure of nature. There man lives, moves and has his being, unaware of and largely unaffected by grace. The *reality of grace* is thereby "elevated" above,

---

1 In their interpretation of original sin, both Schoonenberg and Weger explicitly mark the transition from "natural" (anthropological-philosophical) to "supernatural" (theological) considerations (Schoonenberg, *Geloof,* IV, 156; Weger, *Theologie der Erbsünde,* 121-22, cf. 75).

2 The use of the term "nature" in this section is not wholly univocal with its use in the previous section. There, "nature" was seen primarily in distinction from and as counterpart of "person." In this section, "nature" represents the counterpart of grace and as such specifically *includes* the idea of person and freedom. See, e.g., Schoonenberg, *Man and Sin,* 69; *Geloof,* IV, 218-19; I, 190: "Indeed, in the theological concept of nature, precisely the spiritual qualities of man, his rationality and freedom, stand in the foreground, since primarily these determine man's reaction to grace." As suggested in this quotation, the two concepts are usually distinguished as the philosophical concept of nature (nature as counterpart of person) from the theological concept of nature (nature as counterpart of grace); see, e.g., Schoonenberg, *Geloof,* I, 188, 190, 191, 192; Rahner, *Schriften,* I, 34-35, 341, 406; IV, 229.

3 Rahner, *Schriften,* I, 324, 336; IV, 212, 234.

removed from daily life, a "bewusstseinsjenseitige Überbau."[4] Grace becomes a mysterious plus first encountered and experienced in an equally mysterious act called faith.[5] If the reality of grace is thus placed beyond the pale of man's immediate experiences, any disruption in the "realm of grace," of course, leaves man basically unaffected. In no case can a disruption, such as original sin, be experienced as an inner loss, an interior destitution. An extrinsic connection between nature and grace banishes the doctrine of original sin – from the outset – to an isolated island. And no amount of reinterpretation of original sin, however profound, can in and by itself repatriate this doctrine to the mainland of daily life.

If one of the main motives for reinterpreting original sin is the desire to indicate its universal relevance, it is obvious that the integration of nature and grace is of paramount significance. Both Schoonenberg and Rahner devote extensive articles to an elaboration of an alternative to the conception which views nature and grace as two relatively independent realms related as infra- and superstructure.[6] So radically is this extrinsicalistic conception abandoned, that a novel procedure is applied to the problem of the relationship of nature and grace: the point of departure is no longer nature *and* grace as two given realities in need of subsequent integration. Instead, grace is the exclusive point of departure and orientation. In fact, in harmony with the priority assigned to the reality of grace, it assumes the function of criterion, determining the necessity and essence of nature. Nature emerges as an essential but secondary reality whose existence is required and whose essential quality is specified by the primary reality of grace. This novel procedure yields as its fruit a maximum degree of unity. Surprisingly, that same procedure yields also an indispensable degree of duality between nature and grace. That duality, in other words, is not maintained out of a surreptitious concern for keeping nature intact for its own sake. Rather, entirely consistent with the new approach, that duality is maintained for the sake of *grace*; the duality of nature and grace emerges as the very condition of possibility for a relationship constituted by grace.[7]

4 *Ibid.*, IV, 210; cf. IV, 213, 218-19; I, 324.
5 *Ibid.*, IV, 210-11. See also *Schriften*, IV, 51-99; IX, 113-26, for Rahner's general opposition to an irrationalistic conception of "mystery." Similarly, Schoonenberg, *Geloof,* IV, 155-57.
6 Rahner, *Schriften*, I, 324, 325, 329; IV, 210, 213, 219, 271. Schoonenberg, *Geloof,* I, 124, 189. In view of the interdependence noted earlier (see the introductory paragraphs of ch. I above), Schoonenberg's and Rahner's views on nature and grace and on salvation history will be presented individually or jointly as demanded by the particular facet of these subjects being considered.
7 See *Schriften*, IV, 270 where Rahner insists that the distinction of nature and grace

A. THE UNITY AND DUALITY OF NATURE AND GRACE AS GROUNDED IN GOD

It would be a mistake to suppose that the distinction between nature and grace (or supernature),[8] corresponds to a contrast between spatiotemporal, mundane reality and supratemporal, divine reality. The complex of nature and grace represents, not a horizontal distinction between God and man, but a vertical distinction between two modes of the God-man relationship. The realities designated as nature and grace are both grounded in God,[9] existing only in continuous dependence upon His activity. For that reason, both the unity and the distinction of nature and grace may best be approached initially by considering their source.

Nature and grace originate in distinct but interacting activities of God. In order to indicate the unity of these activities, both Schoonenberg and Rahner stress, in effect, that God's gracious destination of man to a supernatural end is not an afterthought, but a "forethought." God did not, *post factum*, happen to destine an already existent creature to a goal that lies beyond the powers and rights of his natural being. No, God's first thought was loving self-communication, the bestowal of His own inner being, His divine life. It is in order to accomplish this that God "also" creates. In order to give Himself away, an existent creature is needed. Therefore God creates.

Though united with respect to the priority of grace, Schoonenberg and Rahner elaborate that thesis in different ways. When Schoonenberg addresses the question directly, the framework of creation-covenant frequently domi-

---

is essential, not for the sake of defending the inviolability of nature, but in order to safeguard the sovereignty of God's grace. Cf. *Schriften*, I, 345: nature must remain nature "um der Gnade willen."

8 The terms "grace" and "supernatural" can be used synonymously since both express *formally* the gift-character of the *substance* of grace, God's self-communication. The term super-natural represents an explication of this gratuity: the reality of grace *transcends* the essence, powers and rights of nature. See Schoonenberg, *Geloof*, I, 104-105, 117-25, 186; *Covenant and Creation*, 113-16, 130-41, 204-205; "Aantekeningen over Natuur en Genade," *Katholicisme en geestelijke vrijheid: Bijdragen tot een gedachtewisseling* (Utrecht: Het Spectrum, 1951), 16-17; cited hereafter as *Aantekeningen*. Rahner, *Schriften*, I, 334-43; *LThK* IV, 993. For a discussion of contemporary views, including those of Rahner and Schoonenberg, of the relationship of nature and grace, see G. C. Berkouwer, *"Identiteit of conflict? Een poging tot analyse,"* Philosophia Reformata, XXI (1956), 1-44; G. E. Meuleman, "Natuur en Genade," *Protestantse verkenningen na Vaticanum II* ('s-Gravenhage: Boekencentrum, 1967), 65-88; B. Wentsel, *Natuur en Genade: Een introductie in en confrontatie met de jongste ontwikkelingen in de rooms-katholieke theologie inzake dit thema* (Kampen: Kok, 1970).

9 M. C. Smit calls attention to this implication of the duality of nature and grace for the doctrine of God; see *De verhouding van Christendom en historie in de huidige rooms-katholieke geschiedbeschouwing* (Kampen: Kok, 1950), 37 and "thesis IV" appended to that dissertation. See also n. 158 below.

nates that of nature-grace.[10] Nevertheless, the latter remains basic to his reinterpretation of original sin. Rahner, by contrast, methodically refines and elaborates the framework of nature and grace, to which he subordinates that of creation and covenant.[11] Reflecting this difference, we will begin with a brief exposition of Schoonenberg's restatement of the relationship of nature and grace. Subsequently, we will explore that relationship further predominantly with the aid of Rahner's concepts.

1. The Mutual Supposition of Nature and Grace

Schoonenberg expresses the priority of grace[12] and the consequences of that priority by expanding upon the traditional thesis, "grace supposes nature." That thesis is susceptible to the interpretation that "to suppose" means no more than to take into account an already existent reality of nature which as such has no inner affinity with grace. Schoonenberg overcomes this extrinsicalistic conception by supplementing the traditional thesis with its converse: not only does grace suppose nature, but nature also supposes grace.[13] Surprisingly, he arrives at the converse by elaborating the original thesis. To say that grace supposes nature means that God's covenant activity includes as *its* presupposition the activity of creation: created persons must exist if God is to share his covenant love.[14] In his covenant love, God is not dealing with an already existent reality that has its own shape and structure apart from that love. Having been created out of nothing, the world is shaped by nothing other than God's purposes. His primary purpose being covenanting love, grace permeates and moulds creation.[15] Nature is wholly

---

10 It would be possible to trace the development of Schoonenberg's thought in terms of the struggle between the nature-grace, and the creation-covenant conception. Both are found intermingled in *Geloof*, I, 103-132 (see especially 117, 123, 127-29) where "creation and covenant" appears as a sub-heading under the chapter title "Nature and Grace" (cf. *Covenant and Creation* (!), 112-49; in the epilogue of this translation, Schoonenberg states, "... my views on the distinction of nature and grace have become more supple" [210], i.e., since the publication of the first two volumes of *Geloof*; see also the brief comments on nature and grace on pp. 203-206 in this epilogue). Interestingly, in his book *The Christ,* the only sub-heading placed within quotation marks is "Nature and Grace" (p. 32). To trace the ultimate outcome of this "struggle" between two conceptions requires a thorough analysis of Schoonenberg's extensive publications in the area of Christology in recent years (see, e.g., *The Christ*, 22-49).

11 See Rahner, *Schriften*, IV, 264-71.

12 *Geloof*, I, 128-32; *Covenant and Creation,* 143-44, 148-49.

13 *Geloof*, I, 125-27, 130, 191-94; *Aantekeningen,* 18-19, 20, 22, 24; *Covenant and Creation,* 141-43, 147.

14 *Geloof*, I, 125-26; *Covenant and Creation,* 141.

15 *Geloof*, I, 129-30; *Covenant and Creation,* 146.

attuned and directed to grace, so that that directedness becomes nature's "intrinsic mode of being."[16] So fully is nature the supposition *of grace* that nature is modified in its concrete mode of being.[17] But, if the thesis that grace supposes nature implies that nature is modified, then the converse thesis is also true: concretely existent nature supposes grace. Schoonenberg recognizes that the term "suppose" as it occurs in the original thesis and its converse is not strictly univocal, but for him this does not mean that the converse is in any way weakened.[18] Because it is always related to grace, nature's own basic design is modified.[19] Therefore, nature as it concretely exists cannot be correctly viewed and evaluated without taking into account its intrinsic directedness to grace. In other words, grace must always be (pre)supposed as an ordering principle of nature.

2. The Distinction of Nature and Grace

The specific distinction between nature and grace is articulated and elaborated most clearly by Rahner.[20] Stated very simply, grace, in Rahner's view, is God *Himself* in relationship to man, God's *self*-communication to

16 *Geloof*, I, 188; cf. III, 184n.
17 *Geloof*, I, 192.
18 *Covenant and Creation*, 147: "The covenant supposes the creation as foundation, as basis, as point of departure (these terms must be interpreted neither temporally nor spatially), but creation supposes the covenant as purpose." To the objection that "suppose" in the latter instance "is not being used in its real meaning, that it does not mean the same as 'presuppose'," Schoonenberg replies, "Yet to us this certainly appears to be the case, precisely because purposiveness is intrinsic to the creature" (*ibid.*, 148; *Geloof*, I, 130-31).
19 *Geloof*, I, 193.
20 Schoonenberg does not elaborate the distinction between nature and grace as methodically as Rahner. Moreover, although Schoonenberg's conception is frequently in agreement with that of Rahner, their conceptions may not be assumed to be simply identical, not even during the period in which Schoonenberg was busy primarily with the doctrine of original sin. Nevertheless, the significant point of consensus is that the salient features of the nature-grace conception, to be uncovered in this section with the aid of Rahner's analysis, are to be found also in Schoonenberg's reinterpretation of original sin. Hence, at crucial junctures, the conception of nature, e.g., functions as a decisive court of appeal (see ch. IV, sec. A below and, generally, *Aantekeningen*, 19; *Geloof*, I, 123, 193; "De genade en de zedelijk goede act," *Jaarboek 1950*, 203-53). Towards the end of this last-mentioned, extensive article devoted to the integration of nature and grace, the significance of the retention of the thesis *gratia supponit naturam* becomes manifest (see pp. 236-37; cf. "Genade en natuurlijke Godsliefde," *Jaarboek, 1959*, 19-37, especially pp. 29-34.

In Weger's treatment of the doctrine of original sin, the nature-grace framework is not elaborated explicitly but is, nevertheless, clearly present (see, e.g., Weger, *Theologie der Erbsünde*, 122, 124, 125).

man.²¹ The countless formulations of the essence of grace are so many variations of this notion. In grace, God gives Himself *as God*, the infinite itself, in His own reality, His innermost being, His triune life, eternal life.²² Although in his very being, man in some sense participates in God's being,²³ in and by grace man is allowed to participate in God's *own nature*, in His innermost, mysterious life.²⁴ Whereas from the viewpoint of nature God appears only as absolute being and ground of being without further definition, in grace the " 'inhaltliche' Wesen dieses Seins" comes into view.²⁵ Grace involves a highly personal-ontological²⁶ process in which God communicates His own being to man so that man's being is divinized.²⁷ This ontological self-communication constitutes the primary meaning of salvation (*Heil*). As its secondary effect, salvation can, and in the present situation always does, *include* the forgiveness

21 For the accentuation that in grace man encounters God Himself, see, e.g., Rahner, *Schriften,* I, 339; IV, 89-90, 92, 98; V, 129-30, 211, 220; VII, 66, 68; Weger, *Theologie der Erbsünde,* 122.
Regarding grace as God's self-communication, see, e.g., Rahner's helpful summary article on the subject in *Herders Theologisches Taschenlexikon,* ed. Karl Rahner (Freiburg: Herder, 1972-73), VII, 35-38, and in his *Schriften,* IV, 92, 93, 118, 124-27; VII, 66; VIII, 601. Cf. Schoonenberg, *Geloof,* III, 186; *The Christ,* 37; Weger, *Theologie der Erbsünde,* 18, 122.
22 Rahner, *Schriften,* I, 339, 363; IV, 24, 92; V, 116, 120, 123, 199, 386-87; VII, 68; VIII, 358-59; IX, 236; X, 540. Cf. Weger, *Theologie der Erbsünde,* 122-23, 127, 129, 133, 152, 158, 159, 163; Schoonenberg, *Geloof,* I, 123, 187 (clearly displaying the greatest reservation with respect to such expressions).
23 Rahner, *Schriften,* I, 386n; cf. *Hörer des Wortes,* 63-70.
24 Rahner, *Schriften,* I, 37 ("Die Teilnahme am trinitarischen Leben Gottes"); IV, 223, 318; VIII, 358-59; *Hörer des Wortes,* 87; *LThK,* IV, 991-93 ("Teilnahme an der Wirklichkeit, die von sich aus nur die Gottes selbst ist...."). Weger, *Theologie der Erbsünde,* 152. Schoonenberg, *Geloof,* I, 123.
25 Rahner, *LThK,* IV, 1123, cf. 1121.
26 In Rahner's thought "personal" and "ontological" are not to be seen as opposed to one another, as will become evident in the following citation (annotated as n. 29). See also *Schriften,* I, 189-90, 193. Cf. *Schriften,* IV, 72 (ontology as "geheimnisvolle *Ereignis,"* emphasis added); IX, 109.
27 See Rahner, *Schriften,* VIII, 600, where Rahner states that "die Gnade das Wesen des Menschen von dessen Wurzel her vergöttlicht..."; similarly, VI, 31 and "Bemerkungen zum Begriff Offenbarung," *Offenbarung und Überlieferung,* by Karl Rahner and Joseph Ratzinger ("Quaestiones Disputatae," 25; Freiburg: Herder, 1965), 17. See also *Schriften,* IV, 88-90; V, 116, 187, 216, 218; VI, 93; VIII, 358-59, 366; IX, 272. Although Rahner adheres unhesitatingly to the notion of "Vergöttlichung," it must be noted that he wishes to dissociate this idea of all pantheistic notions of what he calls "Vergöttung" (idolization, see *SM*,II, 943; *Schriften,* I, 121). In fact, in Rahner's view, it is precisely the idea of free and sovereign grace which most radically demythologizes the creation – relegating it to the "realm" of "das Nicht-göttliche" (nature); see also, *Schriften,* I, 120-26; IV, 130, 145; IX, 234, 236, 237; *Hörer des Wortes,* 68; *Hominisation,* 72-73. Cf. generally the theme of the "Profanisierung" and demythologizing of the

of and victory over sin,[28] but even as such, salvation is basically a perpetuation of divine, ontological self-communication: "Sie [Erlösung] ist die Mitteilung der göttlichen Gnade, sie geschieht in der ontologischen Wirklichkeit der Selbstmitteilung Gottes, sie ist also auf jeden Fall die Fortsetzung und Durchführung jenes seinshaften Prozesses, der in der übernatürlichen Begnadigung und Vergöttlichung der Menschheit von Anfang an bestand."[29] In Rahner's view, this process constitutes the heart and core of Christianity.[30] Nature or creation[31] is defined in contrast to the strictly *transcendent* reality of grace.[32] Creation can, therefore, be described globally as all that which exists outside the inner-divine life itself.[33] Nature or creation is not the communication of Self, but the constitution of *other*-than-Self.

When Rahner wishes to indicate the essential and radical distinction, as he calls it,[34] between nature and grace, he makes explicit use of the distinc-

---

world (e.g., *Schriften*, V, 129-33, 219): see also n. 80 below. Weger's avoidance of the term "Vergöttlichung" is remarkable in view of his frequent use of expressions such as "das Leben Gottes" in describing the reality imparted to man in grace. Schoonenberg rarely uses the term divinization (see *Geloof*, I, 187; *Man and Sin*, 194; sec. C, 2 below).

28 Rahner, *Schriften*, V, 215; cf. *LThK*, IV, 993.

29 Rahner, *Schriften*, V, 216.

30 The essence of Christianity, in Rahner's view, can be expressed in two words, God's self-communication (see *Schriften*, V, 123; VI, 68-69; VIII, 53, 60. X, 168). Because genuine *self*-communication is involved, however, it means the communication of God's innermost, i.e., *triune* being, namely, the communication of Father (origin-less origin), Son (historical Logos; salvation history) and Spirit (existential relationship of love); see *Schriften*, VI, 184; VIII, 53; cf. IV, 95, 96, 124-27, 133; VIII, 48, IX, 106, 251-52; *Offenbarung und Überlieferung*, 15-16. The fundamental thesis of Rahner's extensive writings on the doctrine of the trinity, namely, the thesis that the economical ("heilsgeschichtliche") trinity *is* the immanent (ontological) trinity and vice versa, may be seen as being rooted in his conviction that in grace man truly participates in God Him*self*, in His inner being as He is in and by himself (see, e.g., *Schriften*, IV, 126n). For Rahner's conception of the trinity, see especially "Bemerkungen zur dogmatischen Traktat 'De Trinitate'," (*Schriften*, IV, 103-33) and "Der dreifaltige Gott als transzendenter Urgrund der Heilsgeschichte," *MS*, II, 371-401.

31 Sometimes Rahner indicates that he wishes to distinguish the concept nature from that of creation and the complex nature-grace from that of creation-redemption (*Schriften*, I, 34, n. 2; *Sendung und Gnade: Beiträge zur Pastoraltheologie* [Innsbruck: Tyrolia-Verlag, 1961], 53-55. Generally, Rahner uses the terms interchangeably or in combination, speaking of the natural creation (*Schriften*, IV, 266, 268) and of the "Wirklichkeit der Schöpfung (als Natur)" (*ibid.*, 422), and defining nature in terms of creation *ex nihilo* (*ibid.*, 90) and creation in terms of nature (*ibid.*, 266).

32 Rahner, *Schriften*, V, 115; VIII, 601; cf. V, 120, 129-30.

33 *Sendung und Gnade*, 62; cf. *Schriften*, III, 96: "Die 'Natur' (im theologischen Sinn) d.h. alles Endliche, das nicht aus und in unmittelbarer Begegnung mit dem freien, redend sich offenbarenden Gott entsteht . . . ."

34 *Schriften*, IV, 91.

tion of efficient and formal causality.[35] Nature and grace are then viewed as two distinct modes of divine activity. The mode of action involved in creation is a unique instance of *efficient* causality by which God constitutes — *ex nihilo* — "das absolut andere von sich,"[36] or, as he frequently refers to it, "das Nichtgöttliche."[37] The reality of grace, by contrast, represents a special instance of *formal* causality[38] because it does not involve making another reality but giving a specific form to an existent reality, the form of God's own inner being, the form of His nature.[39] God imparts Himself as form to that which itself exists by virtue of His efficient causality so that He becomes its determination and finalization.[40] He becomes one with His creation, specifically, with the human person as its "vergöttlichende Zuständlichkeit."[41]

3. The Unity of Nature and Grace

To state the unity of nature and grace, Rahner has recourse to the general ontological relationship that obtains in a *unified, plural* entity, i.e., an entity in which both the plurality of mutually irreducible elements, as well as the inner unity which renders the phenomenon a specific, single entity, are equally real.[42] Rahner states that relationship as follows: To be able to be itself, something (A) creates something other than itself (B) as its own presupposition; although A places B opposite itself as *distinct*, A at the same

---

35 Rahner describes efficient causality as "Aus-der-Ursache-*Heraus*-stellen" and formal causality as "In-der-Grund(forma)-*Hinein*nehmen" (*Schriften*, I, 358). Schoonenberg makes mention of the distinction of nature and grace as efficient and formal causality and states that this conception does not conflict with his own (*God of Mens*, 20).
36 *Schriften*, IV, 90; cf. V, 219.
37 *Schriften*, IV, 122; VIII, 174; IX, 231-32. Cf. III, 44: "das *Leere* des Nichtgöttlichen"; IV, 266: das *"Leere* des Ausser-göttlichen" (emphasis added in both instances).
38 Although both efficient and formal causality are unique when applied to God's activity, Rahner expressly qualifies God's causality in grace as *causa quasi formalis*. He does so in order to underscore the idea that although God truly becomes the formal cause *of* the creature, *this* form retains its *absolute* transcendence, i.e., God retains his immutability, aseity, freedom (*Schriften*, I, 358-59; cf. *Herders theologisches Taschenlexikon*, VII, 36).
39 See especially *Schriften*, I, 354-75. See also *Schriften*, II, 127, where grace is described as "das heiligende Formgesetz des ganzen leib-seelischen Lebens des Menschen"; and on p. 128 the relation of grace to spatiotemporal reality is compared with the relation of soul to body (which relation is implicitly described in terms of form and matter). See also n. 158 below.
40 Rahner, *Schriften*, VI, 93; VIII, 53, 361; IX, 237; X, 71, 73, 540; *LThK*, VII, 292. See also sec. B, 3 below regarding grace as "realontologische Bestimmung," and as a modification of man's *a priori* horizon.
41 Rahner, *Schriften*, VI, 93.
42 *Sendung und Gnade*, 58-59.

time posits and retains B as its *own*, thus ensuring unity.[43]

Applying this framework to the order of redemption-creation, Rahner describes creation as "die unterschiedene Voraussetzung die sich die Erlösungswirklichkeit selber schafft, um selbst sein zu können...."[44] The unity of this complex interrelationship is given with the fact that the lower order of nature exists only for the higher order of grace.[45] More specifically, nature exists, *de facto*, as the condition-of-possibility of and for something else, namely, grace. Here too, unity is real despite the distinctness because grace posits and retains nature as the condition of its *own* possibility.[46]

As is implicit in this abstract, ontological framework, the unity of nature and grace is achieved by assigning total priority to the reality of grace. It is viewed as the origin of both the distinction and unity of the grace-nature complex. The priority of grace as source of unity becomes explicit when Rahner considers grace and nature more specifically as God's activities and capabilities.

God is capable of two fundamental activities. He is capable of freely creating reality distinct from Himself without giving His inner being to that reality. He is also capable of freely giving His self to a reality other than Himself. Although it seems self-evident to regard creation or nature to be the first and more basic reality, as the laying of the foundation on which the reality of self-communication *rests,* Rahner reverses this order when applied to the reality of God's capabilities.[47] Rahner speaks of self-communication as God's "Urmöglichkeit," as the "Urphänomen"[48] and as the factual "Grundakt" of God.[49] Despite the fact that God is free and able to create another reality without giving Himself away, creation remains a derived, restricted, secondary possibility which has its ontological ground in the prior and deeper *Urmöglichkeit* ("nicht Urmüssen!" Rahner adds) of free self-communication, of grace.[50] That possibility of God *ad extra*, in turn, has its prior ground of

---

43 *Ibid.*
44 *Ibid.,* 63.
45 *Ibid.,* 62. The terms higher and lower do not refer to two levels of existence but to an order of principles. Cf. *Schriften,* II, 127, where Rahner speaks of grace as a "Prinzip höheren, d.h. der absoluten, der göttlichen Ordnung...."
46 *Schriften,* VI, 95.
47 This reversal is remarkably similar in form and intent to Schoonenberg's inversion of the traditional thesis *gratia supponit naturam* (see sec. A, 1 above). The *difference* arises from the fact that Rahner recasts the traditional idea of "supposition" into the more modern notion of "condition-of-possibility."
48 *Schriften,* IV, 148.
49 *Schriften,* IX, 237.
50 The fact that the order between creation and self-communication concerns an

possibility in God's reality *ad intra*.[51]

This ontological order of capabilities in the being of God has its repercussions for the ontological order of the reality that appears outside of God the moment the transition is made from God's capabilities to His factual activities *ad extra*. When God in fact communicates Himself *ad extra*, creation takes place, one might say, almost as a matter of course. "Die Welt," says Rahner, comes into being "im Vorgang der Selbstmitteilung Gottes . . . ."[52] As a result, the inner, driving force of all of reality is God's gracious self-communication. Everything that is not itself divine self-communication is necessary context called into being to serve God's central act of grace. Creation, though possible as sole reality, is in fact designed for the greater event of grace. Rahner speaks of the Creator-creature relationship, therefore, as the necessary and indispensable "Wesensstruktur der Wirklichkeit überhaupt," but insists that it does not constitute the "eigentliche Inhalt" of reality: "Gott schafft, weil er sich selbst, sich äussernd und entäussernd, mitteilen will."[53] In line with the empty, receptacle-view of creation as nature, Rahner speaks of nature also as a grammar or vocabulary which God uses for His self-expression, His self-communication.[54] God creates this vocabulary for the sole purpose of communicating Him*self*.

By assigning total priority to the reality of God's gracious self-communication and consigning nature to the subservient role of condition of possibility, grammar, vocabulary; and by casting the totality of nature-grace within a framework that is entailed in any *single,* unified plurality, the unity

---

order of *possibilities* is understandably underscored to safeguard God's freedom in communicating Himself to that creature.

51 Even though the priority of self-communication *ad extra* is one of possibility, that priority is, in Rahner's view, not purely hypothetical, but rooted in God's "necessary" being and activity *ad intra*. Rahner contends that God necessarily expresses Himself internally, for else he would not know Himself and would not constitute absolute self-possession. Accordingly, God expresses Himself internally in the *Logos,* the image or symbol of the Father (*Schriften,* IV, 292). That primary self-expression entails as secondary concomitant the positing of a distinction *within* God. Consequently, God's *opera ad extra,* creation (positing a distinct reality) and grace (self-communication), have both their ground of possibility and their irreversible order in God's *opera ad intra* (*Schriften,* IV, 149). *Schriften,* IV, 293 (emphasis added): "Weil Gott sich innergöttlich 'ausdrücken' *'muss,' kann* er sich auch nach aussen aussagen; die geschöpflich-endliche Aussage nach aussen ist eine (*freie,* weil einen endlichen Gegenstand habende) *Fortsetzung* der innergöttlichen Setzung von 'Bild und Gleichnis' und geschieht wirklich . . . 'durch' den Logos (Jo 1:3)." See also *LThK,* IV, 1121.

52 *Schriften,* IX, 237. Similarly in terms of the relation incarnation-creation, *Schriften,* III, 43-44; IV, 150, 296; VI, 548; cf. *LThK,* I, 626.

53 *Schriften,* VII, 68-69.

54 *Schriften,* III, 44; IV, 149; VIII, 174; also "Addressat": VI, 95; IX, 232, 237.

of nature and grace appears to require no further qualification. Nevertheless, that unity proves to be limited by an indispensable duality.

4. The Indispensable Duality of Nature and Grace

Although the description of nature as vocabulary and grammar for God's self-communication, the description of nature-grace as unified entity, and – taken at face value – the description of nature as the condition for the possibility of grace all combine to suggest an intricate but unalloyed unity, a further analysis reveals a basic duality that is indispensable for the possibility of *grace*.

When the unity of nature and grace is stressed, it appears as if the unity concerned is that of a complex whole in which nature represents simply a constitutive element. Such an element has actual existence only *as* part of and by virtue of the whole. Nature, then, would have its subsistence *in* the complex unity of grace-nature. Or, if nature be conceived as having its own *existence*, it could be viewed, as in the grammar and vocabulary analogy, as a receptacle that has *meaning* only in being filled. The only function of nature would be to function as vehicle, as medium for living self-expression. In either case, an unqualified unity of nature and grace would obtain.

A duality between nature and grace becomes manifest when one observes that grace requires a specifically qualified recipient. What conditions must this reality fulfill in order to qualify as a fitting recipient of grace?

That question cannot be answered by a direct examination of nature. Such a direct approach to nature is precluded by the simple fact of the constant interaction of nature and grace as a result of which nature is not observable as such, but only as affected by the power of grace. Moreover, since nature exists as the condition for the possibility *of grace*, the most obvious (and only remaining) way to determine the character of nature is first to determine the character of grace and then to deduce the conditions that are required for the possibility of *its* existence. Thus the quality of grace determines the quality of nature.

What is grace? Materially, grace, as we have seen, is God's self-communication. Formally, grace is God's *free* self-communication. God's freedom in bestowing grace upon, imparting Himself to the creature is the *sine qua non* of grace. God must be free, not only in his "original" decision to self-communication *ad extra*, but continually, at every moment of the bestowal of grace upon an existent creature.

That elemental characteristic of grace, its gratuity, is of far-reaching significance for determining the quality of nature. The gratuity of grace means that nature is not adequately described when it is characterized as mere emptiness in need of fulfillment, mere vocabulary for divine self-expression; for God is not truly free in His self-communication with respect to *an essential constituent of that self-communication,* nor is He free with respect to a reality whose *only meaning* lies in the bestowal of grace. If the reality and meaning of nature were exhausted by its function as recipient of God's self-communication, that self-communication itself would be destroyed in its character of free gift — grace would be grace no more. Grace can no longer be grace, pure gift to a creature, if creation exists only by virtue of grace. To safeguard the essential gift-character of God's self-communication, therefore, the reality of grace demands, not simply a recipient in need of completion by that communication, but a recipient basically *not* in need of divine self-communication. Only *then* can God's self-communication be received as pure gift: unowed by God, undeserved by man. Nature cannot be a mere constituent of grace, but must in some sense be complete in itself. Nature must have its own existence and its own meaning independent of God's gracious self-communication. Only in this independent status relative to grace can nature constitute the condition of possibility for grace. The introduction of an independent reality, though necessary for grace, means the introduction of a basic duality between nature and grace, a duality that can be removed only at the expense of grace.

That the gratuitous quality of grace requires as the condition for its possibility a concrete reality opposite it with its own quality, namely, independent existence and meaning, can best be illustrated by Rahner's deliberations on the subject.[55]

The moment the distinction between nature and grace appears to be in danger of being blurred due to a tendency to equate the gratuity of grace with God's freedom to create or not to create, Rahner is quick to point out the indispensability of a sharp distinction between nature and grace,[56] a distinction that in fact entails a duality. To safeguard the specific character of grace, Rahner considers an appeal to God's freedom without further qualification insufficient. True, God is free also as Creator. But God's freedom in grace is of a specific kind, for in His self-communication God is free with respect to an *already*-existent[57] reality, a reality that is not dependent on

---

55 As to Schoonenberg's position on this matter, see n. 20 above.
56 *Schriften,* IV, 264-71, in response to Hans Küng's work *Rechtfertigung.*
57 Although the term "already" must be divested of all temporal connotations, as ontological qualification of nature it proves to be indispensable despite the integration of nature and grace. See Rahner, *Schriften,* I, 331, 339; IV, 234, 265; *LThK,* I, 625 and IV,

grace for its existence or being. Nature has its own principle of existence, its own "bleibende Seinsbestand,"[58] or, as Rahner says elsewhere, its own "Daseinsmöglichkeit."[59] In order that grace be truly and continuously free it requires a *Gegenüber* that is relatively autonomous: "Als freie Selbstmitteilung Gottes an sein Geschöpf setzt die Gnade dieses Geschöpf ... schon voraus, und zwar in einem solchen Besitz seines Wesens und seiner Wesensmöglichkeiten, dass er darin in und auf sich selber stehen kann . . . ."[60]

A relative autonomy is ascribed to nature, not only in its bare existence, but also in its concrete meaning. Nature cannot be dependent for its meaning on the bestowal of grace, for, in that case, nature would fall into meaninglessness if grace were not bestowed and, as a result, God (if He is good, wise, righteous, loving)[61] would be obligated to communicate Himself to the work of His hand. Nature would have a right to grace and God would no longer be free, but *obligated* to grant His *grace* — an inner contradiction. Thus again, the character of grace demands, as the condition for *its* possibility, nature with its own meaning apart from grace.[62]

Although God is wholly free, therefore, both in His decision whether or not to create and in His decision whether or not to communicate Himself, if he does choose the latter, he is *not* totally free in the execution of that decision. If He chooses to communicate Himself outside of Himself, he *must* create a specifically qualified recipient: nature qualified as autonomous (in structure and meaning) relative to the reality of grace. As Rahner puts it, because God (freely) wants one thing, namely, to communicate His own being, he *must* also constitute a relatively autonomous recipient.[63] Nature in

992; see also the quotation below (n. 60); Schoonenberg, *Geloof*, I, 105, 129; *Aantekeningen*, 19; *The Christ*, 36-37 (here the question becomes acute whether the covenant-creation or the grace-nature conception is predominant).

58 Rahner, *Schriften*, IV, 265, cf. 268, 269, 270.

59 *Schriften*, I, 336, 340, 342-43; IV, 143, 234, 235.

60 *Schriften*, VI, 547. Rahner goes on to equate this independence with the good creation and to emphasize that this completeness of nature must at the same time be seen as an openness for grace. For explicit references to the required autonomy, see sec. B, 2 below.

61 Cf. *Schriften*, I, 330.

62 *Schriften*, I, 342. Negatively, Rahner repeatedly emphasises that nature is not "sinnlos" without the bestowal of grace (*Schriften*, I, 336, 342-43; IV, 143, 234) and states that man must reckon with the *"sinnvollen* Möglichkeit des Ausbleibens einer absoluten Erfüllung" (*Schriften*, IV, 235).

63 *Schriften*, VI, 97; cf. I, 336-37; IV, 267-68. The idea of a relatively independent recipient as indispensable condition for grace is implied when Rahner states elsewhere that because God wishes His self-communication to be unowed, He must create man *in such a way* that he can receive this self-communication as grace; accordingly, God must not merely give man *a being*, but must constitute him as *"nature"* (*Schriften*, I, 337n).

this specific quality proves to be, more pregnantly and rigorously than that simple formula at first glance suggests, the condition of possibility to which even God in His free self-communication is bound.[64]

In view of the type of condition necessary for the possibility of grace, the indispensability of a real duality between nature and grace emerges forcefully. To smooth over that duality by speaking only of the distinction of nature as constituent element of grace is to obscure, if not to abolish, the specific character of grace. On the other hand, in view of the priority and the primacy of grace as the reality that orders and specifies the reality of nature, a certain unity of nature and grace is achieved — yet a unity limited by the indispensable duality.

How a real, organic unity is conceivable within these bounds is a problem which Rahner states with utmost clarity,[65] but which he solves less clearly. The degree of unity which is in fact achieved will be set forth in the following section (B) in terms of man's situation.

B. THE UNITY AND DUALITY OF NATURE AND GRACE AS MAN'S SITUATION

From the point of view of God's will and activity, it has become clear that in unifying the realities of nature and grace total priority is given to grace. To nature is assigned the subservient role of indispensable condition of possibility. Yet, precisely in keeping with that role, nature emerges as independent counterpart to grace. In the present section, both the unity and the duality of nature and grace will be articulated more fully from the point of view of man's situation. First, the unity of nature and grace as reflected in the human situation will simply be posited as unproblematically and briefly as possible. Thereupon, the essential duality between nature and grace will be analyzed by considering man's situation of grace from the viewpoint of his freedom. Finally, we will focus on the situational unity of nature and grace once more, but now in terms of an idea that, while safeguarding the essential degree of duality, ensures the highest possible degree of unity — the idea of a "supernatural *Existential.*"

---

64 In addition to the references mentioned in the previous note, consider: "die Selbstmitteilung *kann* gar *nicht* anders als ungeschuldet sein; d.h. der Wille zu einer 'bloss' *ungeschuldeten* Selbstmitteilung ist nicht nur Tatsache, sondern *Notwendigkeit*: Gott könnte gar kein Wesen kreatürlicher Art konstituieren, für das diese Mitteilung die normale, selbstverständliche, in ihm zwingend angelegte Vollendung wäre" (*Schriften*, I, 337n).
65 Cf. *Schriften*, VI, 95, 97.

1. The Unity of Nature and Grace

Because gracious self-communication — rooted in God's inner being — is God's first thought, His primary will, His deepest act, it cannot help but stamp man's situation. That effect is reflected in Schoonenberg's statement that grace is an intrinsic mode of being of nature, modifying even its basic pattern.[66] That modifying effect of grace on nature is further illustrated by the fact that both Schoonenberg and Rahner deny that a reality such as nature ever exists as such, as *natura pura*.[67] Because nature exists only as affected by the field of force constituted by grace, not even the specific content of nature can be determined, so that the concept "nature" must remain purely formal.[68] That formal concept can be derived only by a process of abstraction: *concrete*, intertwined reality (grace[d]-nature) minus grace leaves — as *conceptual* residue — pure nature.[69] So unseparated are nature and grace concretely, that even grace never exists by itself — in fact, it cannot. As Rahner puts it, grace exists only as a qualification, as a determination of nature or person.[70] Or, in Schoonenberg's words, "Grace is not simply 'the transcendent,' but the communicated transcendent."[71] In that sense, it can be said that "reality itself is supernatural."[72]

2. The Duality Essential for Grace as Expressed in Human Freedom

That nature and grace are combined to form a closely knit totality, is undeniable, but the kind of knit employed has not thereby been decided. From what has been said previously, it is clear that a simple unity — or even the complex, but homogeneous unity of a whole and its parts, its constituent elements — is out of the question, for in either case grace would be rendered impossible. Grace could no longer be what it is, a gratuitous gift to man as an already (naturally) existing reality.[73] That independence of nature, required by grace, brings with it a proportional degree of duality between these counterparts.

---

66 See sec. A, 1 above.
67 Rahner, *Schriften*, I, 327, 328, 340-41, 342; IV, 230, 233. Schoonenberg, *Geloof*, I, 191-92.
68 See Schoonenberg, *Geloof*, I, 192-93; III, 183.
69 Both Schoonenberg and Rahner describe "natura pura" as a "Restbegriff." Rahner, *Schriften*, I, 327-28, 340, 342. Schoonenberg, *Geloof*, I, 191-92 (with what appears to be an allusion to Rahner, but without direct reference to him); III, 183-87.
70 Rahner, *Schriften*, VI, 93; *Sendung und Gnade*, 53-54. *MS*, II, 410-11.
71 *Aantekeningen*, 18. Cf. Rahner, *Sendung und Gnade*, 54.
72 Schoonenberg, *Man and Sin*, 20.
73 See n. 57 above.

From the point of view of man's situation, that same duality becomes existentially manifest. At every point of God's history of self-communication, grace is in principle recognizable *as* grace, i.e., in its gratuity.[74] That means that the distinction of nature and grace, obtained conceptually by the rigors of abstraction, is not simply an abstraction, but is rooted and grounded in the concrete experience of grace *and* nature.[75] Moreover, the very ground of possibility of this abstraction is the concrete experience of grace as grace – in distinction from nature.[76] Accordingly, only secondarily do nature and grace represent a conceptual distinction. The duality to which that distinction points is primarily of confessional, religious significance: Man must be led to confess, not merely, "Ich bin das von Gott frei Verfügte [nature]," but, "Über mich [nature] verfügte er frei [grace]."[77] An authentic *Christian* confession, in other words, contains the interrelated duality of nature and grace, for the latter cannot be confessed without at least an implicit affirmation of the former, including its independence.

The duality that constitutes an inherent part of the Christian confession is strikingly illustrated by the fact that the distinction of nature and grace can be defended, not only by an appeal to God's freedom, but, with equal validity, by an appeal to man's freedom. Man must be free to accept or to reject grace.[78] Such freedom requires a base of operation of its own. If the possibility of unbelief is to be ontologically accounted for, a concrete reality must exist that is not yet fully incorporated in God's gracious self-communication, a reality that has a viability apart from grace – nature.[79] Even apart from the possibility of a negative response, however, the freedom of God in grace demands as the condition of its possibility an autonomous and free

---

74 See Rahner, *Schriften,* 326, 341; VI, 549.

75 See, e.g., *Schriften,* I, 340-42, where the entire intellectual procedure by which "natura pura" is extracted as conceptual residue from concrete reality is explicitly rooted in the primary experience of grace as gift (see especially p. 340).

76 Without the experience of grace as grace, the process of subtraction (grace[d]-nature – grace = *natura pura*) is impossible, for the "quality' to be subtracted is unknown except for such an experience. Thus even the formal concept *natura pura* seems to be attainable only on the basis of a concretely experienced *gratia pura*.

77 *Schriften,* IV, 265, cf. 234, 264.

78 Although Rahner maintains the necessity of such freedom, he rejects the idea that it entails dual options in equilibrium (see *Schriften,* IV, 271; VIII, 596).

79 Rahner says, for example, that revelation (identical with God's offer or act of self-communication [e.g., *Schriften,* VIII, 70-71]) "auch als durch freien Glauben zu beantwortende im Modus der Ablehnung muss existieren können und sie selbst *diese* ihre Möglichkeit nur schaffen kann, wenn der 'Unglaube' sich nicht einfach dadurch schlechthin aufhebt, also noch Natur und Selbstbewusstsein bleibt, das sich philosophisch auslegen kann" (*Schriften,* VI, 96-97). Elsewhere, Rahner argues similarly for the necessity of maintaining the relatively independent status of nature (*Schriften,* I, 336-37; IV, 268).

counterpart: "Die Autonomie des Geistes als 'Natur' ist die Bedingung der Möglichkeit jenes Gehorsams, in dem allein Offenbarung so angenommen werden kann, wie sie es muss: in der freien Annahme der Gnade."[80] Entailed in the experience of grace — making that experience *possible* — is an experience of self as nature for which God's self-communication comes as an undeserved, i.e., super-natural, gift.[81]

The fact that this kind of counterpart is required for the very possibility of grace etches the human situation deeply. By virtue of its own (viz., gratuitous) character, grace requires nature with its own (viz., independent) character. Stated in this way, grace itself appears to entail requirements that bifurcate the human situation in a way that defies seamless unification. The measure of unity that remains possible under these conditions is expressed in the idea of a supernatural *Existential*, for it represents the bond that holds nature in intimate and continuous relation to grace.[82]

---

80 *Schriften*, VI, 97. Cf. *ibid.*, 96 where in a similar way the necessity of a distinct and free philosophy is argued as being a prerequisite for safeguarding the nature of revelation "weil nur dem Sichselbstverstehenden und so autonom über sich selbst Verfügenden die Selbstersschliessung Gottes in personaler Offenbarung als die Tat der freien Liebe erscheinen kann." Similarly, Rahner holds that, as an element of its own essence, theology posits philosophy in its autonomy, and adds that only in that capacity of being in itself *domina* can philosophy function as *ancilla theologiae* (*Schriften*, VI, 95). This statement of the relationship of theology and philosophy reflects not merely the academic question as to the relative place of the various sciences, for theology represents the articulation of the sovereignty of grace, while philosophy represents the articulation of the autonomy of man as nature (cf. *Schriften*, VI, 91, 92-93, 94, 95; X, 86). Indeed, "die mit Thomas von Aquin einsetzende Selbständigwerdung der Philosophie, ihre Säkularisation, ihre Freisetzung ist der erste Beginn einer legitimen Weltlichwerdung der Welt, die das Christentum selbst letztlich will und hervorgerufen hat" (*Schriften*, X, 86). For the theme of "Freisetzung" or "Freigabe," see *Schriften*, I, 126-27; VI, 91. 96, 97, 100 and cf. the idea of the profanisation, demythologization, denuminuzation, depotentialization, and dedivinization of the world or history (*Schriften*, VI, 129-32, 219; cf. III, 96). Regarding the theme of secularization itself, see *Schriften*, VIII, 637-66; IX, 177-96; X, 504-508.

81 The maximal development of the immanent powers of humanity and the world is invested with eschatological significance by Rahner: precisely by the full development of man's own immanent powers, humanity is broken open "für das Heil von oben," for at the peak of his own powers man experiences the inescapable finitude, tragedy and vanity inherent in human history (*Schriften*, V, 174).

82 Weger adopts Rahner's notion of the supernatural *Existential* directly (see *Theologie der Erbsünde*, 125-26). Although Schoonenberg does not employ the conception of a supernatural *Existential* in elaborating his view of the relationship between nature and grace, he does not differ with Rahner regarding the content of such a reality. This becomes evident by comparing Schoonenberg's conception that every man exists in a salvific *situation* to Rahner's *situational* definition of this *Existential* (see nn. 85 and 103 below) and by considering Schoonenberg's comments with respect to Rahner's conception (*Geloof*, III, 184-85n). In this context he affirms the appropriateness of the term

3. The Supernatural *Existential* as Unifying Bond

The supernatural *Existential*[83] is the embodiment of God's universal salvific will as it impinges upon man, modifying his "natural situation." Since God wills the salvation of all men, everyone exists in a situation that is objectively different than that which would obtain if God had willed otherwise.[84] That situation is constituted by God's offer of salvation to all[85] and the concomitant inner orientation of man as nature to the supernatural goal of God's self-communication.[86] This situation is called man's *Existential* because it represents a fundamental and factually inextricable *relational* structuration of man's being.[87] It is qualified as *supernatural* because this inner orientation is not given with nature as such, but is "added to" nature.[88] This *Existential*, in other words, is a directional force proceeding from grace (supernatural) and initially, but fundamentally, orienting and relating (*Existential*) man to God's self-communication.

This supernatural *Existential* is relational, not in the sense that it constitutes the realization of the personal, existential grace-relationship itself, but in the sense that it constitutes the objective (situational) conditions that make such an existential relationship possible. Accordingly, the supernatural *Existential* is not the bestowal of grace itself, but the *offer* of that grace, the *offer* of salvation to all.[89] In itself an offer could be understood as purely external, so that the extrinsicism that plagues the traditional conception of the relationship between nature and grace would be perpetuated. The idea of

---

Existential for the intended reality, but objects to the qualification of that reality as supernatural. Schoonenberg agrees that this *Existential* may be called supernatural with respect to the *natura pura,* but not with respect to nature as it concretely exists. Rahner could not but agree with this position. A difference would arise as to the existential significance of affirming the supernatural character of this *Existential* with respect to the *natura pura* (for Rahner's position on this score, see the immediately preceding discussion).

83 Rahner, *Schriften*, I, 339-43, 408; II, 252-53; IV, 230, 250; VI, 99, 549; VIII, 359-71; IX, 112, 507; X, 533, 539-41 and *sub voce* "Existential" in *LThK, SM* and *Herders theologisches Taschenlexikon*.

84 *Schriften,* IV, 249-50.

85 *Schriften,* IV, 230; VI, 549; IX, 112; X, 533, 539-41. Weger, *Theologie der Erbsünde,* 125, 126. Schoonenberg similarly speaks of an offer of salvation that is extended to all men by virtue of God's universal salvific will (*Geloof*, III, 203-11, 236-41; IV, 38, 143, 220; *Man and Sin,* 21; *Gods wordende wereld,* 65-70; *Covenant and Creation,* 83-90). This offer is, furthermore, said to constitute man's abiding situation (*Geloof,* IV, 280;*Man and Sin,* 197, cf. 198).

86 *Schriften,* I, 339, 342, 408; II, 252; VIII, 359, 366, 370; X, 540-41.

87 Eicher, 151, n. 2, 356-57 and notes. See also ch. I, nn. 143 and 200 above.

88 *LThK,* III, 1301;*SM,* I, 1298;*Herders theologisches Taschenlexikon,* II, 272.

89 See n. 85 above.

Existential, indicating a fundamental relational structuration, serves to underscore the internal impingement of the offer of salvation. God's offer of salvation, Rahner insists, does not remain external to man but places an indelible stamp upon his being.[90] God's salvific will is not a mere juridical, verbal decree,[91] but man's "realontologische Bestimmung."[92]

So internal is this *Existential* that it effects a change in man's consciousness. As Rahner frequently formulates it, the supernatural *Existential,* far from being "Bewusstseinsjenseitig,"[93] effects a "Bewusstseinsveränderung."[94] This does not mean that a new, in this case supernatural, *object* looms within man's natural horizon;[95] rather, that horizon itself is altered − expanded. Within man's natural horizon God is present as receding, asymptotic goal.[96] By virtue of God's will to communicate Him*self,* that natural transcendence is elevated and thus opened up to[97] an undeserved perspective: the gracious vista of the absolute and *immediate proximity* of God in His innermost being, His trinitarian life.[98] Both in the case of man's natural transcendence and in the case of its supernatural elevation, the

---

90 *Schriften,* VI, 549; cf. IX, 112-13; VIII,359. Cf. Schoonenberg, *Geloof,* I, 129 where he speaks of this orientation as being etched into the creation.

91 Rahner, *Schriften,* I, 324-25.

92 Rahner, *LThK,* III, 1301; cf. *Schriften,* I, 408, 410. Weger, *Theologie der Erbsünde,* 125.

93 *Schriften,* I, 324, 325; IV, 210; V, 122.

94 *Schriften,* IX, 507; X, 540; cf. I, 408-10; IV, 224-28; V, 155; *LThK,* VII, 292. Cf. Schoonenberg, *Aantekeningen,* 20.

95 *LThK,* VII, 292.

96 See ch. I, sec. B, 1 above.

97 Rahner employs a variety of terms to express the "Bewusstseinsveränderung"; besides "elevation" (*Schriften,* IV, 78, 225; VIII, 361; X, 540) and "disclosure" (*Schriften,* IV, 225, 227; X, 168), he speaks of "finalization" (*Schriften,* VIII, 207, 371; X, 73, 540-41; *LThK,* VII, 292), of "determination" (*Schriften,* X, 71-73), and of "Hinordnung auf" (*Schriften,* I, 339, 342). See also, *Sendung und Gnade,* 53-54.

98 *Schriften,* IX, 105-106; cf. IV, 84; VI, 220, 233. Immediate proximity to God's inner being as such is not fully attained, of course, until the *Visio Dei* (*Schriften,* V, 199). Nevertheless, that immediacy is already present in the bestowal of sanctifying grace (*Schriften,* IV, 84-85, 90, 311; VI, 71-72, 550). Even the transcendental *openness for* this bestowal participates in that immediacy, for that elevation and orientation of man's natural transcendence constitutes the necessary condition for the *Visio* (see *Schriften,* IV, 75, 84; V, 201; VIII, 601-602; X, 168). For that reason this orientation and openness of man's transcendence itself can be described as the transcendental divinization of man's fundamental subjectivity, i.e., of the deepest horizon within which man realizes his conscious and free existence (*Offenbarung und Überlieferung,* 17; cf. *Schriften,* VIII, 365). For Rahner's view of the bestowal of grace, incarnation and *Visio Dei* as three phases of one and the same process grounded in the trinitarian mystery, see, e.g., *Schriften,* IV, 86-99, as well as the references mentioned in n. 30 above.

terminus of transcendence is present neither as object nor as external goal, but as an *a priori* horizon.[99] The difference introduced by the *elevation* of man's natural transcendence is that its terminus is no longer the beckoning, yet ever-receding, presence of God as absolute being, but the absolute proximity of God's inner being.[100] *That* terminus becomes the driving dynamic and the inner entelechy of all of existence — by grace.[101]

In conclusion, the idea of a supernatural *Existential* may perhaps best be pictured as a field of force emanating from God's will to communicate His self. That field of force totally envelops and permeates man, drawing, orienting, directing him to God's inner being. At the same time, in being directed to a supernatural goal, i.e., beyond natural powers and rights, man is being drawn and directed *as nature,* principially and ideally capable of experiencing himself as nature and therefore God's self-communication as grace. Or (reflecting the priority of grace), conversely, man is capable of experiencing God's self-communication as grace and therefore himself as nature. In this way, the supernatural *Existential* functions as a dynamic bond that draws nature within the vortex of grace. This bond is such, however, that it preserves the duality between nature and grace that remains indispensable for safeguarding the full existential experience of grace in its gratuity.[102]

Both the duality and the unity of nature and grace are of direct significance for the reinterpretation of original sin. The duality that is maintained raises the question anew regarding the extent to which man, in his concrete existence, is basically affected by grace, and, commensurately, by the disruption of grace crystallized in the doctrine of original sin. In considering that question, the degree of unity that *is* achieved must be kept in mind.

---

99 *Schriften,* V, 122, 155; X, 539-41; *LThK,* VII, 292. Regarding man's natural *a priori* horizon, see ch. I, sec. B, 1 above.

100 Although man's natural transcendence is borne by and made possible by the infinite mystery, that transcendence always remains a movement that takes place *within finitude,* thus always falls short of the *infinite itself.* As Rahner puts it, this natural transcendence takes place literally *before* the infinite, *in* the finite. By contrast, within elevated transcendence the infinite proffers *itself* as *attainable* goal (*Schriften,* X, 168).

101 *Schriften,* IV, 228; X, 540-41. See also IV, 219; V, 155, 203; X, 556.

102 The introduction of the supernatural *Existential* in no way attenuates the duality of nature and grace. On the contrary, being supernatural, that *Existential* itself participates in that duality. As Schillebeeckx has pointed out, by inserting a supernatural *Existential* between nature and grace, the traditional problem as to their relationship merely recedes one step, returning as the problem of the relationship between the supernatural *Existential* and nature (E. Schillebeeckx, *Theologische peilingen, I: Openbaring en theologie* (Bilthoven: Nelissen, 1964), 251. That this is indeed the case is most clearly evident in *Schriften,* I, 329-36, 342-43.

Surprising as it may seem, that unity itself brings with it its own problems for the situational reinterpretation of original sin. Achieved by assigning full priority to grace, the inextricable interrelatedness of nature and grace leads to the conclusion that all men exist in an objective situation of salvation.[103] As noted earlier, that does not mean that all men are *ipso facto* saved (subjectively, existentially), but that all the conditions necessary for salvation are present. Whereas *in itself* (by nature) man's free act cannot yield salvation,[104] *in fact* (by grace) every total moral act does.[105] That positive conclusion, shared by all three situationalists, is significant for their reinterpretation of original sin. For, in view of the fact that salvation is said to be a *universal situation,* the question becomes acute as to what room remains for original sin as situation. That question becomes exceedingly nettlesome by virtue of the fact that original sin, too, is said to constitute a *universal situation.*[106]

Before we turn to the subject of original sin itself, however, the *situation* of salvation must be set in motion and be seen as salvation *history.*

C. THE HISTORICAL GOD-MAN RELATIONSHIP: SALVATION HISTORY

When the proponents of the situational view of original sin speak of salvation history, it involves more than a reiteration of the biblical notion that God acts savingly in history. Rather, their understanding of "salvation history" represents a specific contemporary conception of God's historical acts. The indebtedness of the idea of salvation history to contemporary thought is evident from the very fact that this idea comprises most of the central (historically formed) themes and concepts discussed earlier: grace and nature, divine self-communication and human self-transcendence, freedom and situation.

As constituents of salvation history, these themes and concepts form a relatively new configuration for two reasons. In the first place, these historical themes and conceptions are incorporated into yet another historical conception, the evolutionary view of the world; for salvation history is seen

---

103 Rahner, *Schriften,* IV, 250; *LThK,* III, 1301. Weger, *Theologie der Erbsünde,* 127-37. Schoonenberg, see n. 85 above.

104 Rahner, *Schriften,* II, 98-99; cf. V, 120.

105 Rahner, *Schriften,* IV, 227; VI, 549; VIII, 208; X, 542, 549; (this act is not merely a natural moral act, but an act of faith, hope and love [*Schriften,* V, 147; VIII, 195; X, 533, 536-38]). Weger, *Theologie der Erbsünde,* 124, 131, 133, 134. Schoonenberg, *God's World in the Making,* 83-90; *Gods wordende wereld,* 70-99; *Geloof,* III, 202-206, 238; IV, 38; "Heilsgeschichte und Dialog," *ThPQ,* CXV (1967), 132-38.

106 See chs. V and VI below.

as the final, unique phase of an embracive, ascending process. Secondly, subsumed under salvation history, themes such as nature and grace, freedom and situation combine to form more concrete constellations, converge in tangible historical manifestations: world religions, Israel, Christ, the Church. Both the evolutionary background and the particular historical concentrations of salvation history are important for understanding the place and meaning of original sin reinterpreted as historical situation.

The evolutionary setting aids in assessing the place of the historical situation of original sin in its relation to the overall historical development. As such, the evolutionary framework, entailing an all-encompassing, ascending line of development, suggests a rather optimistic view of salvation history. That suggestion remains despite the presence of a possible neutralizing factor in the core of salvation history, namely, freedom. By injecting an uncertainty factor, the presence of freedom would seem to temper any optimism regarding the development of history. In fact, in view of the unpredictability of freedom, one wonders how the projection of ascending lines of salvation history remains possible — until one realizes that this history comprises not only the freedom of man but especially the freedom of God. The sovereign freedom of His gracious will constitutes the driving force of salvation history. If the phenomenon of freedom, then, fails to render the upward process of salvation history dubious, the question arises whether the phenomenon of original sin, reinterpretated as historical situation, in fact functions as an antidote to an unqualified optimism regarding salvation history.

The conception of particular concentrations of salvation history, too, plays a significant role in the reinterpretation of original sin. As mentioned earlier, the universality that is predicated of the situation of original sin seems to be rendered extremely problematic by virtue of the universality that is predicated also of the situation of salvation[107] and, as we shall see in this section, of the history of salvation. The idea of particular concentrations of salvation history, however, provides a clue to the meaning of the universality ascribed to opposite historical situations.

1. Evolutionary Background — Salvation History as Ascent

One of the salient features of salvation history as conceived by both Rahner and Schoonenberg derives from its placement within the context of

---

[107] See the conclusion of sec. B, 3 above.

evolution.[108] The association of the history of salvation with the process of evolution must by no means be interpreted as entailing a reduction of the former to the latter. As we shall see, basic distinctions between natural and historical development (human feeedom), and between "natural"[109] historical development and salvific historical development (divine freedom) are maintained. The recognition of these distinctions, however, has not prevented the transposition of a basic feature of the evolutionary process to the realm of salvation history, namely, continual upward development. This remnant of an evolutionary conception constitutes the overall framework of salvation history as conceived by both Rahner and Schoonenberg. That evolutionary motif becomes evident by examining their conception of the basic structure of evolution and by comparing that conception to their delineation of the general pattern of salvation history.

The basic category that Rahner (and in dependence upon him, Schoonenberg)[110] applies to the process of evolution is that of self-transcendence, or, technically, self-surpassing.[111] That kind of category, according to Rahner, is needed to do justice to the undeniable phenomenon of "becoming" — specifically, the becoming of something *more*, something essentially and qualitatively *new*[112] Despite this qualitative newness, however, the "plus" embodied in the higher reality does not erupt into being by external addition to existent reality, but emerges into being from and by virtue of the existent lower reality — by its *self*-transcendence.[113] At the same time, the existent lower reality cannot be conceived of as already being in full possession of the higher, emerging reality, for in that case the ensuing reality

---

108 For a discussion of salvation history within an evolutionary context, see Schoonenberg, *God's World in the Making*, 79-130; *Gods wordende wereld*, 71-99; *Man and Sin*, 192-99; *Covenant and Creation*, 197-203; *The Christ*, 22-27, 46-49; "Natuur en zondeval," *TvTh*, II (1962), 173-201; Rahner, especially *Schriften*, V, 183-221; IX, 227-41. Weger speaks extensively of salvation history (*Theologie der Erbsünde*, 127-36) and accepts the idea of evolution (*ibid.*, 42-75), but does not integrate the two themes in the measure that both Schoonenberg and Rahner have done. As a result, Weger's conception of salvation history lacks the dynamic temporal-process-dimension so dominant in the conceptions of Schoonenberg and Rahner.

109 In distinction from the immediately preceding instance, where the term "natural" designates the sub-human realm, here the term "natural" is used in the theological sense, designating that aspect of the human realm that is to be distinguished from grace.

110 See n. 132 below.

111 The terms "Selbsttranszendenz" and "Selbstüberbietung" are frequently used interchangeably (see *Schriften*, V, 191-93; *Hominisation*, 74-78). Sometimes they occur in combination with "Selbstüberschreitung" (*Schriften*, VI, 210-13).

112 *Schriften*, V, 191-93; VI, 10.

113 *Schriften*, V, 191, 193; IX, 235-36; *Hominisation*, 75.

could not be conceived of as *new*, nor the effectuating process as self-transcendence.[114] In the idea of self-transcendence, therefore, both "self" and "transcendence" must receive equal weight.[115] That combination, Rahner contends, constitutes a "denknotwendiger Begriff."[116]

The anomaly that this logically required concept appears to involve an inner contradiction[117] vanishes, according to Rahner, the moment that self-transcendence is conceived of as taking place within the dynamics of absolute being.[118] Similar to the description of the relationship between the higher and the lower reality (not possessing, yet producing the qualitatively new), the relationship between the lower reality in process of becoming and absolute being is dually qualified. On the one hand, absolute being must be interior to that lower reality to such a degree that its self-transcendence is rendered possible. On the other hand, absolute being cannot be interior to that lower reality to the degree that absolute being becomes the essential constituent of the reality in process of becoming.[119] If absolute being were part of the very essence of this lower reality, the process of becoming itself would be annihilated because that reality would already possess absolute fullness of being as its own – not capable nor in need of becoming *more*.[120] In view of its simultaneous immanence and transcendence, therefore, absolute being is said to stand in relationship to the evolutionary process of self-transcendence as "das Innerste und Fremdste zumal."[121]

In its broad sweep, evolution is seen by Rahner as a process in which matter comes to itself and finds itself in spirit, and in which, conversely, spirit

114 *Hominisation*, 64-66; *Schriften*, V, 191, 193. See Eicher, 378.
115 *Schriften*, V, 192.
116 *Ibid*.
117 *Ibid*.
118 The *Deus ex machina* appearance of this resolution of an apparent contradiction is, from Rahner's point of view, sheer appearance. Within Rahner's conception the idea of self-transcendence by the power of absolute being is the *primum datum* of man's experience of himself as transcendental subject. Furthermore, by virtue of the unity of knowing and being (see ch. I, n. 171 above), it is entirely legitimate to deduce the structure of the evolutionary process from the self-transcendence entailed in the human act of knowing, i.e., to deduce the evolutionary process of coming-to-be from the noetic process of coming-to-know. This epistemological (metaphysical) deduction of the structure of evolution is most clearly manifest in the order and the relation of two sections of *Hominisation*: "Der transzendentale Ursprungsort des echten metaphysischen Ursachsbegriffes" (pp. 70-74) and, immediately following it, "Ontologische Sätze über den Werde-, Ursachen- und Wirkensbegriff" (pp. 74-78). See also *Schriften*, V, 192; VI, 210; Eicher, 375-76, 386.
119 *Schriften*, V, 191 ("Wesenskonstitutiv").
120 *Schriften*, V, 191-92; VI, 211; *Hominisation*, 72-76.
121 *Schriften*, V, 192.

comes to possess itself in its material objectifications.[122] In man, therefore, the culmination of evolutionary development, the cosmos, is said to come to itself.[123] Attain what it may, however, the creational process of evolution, though driven by absolute being, cannot attain to the ultimate reality: the inner being of God. That is given, by grace, in the process of salvation history.

Although salvation history is as radically distinct from the process of evolution as grace is distinct from nature, an interrelationship and attunement obtains.[124] Accordingly, despite the fact that God's self-communication, being pure gift, cannot be seen as a necessary extension of the process of evolution, that process does make divine self-communication plausible. The process of evolution displays a dynamic drive towards ever greater fullness and intimacy, towards an ever more proximate and more conscious relationship to its ground. From the viewpoint of evolution, therefore, absolute immediacy with the infinite ground itself can at least be anticipated asymptotically as the absolute goal of evolutionary development.[125] Conversely, because God's free decision to disclose and communicate His inner being constitutes the factual ground of His creational activity, the process of evolution can also be seen from the viewpoint of salvation history. Within that perspective, the core of salvation history (God's self-communication) renders the evolutionary process plausible. Accordingly, both the inner differentiation[126] and the interrelation of the process of evolution and that of salvation history become manifest once more as being rooted in the priority and primacy of grace:

Die Welt kann wirklich eine Werdewelt in Einheit von Geist und Materie und in

---

122 *Schriften,* V, 186, 197, 205.
123 *Schriften,* V, 197, cf. 186.
124 Rahner speaks, for example, of the relationship between evolution and incarnation in terms of mutual compatability, inner affinity and similarity of style (*Schriften,* V, 183-84). Even structurally a remarkable similarity obtains between God's activity in evolution and in grace. In evolution absolute being, though constituting the inner dynamic, is not "Wesenskonstitutiv." Similarly, in grace God's own nature, though constituting the inner entelechy of history, is not "Wesenskonstitutiv" (cf. *Schriften,* I, 328, 332; see also IV, 151).
125 *Schriften,* V, 199; see also V, 183-84; IX, 239.
126 *Schriften,* V, 205: "... wir dürfen ruhig das, was wir Schöpfung nennen, als ein Teilmoment an jener Weltwerdung Gottes auffassen, in der faktisch, wenn auch frei, Gott sich selbst aussagt in seinem welt- und materiegewordenen Logos; wir haben durchaus das Recht, Schöpfung und Menschwerdung nicht als zwei disparat nebeneinander liegende Taten Gottes 'nach aussen' zu denken, die in der faktischen Welt zwei einfach getrennten Initiativen Gottes entspringen, sondern in der wirklichen Welt als zwei Momente und Phasen eines einen, wenn auch innerlich differenzierten, Vorgangs der Selbstentäusserung und Selbstäusserung Gottes in das andere von sich hinein."

einem einbahnigen geschichtlichen Prozess von immer höherer Selbsttranszendenz sein, weil ihr innerstes und gerade so über sie selbst erhabenes Geheimnis das absolute Sein Gottes ist [nature], dessen Grundakt, der auch Gottes Schöpfertum umfasst, die Selbstmitteilung Gottes an das Nichtgöttliche ist [grace]. Die ganze Werdegeschichte der Welt geht darum in immer höher gestufter Selbsttranszendenz auf jenen Punkt hin, an dem diese Selbstmitteilung Gottes als solche angenommen werden kann und angenommen wird. Das Seiende, das in dieser Weltgeschichte als der Geschichte von Selbsttranszendenz wird als das Subjekt, das eine solche Selbstmitteilung Gottes annehmen kann, heisst Mensch.[127]

Salvation history appears as the highest and absolute phase of the world-historical process of self-transcendence, namely, as the "Selbsttranszendenz in das Leben Gottes hinein" that is identical with and made possible by the self-communication of God.[128] This unique phase of world history involves essentially the "Vergöttlichung der Welt"[129] and the "Weltwerdung Gottes,"[130] a unified process that finds its central historical manifestation in the incarnation.[131]

Schoonenberg, too, adheres to an evolutionary conception of the world. Although his conception displays similarities with that of Rahner — as evidenced, for example, by the adoption of the crucial concept of self-surpassing[132] — Schoonenberg has been more profoundly influenced by the thought of Teilhard de Chardin. Despite criticism of elements of Teilhard's thought,[133] Schoonenberg acknowledges that he is indebted to and deeply influenced by him.[134] In fact, it is Schoonenberg's increasing concern to integrate this evolutionary conception more fully into his own theology.[135]

In view of Schoonenberg's general agreement with Rahner's view of the basic structure of evolution as involving a process of self-surpassing, a brief

127 *Schriften*, IX, 237-38.
128 *Schriften*, V, 186, 207.
129 *Ibid.*, 205.
130 *Ibid.*, 187.
131 *Ibid.*, 186-87 and sec. C, 3 below.
132 Sometimes with reference to Rahner (*God's World in the Making*, 61; *Gods wordende wereld*, 48; *The Christ*, 23), sometimes used to express his own position without reference to Rahner (*God's World in the Making*, 63; *Gods wordende wereld*, 50, and [in the epilogue of] *Covenant and Creation*, 199).
133 Schoonenberg wishes to supplement Teilhard's thought by placing greater emphasis upon "man's typical historicity and freedom" (*Man and Sin*, 192; cf. *Covenant and Creation*, 201-202). This emphasis leads Schoonenberg to criticize those statements by Teilhard which postulate "the necessity of evil at *every* level of reality" (*Man and Sin*, 43, emphasis added; see his critique, *ibid.*, 45-47).
134 *God's World in the Making*, 8-9; *Man and Sin*, 192. Elsewhere, Schoonenberg states that he, though not wishing to bind himself to the details of Teilhard's views, sees himself as following in the footsteps of Teilhard (*Covenant and Creation*, 197).
135 *Covenant and Creation*, 197. See also L. Bakker, *TvTh*, XI, 354, 364-68.

outline of Schoonenberg's view will suffice to indicate the evolutionary setting of his conception of salvation history.

The world, says Schoonenberg, is evolutionary in every respect.[136] Wholly in accordance with that view, the entire hierarchy of being — traditionally conceived of as a timeless vertical structure — is seen as a horizontal temporal process. By introducing the factor of time, the analogy of being is seen as extending through a linear process of becoming.[137] Ever higher centers of independent activity (the "Within") are integrated with ever more complex extensions of passivity (the "Without"), until this process unfolds at its highest level in self-consciousness and self-determination.[138] Culminating in man, this development is seen as "growth towards God's image."[139]

Although the development of the world after the appearance of man is significantly different from the preceding process due to the introduction of personal freedom and thus of history,[140] the impact of the evolutionary view of reality does not stop at the threshold of man's appearance. In fact, Schoonenberg considers Teilhard to be worthy of "even more praise for his speculations concerning the fulfillment of evolution in man and in its hominized continuation than for those concerning evolution before the appearance of life."[141] The extension of an evolutionary framework into the area of history is legitimate, in Schoonenberg's opinion, because concepts such as growth, genesis, becoming and ascent apply to both.[142] That evolutionary framework extends even beyond historical development as such — to salvation history.[143]

---

136 *TvTh*, II, 175.

137 *God's World in the Making*, 29; *Gods wordende wereld*, 24. Since it is God who constantly actualizes this world as an evolving world, evolution can be said to be "a proof for his existence" (*God's World in the Making*, 44; *Gods wordende wereld*, 36; see also, respectively, 36-46 and 29-38). In an interesting and significant simile, Schoonenberg states that the traditional conception of the analogy of being "shows us the steps of evolution, but without time and movement, like a tidal wave that is frozen" (*Gods wordende wereld*, 18; *God's World in the Making*, 21 [translated as "like a frozen fountain"]).

138 *God's World in the Making*, 26-29; *Gods wordende wereld*, 22-24.

139 *After* the appearance of man, history is seen as a growth *of* that image, *God's World in the Making*, 45; *Gods wordende wereld*, 36-37.

140 See note 133 above, and *God's World in the Making*, 81; *Gods wordende wereld*, 63.

141 *Covenant and Creation*, 202.

142 *God's World in the Making*, 81; *Gods wordende wereld*, 62. Schoonenberg points out that, as in pre-human evolution, the ascending line of human history repeatedly branches out into dead ends and is interrupted by regressions (*God's World in the Making*, 81-82; *Gods wordende wereld*, 63).

143 Schoonenberg distinguishes evolution and salvation history from the viewpoint

Schoonenberg himself describes his view of the historical development of salvation as one that is inspired by an "evolutionistic conception of salvation history."[144] This specific instance of the integration of evolution and theology comes to expression in a key concept of Schoonenberg's view of salvation history: "ascent." From the primitive, anonymous religion of primordial man, through the confused dialogue of pagan religions and the clarification that took place in Israel, salvation history sweeps upward to its culminating midpoint, fullness in Christ.[145] All of these (partially contemporaneous, partially successive) stages, including pagan religions, are seen as a preparation for and as an ascent to Christ.[146] That process of ascent does not stop at the incarnation, but moves on in a further ascent to the point Omega, to God all and in all.[147] Schoonenberg describes this final stage of God's self-communication as the greatest leap that has ever occurred either in evolution or in history, for at that point evolution, history and also salvation history are all elevated and terminated in eternal fulfillment.[148] To summarize Schoonenberg's view of salvation history as ascent in his own words, "the whole history of salvation is directed towards Christ, not only towards Christ's life on earth, not only towards his death on the cross and his resurrection, but also towards the growing presence of the Lord in his Spirit, which will find its completion in the renewed and divinized universe of the final fulfillment."[149]

---

of *God's* activity as *transcendent* causality with respect to evolution in distinction from His self-communication in salvation history. Nevertheless, in comparison to evolution, salvation history is said to display "a similar, analogous ascent" (*God's World in the Making*, 98, cf. 96-97; *Gods wordende wereld*, 74, cf. 74-75).

144 *TvTh*, IV, 63. Even the relation of nature to grace is cast within this evolutionary framework: "Thus one might say that today's 'nature' or person is yesterday's grace" (*Covenant and Creation*, 204).

145 *God's World in the Making*, 91-127; *Gods wordende wereld*, 70-99; *Man and Sin*, 107, 109; *ThPQ*, CXV, 133-34.

146 *Man and Sin*, 107, 109; *God's World in the Making*, 108-109; *Gods wordende wereld*, 84-85; *TvTh*, II, 193; *ThPQ*, CXV, 133-35. This view of salvation history has its repercussions for the evaluation of all that is "non-Christian." Schoonenberg assesses that which exists outside the pale of Christianity as being "pre-Christian and hence... on the way," points to the possibility of concealed Christian forces operative in non-Christian religions, and postulates the presence of a way that ultimately leads to Christ's fullness even in the secular, *post*-Christian cultural-historical currents (*God's World in the Making*, 124-25; *Gods wordende wereld*, 96-97; cf. *ThPQ*, CXV, 135-37).

147 *God's World in the Making*, 95, 119-27; *Gods wordende wereld*, 74, 93-99; *Man and Sin*, 194.

148 *God's World in the Making*, 96-97; *Gods wordende wereld*, 74-75.

149 *Man and Sin*, 194.

2. Salvation History as Mediated Freedom

From the viewpoint of both participants — God and man — the combination salvation-*history* is appropriate by virtue of the broad definition of history as being a phenomenon grounded in free decisions.[150] Certainly God's self-communication qualifies as a preeminently free (gracious) act. By that definition, even God's *offer* of self-communication constitutes an historical act. By the same token, salvation history is truly historical also by virtue of the human activity entailed. As we have seen, grace requires as the condition of its possibility the free decision of man.[151] Salvation is realized in and through (though not by virtue of) man's *free* acceptance of God's free self-communication, i.e., in and through *human* history. In salvation history both participants act historically.

As in the case of history generally, freedom alone does not suffice to make salvation *history*. If God's freedom as such rendered His acts historical, creation too would constitute an historical act.[152] In fact, however, only God's acts of grace are fully historical, for (unlike the act of creation) they involve not merely freedom, but freedom with respect to and in terms of an already-constituted human being-in-his-world.[153] Such acts are not world-creating, but *inner*-worldly acts.[154] If Schoonenberg's definition of history[155] were employed, God's gracious initiative could be defined as a unique instance of the interaction of free decision and situation: God freely offers Himself in the already existent situation of creation and thus effec-

---

150 See above, ch. I, the opening paragraphs of sec. A, 3 and of sec. B, 2, b.

151 See sec. B, 2 above.

152 Rahner describes God's act of creation (in an inescapably contradictory expression) as "pre-historical" (*Hörer des Wortes*, 194). Elsewhere, Rahner describes creation as involving an act of *metaphysical* freedom (*Schriften*, I, 100). This distinction between God's act of creation and His act of grace becomes somewhat problematic in view of the fact that, in an evolutionary conception, God's creative activity itself seems to take place within, or at least in relation to, time. Nevertheless, the distinction is maintained insofar as the *mode* of God's creational activity can be said to remain transcendent with respect to time. See Rahner, *Hominisation*, 59-60, 80-81; *Schriften*, I, 120-21. Schoonenberg, see n. 143 above.

153 Rahner, *Hörer des Wortes*, 194; *Schriften*, I, 100. The term "already" must again be divested of all temporal connotations; see n. 57 above.

154 Rahner, *Schriften*, I, 100: "diese metaphysischen Freiheit [of creation] darf nicht mit der innerweltlichen Freiheit Gottes innerhalb der schon konstituierten Welt verwechselt werden."

155 See ch. I, the opening paragraphs of sec. A, 3 above. Schoonenberg himself first formulates this definition of history in an attempt to come to grips with the nature of God's historical activity (*Geloof*, I, 37-38); cf. *God's World in the Making*, 91; *Gods wordende wereld*, 70.

tuates a new (salvific) situation. Within that frame of reference, it becomes understandable that Rahner speaks of the salvation history of the supernatural *Existential*.[156]

The definition of the grace relationship in terms of free decisions and situation, simply stated as such, does not mark a significant advance beyond the ahistorical, static framework of grace and nature. That framework is hardly devoid of dynamics, but it does not bring salvation into view as a dynamic process *through space and time*. As mentioned, however, God's acts of grace are precisely that, inner-worldly acts, i.e., acts that are inescapably affected by, implicated in a *spatiotemporal* world. God's gracious activity is (freely) subject to the phenomena of before and after, of yesterday, today and tomorrow, of here and there. God's saving acts extend through space and time; in short, they are spatiotemporally mediated. Only by virtue of that mediation do God's saving acts constitute salvation *history*. To use Rahner's recondite terminology, in salvation history God manifests himself in material reality (which He has posited by creation) and in doing so adopts it as His own self-expression (grace).[157] Somewhat less formally, he describes salvation history as the "fortschreitende geschichtliche Inbesitznahme der Welt durch Gott . . . ."[158] In God's gracious self-*ex*-pression, His self-communication to the world, that world becomes God's *own* and, being a spatiotemporal world, that world becomes God's own *history*.[159]

From the viewpoint of mediation, the grace relationship fully qualifies as salvation history also in terms of man's participation. Not even the supernatural *Existential* can be experienced in the inner recesses of man, isolated

---

156 *Schriften*, VIII, 361.
157 *Schriften*, V, 205; cf. IV, 292-96, 148-51.
158 *Schriften*, I, 187. By positing that God takes possession of the world *in grace*, Rahner does not deny that this world is already God's as *creation* (nature). As nature, however, creation is God's simply as "das *Nicht*göttliche" – in grace God appropriates creation so that it is "vergöttlicht." This double relationship indicates how deeply the duality of nature and grace penetrates into the being and activity of God. Formally parallel to man's relation to his material nature (as well as to his situatedness), God stands in relation to creation as to "His" *Gegenüber* which He increasingly makes His own by the personal free act of grace. As noted earlier, Rahner explicitly draws a parallel between God's relationship to the world in grace and the relationship of soul (free person) to body (see n. 39 above). The relationship God-world is distinct from that of soul-body in that God freely posits the world in absolute creativity and remains continuously free as to whether or not to appropriate this otherness by grace. For that reason Rahner objects when God is viewed as "anima mundi" without (dual) qualification (see *Schriften*, III, 94; V, 130).
159 *Schriften*, V, 215.

from space and time.[160] Salvation is never an esoteric experience of the transcendental drive as such, but an experience mediated by the spatiotemporal world.[161] Man experiences his supernatural relationship with God in terms of and by means of existent religious expressions: cultic practices, symbols, confessions, words, institutions, philosophy, morality, daily life.[162] These expressions are simultaneously shaped by others and are his *self*-expressions.[163] These, in turn, impinge internally upon others, so that each person can be said to play a mediating role for his fellowman.[164]

Salvation history is therefore fully and concretely historical because it involves mediated freedom on the part of both God and man. In Rahner's words these free acts between God and man can be called salvation history "weil es sich sowohl von seiten Gottes wie des Menschen um wirkliche Entscheidungen und Taten der Freiheit, um gegenseitige personale Kommunikationen handelt, die konkret vollzogen werden in und am Material der profanen Geschichte."[165] The spatiotemporal medium of salvation history functions literally as the mid-point common to God and man. At and through that common mid-point, God's self-communication comes to itself in man and man comes totally to himself in God.[166] Salvation history is truly the history of God and of man in one.[167] Indeed, at a certain *time* and *place* God's self-communication and man's self-transcendence,[168] God's acceptance of the world and the worlds acceptance of God,[169] the yes of God and the yes of man[170] become (and remain) *historically* manifest as *one* – unmixed and unseparated.[171]

---

160 See Rahner, *Offenbarung und Überlieferung*, 18. Weger, *Theologie der Erbsünde*, 125.
161 Rahner, *Schriften*, IV, 320; V, 116, 117, 146-47, 151; VI, 70-71. See Weger, *Theologie der Erbsünde*, 127-37.
162 Rahner, *Schriften*, V, 116, 124, 147-48, 150-52, 154; VIII, 370-71; X, 540-42.
163 *Schriften*, V, 151; VI, 547.
164 Rahner, *Schriften*, VIII, 218-235. Schoonenberg, *Man and Sin*, 119. Weger, *Theologie der Erbsünde*, 134, cf. 130, 136.
165 *Schriften*, V, 123-24. Cf. Schoonenberg, *God's World in the Making*, 91; *Gods wordende wereld*, 71.
166 Rahner, *Schriften*, IX, 212; cf. X, 112, 122; IV, 90; V, 140, 204.
167 *Schriften*, IX, 213; cf. V, 201.
168 *Schriften*, V, 186, 207; IX, 239.
169 *Schriften*, IX, 239.
170 *Schriften*, VII, 70.
171 *Schriften*, V, 207, 212; VI, 71-72, 229; IX, 212-13. Cf. Weger, *Theologie der Erbsünde*, 127-128.

3. Universal Scope and Particular Concentrations

Salvation history is considered to be a universal phenomenon by all the situationalists.[172] Of them, Rahner articulates the nature of that universality most clearly. He defends the thesis that salvation history is coextensive with profane or secular history.[173] This coextension obtains transcendentally by virtue of God's (salvation) history-making decision to communicate His inner being to man. As we have seen, that decision effects a modification of man's natural mode of existence.[174] Although it may appear strange to designate as *salvation history* that which in fact constitutes an abiding, constant structuration of man's existence, an ontological determination of his being, this designation is entirely appropriate because this universal phenomenon proceeds from and continuously exists by virtue of God's free decision with respect to an existent situation.[175] In this sense, salvation history is strictly universal, spatially and temporally coterminous with world history.[176]

Since the relationship of grace cannot be sealed within the transcendental supernatural *Existential,* salvation history is universal also in its spatiotemporal mediation, i.e., in the religious expressions mentioned earlier. The universality of these legitimate objectifications cannot, of course, be as strict and unqualified as in the case of the transcendental relationship itself.[177] Nevertheless, these objectifications of man's relationship to God's grace are universal in the sense that they are found everywhere, though in varying degree, intensity and purity of expression.[178] In view of this variation, the universality of salvation history in space and time does not exclude the formation of particular concentrations.

Although salvation history is to be found everywhere and is in that sense coextensive with world history, salvation history is not simply identical

---

172 Schoonenberg, *God's World in the Making,* 79-130; *Gods wordende wereld,* 61-99; *Geloof,* III, 204; *ThPQ,* CXV, 137. Weger, *Theologie der Erbsünde,* 123-37.
173 *Schriften,* V, 121. Weger, *Theologie der Erbsünde,* 132.
174 Above, secs. A, 1; B; and C, 2.
175 See secs. A, 4 and C, 2 above.
176 Rahner, *Schriften,* V, 123; VI, 98.
177 A strict universality can be predicated of salvation history only when the term "salvation" is employed in the generic sense as all that which pertains to "Heil," thus including "Un-heil." At some points Rahner appears to speak of the coexistence of salvation history and world history in this generic sense (see, e.g., *Schriften,* VI, 98; VIII, 361; X, 71). Certainly A. Darlap, in an article on salvation history that is strikingly similar to Rahner's treatment of the subject, speaks of the universality of salvation history explicitly in the generic sense (*LThK,* V, 156).
178 *Schriften,* V, 124-25. See Schoonenberg, *Geloof,* III, 207.

with that profane world history.[179] This non-identity is partly due to the fact that man's rebellion against God's ubiquitous offer of salvation converts "Heilsgeschichte" into "Unheilsgeschichte."[180] This is not the sole, nor even the most fundamental, reason for the non-identity of salvation history and secular history. Between these lies a structural difference, one that runs entirely parallel with the differentiation of grace and nature.[181]

By its very nature, history is a provisional, ambivalent and ambiguous reality.[182] Although salvation occurs and is objectified in the spatiotemporal dimensions of ordinary history, that history as such remains ambiguous; it is always in flux, so that any one of its moments is relativized by the next.[183] As a result, the salvific quality of a particular historical manifestation cannot be definitively inferred from that manifestation.[184] Salvation is, at one and the same time, expressed in, and concealed by history.[185] Both the unity and differentiation of history and salvation can be stated in this way: although it is known with certainty *that* all salvation finds its objectification in history, that historical objectification as such cannot be known with certainty *as* salvation history.

Upon taking cognizance of such negative judgments regarding the knowability of salvation history, one wonders whether it is possible to know, and hence to speak of, salvation *history* in any concrete way. Moreover, in

---

179 Rahner, *Schriften*, V, 121. Rahner uses the terms "Weltgeschichte" and "Profangeschichte" interchangeably in his essay entitled "Weltgeschichte und Heilsgeschichte" (*Schriften*, V, 115-135). Sometimes he combines them and speaks of "profane Weltgeschichte" (*ibid.*, 121).

180 *Schriften*, V, 117.

181 Rahner, *Schriften*, V, 134. See Franz Schupp, "Die Geschichtsauffassung am Beginn der Tübinger Schule und in der gegenwartigen Theologie," *ZKTh*, XCI (1966), 163.

182 Rahner, *Schriften*, V, 115, 117, 119, 130, 131. Similarly, nature generally is qualified as "bivalente Natur" in contradistinction from "die eigentliche Gnade" (*Schriften*, VI, 268). And in both cases this bivalence, and with it the dualism of Christianity and history (*Schriften*, V, 130), is necessary to safeguard the gratuity of grace and to account for the possibility of belief and unbelief; compare *Schriften*, V, 268 and VI, 96-97 to V, 118, 120.

183 *Schriften*, V, 211; IX, 107.

184 *Schriften*, V, 120-21.

185 *Schriften*, V, 117, 118, 119, 130-31. Rahner gives two reasons for the hiddenness of salvation history (*Schriften*, V, 119-20), one from the viewpoint of man's, the other from the viewpoint of God's free decision. 1) Salvation involves man's free decision the deepest quality of which cannot be inferred from its objectification ; only God judges the heart. 2) Salvation is not simply the *result* of nor does it lie within the powers of man's free decision. It is the result of God's free decision; in fact, salvation *is God himself*. In this dispensation, however, before the immediate *Visio Dei*, God, though present in His own being (*Schriften*, V, 116), is not experienced immediately, but *mediately*.

view of the fact that, in contrast to history, salvation is fundamentally not provisional, not relativized by a new historical act – not even by any act of God –[186] history and salvation appear to represent incommensurable magnitudes. In that case, not only would salvation be historically unknowable, but salvation-history would be a contradictory combination. When Rahner speaks of the impossibility of univocal interpretation of history as salvation history, however, he always appends a qualification such as "of itself" or "in itself."[187] Of, by and in itself secular history does not allow a definite interpretation with respect to its salvific quality. Nevertheless, a particular segment of what would otherwise remain ambiguous, provisional history is interpreted as to its quality of *Heil* or *Unheil* by *God,* through His Word.[188] This divine interpretation sets apart a sector of secular history and of the *universal* history of salvation as *special* salvation history. In this particular concentration, salvation becomes historical in the strictest and fullest sense:[189] it is lastingly present and knowable in objectified, institutional form.[190]

Special concentrations of salvation history occur in Israel (and the Old

---

186 Because salvation *is* (our participation in) God *Himself* (see *Schriften,* V, 211; see also V, 115, 120, 129-30; IX, 207).

187 *Schriften,* V, 118, 119, 120.

188 *Schriften,* V, 125. Whether the paradigm of salvation as an *immediate* relationship to the inner being of God as He is *in Himself* allows an integral unity between salvation and history appears to be questionable: history entails finite mediation – salvation in principle excludes such mediation (*Schriften,* IX, 107). The solution that Rahner offers is a dialectic unity of opposites: "Vermittlung-durch-Unmittelbarkeit Gottes (*Schriften,* VI, 72, cf. 71). Cf. *Schriften,* IV, 90: "Das in Gnade und Inkarnation Gegebene ist nicht etwas von Gott Verschiedenes, sondern Gott selbst. Die Kreatur vermittelt ihn nicht, insofern sie durch ihre geschaffene Wirklichkeit auf Gott verweist, sondern Gott selbst vermittelt sich durch sich selbst an die Kreatur" (cf. *Schriften,* IV, 311). Rahner at one point states that the possibility of such an immediate relationship to the infinite mystery "als es selbst" can be known only by revelation (*Schriften,* IV, 84). Such an appeal to revelation, however, appears to reintroduce into the heart of Rahner's theology the conception of mystery that Rahner is determined to banish radically (in that very essay, IV, 51-99). True, Rahner's certainty of that mystery is (correlatively) anchored "subjectively" in the conviction that in grace man truly encounters God *Himself* (see n. 30 above) and "objectively" in the revelation of the unmixed and undivided unity of God and man in the incarnation (see C, 3 above and *Schriften,* IV, 90; V, 211; VI, 71-72). Nevertheless the question must be asked whether that "subjective" conviction has not been detrimentally influenced by a tradition which opposes God-in-Himself to God-*in-relation*-to-the-creation and whether the "objective" anchorage does not rest upon a tacit ascription of revelatory significance to the Chalcedonian christological formulations.

189 *Schriften,* V, 119, 120, 123, 124.

190 See *Schriften,* VI, 86.

Testament), Christ (and the New Testament) and, presently, in the Church. Although Christ represents the preeminent and pivotal manifestation of these concentrations, from Rahner's characterizations of the specific features of special salvation history it is obvious that previous concentrations are *presently manifest* only by virtue of an indefectible, infallible and efficacious institution, the Church. Since the previous concentrations converge in the Church, it is not surprising that this institution should function as the orientation point and criterion for reflecting upon those previous forms of special salvation history. In view of this ecclesiastical retrospection, we will briefly describe Rahner's conception of the three main phases in reverse order, beginning with the Church.[191]

The embodiment of salvation history in the Church is characterized by the fact that in this institution salvation receives a *definitive* and *reliable* historical form. This form is historical in the strictest and fullest sense, for that which is normally largely concealed within history as its deepest drive is historically manifest and manifestly historical in a concrete institution, in its tangible words and deeds.[192] Within history and as a part of history, one agency is demarcated from the rest of history to the extent that its meaning and significance is not subject to the exigencies of normal history, namely, to relativity and ambiguity. The Church is not susceptible to a host of subjective, divergent interpretations. The Church exists as a divinely interpreted segment of salvation history, as official and explicit salvation history.[193]

Both the notions "explicit" and "official" are crucial in describing the distinctiveness of the Church as the current instance of particular salvation history. The term "explicit" has reference especially to the *Word* of God, while the term "official" designates the authoritative character of that Word.[194] For, although God's acts of salvation occur everywhere, it is their authoritative interpretation and expression that renders those acts wholly

---

191 In Schoonenberg's view of salvation history a conception of the Church resembling Rahner's plays an equally significant role. Since Schoonenberg's conception of the Church and its function emerges most clearly in his reinterpretation of original sin (see chs. V and VI, below), his views will be dealt with directly in that context. In this section, views of Schoonenberg similar to those of Rahner will be referred to in the footnotes.
192 *Schriften*, V, 119-20, 123-24.
193 *Schriften*, V, 125.
194 Hence the frequent combinations, "amtliche und ausdrückliche Heilsgeschichte" (*Schriften,* V, 125), "amtliche besondere" (V, 127; cf. 128-29), "spezielle, amtliche begrifflich-worthafte Offenbarungsgeschichte" (VI, 98), "Heilsgeschichte ausdrücklich worthafter, gesellschaftlicher und sakramentaler Art" (V, 129).

present historically and capable of being experienced as such.[195] The Church may be seen as the (present) apex at which God's self-communication fully comes-to-itself and is present-to-itself historically.[196] Its content objectified, grace is *reflexively* present and hence can be explicitly known. The Church is the abiding *historical* presence of the eschatological Christ-event.[197] That privilege of the Church finds its reliable manifestation specifically in the infallible authority of the magisterium and in the *opus operatum* efficacy of the sacraments.[198] The Church is not an independent concentration of salvation, however, but one that is rooted in the historical appearance of Christ.

In Jesus Christ the process of God's self-communication attains its first definitive historical manifestation.[199] The broadest term which Rahner uses to designate that definitive quality of salvation history in Christ is the term "eschatological."[200] The incarnation is eschatological in that it represents a *final* and *irrevocable* event.[201] As in the case of the Church, the definitiveness of the incarnation attaches to it not merely ontically but historically, i.e., manifest in space and time.[202] The undivided and mixed unity of God's self-communication and of its acceptance by man becomes historically manifest by the interpreting word. Although the apex of God's self-revelation, too, can be *univocally* interpreted only by God's word, that interpretation becomes historically manifest only by way of the human word.[203] Accordingly, without wishing to minimize the basic and essential facticity involved, Rahner does emphasize that the facticity of the hypostatic union has its "innere, notwendige und mitkonstitutive Fortsetzung in dem absoluten Soh-

---

195 *Schriften*, V, 125-26. See also Rahner, "Kirchliche und ausserkirchliche Religiosität," *StZ*, CXCI (1973), 6, 10.

196 *StZ*, CXCI, 6: "Die Verkirchlichung dieser heilshaft ausserkirchlichen Frömmigkeit ist das volle Zusichselberkommen einer durch die Gnade schon immer gegebenen Frömmigkeit in der ausdrücklichen Begegnung mit Jesus und seiner institutionell verfassten Glaubensgemeinde." Cf. *Schriften*, V, 140, 155; *LThK*, VII, 292-93. The absolute apex ·is attained, of course, in the *Visio* which entails the "Aufhebung" (triple sense?) of history (*Schriften*, V, 120, cf. 115, 117).

197 *Schriften*, III, 295-96; IV, 18-19; VIII, 340, 365; IX, 252; *Kirche und Sakramente*, 13, 17-18. Cf. Schoonenberg, *Geloof*, III, 239; *God of mens*, 25.

198 Rahner, *Schriften*, VII, 70; *Kirche und Sakramente*, 22-30; Weger, *Theologie der Erbsünde*, 128-29.

199 See *Schriften*, V, 202, 203, 206-207; IX, 213. See also the final paragraph of sec. C, 2 above.

200 *Schriften*, V, 148; IX, 238.

201 *Schriften*, V, 128-29, 148-49, 202-203, 206; IX, 239.

202 *Schriften*, V, 202-203.

203 *Ibid.*, 126-27.

nesbewusstsein des Menschen Jesu ...."[204] Because the hypostatic union represents an *absolutely transcendent* mystery, it is present in our historical dimension only via the self-revelation of Jesus *in His human word.*[205] For that reason, the incarnation event can be translated as an apex of special salvation history: Christ-Jesus represents the univocal interpretation by God's word (special) of His act of self-communication and of man's act of acceptance in irrevocable unity (salvation) objectively manifest in the human word of Christ's self-testimony.[206]

From what has been said about the Church and about Christ, the nature of the concentration of salvation history in Israel can largely be anticipated. The history of Israel qualifies as salvation history because of its elements of legitimate religion, i.e., elements truly willed by God and, furthermore, to some extent objectified in legitimate institutions.[207] Moreover, this salvation history of the old covenant qualifies as *special* salvation history, because within it the possibility of distinguishing between legitimate and illegitimate elements of its religion was given in the institution of the prophets.[208] Nevertheless, this similarity between Israel and the Old Testament, on the one hand, and Christ, the New Testament and the Church, on the other, is limited. The prophets arose only sporadically and were opposed by *false* prophets.[209] What was lacking was an official institution that stood above both as an objective, infallible criterion. In the absence of such an institution, the decision as to the true and the false prophet was left up to each individual conscience. Even if objective criteria for testing the spirits were available, says Rahner, the employment or application of these criteria could not (yet) be left up to an "ecclesiastical" agency within Israel, for even such an agency could and did fail.[210] In Israel, no objective "Dauerinstitution" as yet existed.[211]

---

204 *Ibid.,* 126.
205 *Ibid.,* 126-27.
206 See *ibid.,* 126-29, 202-203.
207 *Ibid.,* 149, 154.
208 *Ibid.,* 148, 153-54.
209 *Ibid.,* 148-49.
210 *Ibid.* Behind this last stamenent lies Rahner's fundamental thesis that in distinction from the Church, Israel was basically and perpetually defectible (see also *Schriften,* IV, 18-19). For an analysis, see G. C. Berkouwer, *Vatikaans concilie,* 256-62; *The Second Vatican Council,* 207-12; *idem, De Kerk I,* 213-14. For the discussion with Hans Küng on the issue of infallibility or indefectibility, see *Zum Problem Unfehlbarkeit: Antworten auf die Anfrage von Hans Küng,* ed. Karl Rahner ("Quaestiones Disputatae," 54; Freiburg: Herder, 1971), 9-70.
211 *Schriften,* V, 148-49. Cf. Schoonenberg, *Geloof,* III, 207.

As becomes manifest in Rahner's description of salvation history in Israel, the criterion by which any one stage of salvation history is assessed is the Church as unique medium of grace. In the course of the following chapters, it will become clear that a conception of elevating-sanctifying grace uniquely transmitted by the Church plays a decisive role in the reinterpretation of original sin as the situational privation of grace.

PART II

ORIGINAL SIN
AS
HISTORICAL SITUATION

CHAPTER III   *SITUATIONAL PRIVATION*
OF GRACE AS SIN

A. PRELIMINARY DEFINITION AND QUALIFICATION
OF ORIGINAL SIN AS SITUATION

It is almost impossible to provide a simple definition of the situational conception of original sin, for any definition of that conception must draw upon many of the complex themes and concepts discussed in the previous section, namely, situational *Existential* spatiotemporal mediation, grace and salvation history. Moreover, the existential impact of the reality thus defined becomes apparent only in its interaction with the counterparts of the themes and concepts just mentioned, namely, freedom, person, appropriation, nature (as "theological" concept). A definition of original sin as situation, therefore, obtains its full meaning only in terms of the framework considered in part I and by way of the application of that framework to be explored in part II. Nevertheless, as point of reference, a brief definition at this stage may be of some help for understanding the subsequent discussion. For present purposes, then, original sin may be defined as the situational privation of sanctifying grace that renders every human being (analogously) guilty from the moment of birth.[1]

The limited value of this definition is obvious, for it raises more questions than it answers, questions concerning 1) the essence of original sin (of what is man deprived and in what sense can this privation be called sin or guilt? chapter III); 2) solidarity and freedom (in what sense can one speak of *solidarity* in sin and how radical is the effect of such solidarity? chapter IV); 3) the universality of this situation (in what specific way is every human being deprived of grace? chapters V and VI). To facilitate an analysis of the

---

1 This terse provisional definition can be compared to the more complete definitions or circumscriptions given by Schoonenberg (*Geloof* IV, 155; *Man and Sin,* 118-23; *MS,* II, 895-97, 928-32), Rahner (*Schriften,* IX, 267-69; *Exkurs,* 187-89; *SM,* I, 1110-1112, *SMe,* IV, 331) and Weger (*Theologie der Erbsünde,* 161 and 174).

essentially structural problems entailed in the first two questions, the question concerning the *precise way* in which man can be said to be deprived of grace will be kept in abeyance in this and the next chapter. This provisional simplification is in keeping with the situationalists' frequent description of original sin in terms of an unspecified absence of grace.[2] The specific way in which grace can be said to be situationally lacking will be examined in answer to the third question (chapter V as well as VI).

Still, although an exact specification of the situation of original sin can be postponed, a general qualification of that situation is required at this point. That qualification is necessary to avoid the suggestion that the idea of a situational *lack* of grace flatly contradicts the conception of the universal (situational!) *presence* of grace that is held by all the situationalists.[3] That presence of grace, in fact, constitutes an ineradicable *Existential*, an ontological determinant, an irreversible aspect of the situation of every human being.[4] The lack of grace that constitutes original sin, therefore, does not involve or affect this universal *Existential* (or situation) of grace.[5] To clarify this seemingly contradictory juxtaposition of the situational presence and absence of grace, a distinction within the idea of situation is mandatory. Because the universal grace-*Existential* or grace-situation is real regardless of the specific historical, cultural or familial situation, it is aptly described as a *transcendental* situation (or *Existential*).[6] The specific cultural-historical constellation that constitutes man's concrete situation can then be distinguished as man's *spatiotemporal* situation (or *Existential*).[7] The exact but rather

---

2 See the circumscriptions of the situation of original sin mentioned in the preceding footnote. Cf. such terminology as "the grace-less 'world' " and "a universe deprived of grace" (Schoonenberg, *Man and Sin,* 179 and 120; *Bijdragen*, XXIV, 376 and 366 ["genadeloze ruimte," "genadeloosheid" as " 'existentiale' situatie"]); "gnadenlose Welt" (Weger, *Theologie der Erbsünde,* 139, 144, 159, 160).
3   See ch. II, secs. B, 3 and C, 3 above.
4   *Ibid.*
5 Rahner, *SM*, I, 1114; cf. 1109, 1110, 1113; *SMe*, IV, 333; cf 330-32. Weger, *Theologie der Erbsünde,* 126, 151. Materially Schoonenberg is in essential agreement with Rahner's and Weger's view of the coexistence of a universal presence and lack of grace (see ch. VI below).
6 The term "transcendental" must be distinguished from the term "transcendent". A transcendental situation is not transcendent in the sense of being simply elevated above man, for it is precisely *man's* situation.
7 At one point, Weger explicitly employs these designations: "So kann man aber nicht nur von einem vorpersonalen, *transzendentalen* Existential des Menschen sprechen, sondern gleichzeitig auch von einem *kategorialen*, mitmenschlichen Existential..." (*Theologie der Erbsünde,* 115-16, emphasis added). See also ch, I, secs. B, 1 and B, 2, b and ch. II, sec. C, 2 above for the idea of spatiotemporal mediation.

abstruse distinction between the spatiotemporal and the transcendental situation may be rendered more comprehensible by thinking, respectively, of the "atmosphere" and of the "horizon" of human existence. Both of these represent (distinct) *situational* realities.

With the aid of that distinction, original sin can be defined more precisely as a *spatiotemporal* privation of grace. That privation represents a negation of the intended spatiotemporal *presence* of grace. Grace was intended to be present as the atmosphere of human existence. God's grace was not meant to be communicated purely transcendentally — via man's horizon — so that the presence of grace as the atmosphere enveloping the individual would need to be created anew by that individual, i.e., by his positive response to the horizon. Rather, God wishes to communicate Himself transcendentally *and* spatiotemporally, so that each human being is to act as spatiotemporal, historical mediator of grace *for his fellowman.*[8] Each human being plays this mediating role not only for his contemporaries but also for future generations. In fact, this historical mediation takes place most incisively in what might be called the smallest link of history, the family, specifically in the relation of parent to child.

The entrance of sin into the world brings with it a disruption of this spatiotemporal communication of grace, a disturbance in the atmosphere of human existence, for in its deepest sense, sin entails a rejection of God's grace.[9] The effect of such resistance to grace is a spatiotemporal privation of grace for one's fellowman. Although God continues to orient man to, and situate man by grace transcendentally, the spatiotemporal mediation of grace is thwarted.[10] God's gracious love and man's sinful resistance coexist, with the result that each human being is situated simultaneously by a *transcendental presence* of grace and by *spatiotemporal lack* of grace. Whenever original sin, therefore, is described by the situationalists themselves or in the following chapters as the absence or privation of grace, the qualification "spatiotemporal" must always be supplied by the reader.

---

8 Schoonenberg, *Geloof,* IV, 186-88, *Bijdragen,* XXIV, 365, *Man and Sin,* 119; Rahner, *Schriften,* VIII, 231. Weger, *Theologie der Erbsünde,* 127-37.

9 Schoonenberg, *Man and Sin* 21, 23-24, 107, 118-19; *Bijdragen,* XXIV, 357-58, 365; *Geloof,* IV, 38-39, 153; *MS,* II, 891-98. Rahner, *Schriften,* V, 216. Weger, *Theologie der Erbsünde,* 133-40.

10 See the references in note 8 above.

B. HERMENEUTICAL PROBLEMS

1. Choice of Starting Point and Traditional Options

Aside from the situational framework of reinterpretation, the most obvious consensus obtaining among the situationalists is the negative or privational definition of original sin. Schoonenberg describes the situation of original sin by contrasting it with the model, the situation of the child.[11] In comparison to that model, the most important distinguishing feature of the situation of original sin, he says, is its supernatural character.[12] The situation of original sin, Schoonenberg explains, does not have its origin in man's natural relationship to God and to fellowman, but "in a fall out of supernatural love, in a breach in the covenant relationship between God and man."[13] The resultant situation of original sin is accordingly described in terms of a privation of "supernatural grace"[14] or "supernatural life,"[15] or simply in terms of "gracelessness."[16] Rahner and Weger similarly proceed from the idea of supernatural grace (though with a stronger emphasis on the idea of *sanctifying* grace)[17] to arrive at their negative definition of original sin.[18] That privational definition involves a hermeneutical step of great import, for this definition reveals a basic choice that has been made with respect to the starting point of reinterpretation. The privational view of original sin represents the expression of a choice between at least two options presented to the interpreter by tradition.

As we have seen, a survey of the theological tradition reveals roughly two contrasting approaches to the doctrine of original sin. On the one hand, man's condition is understood primarily in terms of his present resistance to

---

11 *Geloof*, IV, 152-53. For a discussion of that model as such see ch. I, sec. A, 3, b above.

12 *Geloof*, IV, 153. Although the qualification of sin as "supernatural" may at first glance seem strange, it is entirely appropriate to Schoonenberg's intentions, namely, to point out the reality which sin affects most deeply, namely, grace. C. Dumont's criticism of this terminology as a "gaucherie dans l'expression" is rather fastidious and his postulation of an error in translation is incorrect (C. Dumont, Review of *L'homme et le péché*, by P. Schoonenberg (Tours: Mame, 1967), *NRTh*, XC (1968), 716.

13 *Geloof*, IV, 153.
14 *Ibid.*, 155.
15 *Ibid.*, 154.
16 See n. 2 above.
17 See the introductory paragraphs of sec. C, 2, b below
18 See n. 1 above and sec. C, 2, b, i below

and rebellion against God. This active inclination of the will is viewed as a manifestation of the solidarity of the human race in sin. In this view, articulated by Augustine, the core of original sin is an original *aversio a deo* in the heart of each human being. This positive definition of original sin as *aversio* find its negative counterpart in the understanding of original sin as a *privatio*, an absence or lack either of special supernatural gifts or of the central gift of sanctifying grace. This tradition has its antecedents in the mainstream of the theology of the Greek Fathers, gains a foothold in Western theology via Anshelm and Aquinas, and becomes predominant in post-Tridentine Roman Catholic theology.

The situationalists' choice of the negative, privational approach to original sin has repercussions for every aspect of their reinterpretation. Hence it may be well to ask concerning the possible reasons for this choice.

Several reasons for their choosing a privational conception of original sin suggest themselves. In the first place, the central category of their reinterpretation, situation, would seem — because of its passive character — to facilitate, if not dictate, a passive conception of original sin. Though seemingly obvious, this explanation is rendered problematic if one asks whether the inverse procedure is not more likely, namely, that the privational understanding of original sin opens the way for a situational interpretation of original sin. Surely the situationalists intend to mould their central categories to serve the matter being reinterpreted, not vice versa.

As a second possible reason for the situationalists' choice for the negative definition of original sin one might point to the teaching of the Council of Trent regarding original sin. Its second canon, as we have seen, teaches that Adam lost holiness and justice not only for himself but also for his descendants.[19] Also this appeal to Trent, however, fails to reveal an adequate ground for opting for a privational understanding of original sin. Though teaching that Adam lost "holiness and justice" for his progeny, this canon as well as others describe the resultant condition of original sin rather unproblematically in terms of notions such as sin and guilt.[20] Moreover, it is striking that none of the situationalists argues that the magisterium explicitly or directly teaches the idea of original sin as a private condition.[21] On the contrary, a privational understanding of original sin necessitates, as we shall see, a

---

19 *DS*, 1512 (see Introduction, sec. A, 8 above.).
20 See canons 2, 3, 4 and 5 (Introduction, sec. A, 8 above) and ch. I of Trent's decree on justification (*DS*, 1521)
21 Schoonenberg, Rahner and Weger all deal with this privative conception of original sin as an increasingly dominant *theological* tradition (Schoonenberg, *Geloof*, IV,

reinterpretation of certain elements of the official teaching of original sin that appear to be at odds with the privational conception.[22]

If neither the central category of the situational reinterpretation nor the texts being reinterpreted directly sanction the choice of the privational conception of original sin, the situationalists' seemingly unquestioned adoption of that conception is remarkable, indeed. Especially surprising is Schoonenberg's adoption of this conception, for if anyone is averse to adopting a relatively late doctrinal or theological conception as a point of departure for further elaboration, it is Schoonenberg. As noted, he constantly attempts to nourish, perhaps even to revive, the core of a doctrine by digging beneath its later historical expression to its original, often richer soil.[23] For the doctrine of original sin that soil is the biblical theme of solidarity in sin.[24] Between the biblical notion of solidarity in sin and the medieval or post-Tridentine conception of original sin as the privation of grace yawns a historical chasm of centuries. Nevertheless, in the process of reinterpreting original sin, Schoonenberg traverses that chasm so effortlessly that it hardly seems to exist.[25] The bridge that makes this feat possible is the category "situation," which is applied to both the idea of solidarity in sin and the privational conception of original sin.[26] Whether Schoonenberg's bridge provides an integral link between the biblical notion of solidarity in sin and the contemporary interpretation of original sin in terms of the situational privation of grace cannot be decided in abstraction, i.e., apart from the product of his reinterpretation.

The ultimate ground for the situationalists' choice of a privational view of original sin is difficult, perhaps impossible, to recover. Nevertheless, the question concerning that ground is not meaningless. It has been raised at this stage in order to uncover a central problem of the situational reinterpretation that remains concealed when the privational conception of original sin

---

177-78; Rahner *SM,* I,1107-1108; *SMe,* IV, 329-30; Weger, *Theologie der Erbsünde,* 17: "Nun gibt zwar das Trienter Konzil keine ausdrückliche Definition der Erbsünde (es sei denn, man wolle die 'Heiligkeit und Gerechtigkeit,' die Adam von Gott empfangen und für uns aller verloren hat, als solche betrachten), aber die katholische Theologie sieht zumindest heute und zu Recht das Wesen jeder menschlichen Schuld im Fehlen der heiligmachenden Gnade Gottes, im Fehlen des Lebens, das Gott selbst ist . . . .")

22 See secs. C, 1, a and C, 2, a below.
23 See ch. I, sec. A, 1 above.
24 *Ibid.*
25 Note the transition between Schoonenberg's rather general use of the term "situation" to describe the scriptural theme of solidarity in sin and enslavement to the power of sin (*Geloof,* IV, 93, 95, 96, 101, 105, 106, 142, 144, 158; *Man and Sin,* 103-105) and his specific use of that term to describe man's being deprived of grace (*Geloof,* IV, 153-55; *Man and Sin,* 110, 118-120).
26 See the references in the preceding footnote.

becomes the unquestioned point of departure. The fact that this point of departure represents a choice of great hermeneutical significance must be kept in mind as the actual process of reinterpretation is traced. In no case may that choice be obscured either by the suggestion that a privational understanding is self-evident, or by an appeal to a consensus or convergence of theological opinion.[27]

2. Encounter of Past and Present in the Question of Guilt

The question as to whether and in what sense guilt may be ascribed to the reality of original sin arises in the first instance because the magisterium speaks rather unproblematically of original sin as involving guilt and therefore requiring remission of sin in a true sense.[28] That fact alone necessitates reflection upon the relation between the situational conception of original sin and the reality of guilt. The fact that this central traditional datum becomes rather problematic for the situational understanding of original sin represents another aspect of the hermeneutical question raised previously with respect to the privational definition of original sin.

Relative to the privational definition, the guilt question represents both an extension and a shift of the hermeneutical problem: an extension insofar as a purely privational interpretation of original sin in itself renders the traditional datum of guilt problematic; a shift in that the confrontation of the past (the relatively late passive-privational conception of original sin) with a more distant past (an earlier active-directional understanding of original sin and, still earlier, the biblical theme of solidarity in sin) becomes less dominant. In the question of guilt, the confrontation of past and present becomes central. To be sure, the present is also inescapably involved in the situationalists' privational understanding of original sin, namely, in the person of the interpreter, his choice of starting point and his employment of a category such as situation. Nevertheless, with the question of guilt the confrontation of past and present erupts more powerfully.

Two reasons may be given for that forward shift in the center of gravity. In the first place, although the privational definition itself tends to render the guilt-character of original sin problematic, that difficulty, though not resolved, was at least mitigated in the past by means of a thought-form which made it possible to conceptualize each man as in some way included in Adam

---

27 Cf. n. 21 above.
28 *DS*, 223, 1514.

by virtue of "human nature." Accordingly, theologians who defined original sin primarily in privational terms could at the same time speak of original sin as a *peccatum naturae*.[29] With the aid of such conceptions, guilt by participation remains conceivable. When the idea of the privation of grace is interpreted with the aid of the modern category "situation," however, any appeal to such a thought-form is radically precluded, far that which corresponds to situation is person, and a person is culpable only on the basis of his own free acts. That contemporary thought-form makes far more pressing the question as to whether and in what sense the situational privation of grace can properly be qualified as sin and guilt. The intensity with which the situationalists struggle with this question must not be deprecated as being merely a desperate *ex post facto* attempt to sanction an independently attained conception of original sin by a subsequent *re*interpretation of the ecclesiastical doctrine. Rather, since the situational conception of original sin intends from the outset to be a re*interpretation of that doctrine,* the intense and relentless grappling with the question of the guilt-character of original sin constitutes an *inherent* part of the situational reinterpretation of original sin. That struggle takes place as a confrontation of two historical periods, that of the interpreter and that of the texts, with their undeniably different understanding and experience of reality.

The present becomes more central in the question of guilt not merely due to the direct confrontation of past and present, for in such a confrontation the orientation could obviously still be (from the present) towards the past. The present becomes even more central for a second reason. Behind the question as to whether original sin can be qualified as guilt lies the more general but all-important question as to whether the reinterpretation of original sin *as situation* renders the content of the ecclesiastical doctrine conceivable as a reality that is experienced existentially in the present.[30] That issue becomes acute in the question of guilt because guilt represents sin in its deepest existential expression.[31] The answer to the question concerning the guilt-character of the privation of grace represents a partial answer to the question concerning the existential significance of original sin understood as situation.[32] Thus the center of gravity is shifted forcefully towards the present.

---

29 See Gross, III, 17-19; Schoonenberg, *Geloof,* IV, 163-67, 175-76.

30 Schoonenberg, *Geloof* IV, 144; Rahner, *SM,* I, 1105-106; *SMe,* IV, 328-29; Weger, *Theologie der Erbsünde,* 10, 41-42, 107.

31 See Schoonenberg, *SM,* IV, 773; Weger, *Theologie der Erbsünde,* 141, 165, 175.

32 An assessment of the *full* existential significance of original sin conceived of as situation must also take into account the material presented in the next two chapters.

It is a *shift toward* the present, however, not simply a *transition to* an isolated present, severed from the past. For that reason the question of guilt remains a hermeneutical question, an interpretation in and for the present (interpreter, categories of interpretation, relevance for modern man) of the past (a confessional ecclesiastical expression).

C. SITUATIONAL PRIVATION OF GRACE AS ANALOGICAL GUILT

The question concerning the guilt-character of original sin will be dealt with in two stages. In order to bring to the fore the hermeneutical problem that is always implicit in this question, Schoonenberg's procedure will be presented first, for he, more than Rahner and Weger, deals with this question in explicit confrontation with the rather unproblematic fusion of guilt and original sin in the teaching of the Church. Thereupon, we will consider the various ways in which both Rahner and Weger attempt to demonstrate the analogical guilt-character of the situational privation of grace.

1. Original Sin as Sin by Attribution: Schoonenberg

At first glance the question of guilt appears to present no real problem for Schoonenberg's situational view of original sin, for, on the one hand, guilt is directly associated with personal sin (a free act)[33] and, on the other hand, situation has been rigorously delimited by dissociating it from person and freedom.[34] Against that background, what appears to be a simple elimination of guilt from the situation of original sin comes as no surprise: "We must cease viewing original sin as a sinful attitude, as sin and guilt in the same (be it diluted) sense as personal sin."[35] Elsewhere, Schoonenberg states categorically that original sin is not an act or attitude and therefore cannot be seen as guilt.[36] Rather than simply cutting the Gordian knot that has traditionally tied guilt and original sin rather indiscriminately together, Schoonenberg painstakingly unravels it. Only after this analytical dissociation does Schoonenberg join the ends once again by means of the more refined link of analogical association.

a. *Analytical Dissociation*

Schoonenberg himself points out that the Council of Trent explicitly calls the state of original sin "sin" and even "guilt," and that the Council of

---
33 *Man and Sin,* 16-20; *SM,* IV, 770-73; *Geloof,* IV, 214.
34 See ch. I, sec. A, 3 above.
35 *Ex Auditu Verbi,* 262.
36 *Geloof,* IV, 160; cf. 158, 171.

Orange applies a text with a preeminently *personal* thrust ("The soul that sins shall die.") to *original* sin.[37] More generally, Schoonenberg observes that the magisterium speaks of "original sin in terms derived from personal sin."[38] Even infants are, according to the teaching of the Church, baptized unto the remission of sins in a true sense.[39] As to Scripture, Schoonenberg has pointed out that it speaks of a communal participation in sin, contains confessions of collective guilt, and does not treat original sin as distinct from personal sin.[40]

Despite this coalescence of personal guilt and solidarity in sin within Scripture and tradition, Schoonenberg proceeds to dissociate personal and original sin — with an appeal to both sources. As to Scripture, it suffices to recall Schoonenberg's delineation of a development within the Bible towards a separation of personal sin from communal sin.[41] That development functions as an implicit santion of the elimination of guilt from the reality of original sin.[42] The principle of personal responsibility precludes the understanding of solidarity in sin as involving the inheritance of the personal guilt of one's predecessors.[43] As to tradition, Schoonenberg appeals, on the one hand, to elements that require and, on the other hand, to elements that allow for the elimination of the notion of guilt from the reality of original sin. Appealing to these elements, Schoonenberg demarcates a unique realm of original sin, a realm that is delimited by two adjacent realms: that of personal sin on the one side and that of mere punishment on the other. In order to determine the precise nature of original sin as conceived by Schoonenberg, we will attempt to establish the boundaries that separate the realm of original sin from these adjacent realms.

The elimination of guilt from the reality of original sin is *required* by the presence of an implicit analogy in the Church teaching.[44] That analogy points to a boundary between original sin and personal sin. Schoonenberg contends that, despite the fact that the magisterium uses personal terms such as sin and guilt in connection with original sin, the analogical meaning of such terms is implicitly recognized:

37 *Geloof,* IV, 161; Eze 18:20; *DS,* 371.
38 *Geloof,* IV, 161.
39 *DS,* 223, 1514.
40 See ch. I, sec. A, 1 above.
41 See *ibid.,*
42 *Geloof,* IV, 157, 158;
43 *Geloof,* IV, 157.
44 Here only the *difference* involved in the analogy will be examined. In the following section both the similarity and the difference involved in the analogy between personal and original sin will be examined.

When both the councils of Carthage and Trent point to this original sin in "infants who have not yet been able to commit any sins of themselves" (*DS*, 223, 1514), a fundamental distinction is thereby made in these very teachings between original sin and personal sin. That same distinction also applies to the difference between the "guilt" of original sin (*DS*, 728: *culpa*; *DS*, 1515: *reatus*) and one's personal, one's "own guilt," as well as to the difference between the "forgiveness" (*remissio*) of the former and that of the latter.[45]

The analogy that Schoonenberg singles out as being implicitly affirmed by the magisterium has been elaborated and explicated, he points out, in theological reflection.[46] Schoonenberg does not, however, simply adopt the notion of analogy as it has been applied to original sin in the theological tradition. Rather, he carries that analogy further by, as he himself says, placing an even greater emphasis on the *difference* involved in the analogy.[47] In fact, Schoonenberg accentuates this difference in such a way that little inherent similarity between personal sin and original sin appears to remain: on his construction they seem to lack a crucial common feature. Traditionally, that common feature was voluntariness. The ascription of guilt to the condition of original sin was plausible on the basis of and to the extent that a kind of voluntariness was ascribed to that condition, be it "voluntarium voluntate Adami."[48] Schoonenberg, however, methodically expunges even the minimum of voluntariness traditionally attributed to the reality of original sin.[49] Voluntariness through the will of another person appears to be a contradiction, he says, as is the idea of passively incurred guilt. He therefore eliminates both *voluntarietas* and *culpa* from the condition of original sin and calls that which "the person encounters as arising from the act of another: *situation*."[50] As might be expected in view of the intrinsic link between guilt and voluntariness, Schoonenberg justifies the *elimination* of the latter by appealing once again to the fact that the magisterium describes the infant subject to original sin as not yet being able to commit any (personal) sins.[51]

Thus, the teaching of the Church that *requires* the elimination of all personal elements (epitomized by guilt) from original sin has revealed the boundary that demarcates original sin as situation from personal sin. The

45 *Geloof*, IV, 162; cf. 181. See also *Man and Sin*, 172.
46 *Geloof*, IV, 162, 163, 181.
47 *Ibid*.
48 *Geloof*, IV, 177, 178.
49 *Ibid.*, 179, 182n; *Man and Sin*, 181; *MS*, II, 929.
50 *Geloof*, IV, 179-80.
51 *Man and Sin*, 172; *MS*, II, 923: "Den Charakter eines Aktes oder eines 'aktiven Habitus' oder eine *eigene* 'voluntarietas' im Kinde (zumindest während seines individuellen Daseins) kann man also nach dem Tridentinum dem erbsündlichen Zustand nicht zuschreiben."

teaching that *allows* the elimination of guilt reveals the boundary on the other side, demarcating original sin from mere punishment.[52]

As Schoonenberg points out, the Church clearly teaches that original sin is to be understood as sin and is not to be equated with a mere punishment for sin.[53] This teaching is especially significant in view of the fact that the Council of Sens condemned the thesis of Abelard that original sin constitutes only punishment rather than guilt.[54] Thus, the magisterium maintains the boundary between original sin and mere punishment by pointing to the guilt-character of original sin. But Schoonenberg has thoroughly eliminated guilt from the situation of original sin. The question arises, therefore, how Schoonenberg can maintain the boundary that separates original sin from mere punishment while eliminating the element of guilt to which the magisterium points precisely in order to demarcate original sin from mere punishment.

Schoonenberg is of the opinion that the teaching of Sens does not preclude his elimination of guilt from original sin. He contends, in effect, that the scope of what is positively expressed by the terms guilt and sin is determined by what is negatively rejected in the term punishment.[55] The purpose

---

52 In addition to these boundaries, Schoonenberg points to two other points of agreement between the traditional doctrine and the situational interpretation that justify the dissociation of original sin and guilt. The first concerns the interiority of original sin: the magisterium teaches that original sin is "proper to each, unicuique proprium" (*DS*, 1513); the same is true of situation in that it represents an inner determination of each person (*Geloof*, IV, 162, 180; *Man and Sin*, 173, 180; *MS*, II, 928-29; cf. 891). The second point of agreement concerns the seriousness of original sin: the magisterium describes the radicality of original sin in terms of a "death of the soul" (*DS*, 372, 1512); the same is true of being-situated by sin, "for the situation of original sin consists of a deprivation of grace and an inability to love." (*Geloof*, IV, 162). For a further discussion of both points, see ch. IV below.

53 *Geloof*, IV, 161, with reference to *DS*, 372, 728, 1512. Cf. *Man and Sin*, 171-72; *MS*, II, 923.

54 *Geloof*, IV, 161; *DS*, 728.

55 The procedure followed in this instance represents the application of a basic hermeneutical principle utilized by Schoonenberg. The meaning of "generatione" and "propagatione," for example, is determined by what was rejected in the *negative* phrase, "non imitatione." Schoonenberg argues on that basis that a theory (such as his own) that does not interpret "generatione" and "propagatione" in a direct causal way is not for that reason illigitimate. The legitimacy of a new theory concerning the transmission of original sin depends upon whether this new theory excludes Pelagianism as effectively as "generatione" did in its time (see *Geloof*, IV, 188, 190). For the concrete application of this principle in the construction of the situation theory, see ch. I, secs. A, 3, a and A, 3, c above. For an elaboration of the principle itself, see *WuW*, XXII, 337-46, esp. 742-46. "Wenn eine Lehräusserung gegen eine bestimmte Meinung gerichtet ist, so wird man auch dasjenige, was darin positiv ausgesagt wird, in erster Linie als eine Ablehnung der verurteilten Meinung interpretieren müssen und nicht notwendigerweise als die einzig mögliche Umschreibung des Glaubensgeheimnisses, das gegen die verurteilte Meinung geschützt wird" (*ibid.*, 743).

of an ecclesiastical arrow, one might say, cannot be deduced from its shaft but only from its point, which is most sharply felt at its impact with the target. The target of statements regarding the guilt-character of original sin, according to Schoonenberg, is the identification of original sin with punishment conceived of as *malum physicum*.[56] That identification eliminates original sin from the moral-religious realm. Although evil as punishment has its *occasion* in the moral-religious domain, as *physical* evil it itself stands outside that realm.[57] Thus in negating the idea of punishment, Schoonenberg argues, the Church affirmed the moral-religious character of original sin. In doing so, it made use of the terms sin and guilt. Although these terms do indicate that some kind of guilt was *presupposed* in the teaching of original sin,[58] they *intend* to teach (as is evident from their target) no more than the moral-religious character of original sin — and no less. In distinction from the idea of guilt itself, this moral-religious character of original sin is not a dispensable presupposition. "On the contrary," says Schoonenberg, "it constitutes an essential implication without which the Church's language concerning sin, guilt, justification, etc. is robbed of its content."[59] In view of that analysis, the question becomes acute as to the sense in which original sin conceived of as *situation* can be said to belong to the moral-religious realm.

b. *Analogical Association*

To understand the sense in which Schoonenberg qualifies the situation of original sin as sinful, consideration will first be given to his argumentation that original sin conceived of as situation is entirely coextensive with the area that lies between the realm of personal sin and the realm of physical evil. Thereafter, Schoonenberg's explicit qualification of original sin as sin will be considered.

Schoonenberg argues that the conception of situation is ideally suited to fall precisely within the area delimited on the one side by personal sin and on the other side by physical evil:

> The utilization of this notion makes it possible to demarcate original sin both from the area of the purely natural, not yet moral, and from the domain of personal decision. Being-situated by sin... is not a pure given-of-nature, but arises

---

56 See *DS,* 372 where the idea of original sin as constituting merely the punishment of physical death (the death of the body) is rejected, and the idea that sin itself ("the death of the soul") is passed on is defended. Cf. *DS,* 1512 (Introduction, sec. A, 8, b above).
57 *Man and Sin,* 180, cf. 171-72. Cf. the traditional definition of punishment as *malum physicum inflictum propter malum morale* (*Geloof,* IV, 201).
58 *Geloof,* IV, 161, 181.
59 *Bijdragen,* XXIV, 370, 371; *MS,* II, 923.

out of a history, out of free sinful decisions. On the other hand, these decisions are not those of the person situated in this way, so that being-situated is not a personal attitude, not an active *habitus*.[60]

The same boundaries are in view when Schoonenberg characterizes his reinterpretation of original sin in terms of situation as a "middle way between, on the one hand, a natural or essentialistic view and, on the other, a personalistic or existentialistic view."[61] In defending this *via media*, Schoonenberg consciously chooses position both against what he considers to be the dominant tendency of Catholic theology to date,[62] as well as against the dominant tendency of Protestant theology.[63]

Concerned to safeguard the objective reality of original sin, Catholic theology has displayed a proclivity for nonpersonal, natural categories, categories which jeopardize the moral-religious character of original *sin*.[64] Dissociating himself from this "naturalism," Schoonenberg emphasizes the fact that, although original sin as situatedness precedes personal decision, "it belongs in essence to the (inter-)personal domain because it arises from personal decisions (of others)."[65] Thus, free decision is basic with respect to the *origin* of the reality of original sin.

Although Schoonenberg stresses the personal element as being basic to the reality of situation, he is equally adament in rejecting the Protestant understanding of original sin. He characterizes this Protestant view as a personalistic or existentialistic conception which identifies original sin with a basic sinful attitude.[66] Schoonenberg acknowledges that the Protestant emphasis on man's basic stance (*aversio a deo*) reflects a legitimate concern for doing justice to the depth dimension of sin. However, because it can be restricted to the individual person, this depth perspective as such is, according to Schoonenberg, of little value for bringing into view the *specific scope* of the doctrine of original sin.[67] The emphasis of the depth dimension of sin, however valuable, fails to uncover the unique dimension expressed in this doctrine: the "breadth dimension" of sin.[68] It is out of concern for this

60 *MS*, II, 929.
61 *Ibid.* Cf. *Man and Sin*, 198.
62 *MS*, II, 930-31.
63 *Ibid.*, 930.
64 *Ibid.*, 931; *Ex Auditu Verbi*, 266.
65 *MS*, II, 931.
66 *Ibid.*, 929-30. Cf. *Ex Auditu Verbi*, 266.
67 *Ex Auditu Verbi*, 262.
68 Cf. *ibid.* Schoonenberg often speaks of this unique element of original sin which he wishes to safeguard as the *social* dimension of sin to which the social dimension of salvation corresponds (*Bijdragen*, XXIV, 349; *WuW*, XXII, 737; *ThPQ*, CXVII, 123; *SM*, IV, 776, cf. 768.

dimension that Schoonenberg dissociates himself from the existentialistic interpretation by emphasizing that in his own interpretation "the condition of original sin is unequivocally demarcated from every personal sin."[69] In his view, original sin is not an existential act, but a situational *Existential.*[70]

If original sin, conceived of as situation, falls precisely within the boundaries that demarcate it from personal sin, on the one hand, and from physical evil, on the other, in what sense can this situatedness itself be called *sin?* In answer to that question,[71] Schoonenberg employs the idea of analogy, but then a particular kind of analogy, namely, the analogy of attribution in distinction from the analogy of proportionality. To understand the precise way in which Schoonenberg qualifies the situational privation of grace as sin, therefore, a brief description of the idea of analogy, specifically, of the two major types of analogy is necessary.[72]

In general, analogy stands mid-way between *univocity*, the use of a term in the same sense (e.g.: a mouse is an "animal"; an elephant is an "animal") and *equivocity,* the use of a term in a different sense (e.g.: the "bark" of a tree and the "bark" of a dog). *Analogy* is the use of one term in a partially similar and, simultaneously, in a partially different sense. In other words, in the case of analogy, one cannot abstract from the differences to arrive at univocity (mouse and elephant: animal), nor discount the similarity to arrive at equivocity. Two basic types of analogy are pertinent to our topic, the analogy of proportionality and that of attribution.

The analogy of proportionality presupposes that the essence or quality (*analogum*) designated by a single term is intrinsic and essential to all of the entities in question (*analogata*).[73] Thus the term "part" is properly predicated of an arm and a wheel: an arm is a part of the human body; a wheel is part of a car. In each instance, the term "part" refers to the *same* concept and

---

69 *MS,* II, 929: "In unserer Deutung wird das erbsündige Dasein eindeutig gegen jede persönliche Sünde abgegrenzt."
70 *Ibid.,* 930. See also ch. I, sec. A, 3, c above.
71 *Geloof,* IV, 180.
72 For the following description of the analogy concept see John A. Peters, *Metaphysics: A Systematic Survey,* trans. Henry J. Koren ("Duquesne Studies, Philosophical Series," 16; Pittsburgh, Pa: Duquesne University Press, 1963), 94-103; and Angelius (O.F.M. Cap.), *Algemene zijnsleer,* edited and completed by Martinianus (O.F.M. Cap.) ("Bibliotheek van Thomistische Wijsbegeerte"; Utrecht: Het Spectrum, 1947), 219-46. Charles Boyer, *Handboek der wijsbegeerte,* I, trans. and ed. H.G. Rambonnet ('s-Hertogenbosch: Malmberg, [1947]), 76-77, 346-60.
73 For example, causality is the *analogum,* while the *analogata* are effective cause, final cause, formal cause, material cause. The term *analogatum (-a)* will be translated as "analogue (-s)," while the term *analogum* will be left untranslated.

the *same* reality, namely, the relationship of part-whole. Simultaneously, the term "part" refers to a *different* concept and a *different* reality, namely, to the organic and to the mechanical part-whole relationship, respectively. The important thing to note, for our purposes, is the fact that, despite the real difference between the analogues, in the analogy of proportionality the thought content of the *analogum* (quality or essence) is *intrinsic* to each entity (analogue).

In the analogy of attribution, by contrast, a specific thought content is intrinsically present only in one entity, in one of the analogues. That analogue may therefore be designated as the *analogatum primarium* or *princeps analogatum*.[74] The thought content of the analogical concept applies to the other entities (the *analogata secundaria*) not intrinsically but by virtue of their relationship to the *analogatum primarium*.[75] A classic illustration of the analogy of attribution is the use of the term and concept "health" to describe a person, a food and a person's complexion. The quality health is intrinsic only to a living organism, in this case to the person. With reference to food, "health" does not describe its intrinsic condition (for that reason unhealthful food is not said to be "ill"), but its effect upon the inner condition of a living organism. Similarly, a complexion is called healthy only because it is a manifestation of the condition of a person (accordingly, an unhealthy complexion is not a skin disease). The secondary analogues, therefore, are related to the primary analogue (living organism) as cause (food) or as effect or sign (complexion). Other examples of secondary analogues which are the *effect* of the primary analogue are manifest in the expressions "a clever piece of work," "an intelligent book," "a sensitive still life."[76] Cleverness, intelligence and sensitivity are not intrinsically present in that an artifact is not inventive, a book does not have an IQ, and a still life does not feel. In each case, the specific quality belongs to the secondary analogue by virtue of its being an effect or product of the primary analogue (a clever, intelligent or sensitive person). In both relational directions (secondary analogue as cause and as effect), the analogy of attribution proves to be of particular value in setting forth the sense in which a situation may be qualified as being sinful.

In the first instance, Schoonenberg explicitly employs the analogy of attribution in order to explain the legitimate qualificiation of being-situated by sin as itself (original) *sin:*

---

74 See, e.g., Schoonenberg, *Geloof,* IV, 162, 181.

75 For that reason the analogy of attribution is also called the analogy of relationship or even of external relationship.

76 These are mentioned by Schoonenberg (*Geloof,* IV, 181). Similar examples are used by Angelius (pp. 238-39).

> ... we see in original sin not a lower degree, a more limited realization of what "sin" is in comparison with personal sin, but a directedness to personal sin. The concept "sin" is attributed to original sin because one thinks of original sin in relation to ("analogia") personal sin, but this relation is, in the first instance, not that of a lower to a higher degree ("analogia proportionalitatis"), but of a "belonging-to" ("analogia attributionis").[77]

In this case, sin is the *analogum*, and personal sin and original sin are the *analogata*. Personal sin is the primary analogue and original sin the secondary analogue.[78] The relationship to personal sin by virtue of which a situation may be qualified as original *sin* can be further specified in terms of the two main ways in which a secondary analogue may be related to a primary analogue, namely, as cause and as effect. Both of these relational directions apply to the situation of original sin, for, as Schoonenberg says, this situation "*arises from* and *inclines to* personal sin."[79]

Though stressing that primarily the analogy of attribution is applicable to original sin conceived of as situation, Schoonenberg contends that the analogy of proportionality is not entirely excluded.[80] As evidence of a similarity within a difference of degree (analogy of proportion) between personal sin and the situation of original sin, Schoonenberg adduces several facts: in the first place, original sin is a situation that is determinative for one's inner being and "therefore can be called a passive *habitus* or condition; furthermore, this situation is not simply a neutral absence, but a real deprivation of grace; and finally, this situation is a curtailment of the spiritual dynamism of our nature, its directedness towards love."[81] On the basis of these facts, Schoonenberg concludes that original sin, interpreted as situation, may also be seen as an instance of the analogy of proportionality. In the very next sentence, however, he adds a qualification which is tantamount to the demolition of the foundation for that analogy: "But this similarity [in a lower degree] does not extend to all elements: *voluntarietas* is restricted to personal sin."[82] Though

---

77 *Geloof*, IV, 181.
78 *Ibid.*, 162, 181.
79 *Geloof*, IV, 181. Cf. *Man and Sin*, 104; *MS*, II, 890. This description of original sin as situation is significant, for it is an allusion to Trent's description of the concupiscence that remais after baptism. Trent teaches that "the guilt of original sin" and "everything having the true and proper nature of sin" is removed by baptism. Concerning the concupiscence that remains the Council declares "that the Catholic Church has never understood that it is called sin because there is, in the regenerated, sin in the true and proper sense, but only because it is *from sin* and *inclines to sin, ex peccato est et ad peccatum inclinat*" (*DS*, 1515, emphasis added; see Introduction, sec. A, 8, e above).
80 *Geloof*, IV, 181.
81 *Ibid.*, 181-82.
82 *Ibid.*, 182.

wholly in keeping with Schoonenberg's conception of situation, this elimination of voluntariness is presented as far too innocuous a procedure. Presented as merely one of several elements of personal sin, voluntariness seems capable of elimination without jeopardizing the applicability of the analogy of proportionality that was posited in the preceding sentence. Voluntariness, however, is not merely one of several elements of personal sin but its *indispensable* element, its *sine qua non*. In fact, in Schoonenberg's conception, voluntariness is the indispensable element of the *analogum* itself, i.e., of sin.[83] If original sin is to represent a true instance of the analogy of proportionality, a degree of voluntariness must be intrinsically present in the situation. But here and elsewhere, Schoonenberg expressly and methodically excludes every trace of voluntariness from situation.[84] Not only has he eliminated voluntariness from the situation generally, but also from each element now adduced as evidence of the analogy of proportionality.[85] That does not mean that original sin conceived of as situation cannot be qualified in any way as sin. It does mean that it cannot be qualified as being a lower degree of sin.

The specific way in which the situation of original sin can legitimately be qualified as sin can be elucidated by returning to an earlier question: In what sense does this situation fulfill what Schoonenberg considers to be the indispensable condition of the doctrine of original sin, namely, that it fall within the boundaries of the moral-religious realm?[86] Since the basis for that realm is free act,[87] original sin as situation does not belong to that realm *intrinsically*, for situation is expressly defined as a datum for free decision, as a passive reality (*being* situated). Situation belongs to the moral-religious realm, not by virtue of an (active) quality of its own, but by virtue of its *relationship to* (analogy of attribution) free, personal decision, namely, as a datum-*for-free-decision*. The legitimacy of speaking of the situation of original sin as a moral-religious reality – as sin – is derived from its context, namely, the personal decisions at its origin and at its point of impact in the present.

Although this limited qualification of original sin as a moral-religious reality is entirely legitimate, the question arises whether Schoonen-

---

83 *SM*, IV, 773: "Das, was die Sünde zur Sünde macht, ist die Schuld. Sie besteht gerade in der freien Entscheidung zum Bösen, nämlich gegen Gott und Mensch."

84 See sec. C, 1, a above

85 From the *passive* habitus (*Geloof*, IV, 177, 182n, *MS*, II, 929-30), from the *situational* deprivation of grace (*Geloof*, IV, 177), and from the *natural* (in contrast to personal) dynamism of man's nature (*Geloof*, IV, 179).

86 See sec. C, 1, a above.

87 *Man and Sin*, 19, 171; *MS*, II, 853, 923; *Geloof*, IV, 48-49.

berg's critique of the identification of original sin with physical evil does not rebound with equal force upon his own construction: the identification of original sin with being situated by sin. Applied to the situation theory, that critique can be formulated as follows: Although the sinful situation has its origin in the moral-religious realm, as *situational* sin it stands outside that realm.[88] It is true that, in comparison to physical evil, situational sin stands "closer" to the moral-religious realm in that this situation has personal sin as its exclusive *source*. Nevertheless, in its *existence* situational sin, like physical evil, represents a mode of being which is opposite to the mode of being of the reality that constitutes the indispensable basis for the moral-religious realm, namely, the reality of free act. Whereas the uniqueness of a moral-religious phenomenon consists in active freedom, the uniqueness of "being situated" is its passive givenness.[89] The situation of original sin is therefore legitimately qualified by the moral-religious category "sin" only by virtue of the double relationship of this situation to ("arising from and inclining to") personal sin. In other words, conceived of as situation, original sin may be called sin only on the basis of the analogy of attribution.

Whether and in what sense the situation of original sin can be drawn more deeply and more intrinsically into the moral-religious realm by the personal sins of the present is a question that will be considered in the following chapter. First, the struggle of Rahner and Weger with the problem of the guilt-character of the situation of original sin must be considered. Perhaps their combined intellectual strength, directed as it is along paths not travelled by Schoonenberg, will uncover a relationship between guilt and the situation of original sin that is more intrinsic than that which has been established to this point.

2. Guilt as *Terminus a quo* or *ad quem*: Rahner and Weger

In view of the strong emphasis that both Rahner and Weger place upon the analogical character of original sin, one might expect them to specify the nature of this analogy in terms of the two major types to which Schoonenberg appeals. This expectation is heightened when one observes that Rahner is of the opinion that the merely analogical similarity between personal and original sin has, up to the present time, been insufficiently elaborated[90] and

---

88 Cf. sec. C, 1, a above.
89 See ch. I, sec. A, 3 above.
90 *SM*, I, 1107-108.

that Weger considers the demonstration of the analogical guilt-character of original sin to be the principal theme of his study.[91] Neither Rahner nor Weger, however, provides a formal explication of the type of analogy that is entailed. Instead, they at times set out from an undifferentiated notion of guilt and from that point attempt to arrive at an understanding of original sin ("a"); at other times, conversely, they set out from a very specific conception of original sin and from there attempt to arrive at an understanding of its guilt-character ("b"). The point of departure, direction and progress of these two approaches can usually be charted more clearly in terms of Rahner's essays, while the existential struggle in following these routes becomes more palpable in Weger's treatment. We shall use Rahner as the main guide along the common routes ("a" and "b, i, ii");[92] thereafter, we shall briefly retrace Weger's journey along these same routes before joining him as he sets out on a path not trodden by Rahner ("b, iii").

a. *From "Guilt" to "Original Sin"*

The point of departure from which the question as to the guilt-character of original sin is approached emerges with great clarity in Rahner's essays because of his concentric method of theologizing, a method in which every specific doctrine is initially reduced to the central message of Christianity.[93] The danger of this method is, of course, that the multifaceted confessions that have arisen in concrete historical situations are reduced to a meagre theological residue.[94] However real this danger may be, it is remarkable that this method yields basically two different answers to the question concerning the primary ground of the doctrine of original sin and thus provides two different points of departure for demonstrating the guilt-character of original sin. One of these will be considered in this section ("a").

In one of his essays on original sin, Rahner begins by setting forth some fundamental methodological principles. In doing so, he also gives an initial answer concerning the basis and core of this doctrine. The doctrine of original sin, says Rahner, is a theological-protological given. Even in its New Testament form that doctrine is not itself primary revelation and thus not an origi-

---

91 Weger, *Theologie der Erbsünde*, 29.
92 In these sections, Weger's appeal to arguments similar to those of Rahner will be indicated in the footnotes.
93 What we call concentric method, Rahner himself describes as a procedure involving a "reductio in mysterium" (*Schriften*, IX, 113-26; cf. IV, 82-99; VIII, 49-65). Formally this method is entirely parallel to the centripetal method which Schoonenberg advocates (see ch. I, n. 12 above).
94 Rahner is not unaware of this danger (see *Schriften*, IV, 82-83).

nal point of departure but a theological unfolding of and deduction from that primary revelation.[95] In other words, the doctrine of original sin is not simply one among many other revealed data that, as revelation, constitute a plurality of coordinate primary givens. Rather, the doctrine of original sin (like other doctrines) is itself a derivative of the more original revelation. That doctrine is understood, therefore, only by going beneath it in etiological retrospection to that *primum datum:* revelation. In this context Rahner goes beyond these methodological remarks to describe the original revelation from which the doctrine of original sin is derived. That revelational point of departure is, according to Rahner, man's knowledge of himself in the Christian *Grundoffenbarung* as a sinner who obtains forgiveness and salvation (*Heil*) only through Jesus Christ.[96]

That in this context forgiving grace should take on central importance as the ground of the doctrine of original sin is a remarkable and significant outcome of Rahner's concentric approach. Since the central mystery of Christianity is, in Rahner's view, elevating or divinizing grace,[97] one would expect this mystery to be uncovered at the outset as the ground of the doctrine of original sin. That this is not the case is evidence of the fact that in this context Rahner's concentric method and his conception of the core of Christianity are linked sufficiently loosely to allow the concrete material to control the outcome of his enquiry concerning the ground of the doctrine of original sin. Although this flexibility pleads for the care with which Rahner employs his method, its initial result does present an internal problem: how can forgiving grace, as ground of the doctrine of original sin, yield the privational definition of original sin, a definition that is grounded, as we shall see, in the idea of divinizing grace?

One could argue that a basis for that privational conception of original sin is already present in the context now under consideration, namely, in Rahner's juxtapositioning of *Heil* and *forgiveness,* since in Rahner's thought the term *Heil* designates primarily the idea of divinizing rather than forgiving grace.[98] Divinizing grace, however, has as its counterpart man as nature. Since, in the present context, Rahner speaks explicitly and exclusively of man as sinner, it is illegitimate to weaken the clear emphasis on forgiving grace by

---

95 *Schriften,* IX, 261.
96 *Ibid.* Cf. Weger, *Theologie der Erbsünde,* 16, 24, 28, 161, 162 (in connection with baptism "in remissionem peccatorum").
97 See ch. II, A, 2 above. In the following discussion preference has generally been given to the term "divinizing grace" because it designates the sense in which man is "elevated."
98 See ch. II, sec. A, 2

an appeal to the as yet undefined term *Heil*. In any case, the central role initially assigned to the notion of forgiving grace within the context of the doctrine of original sin becomes even more explicit when Rahner again returns to the focal point of revelation. There Rahner again emphasizes that in Scripture the salvific efficacy of Christ (*Heilsursächlichkeit Christi*) is always seen as being directed to man as sinner and not only to man as a being for whom God's grace as divinization is unowed (man as nature).[99] This accentuation is the more striking in that it represents an inversion of the more prevalent emphasis: grace is divinization, not only forgiveness.[100]

Before turning to the idea of divinizing grace as point of departure for determining the guilt-character of original sin, the salient features of the initial departure from grace as forgiveness may be summarized. On the one hand, in proceeding from grace as forgiveness, divinizing grace is not out of the picture. On the other hand, more significant is the way in which divinizing grace comes into view, namely, in initial subordination to grace as forgiveness. Whether this clear and methodic subordination of divinizing grace is maintained cannot but become manifest in terms of the question as to the guilt-character of original sin. As Rahner's initial steps indicate, the notions of sin and guilt have an inherent tendency of drawing the idea of forgiving grace into a position of predominance. Especially in determining the guilt-character of original sin, therefore, the notion of grace as forgiveness may rightly be expected to fulfill the dominant role.

b. *From "Divinizing Grace" via "Privation of Grace" to "Guilt"*

That Rahner's and Weger's interpretation of the doctrine of original sin should be *centrally* based upon the idea of divinizing grace is as such not surprising in view of the preponderance of this notion in their general theological framework.[101] Nor is the fact that they appeal to the notion of *both* forgiving *and* divinizing grace surprising, for in their conception these two notions are clearly compatible.[102] Nevertheless, the appeal to the notion of divinizing grace in this context remains startling for three interrelated reasons. In the first place, the attempt is made to derive the guilt-character of original sin from a notion of grace that as such has no intrinsic reference to sin and guilt. Secondly, despite its lack of intrinsic reference to the notion of sin,

---

99 *Schriften*, IX, 271-72.
100 See ch. II, sec. A, 2 above.
101 See ch. II above.
102 See ch. II, sec. A, 2 above.

divinizing grace becomes the *preponderant* idea for determining the guilt-character of original sin. Thirdly, the notion of divinizing grace becomes preponderant as primary ground despite the fact that Rahner also points to another ground for the doctrine of original sin, namely, the *Grundoffenbarung* that discloses man as *sinner* before God's *forgiving* grace.

The transition from forgiving grace to divinizing grace as ground of the doctrine of original sin and basis for determining its guilt-character may well be legitimate, but then one would expect its legitimacy to become transparent, especially in view of the fact that Rahner's concentric method repeatedly occasions the question as to the ground of a particular doctrine. If that very method applied to a single doctrine yields what appears to be two grounds, one may rightly expect a further application of that method to indicate how one ground in fact derives from the other. That inner connection, however, is not demonstrated in this case.

The fact that neither Rahner nor Weger indicate the inner connection between divinizing and forgiving grace need not mean, of course, that no inner connection in fact exists. To Rahner and Weger the connection between these grounds may seem so self-evident and so intrinsic that its demonstration is considered to be superfluous.[103] Since this hypothesis is not verified at the *starting point* of the path that leads from divinizing grace, it must be tested at the *terminal point* of that path. Proceeding from the idea of divinizing grace, Rahner's and also Weger's destination is a notion of original sin as real, analogical guilt. If the notion of guilt *arrived at* in this way is closely akin to the notion of guilt from which Rahner *started* by positing forgiving grace as original ground, the conclusion is warranted that what appeared to be two disparate grounds are in fact intrinsically related and may perhaps even be reduced to a single, genuinely primary ground.

At a later point in the essay which he began by designating the complex "man as sinner – forgiving grace" as the *Grundoffenbarung* on which the doctrine of original sin rests,[104] Rahner returns to the question concerning the original datum from which this doctrine may be derived. Here he posits the same ground that he posited at the beginning but now adds a qualification which represents an inversion of an immediately preceding emphasis: he has just emphasized that grace is not merely divinization,[105] but now emphasizes that grace is not merely forgiveness. In the final analysis, Rahner contends, the doctrine of original sin is a direct implication of the truth a) that all men

---

103 See *Schriften*, IX, 272.
104 See the immediately preceding section ("a").
105 See *ibid*.

as inners need to be redeemed by way of Christ and b) that this redemption consists not merely of some kind of liberation from guilt, but of that justifying sanctification in which God communicates His own holiness in His Holy Spirit.[106] Both Rahner and Weger indicate that the latter conception of grace is decisive for a proper understanding of the doctrine of original sin.[107]

The decisive significance of this concept of grace for the doctrine of original sin becomes explicit when in the "Preliminary considerations" that precede his elaboration of this doctrine Rahner once again raises the question concerning its ground.[108] Remarkably, Rahner answers that question without any reference to the ground adduced elsewhere as basic to the doctrine of original sin, namely, forgiving grace. Rejecting the notion that original sin represents an irrational mystery, Rahner posits the mystery of sanctifying grace as the *proper ground* of the mystery of original sin.[109] Sanctifying grace as such does not refer to a process in which man is cleansed from sin. Accordingly, Rahner explicates this concept of grace wholly with reference to man conceived of as "nature," i.e., as recipient of elevating grace. Sanctifying grace, he says, involves the *self*communication of the essentially (ontologically) holy God. The holiness that is communicated to man is *proper* only to God.[110] This explication represents a restatement of the conception of grace which was examined earlier, namely, grace as the free communication (mode of "grace") of God's inner nature itself (the content of "grace").[111] For the

106 *Schriften,* IX, 272: "...die Erbsündenlehre [ist] letztlich eine schlichte Implikation... in der Wahrheit, [a] dass wir alle als Sünder von Christus her erlöst sind und erlöst werden müssen, [b] dass diese Erlösung nicht bloss in irgendeiner Schuldbefreiung, sondern in jener rechtfertigenden Heiligung besteht, in der Gott die eigene Heiligkeit in seinem heiligen Pneuma mitteilt, und [c] dass in diesem ganzen Heilsgeschehen der Einzelne immer gemeint ist, insofern er auch Glied der einen Menschheit ist, die Christus sowohl voraussetzt als auch konstituiert." The third aspect ("c") has been touched upon when the situational privation of grace was qualified as being spatiotemporal (sec. A above) and will come into view once more in the discussion of God's will with respect to the communication of grace (sec. C, 2, b, ii below).

107 Weger, *Theologie der Erbsünde,* 18; Rahner, *Exkurs,* 187, n.16. Whether this conception of grace is legitimately raised to a norm by stating, as Rahner does, that it is decisive for understanding *the orthodox* doctrine of original sin (*ibid.*) may, at this stage of our discussion, remain a moot point. In the present context, it is sufficient to establish that this conception of grace is decisive for *Rahner's* (as well as Weger's) understanding of the orthodox doctrine of original sin.

108 *SM,* I, 1108, *SMe,* IV, 330.

109 *Ibid.*

110 *Ibid.*

111 Ch. II, sec. A, 2 above. See also *Schriften,* IV, 73-75 where Rahner articulates the central mystery of Christianity (man's relationship to God's inner being) as being a *holy* mystery: "... *Gott* [ist] wesentlich *als* heiliges Geheimnis dem Menschen gegeben..." (*ibid.,* 75).

purpose of explaining the nature of original sin, however, Rahner has restated this conception in terms of "holiness." Since it is God's very own nature, this ontological holiness (content) can become a *quality of man* only *by grace* (mode), i.e., by virtue of God's free decision to share His own inner being with another being. In the present context, therefore, Rahner speaks implicitly of man as nature when he says that *of himself* man lacks this holiness and when he describes man accordingly as an *ambivalent* creature.[112] In contrast to God, man by (his proper) nature lacks this quality of holiness and is in that sense "by nature" *not* holy. This ambivalence is overcome *in* and *by* grace: God freely communicates Himself to man, conferring His holiness upon him. Grace is thus seen to be essentially *sanctifying* grace: divine holiness becomes a (bestowed) quality of human nature.

In the context of the doctrine of original sin and especially with reference to the question of guilt, this translation of the framework of grace-nature into holiness-unholiness is crucial, for the latter pair introduces an "ethical" category,[113] though of a peculiar type. As both Rahner and Weger emphasize, in its common sense, ethical qualification applies only to a reality involving man's free decisions. No *creaturely* reality is in itself ethically qualified as holy (or unholy), but is taken up into the moral order by personal, free decisions.[114] The term "ethical" is a qualification of man's voluntary good (or evil) conduct, of his existential acts. The reality of *grace*, however, introduces a decisively different ethical qualification into the human realm.[115] Because God is *essentially* holy, the communication of His nature renders man holy *pre*personally, i.e., *before* (ontically, not necessarily temporally) his free decisions.[116] In the present context, therefore, holiness is truly a quality *of* man but it does not proceed *from* man, does not have its origin in man; by grace it is *man's divine* quality. In short, the quality of

112 *SM*, I, 1108, *SM*e, IV, 330. Rahner frequently speaks explicitly of nature as being inherently ambivalent (see ch. I, n. 182 above).
113 Cf. Rahner, *Exkurs*, 187-88, n. 16.
114 Weger, *Theologie der Erbsünde*, 17-18, 151, 163; Rahner, *Exkurs*, 187-88, n. 16.
115 Cf. Weger, *Theologie der Erbsünde*, 18. In view of the *analogical* sense of "guilt" that will be based upon this (divine) "ethical" quality of man, it must be noted that the term ethical as predicated of man by virtue of his divine quality of holiness, on the one hand, and by virtue of his own free acts, on the other, represents an *equivocal* use of that term.
116 Weger, *Theologie der Erbsünde*, 17-18, 151; Rahner, *SM*, I, 1108, 1111, *SM*e, IV, 330, 331. Cf. Rahner's description of grace as an *"existential, vorexistentiell* durch Gottes eigene Heiligkeit mitgeteilten Heiligkeit . . ." (*Schriften*, IX, 268, emphasis added). In this context, it becomes manifest that the duality person-nature cuts through the duality nature-grace. To indicate this interpenetration of the two complexes the theological concept of "nature" (see ch. II, n. 2 above) will be designated by the capitalized

divine holiness imparted to man is a (preexistential) relational ontological determination — man's supernatural *Existential*.[117]

i. *Privation of grace as "unholiness"*

On the journey that proceeds from the idea of divinizing grace and has as its goal an understanding of the guilt-character of original sin, both Rahner and Weger begin, as we have seen, by appealing to the fact that this grace entails the communication of God's *holiness*. They contend that without this conception original sin cannot be understood as man's real guilt before God.[118] Weger argues that because only God Himself can render man holy even prior to man's personal decision, the guilt of original sin *must* consist of the absence of God's sanctifying grace. Only in this way can original sin be maintained as inherited *sin* ("Erbsünde") rather than being reduced to inherited *evil* ("Erbübel").[119] Rahner argues this position more clearly. The idea of grace as the self-communication of the *essentially holy* God is indispensable for understanding the doctrine of original sin, he contends, because in a purely "natural" order no *ethical* goodness, no righteousness and holiness that precedes the moral decision of a person can exist. Accordingly, in such an order no moral evil anterior to the free self-disposal (and thus the personal sin) of the individual can exist.[120] In an order of grace, however, an order in which God communicates His own holiness to man, a prepersonal ethical qualification *is* possible: the situational privation of grace (divine holiness) renders man un-holy anterior to his free decision. This privation of holiness is man's original sin.[121]

At this point, the question becomes acute as to the sense in which this situational privation of holiness may be called sin and guilt. If anywhere, it is in this context that the term *Schuld* appears to be used merely in its minimal sense of "debt,"[122] in this case an inherited debt: the absence of something that might and should have been present, but isn't because of the sins of the fathers. This minimal conception of *Schuld* seems the more plausible insofar

---

term Nature: Man's quality of holiness is *grace,* i.e. a free gift that God bestows upon man, who of himself is simply *Nature*; since this gift of grace constitutes a prepersonal ontological determination of man, however, it represents *nature* in relationship to man as free *person*.

117 See ch. II, B, 3 above.
118 Rahner, *Exkurs,* 187-88, n. 16; Weger, *Theologie der Erbsünde,* 17-18.
119 Weger, *Theologie der Erbsünde,* 151; cf. 17, 163.
120 *Exkurs,* 187, n. 16.
121 *Ibid.*, 188, n. 16.
122 The German term *Schuld* can denote both the idea of *debitum* (debt) and the idea of *culpa* (guilt).

as it is in accordance with the medieval tradition within which the situationalists stand, namely, the tradition which characterizes original sin as *privatio debitae justitiae*.[123] Despite its seeming plausibility, however, this minimal conception of *Schuld* is manifestly unacceptable to both Rahner and Weger in their reinterpretation of original sin. If they could have been satisfied with this notion of *Schuld,* the guilt-character of original sin would not have presented them with any problem whatsoever. But as their arduous argumentation indicates the question as to the meaning of the term *Schuld* with respect to original sin represents a genuine problem precisely because the primary referent (analogue) of original sin is and remains personal sin, i.e., guilt and sin in their proper sense. Accordingly, both Rahner and Weger are at great pains to point out that the situational privation of grace entails real guilt and may in a true sense be called sin.[124] Moreover, the present argument based on the idea of grace as the communication of divine holiness is in itself a clear indication of the fact that Rahner and Weger wish to move beyond a conception of original sin as debt.

The question remains, therefore, in what sense this situational deprivation of holiness can be described as sin and guilt of the person thus deprived? If holiness were taken to be a quality attributed to man by virtue of his moral conduct, the association of unholiness with sin or guilt would be beyond dispute. But every ethical qualification deriving from *man's* free decision has been expressly and unequivocally excised from this concept of holiness. This holiness consists of God's own being and can therefore be a quality of man only by virtue of *God's* free decision to self-communication. Even though it must be granted that within the nature-grace framework the *presence* of this holy quality in man may be qualified as ethical in a unique (prepersonal) sense,[125] it is difficult to conceive how the situational *absence* of that holy quality can be characterized as being an *ethical* reality — even in the unique sense of the term "ethical." In this context, "unholy" appears to mean nothing more than "*non*holy," i.e., a situational absence of a prepersonal holiness that might have been. That absence of holiness is indeed brought

---

123 See Introduction, A, 6 above.
124 Rahner, *Schriften,* II, 101; IX, 25, 268, 272; *Exkurs,* 192; *SM,* I, 1111, *SMe,* IV, 331; Weger, *Theologie der Erbsünde,* 16, 17, 18, 31, 152, 158-59, 161. Although Rahner expresses indifference with respect to the term "original *sin*" ("Erb*sünde*"; *Schriften,* IX, 263; cf. V, 69-70; *Exkurs,* 192), he also says that the reality intended is legitimately called a condition of sinfulness ("wird mit Recht ein Zustand der Sündigkeit genannt"; *Schriften,* IX, 268; cf. 272).
125 This is not entirely unproblematical due to the equivocal use of the term ethical (see nn. 115, 116 above).

about by the guilt of preceding generations, but for the succeeding generations this situation represents the fate of inescapable deprivation.

As one of the steps between the idea of grace as divinization and the guilt-character of original sin, the argument that the situational privation of this grace renders man unholy must carry its own weight.[126] At the same time, it must be kept in mind that this argument is frequently combined with an appeal to the idea that the situational privation of grace is counter to God's will. In other words, holiness as a prepersonal but concrete quality of every human being is not merely a situation that might have been, but a situation that ought to have been.

ii. *Situational privation counter to God's will*

At times Rahner indicates that the situational absence of a divine quality of holiness is insufficient ground for understanding original sin as guilt.[127] He then appeals to the idea that God wills to communicate his grace via other human beings. In the communication of grace, God wishes to work via the historical solidarity and continuity of mankind. This mode of grace-communication has already been touched upon in connection with the spatiotemporal nature of the privation of grace.[128] In connection with the problem of guilt, all the emphasis falls upon the idea that God *wills* this mode of communication.[129] Consequently, original sin is usually defined as an absence of holiness counter to God's will;[130] or, more positively, as an absence of holiness experienced in confrontation with God's will which demands its situational presence.[131] This more positive formulation is significant for the conception of Rahner and Weger, for in itself the frequent appeal to the idea that God demands the situational presence of grace appears tantamount to an arbitrary appeal to an equally arbitrary divine decree.[132] Although the appeal to a divine decree is undeniable, for Rahner and Weger

---

126 Accordingly, the guilt-character of original sin is frequently assumed to be demonstrated by a casual appeal to the present argument (see Weger, *Theologie der Erbsünde,* 17, 18, 23, 151, 163; Rahner, *Exkurs,* 187-88, n. 16; *SM,* I, 1111, *SM*e, IV, 331.

127 *SM,* I, 1111, *SM*e IV, 331; *Schriften,* IX, 268-69.

128 Sec. A above.

129 This emphasis is formally wholly in accord with Anselm's understanding of *debitum* (See Gross, III, 20-21).

130 Cf. Rahner, *SM,* I, 1108: "Das *nicht sein sollende* Fehlen dieser 'Heiligkeit' . . . ." Cf. Weger, *Theologie der Erbsünde,* 154.

131 Rahner, *SM,* I, 1108, *SM*e, IV, 330; *Schriften,* IX, 269.

132 See Schrofner, "Theologie der Erbsünde mit und ohne Fragezeichen," *ZKTh,* XCIII (1971), 204.

this decree is not simply deduced from or postulated upon the basis of word-revelation but is manifested and experienced in God's present act-revelation.[133] That God indeed wills to mediate his grace via interhuman communication is not a conclusion drawn from speculation regarding a *primordial* state of affairs, but a reality disclosed by the *present* order of salvation:[134] despite modifications necessitated due to the disruptive effect of sin, God continues to communicate Himself to the individual only via his solidarity with fellowman.[135]

The fact that God wills the interhuman, prepersonal communication of grace provides a ground for understanding the privation of that grace as guilt, for guilt always implies an "ought," a legitimate demand which is not complied with. The fact that, due to the disruptive effect of sin, solidarity with mankind and historical rootedness in the lineage of generations does not adequately and reliably communicate grace to the individual is contrary to God's will. In that sense, privation of grace and personal sin are analogical phenomena: they are *similar* in that both involve falling short with respect to God's demand; they *differ* in that personal sin goes counter to the will of God as law-giver, while original sin goes counter to the will of God as self-communicating Creator. As law-giver God demands that the personal decisions of the individual comply with ethical norms. As self-communicating Creator, God designs a certain structure within which these personal decisions are to take place: He demands that the situational presence of grace constitute the prepersonal spatiotemporal *Existential* of each human being.[136] Because the situational absence of grace represents not a mere *Nichtgegebensein*, but a *Nichtgegebensein* in face of a *Gegebenseinsollen*, it involves analogical guilt.[137]

What is the nature of this guilt? In this context, the minimal meaning

---

133 Rahner, *SM* I, 1113-14, *SMe*, IV, 332-33; *Schriften*, IX, 261, 271. Weger, *Theologie der Erbsünde*, 34, 108.

134 Accordingly, Weger continually emphasizes that, rather than appealing to an *original* (but abrogated) divine decree, he will appeal only to *presently* functioning anthropological and redemptive historical structures (*Theologie der Erbsünde*, 75, 107-108, 136, 139, 150, 153).

135 Rahner, *Schriften*, IX, 267-68, 272; *Exkurs*, 188-89; Weger, *Theologie der Erbsünde*, 127-37.

136 Rahner, *SM*, I, 1108, 1109, 1111; *SMe*, IV, 330, 331; *Schriften*, IX, 268, 270; *Exkurs*, 190. Though Rahner often speaks simply of God's *"creative* will" in this context, he means the factual, i.e., self-communicating Creator. Accordingly, Rahner at one point refers to this divine will emphatically as the *"konkreter* Schöpfungswille" (*SM*, I, 1111, *SMe*, IV, 331).

137 Rahner, *Schriften*, IX, 269. Cf. Weger, *Theologie der Erbsünde*, 126, 162.

of *Schuld* discussed earlier appears to gain the upperhand once again, except that now the "ought" implied in that concept has come more clearly into focus. The situational privation of grace constitutes a debt of *mankind* because, as self-communicating Creator, God legitimately demands the situational presence of grace. At the same time, the very clarification of the unique "ought" entailed in the *Schuld* given with the privation of grace increases the difficulty encountered in understanding this privation as sin, for without any fault of his own the individual can in no way comply with this particular demand of God.[138] But in that case, in what sense can God's *continuing demand* for the situational presence of grace be legitimate?

Rahner is not unaware of the difficulty encountered in the attempt to derive the analogical character of original *sin* from the idea of God's *will* as self-communicating Creator. When this problem becomes explicit, however, he has recourse to the argument that the privation of grace renders man "unholy." Rahner acknowledges that the privation of grace is not sinful simply because it is against God's will, for a mere *consequence* of sin is also contrary to God's will; yet it as such does not render anyone unholy. By contrast, the privation of *ontological holiness* (grace) does render man unholy.[139] Although this unholiness as such is entirely conceivable within Rahner's theological framework,[140] the recourse to that conception at this critical juncture does not solve the problem at hand. Instead of demonstrating that situational privation of grace counter to God's will is sin, this reversion to the argument from prepersonal holiness leads to circular argumentation: privation of grace counter to God's will is sin because, deprived of holiness, man is unholy; but this unholiness is sin only because it is counter to God's will.[141] The axis of this argument is the ambiguous use of the term "sin." In the context of God's will it connotes *"Schuld"* in the sense of debt. In the context of unholiness it connotes "impurity," "stain." In neither case, however, can an intrinsic analogy between original sin (privation of grace) and personal sin be sustained, for man is conceived to be in debt but in no way culpable; unholy but in no way stained.

iii. *Development from prepersonal privation to personal sin*

While Rahner leaves us in a seeming impasse, Weger in effect, attempts

---

138 *SM*, I, 1108, 1111; *SM*e, IV, 330, 331.
139 *SM*, I, 1111; *SM*e, IV, 331.
140 See ch. II, sec. A, 2.
141 See also Rahner, *Schriften* IX, 269; Weger, *Theologie der Erbsünde*, 126, 162.

to liberate the idea of original sin from the circle that confines it to a situational debt of holiness; he does this with a view to linking original sin intrinsically to personal sin. In order to capture the climactic significance accruing to this last phase of Weger's restless odyssey in search of the analogical nature of original sin, his prior itinerary, already presented in substance, will be briefly recapitulated.

From the outset Weger has placed the question of the guilt-character of original sin central to his entire reinterpretation. He has done so by positing, as an indispensable element of this doctrine, the idea that original sin constitutes real guilt on the part of those subject to this condition,[142] and by calling the demonstration of the precise nature of the analogy between personal sin and original sin the principal theme of his subsequent investigations.[143] After having set forth the anthropological as well as the theological framework for reinterpreting original sin, and having demonstrated that the interiority of historical situatedness can be transposed directly to the specific situation of original sin, Weger comes to what he calls the critical point of every reinterpretation of this doctrine.[144] He formulates that point in terms of the question whether being situated by sin itself constitutes real guilt, i.e., whether this prepersonal situatedness is sin. He explicates this question by asking what constitutes the analogy between personal and original sin.[145]

The analogy which Weger uncovers can be summarized in terms of its constituents, namely, similarity and difference. The first and central similarity between personal and original sin to which Weger points is that both involve a loss of grace; and since grace is God's holiness (God Himself), its loss renders man unholy.[146] Moreover, the situational privation of grace is against God's will.[147] Finally, like personal sin, original sin is "one's own" sin, for it is one's *interior Existential*.[148] The basic difference between personal sin and original sin is that the absence of grace in the former is caused by and consists of *personal* resistance to God, and in the latter is caused by others and consti-

---

142 Weger, *Theologie der Erbsünde*, 16. Here and elsewhere, Weger grounds the necessity of affirming the guilt-character of original sin in the fact that infant baptism is performed "in remissionem peccatorum" (cf. *ibid.*, 24, 28, 158, 161, 162).
143 Ibid., 29; see also Weger, *Erbsünde heute: Grundlegung und Verkündigungshilfen* (München: Don Bosco, 1972), 10, 19.
144 *Theologie der Erbsünde*, 151.
145 *Ibid.*
146 *Ibid.*, 151-52; cf. *Erbsünde heute*, 23-24.
147 *Theologie der Erbsünde*, 126, 152, 154, 161, 162.
148 *Ibid.*, 152, 154-55, 157, 161, 163.

tutes a *prepersonal* spatiotemporal situation.[149] The conjunction of these essential differences and similarities is indicative of an analogical relationship between personal and original sin. From that point of view, Weger has indeed demonstrated the reality of a "fremdverursachte, dem Menschen aber trotzdem innere und eigene Schuld vor Gott."[150] The analogy having been established, one would expect Weger to proceed simply by elaborating and refining this analogical reality. Interestingly, however, that which is frequently presented and appealed to as solid ground for the guilt-character of original sin suddenly crumbles. This occurs when, in a discussion of "original sin in the unbaptized infant,"[151] Weger openly admits the inadequacy of the case established so far. Before examining Weger's surprising admission, a comment must be made regarding the possibility that this admission is neither surprising nor significant in view of the unique case being considered, namely, the case of the infant. The inadequacy which Weger admits could be restricted to this unique case.

That restriction seems plausible in the light of some of Weger's statements that suggest that one cannot speak of free decisions in the case of an infant.[152] In that case, the infant constitutes a radically unique human being and the inadequacy of Weger's previous case for the guilt-character of original sin obtains only with respect to the infant. Though seemingly plausible, this restrictions does not in fact hold, for it must be kept in mind that the guilt-character of original sin which Weger has established earlier is carefully and emphatically demarcated from the free decisions that constitute personal sin: original sin, not only in infants but also in adults, is (ontically) a *pre*-personal reality. Moreover, Weger acknowledges that some kind of freedom is present in the infant too. On that basis the infant is treated – as a borderline case, to be sure – from the viewpoint of adult personal decisions.[153]

Weger's discussion of the unbaptized infant represents a final concentration upon the vexing question concerning the guilt-character of original sin.[154] Although he considers the sinfulness of an unbaptized infant to be a fact that is beyond dispute for Catholic theology, he recognizes the difficulties that stand in the way of understanding that sinfulness as real guilt.[155] It is at this point that Weger makes the astonishing admission that these difficul-

---

149 *Ibid.*; cf. *Erbsünde heute*, 23-24.
150 *Theologie der Erbsünde*, 152.
151 *Ibid.*, 161-75.
152 *Ibid.*, 164, 172.
153 *Ibid.*, 69, 108, 137, 161-64.
154 *Ibid.*, 161.
155 *Ibid.*, 162.

ties are not resolved by the *correct* observation that the infant is deprived of sanctifying grace (God's holiness), on the one hand, and, that this absence is contrary to God's will, on the other.[156] But these are the principal arguments which Weger has employed thus far to demonstrate the guilt-character of original sin. Why do they fail him now?

Weger ascribes the inadequacy of these arguments to the contemporary personalistic climate of thought. Within that pattern of thought, concepts such as grace and sin are closely conjoined with man's personal, free acts. As a result, Weger contends, there is no room for a conception of prepersonal grace and even less for a notion of *pre*personal *sin*.[157] Our time no longer possesses a *Verständnishorizont,* says Weger, within which such notions can be placed.[158]

This diagnosis of the source of the difficulty encountered in understanding the privation of grace as guilt touches upon the hermeneutical dimension of that problem: a discrepancy is discovered between the past horizon of understanding within which the doctrine of original sin was developed and the present horizon within which that doctrine is being reinterpreted. That diagnosis calls for a choice with respect to the remedy for resolving the present difficulty. The interpreter can demonstrate the legitimacy of the old horizon, accept the reality of the modern horizon, or point out the contours of a third and broader horizon. Both the first and the last choice entail a critical stance with respect to the modern *Verständnishorizont.*

At first glance, Weger's very formulation of the problem suggests that he indeed criticizes the modern thought-horizon as being illegitimately constricted: this horizon is so narrow that it cannot accommodate the indisputable fact of a prepersonal sinfulness of the infant. It soon becomes evident, however, that Weger does not present a fundamental critique of modern man's horizon of understanding, nor does he attempt to widen that horizon. Instead he accepts and attempts to work within it, for he wishes to uncover the sinfulness of the unbaptized infant by proceeding from the *personal* sin of the adult.[159] Weger adopts the modern horizon but says, in effect, all is not horizon: personal sin is the *horizon;* original sin is a phenomenon *within* that horizon, namely, the "*vor*personale Sündigkeit," the *pre*personal "Unheils-

---

156 *Ibid.,* 161-62

157 *Ibid.,* 163. From the outset Weger has pointed to this problem as constituting the principal difficulty that stands in the way of an understanding of the doctrine of original sin by modern man (*Theologie der Erbsünde,* 28).

158 *Ibid.,* 163.

159 *Ibid.,* 163-64; see n. 153 above.

situation."[160] Weger does not criticize the modern horizon; he takes modern man to task for being so obsessed with his horizon as to be oblivious of indispensable elements that loom within that horizon. With that the stage is set for Weger's final attempt to demonstrate the reality of prepersonal *sin*.[161]

Weger speaks of the infant as a borderline case of human sinfulness.[162] He does so because while sin is closely linked with free personal acts, the infant is not fully capable of such acts.[163] That does not mean that in Weger's view the child does not possess freedom, for freedom belongs to the essence of man.[164] Even if one wishes to ascribe to the child only the *possibility* of a *later* exercize of that freedom, Weger contends, even then that possibility must be acknowledged as being an inner *reality* that is *present* in this child.[165] If one wishes to *describe* this freedom, however, one cannot proceed phenomenologically in the sense of proceeding from the behavior and expressions of the infant. Rather, Weger continues, to clarify what freedom involves, one must proceed from the freedom of the adult.[166]

Applied to original sin, this approach proceeds from the free act of personal sin in an attempt to demonstrate that even an infant incapable of such acts stands in guilt before God. Weger describes this procedure as a *backward* movement, a regression from personal sin and says it is aimed at arriving at the very first beginnings of prepersonal sinfulness in man.[167] This *methodological* regression presupposes for its validity, however, a corresponding *actual* progression, namely, the development of man from infant to adult. Accordingly, Weger's present argument is suffused with terms such as becoming, growth, consummation, unfolding and realization.[168] This development, Weger holds, applies also to man's involvement in sin. Man's prepersonal sin-

---

160 *Ibid.,* 163-64.
161 This argument from development occurs in a discussion in which the question as to the efficacy of the sacrament of baptism also plays an important role. In the following presentation of the argument from development, its essential structure has been distilled from that discussion. The question as to the relation of sacramental grace and original sin will be considered in chapter VI below.
162 *Theologie der Erbsünde,* 161, 162, 163, 174.
163 *Ibid.,* 164; cf. 28, 172.
164 *Ibid.,* 164.
165 *Ibid.,* 163. The problem encountered in a slightly different form in Schoonenberg's appeal to the case of a child retaining only the capacity of freedom (ch. I, n. 142 above) emerges also in Weger's argumentation. That problem can be formulated as a paradoxical question: is a *real* inner *possibility* real if its realization is impossible? Or, to formulate the same problem differently, if freedom is an act, can it ever be pure potentiality?
166 *Theologie der Erbsünde,* 164.
167 *Ibid.,* 164; cf. 69, 167, 174.
168 *Ibid.,* 166-67, 171-74.

fulness progresses through the various stages of personal development.[169] Hence, prepersonal gracelessness (original sin as situation) is not a static, changeless phenomenon, but a dynamic, growing sinfulness which allows of an initial stage of inception and which attains its full reality in personal sin.[170] That, in a nutshell, is Weger's final argument for the guilt-character of original sin conceived of as the situational privation of grace. Does this final route succeed in breaking through the circle that confines the reality of original sin to an inculpable nonholiness counter to God's will?

The present argument appeals to two facts: in the first place, the reality of personal development with its concomitant possibility of development in personal sin and, secondly, the variety that obtains with respect to the situation of prepersonal sinfulness. Both are incontrovertible facts. The crucial point at issue, however, is whether development *of the kind* suggested by Weger is possible. Weger suggests not a mere progression in personal sin in *combination with* variations in prepersonal sinfulness but a continuous progression *from pre*personal sinfulness *to personal* sinfulness. But to move from prepersonal to personal sin involves not continuous growth, as suggested, but a *metabasis eis allo genos*. It involves a development from the *Existential* of gracelessness to the existential act of personal sin, from passive datum to active freedom, from "being situated" to "self-situating." Both realities, prepersonal and personal sin, always coexist; in fact, they continuously interact, but prepersonal "sin" — the situational privation of grace — cannot grow by continuous development into personal sin. Yet that is the kind of development Weger suggests when he says that by freely appropriating prepersonal sinfulness in his personal sin, man *becomes* what he already is.[171] Although the idea of appropriation is worthy of separate attention,[172] it must be pointed out with respect to the question under consideration that *this* conception of the relation "being-becoming" presupposes what it purports to prove. If, by continuous progression, man becomes (personal sinner) what he already is (prepersonally sinful), then "being situationally deprived of grace" must first be demonstrated to be sin in a true, be it (proportionally) analogical, sense. But *this* analogy is not demonstrated by positing a continuous progression from prepersonal privation to personal sin.[173]

169 *Ibid.*, 166.
170 *Ibid.*; cf. *Erbsünde heute*, 81-82.
171 *Theologie der Erbsünde*, 166; see also *ibid.*, 120, 135, 149-50, 169-70, 171, 174.
172 See chapter IV below.
173 This critique of Weger's final argument does not rest on a denial of one of his basic theses, namely, that man *is* also his *Existential* (in this case the situational privation of grace). Within a situationalist framework that thesis is incontrovertible: man *is* also his

Weger himself appears not to be unaware of the inadequacy even of this final argument, for even after having concluded — on the basis of this argument — that original sin (privation of grace) unfolds into personal sin, he himself states that the essential question remains to be answered: "Trotzdem bleibt noch zu fragen, worin nun näherin diese wirkliche Sündigkeit im ungetauften Kind besteht, wie das Fehlen der kategorial-geschichtlich zu vermittelnden Gnade Gottes allererstes Stadium menschlicher Schuld sein kann."[174] Weger's acknowledgement that this central question remains unanswered raises the expectation that the argument from human development will be further refined, or even that a new argument might possibly be introduced. Unfortunately, in what follows Weger reverts to the earlier argument that since grace renders man pre-personally holy its absence renders man correspondingly unholy. Only the *form* of that argument is changed in that sanctifying grace from which the argument proceeds is now explicated in terms of the grace dispensed in the sacrament of infant baptism.[175] Then, after this explication of sanctifying grace, Weger combines this earlier argument with the argument from development and concludes his study by summing up what he calls the decisive point of his reflection: on the basis of human *Unheilsgeschichte* a guilty absence of the sanctifying grace that should have been spatiotemporally mediated exists; this absence constitutes an interior determination of man's freedom that precedes personal sin, yet in an analogical way renders man guilty before God.[176]

That indeed accurately sums up not only the results of Weger's reinterpretation of original sin but also the essential question that remains: How within the horizon of personal freedom can the prepersonal absence of grace come into view as intrinsically analogical to personal sin. Having come to the very end of his tortuous odyssey in search of a solution to that problem,

---

situation; or more accurately, to-be-man is (also) to-be-situated (see ch. I, secs. A, 3 and B, 2, b above). The problem arises precisely when one grants this thesis, keeps in mind the nature of an *Existential* and attempts to conceive of a continuous development from a specific spatiotemporal *Existential* to personal sin, for to-be-situated and to-be-free-act, though unified in man, represent two distinct and opposite modes of being.

174 *Theologie der Erbsünde*, 167.

175 *Ibid.*, 167-73. The implications of the sacramental communication of grace for the situational reinterpretation of original sin will be given separate treatment (see chapter VI below).

176 *Theologie der Erbsünde*, 174: "Es gibt auf Grund menschlicher Unheilsgeschichte schuldhaftes Fehlen der kategorial zu vermittelnden, heiligmachenden Gnade. Dieses Fehlen göttlichen Gnadenangebots liegt der persönlichen Sünde des Menschen schon immer voraus und bestimmt seine Freiheit innerlich, es macht den Menschen in einer zur persönlichen Schuld analogen Weise schuldig vor Gott."

Weger, in a remarkable statement, tacitly admits that his goal remains essentially elusive. Moreover, this statement captures – perhaps unintentionally – one of the basic reasons for the insolvability of the posed problem: "Zugegeben . . ., es ist nicht leicht, einen wesentlich *personalen Vollzug*, was es die Sünde ist, im *vorpersonalen Bereich* zu beschreiben . . . ."[177] Having taken cognizance of Weger's reinterpretation of original sin, some commentators conclude that a description of *pre*personal *sin*fulness is not merely difficult but simply impossible.[178] Less categorically Schrofner concludes, to his disappointment, that Weger's promising approach has failed to clarify how one's being situated in a specific historical way can conceivably become one's (be it analogical) guilt.[179] Schrofner's disappointment is fully understandable; for, as we have seen, Weger himself has called such guilt an indispensable element of the doctrine of original sin, an indisputed fact and a principal theme of his investigations. Moreover, this disappointment is not mitigated by the correct observation that Weger has demonstrated the situational privation of grace to be *Schuld* in a minimal sense, namely as inculpable *debitum*. For as revealed by his introduction of the new argument from development, his sudden reversions to an earlier stage of argumentation[180] and his repeated indications of dissatisfaction with the intermediate and even ultimate results achieved,[181]

---

177 *Ibid.*, 174-75, emphasis added.
178 Julius Gross: "Eine solche der freien Willensentscheidung vorausliegende Sündenverfallenheit kann unmöglich schon Sünde sein. Sie wird missbräuchlicherweise Sünde genannt. Wäre es nicht an der Zeit, mit diesem auf Augustin zurückgehenden Missbrauch endlich Schluss zu machen?" ("Katholische Erbsündentheologie heute" [review of Weger's *Theologie der Erbsünde*], *Zeitschrift für Religions- und Geistesgeschichte*, XXII [1970], 376-77). Herbert Haag: "But to derive an 'original sin' of the individual as 'guilt before God' from mankind's solidarity in sin is illogical and conflicts with the testimony of scripture" (*JESt*, X [1973], 273-74). The German original indicates that Haag's difficulty remains despite the fact that the term *Schuld* has a broader meaning than the term guilt: "Aus der Solidarität der Menschheit in der Sünde aber eine *Erbsünde* des einzelnen als *Schuld vor Gott* abzuleiten, entbehrt der Logik und widerspricht dem Zeugnis der Schrift" *ThQ*, CL [1970], 448).
179 "Wie . . . das Hineingebundensein des Menschen in eine bestimmte Geschichte diesem zur – wenn auch nur analogen – Schuld werden soll, ist trotz aller Bemühungen des Verfassers einfach nicht einzusehen. . . . Der Übergang von der vorpersonalen Bestimmung der menschlichen Freiheit durch die Unheilsgeschichte zur Schuldhaften Identifizierung des Menschen mit dieser Unheilsgeschichte (149f u.ö.) bleibt unbewiesene Behauptung und wird auch durch noch so häufiges Wiederholen nicht einsichtig" (Schrofner, *ZKTh*, CXIII, 203-204). Stenzel is of the opinion that on Weger's construction one cannot speak of man in original sin as a "schuldhaft gnadenloses Mensch" – not even in an analogical way (Alois Stenzel, Review of *Theologie der Erbsünde*, *ThuPh*, XLVI [1971], 560).
180 See, e.g., *Theologie der Erbsünde*, 169-70, 171-72, 174.
181 See, e.g., *ibid.*, 162-63, 167, 175.

Weger himself sought and held in the offing more than that minimal conception of *Schuld*.

* * *

In retrospect, it remains to determine the relative positions of Schoonenberg, Rahner and Weger regarding the issue under consideration. Weger's third route has failed to bring us any closer to a discovery of the guilt-character of original sin than did Rahner's reflections. Their common position, in turn, represents an advance relative to the position of Schoonenberg in that they elaborated the definition of original sin as the situational privation of grace, showing that it involves a prepersonal *unholiness counter to God's will (Schuld)*. That elaboration disclosed additional similarities between the situational privation of grace and personal sin. At the same time, however, this elaboration clarified the fact that in contrast to personal sin the *Schuld* of original sin does not involve culpability for the person deprived of grace and that the unholiness incurred is simply the privational *non*holiness that constitutes an interior *Existential*. In effect, therefore, this further elaboration by Rahner and Weger has also clarified the fact that with respect to the key question regarding the intrinsic (proportional) similarity between the *essence* of personal and original sin their position coincides with that of Schoonenberg: conceived of as the situational privation of grace, original sin may be called sin because of its (structural) association with personal sin, for this situation originates from and subsequently accompanies and inclines to personal sin.

That substantial consensus regarding the sense in which the situational privation of grace may be called sin and guilt represents an important hermeneutical problem. Although the documents being reinterpreted make a distinction between personal and original sin, they speak of original sin unproblematically as sin and guilt in the proper sense of those terms.[182] Within the situational reinterpretation, by contrast, the predications "sin" and "guilt" describe neither the essence nor the intrinsic quality of original sin. Indeed, the situationalists have accomplished by the very process of reinterpretation that which the documents being reinterpreted claim is accomplished by the sacrament of (infant) baptism, namely, the elimination of "the guilt of original sin" and the removal of "everything having the true and proper nature of sin."[183] Accordingly, that which in the situational interpretation constitutes *original sin itself* is qualified as "sin" formally in the same way in which Trent defines *concupiscence* as an essentially sinless *remnant* of original sin.[184]

---

182 See Sec. C, 1, a above.
183 *DS*, 1515 (see Introduction, sec. A, 8, e above).
184 *DS*, 1515. This formal similarity between the way in which Trent qualifies con-

Having examined the implications of the situationalists' conception of the structure of original sin (spatiotemporal situational *Existential*) for their understanding of the essence of original sin (privation of sanctifying grace as "sin"), we now turn to analysis of the impact of this situation of original sin upon man's existential acts.

---

cupiscence (*ex peccato est et ad peccatum inclinat*) and the way in which original sin as situation may be qualified as sin does not mean that the situation of original sin is materially identical with concupiscence, as Scheffczyk suggests (L. Scheffczyk, "Versuche zur Neuaussprache der Erbschuldwahrheit," *MThZ,* XVII [1966], 257). For all the situationalists, the essence of original sin is the privation of grace, which is distinguished from its consequences (see Schoonenberg, *Geloof,* IV, 153-54; Rahner, *SM,* I, 1112-13; *SMe,* IV, 331; Weger, *Theologie der Erbsünde,* 157-60; see also chs. IV and V below). Despite Weger's arguments to the contrary, Stenzel remains of the opinion that Weger fails to demonstrate that his conception of original sin places it in a category other than that of concupiscence (ThuPh, XLVI [1971], 560).

CHAPTER IV *THE SITUATIONAL IMPACT*
OF ORIGINAL SIN UPON FREE ACTS

If original sin is a situational *Existential* and consists of the spatiotemporal privation of grace, how deeply does that situation affect man's existence? To bring this issue into clear focus we will assume, as we did in the preceding chapter, a total spatiotemporal absence of grace. What power does such a situation have over man's free acts? This crucial issue will be explored in three stages. First, the drastic effect attributed to the situation of original sin by Schoonenberg. Then, the process of inevitable and free appropriation of one's situation will be considered. Finally, the effect of concupiscence upon man's free acts will be assessed.

A. SITUATIONAL BONDAGE OF THE FREE WILL

Schoonenberg holds that the situation of original sin brings with it man's absolute moral inability.[1] So closely is this inability linked with the situation of original sin itself that he includes this impotence in the very definition of original sin: "Original sin in us is the situation of being deprived of supernatural grace and of being impotent with respect to all love."[2] This drastic concomitant of the situation of original sin is formally identical with the result of the model situation, the child born into a family in which the value of honesty is completely lacking.[3] In both cases an absolute inability results. The concomitants of these situations differ significantly in that the child in the model situation is said to be absolutely incapable of a *particular* virtue,[4] whereas all those subject to original sin are said to be incapable of the *root* of virtue, love, and thus incapable of all that is fully virtuous.[5] The

---

1 *Geloof,* IV, 153-55, 229; *Man and Sin,* 77, 122, 180; *MS,* II, 877, 894-95.
2 *Geloof,* IV, 155.
3 See ch. I, sec. A, 3, b above.
4 See *ibid.*
5 *Geloof,* IV, 39, 153, 224; *Man and Sin,* 72-73; *MS,* II, 850.

grounds for that astounding conclusion warrant further examination.

The basis for positing an absolute moral inability as a concomitant of the situation of original sin was laid in an extensive and penetrating essay which Schoonenberg wrote some time before he introduced the situational interpretation of original sin.[6] In this essay Schoonenberg argues that grace is absolutely necessary not only for a salvific act (*actus salutaris*) but also for a morally good act (*actus moraliter bonus*),[7] not only for supernatural love but also for natural love.[8] Schoonenberg gives two basic reasons why grace is necessary for an act of *supernatural* love. In the first place, man's supernatural goal wholly transcends his natural powers. In the second place, due to sin man is no longer positively directed towards this transcendent goal, but lives in a *status aversionis a deo*.[9] The thesis that grace is necessary for supernatural acts is hardly startling. The significance of Schoonenberg's essay lies in the fact that that traditional thesis is used as a basis for arguing that grace is necessary even for a morally positive natural act. Schoonenberg gives two basic reasons for the necessity of grace for an act of *natural* love. In the first place, nature and grace constitute a unity[10] so that it is simply impossible to separate a natural act from a supernatural act. Rather, a positive natural act is always taken up into a supernatural act of love.[11] In fact, because nature is integrally directed to the supernatural goal, the natural and the supernatural act represent a single reality.[12] Grace is necessary for an act of natural love,

---

6 "De genade en de zedelijk goede act," *Jaarboek 1950*, 203-53.

7 *Jaarboek 1950*, 203.

8 Because they are less cumbersome, the terms "natural" and "supernatural love," which become more prevalent in Schoonenberg's later writings (see *Jaarboek 1959*, 27-35; *Geloof*, IV, 221-23; *Man and Sin*, 71), will be used as equivalents of the terms "morally good act" and "salvific act" found in his essay of 1950.

9 *Jaarboek 1950*, 208, 217-19, 229, 237-40, 252; cf. *Jaarboek 1959*, 27-28.

10 See ch. II, secs. A, 1 and B,1 above.

11 *Jaarboek 1950*, 208, 211, 222-42; *Jaarboek 1959*, 28-30; *Geloof*, IV, 220-21; *Man and Sin*, 70-71.

12 *Jaarboek 1950*, 203, 208, 209, 210-12; *Jaarboek 1959*, 31. A salutary and a morally good act are distinguished, according to Schoonenberg, in that the term "salutary" points to the goal and fruit of the morally good, whereas the term "morally good" points out the way along which salvation is attained (*Jaarboek 1950*, 209).

Interestingly, Schoonenberg defends his thesis that the natural and supernatural act are one by appealing to the Church's anti-Pelagian teachings, for in these, he points out, the distinction of nature and grace was not yet operative. Consequently, a statement regarding the necessity of grace in these teachings may not be restricted as if it applied only to the necessity of grace for attaining to the *supernatural* goal. Because that restriction introduces a distinction that arose later in history, this procedure, Schoonenberg argues, represents an anachronistic misinterpretation of the anti-Pelagian teachings (*Jaarboek 1950*, 213-16; cf. *Jaarboek 1959*, 26).

in the second place, due to the nature of love. Love is a positive decision with respect to all of reality. Consequently, a decision that concerns only man's natural relationship to God, even if such a decision were possible, cannot be characterized as love.[13] Schoonenberg concludes, therefore, that grace is necessary for all love and, since love is its root, for all virtue.[14]

On the basis of Schoonenberg's thesis regarding the integral dependence of love upon grace, its corollary — without grace no love is possible — seems self-evident. That self-evidence, in turn, seems wholly transferable to the concomitant of original sin. Defined as the situational absence of grace, original sin seems indeed to bring with it an inability with respect to all love.

Nevertheless, it is precisely as a concomitant of original sin as situation that this inability becomes less plausible. If original sin meant that grace were wholly absent, a purely natural love would be possible once more, for it would represent a positive decision with respect to all the reality accessible to man, in this case his natural relationship to others and to God.[15] As has been pointed out, however, in the situation of original sin man is deprived of grace in a specifically qualified way, namely, spatiotemporally.[16] Despite this spatiotemporal privation of grace, every human being is transcendentally situated by God's continued offer of salvation.[17] Against that background Schoonenberg's surprising argument for the impossibility of an act of natural love in the situation of original sin becomes understandable. Schoonenberg ascribes that impossibility not, as might be expected, to the fact that in the situation of original sin grace is *absent*, but to the fact that, despite original sin, grace is *present*. It is due to that presence of grace that a purely natural act is excluded.[18] Precisely because God continues to extend his grace, man cannot respond only in an act of natural love.[19] That argument, however, raises the problem whether the inability with respect to all love remains tenable as a concomitant of the situation of original sin. Although a *purely*

---

13 *Jaarboek 1950*, 212; *Jaarboek 1959*, 30; *Geloof*, IV, 221-23; *Man and Sin*, 71.
14 *Man and Sin*, 72-73; *Geloof*, IV, 224.
15 Surprisingly, in his article in *Mysterium Salutis*, Schoonenberg speaks only of the impossibility with respect to a *supernatural* moral act (*MS*, II, 929). Whether this restriction is deliberate is difficult to determine. A deliberate restriction seems unlikely since it would mark a regression in Schoonenberg's attempt to unify nature and grace. Cf. *Bijdragen*, XXIV, 377 (roughly the basis for the *MS*, II essay) and *Man and Sin*, 180, where Schoonenberg still speaks of an inability with respect to *all* love.
16 Ch. III, sec. A above.
17 See ch. II, n. 85 above.
18 *Geloof*, IV, 222-23.
19 *Ibid.*, 223.

natural act of love is rightly said to be impossible due to the permeating, transcendental presence of grace *despite* the spatiotemporal situation of original sin, can the impossibility of a *complete* (natural-supernatural) act of love be maintained *on the basis of* original sin?

One of the intriguing aspects of the problem regarding the drastic effect which Schoonenberg ascribes to the situation of original sin is the fact that a key argument employed in his essay of 1950 that might have rendered that effect plausible is not maintained later. Moreover, this argument for the paralyzing effect of original sin is excluded, ironically enough, precisely by Schoonenberg's subsequent reinterpretation of original sin as situation.

In his essay of 1950, the thesis that without grace love is impossible was centrally supported by the argument that due to sin man is turned away from God (*status aversionis a deo*). In that essay Schoonenberg proceeds from the Augustinian idea that man's acts are driven either by love for God or by self-love.[20] Accordingly, Schoonenberg maintains that for the realization of man's love of God and for the avoidance of self-love grace is necessary.[21] The *aversio*-effect of sin is overcome by the *conversio*-effect of grace.[22] Moreover, in that essay man's *aversio* was said to be not merely the result of personal sin, but an essential element of *original sin.*[23] Reinterpreted as situation, however, original sin, as Schoonenberg points out, in no way involves a moral-religious attitude or inclination,[24] so that man cannot be said to be morally turned away from God on account of this situation.[25] Instead, the correlate of being thus situated is usually man's free decision, which as such is unqualified as to direction. Despite this significant shift in the interpretation of original sin from *aversio* to *situation*, Schoonenberg maintains that the effect of original sin remains unchanged: the inability with respect to all love. That means that this drastic effect must now be ascribed wholly to the spatiotemporal, situational absence of grace. Moreover, this inability must hold true despite the transcendental presence of grace. Whether even the total spatiotemporal privation of grace can effect a total moral paralysis must be explored now.

Completely in harmony with the structure of the situation theory,[26]

---

20 See n. 9 above.
21 *Jaarboek 1950*, 220.
22 *Ibid.,* 218.
23 *Ibid.,* 217-19, cf. 238-39.
24 See ch. III, sec. C, 1 above.
25 See *Geloof,* IV, 223 where Schoonenberg concludes from the fact that original sin is a situation that man cannot be asked to repent from original sin as such.
26 See Ch. I, sec. A, 3 above.

Schoonenberg points out that in a situation such as that of original sin man's will remains free, but lacks the room and the fellowship required for the attainment of love and genuine virtue.[27] Man's freedom is bound and restricted by the situational absence of grace that constitutes original sin.[28] As is evident from this terminology, Schoonenberg considers the situation to effect some kind of bondage of the will. The situation of original sin binds man's freedom so severely that it is incapable of any love. Accordingly, as in the traditional view, in the situational interpretation original sin is said to inflict a fatal blow that causes the "death of the soul."[29]

Despite this bondage, or rather, within this bondage, man's will remains free. If one were to attempt to place Schoonenberg's view of the effect of original sin in terms of the classic controversy regarding man's will, one would classify him as defending not simply a *liberum arbitrium*, nor simply a *servum arbitrium*, but rather a *servum liberum arbitrium*, i.e., the situational bondage of the *free* will. That remaining freedom deserves further attention. Appealing to the magisterium's defense of the free will — especially against the theses of Baius and the Jansenists[30] — Schoonenberg emphatically posits that in man's natural capacities nothing is impaired.[31] By virtue of man's nature, Schoonenberg contends, the capacity of the free will is radically invulnerable and hence radically unimpaired.[32]

It is in light of Schoonenberg's seemingly absolute statements regarding the free will that the scope of his similarly absolute statements regarding man's moral inability due to the situational bondage of original sin become very difficult to understand. That difficulty becomes manifest when one

---

27 *Geloof,* IV, 228; *Man and Sin,* 76-77. In the Dutch original, Schoonenberg treats "the sequels of sin," not before, as in the English edition (*Man and Sin,* 63-97), but after his treatment of the doctrine of original sin. As a result, in the Dutch edition Schoonenberg explicates the specific consequences of *original* sin more frequently than in the English edition (*Geloof,* IV, 214, 222, 228, 229, 235, 236, 238, 239, 240, 241, 248, 255, 256; *Man and Sin,* 76-77). From these explications it becomes clear that whether the situation is the result of one's own personal sin or the result of the sins of others, Schoonenberg considers the *effect of being-situated* to be the same in both cases. The two conditions differ in that the situation springing from one's own sin involves a wrongly inclined free will, whereas the situation of original sin does not (see *Geloof,* IV, 239-40; *Man and Sin,* 122; see also the section on venial and mortal sin: *Geloof,* IV, 50-72; *Man and Sin,* 25-40).
28 *Geloof,* IV, 228; *Man and Sin,* 122.
29 *Geloof,* IV, 228; *Man and Sin,* 122. Cf. *Jaarboek 1950,* 240.
30 See esp. *DS,* 1927-30, 1937, 1965, 2401-406, 2438-42.
31 *Geloof,* IV, 226-29; *Man and Sin,* 74-77; *Jaarboek 1959,* 33-34; *Jaarboek 1950,* 225-37, 250-51.
32 *Geloof,* IV, 229, cf. 228.

notes that Schoonenberg defines morality as having as its basis free decision and as its norm a total decision with respect to the whole of reality.[33] In view of that definition, it would seem imperative to ascribe the possibility of a positive moral choice to a will that remains radically free. Schoonenberg avoids that conclusion by pointing to the effect of being situated. Is the counter-effect of being situated, however, sufficient to totally squelch the radical freedom that remains? As was noted with respect to the model, living in a family in which lies and deceit are the order of the day effects the child's absolute inability with respect to honesty.[34] Even with respect to that model, the question may legitimately be raised whether an inner aversion, be it ever so slight, to this tragic situation must not be judged as being a positive moral decision on the part of the child. Whatever the answer to that question may be in the case of Schoonenberg's model, that question becomes even more acute with respect to the reality approximated by that model, the situation of original sin. Since that (spatiotemporal) situation coexists with an encompassing (transcendental) situation of grace, must one not assume that man is capable of a positive response by virtue of his radically invulnerable freedom? Schoonenberg's answer is that man's disability remains despite his "radical" freedom because the (spatiotemporal) situation also reaches to the "root."[35]

Two explanations for this radical effect of being-situated may be given. On the one hand, the free will may be reduced to a merely latent capacity, as was done in the case of the model.[36] On the other hand, due to the unity of man as embodied person and personalized body,[37] the free will may be assumed to be incapable of coming to *concrete* (positive) *expression* within an adverse (negative) situation. The first explanation is extremely problematical. As has been pointed out,[38] precisely because freedom represents the heart of man and because freedom is by nature an *act*,[39] it seems impossible to reduce the capacity of free decision to a pure potentiality.[40] Hence an

33 *Man and Sin*, 19, 21, 42-43; *Geloof*, IV, 48-49, 66; *MS*, II, 851.
34 See ch. I, sec. A, 3, b above.
35 *Geloof*, IV, 229. Here again that situation is said to be due either to original sin or to one's own sin. Cf. *Man and Sin*, 77.
36 See ch. I, sec. A, 3, b above.
37 See ch. I, sec. A, 2, b above.
38 Ch. I, n. 142 above; cf. ch. III, n. 165 above.
39 *Jaarboek 1950*, 238; *Man and Sin*, 33, 111; *Geloof*, IV, 61; cf. ch. I, sec. A, 2, a above.
40 The expedient of reducing a capacity to mere potentiality was somewhat more plausible in the case of the model (ch. I, sec. A, 3, b above) because the childs inability with respect to honesty concerned a *particular* "faculty" which, it may be assumed, can

adverse situation *can* account for a limited inability, namely, the inability of expressing a free act fully and concretely in the dimensions of space and time. But can a situation, however adverse and however interior, absolutely rule out a positive moral decision?

One can search for an answer to that question within Schoonenberg's own framework by observing his analysis of the effect of inescapable, monolithic situations in which man finds himself, such as an incurable disease or death. In such boundary situations, as Schoonenberg calls them, the subject's free decision can in no way effect a change in his situation. Nevertheless, even in such inexorable and immutable situations, Schoonenberg points out, man makes an inner personal decision. He does so by assuming an attitude of rejection or acceptance with respect to the determinative, inescapable situation that impinges upon him interiorly.[41] In this way, man can always give meaning to his life and its impinging situations.[42] Yet in the case of the situation of original sin, Schoonenberg speaks *categorically* of a moral inability despite the fact that man retains his "physical" ability to choose.[43] This *physical* ability to choose freely is even entailed in man's *moral* inability, according to Schoonenberg, because a moral inability is one that has its origin and existence in a free decision. And a free decision always presupposes the (natural) *possibility* of choosing otherwise.[44] Although the nature of this moral *inability* is difficult to understand since its *moral* quality depends on the simultaneous possibility of choosing otherwise, this definition of moral inability in terms of freedom once again uncovers the even greater difficulty of ascribing the cause of an absolute moral inability, not to man's free decision, but to his situation.[45] In view of this difficulty, it is more in keeping with Schoonenberg's own framework to conclude that the moral

---

be re-activated in more favorable circumstances by the child's central, personal freedom which remains. When Schoonenberg speaks of the capacity that remains despite the situation of original sin, however, it involves not a mere "faculty" but man's *power* of making a *central* free choice.

41 *Geloof,* I, 96; III, 147, 150; IV, 61-62; *Gods wordende wereld,* 21, 46; *God's World in the Making,* 25, 58.

42 *Geloof,* IV, 145-46; cf. *Man and Sin,* 111.

43 *Geloof,* IV, 229; *Man and Sin,* 77. The term "physical" in this context should be taken as an equivalent of "natural," primarily in its *philosophical* sense (cf. *Jaarboek 1950,* 243-53; *Jaarboek 1959,* 31-35).

44 *Jaarboek 1950,* 251.

45 In the essay of 1950, a moral inability is defined as one that has its origin and existence in a free decision (*Jaarboek 1950,* 248-52). The absoluteness of such inability lasts only while man freely persists in evil. By definition such moral inability cannot be said to be caused by a negative situation.

inability that can legitimately be ascribed to being-situated is itself strictly situational: in the concrete (spatio-temporal) situation of original sin (absence of grace) man is incapable of creating a new, positive situation that is the expression of love. At the same time, it must be concluded that even in this negative situation of original sin man is still capable of making the right moral choice, namely, hate towards and rejection of this situation and loving acceptance of his transcendental situation of grace.

The problem encountered in understanding the way in which the situation of original sin can be said to effect an inability with respect to all love gives rise once more to the question as to *the degree of interiority* of situatedness. The frequent criticism that situation is a reality that is, without further qualification, exterior to man is clearly unfounded. Both Schoonenberg and Weger rightly refute *this* charge of exteriority by pointing out that the phenomenon intended by the concept "situation" does not constitute simply a complex of external *circum*-stances, but *man's being*-situated, his *interior* situation or *Existential*.[46] Schoonenberg expresses this interiority well when he casually refers to being situated as a *Daseinsweise* of man.[47]

Despite this consistent emphasis on the interiority of being-situated, the problem that is thereby demonstrated to be nonexistent at a certain level returns at another, deeper level. Interiority and exteriority are relative terms, presupposing a point of reference. When the point of reference is simply "man," being-situated must clearly be qualified as interior. All criticism of the situation theory that overlooks this level of interiority blocks the path to a fruitful discussion of the problem of exteriority.[48] The discussion

---

46 Schoonenberg, see ch. I, secs. A, 3 (introductory paragraphs) and A, 3, c. Weger, *Theologie der Erbsünde,* esp. 145-50. Cf. Rahner, *SM,* I, 1113; *SMe,* IV, 332.

47 *MS,* II, 929-31.

48 This shift (rather than solution) of the problem explains why the "exteriority-criticism" persists even after Schoonenberg has elucidated the sense in which being-situated is interior to man. Seybold's criticism regarding the exteriority of being-situated, for example (see ch. I, n. 105 above), is levelled at the German edition of Schoonenberg's book on sin which, like the English edition, greatly clarfies the interiority of "being-situated."

In a recent article (Reinhold Weier, *"Erbsünde und Sünde der Welt: Probleme der Erbsündenlehre Piet Schoonenbergs und Teilhards de Chardin,"* TThZ, LXXXII [1973], 154-71), the essential problem of the exteriority of Schoonenberg's situation concept is instructively elaborated once more. This stimulating article demonstrates the precise problem entailed in the situation theory. It does so *despite* the lamentable fact that Schoonenberg's situation theory is misrepresented at several points as entailing an Aristotelian conception of situation, i.e., situation as a complex of external circumstances (*ibid.,* 156, 158, 159-60). Amazingly, the incorrectness of this interpretation is demonstrated by the material which Weier himself supplies in the immediately preceding pages (ibid., 155-56).

penetrates to a deeper level of the current problem when one observes that "man" without further qualification is not the only, nor even the most significant point of reference for the alternative exterior-interior. The critical point of reference is not simply man, but the essence, the heart of man, man as free person. Implicitly or explicitly, Schoonenberg, Rahner and Weger all speak of freedom as the innermost center of man's being.[49] Relative to *that* point of reference, being-situated must be qualified as exterior.[50]

It is by virtue of this relative but crucial exteriority of being-situated that Rahner emphatically insists that, not man's freedom, but man's "Freiheits*situation*" is "determined" by the decisions of others,[51] and that Schoonenberg can maintain a radically unimpaired freedom within a totally negative situational *Existential*.[52] No matter how radical being-situated is

There he rightly indicates that Schoonenberg introduces an "Aristotelian" definition of situation only in order to supersede it. Indeed, Schoonenberg introduces the idea of situation as *Um-Welt* only to reject it because of its exteriority and to use it as a platform for penetrating to the more interior level of being-situated (see *Geloof,* IV, 145-146; *Man and Sin,* 104-106, 115-18; *MS,* II, 890-91, 930). In view of the fact that Weier begins by recognizing Schoonenberg's non-Aristotelian situation concept, his subsequent Aristotelian interpretation of this concept can plausibly be explained as follows: correctly perceiving that the problem of exteriority continues to plague the situation theory despite Schoonenberg's overt *re*-definition and *re*-formulation of situation as an interior *being*-situated, Weier wrongly concludes that this persistent exteriority *must* be due to a covert retention of an Aristotelian situation concept. That this conclusion is false is demonstrated not only by Schoonenberg's exposition but also by Weier's own attempt to overcome the exteriority problem with the aid of Sartre's and Jaspers' conceptions of − essentially − *self*-situating. The interiority that Weier indeed attains *in this way,* stands in polar tension with the exteriority of his own existentialistic (non-Aristotelian) situation concept (see *ibid.,* 158-66).

49 Aside from Schoonenberg's explicit adoption of the Teilhardian terms "the Within" and "the Without," the former of which stands for man's freedom (see ch. I, sec. A,2,b [esp. n. 85] above), there are other instances in which the terms "interior" and "one's own" are used to describe man's free act (Schoonenberg, see sec. B,1 below; cf. Weger, *Theologie der Erbsünde,* 114-15, 151-52, 154). Generally man's freedom in its uniqueness is described in terms of interiority (see Schoonenberg, *Geloof,* IV, 48-50, 62; *Man and Sin,* 19, 33, 105; Rahner, *Schriften,* I, 392-93). Significantly, when Weier (see preceding footnote) attempts to overcome the exteriority of Schoonenberg's *situation* concept, he penetrates to the interiority of *personal free choice* (*TThZ*, LXXXII, 160-61, 163-65). This interiority is, of course, not at all foreign to Schoonenberg's thought. Only a *terminological* difference is involved insofar as Schoonenberg generally avoids speaking of this interiority in terms of situation; a *material* difference is involved in that Schoonenberg does not posit a paradoxical identity between the exteriority of being-situated and the interiority of self-situating (see ch. I, sec. A,3 above, and sec. B,1 below) as Weier does (*TThZ*, LXXXII, 165-66).

50 See sec. B,1 below.
51 *Exkurs,* 219-20.
52 See sec. A above.

said to be, it is never as radical as man's freedom. Not situatedness but freedom is the *radix* of man. When Schoonenberg, therefore, considers the coexistence of being-situated and being-free and asks whether this situational bondage of freedom does not destroy the latter, he formulates his view very precisely in his answer. The simultaneity of being-situated and being-free involves no contradiction, he replies, for freedom means precisely not being determined *from without*,[53] but *freely determining oneself from within*.[54] That, however, is as clear a formulation of an answer as it is of the lingering problem. It is the problem of the limited degree to which one can derive a moral inability from man's being situated. If man always retains his radical freedom, the specific content of his situational *Existential* can certainly vary the range of concrete self-expression; it cannot destroy the reality of self-determination.

However interior, being situated by sin remains a bondage of the *free will*, a will that enjoys or detests these bonds. Accordingly, the ultimate effect of this bondage cannot be inferred from the aspect of situatedness as such, but can be determined only by keeping in view also the central free act in which man adopts an attitude of either acceptance or refusal with respect to the drastic and tragic situation of original sin.[55] At a level that is even more interior than his situatedness, man is free to reject or appropriate his specific situation.

B. ORIGINAL SIN AS SITUATIONAL DETERMINANT AND APPROPRIATION AS FREE SELF-DETERMINATION

1. The Interaction between Being-situated and Self-situating

From the outset of his reinterpretation of original sin as situation, Schoonenberg has acknowledged that by his free decision man always assumes a certain attitude towards the situation in which he finds himself.[56] In this way, man also creates *his own* situation; he situates himself.[57] Nevertheless, Schoonenberg consistently and methodically abstracts from this active element in order to distill the unique, passive factor of *being*-situated.

---

53 This represents a formulation of the essence of *being*-situated.
54 *Man and Sin,* 105; *Bijdragen,* XXIV, 355; *MS,* II, 890-91, 930. Cf. *Jaarboek 1950,* 231.
55 Schoonenberg speaks of the situation of original sin as being "the most tragic situation of man" (*Geloof,* IV, 169).
56 *Geloof,* IV, 145-46; *Man and Sin,* 105, 116, 181; *MS,* II, 890-91.
57 *MS,* II, 930: "Selbstsituierung."

By means of this process of abstraction it is possible to obtain a notion of situation as a phenomenon that precedes every personal decision,[58] a phenomenon that is unambiguously demarcated from every personal element.[59] It is exclusively *this* rigorously delimited notion of situation that Schoonenberg employs to reinterpret the reality of original sin. The consistent maintenance of this restriction does not mean that Schoonenberg ever loses freedom from view. On the contrary, as has been noted, implicitly or explicitly freedom remains the preponderant idea.[60] Due to the rigorous delimitation of the passive element of being-situated, however, freedom usually comes into view *explicitly* only in terms of "free decisions" that are not further qualified as to their centrality. Such rigorous delimitation may be necessary in order to obtain clarity of distinction. It is unfortunate, however, that Schoonenberg rarely returns from that clarity to reintegrate the abstracted element of being situated, not merely with free decisions in general but with that central free decision by which man gives meaning to his being situated.

Freedom in this profound sense cannot be permanently kept in abeyance. It reasserts itself if only because the effect of man's being situated by original sin must ultimately be measured *in* the heart of man. Moreover, Schoonenberg introduces the category "situation" in order to indicate the *inner connecting link* that joins the personal sins of one generation to those of the next.[61] If that inner connection is to be demonstrated, one cannot stop at pointing to man's interior *Existential* but must proceed by exploring its existence in man's free self-determination.

After having reinterpreted original sin strictly in terms of being situated, therefore, Schoonenberg is confronted once more with the central free act that was initially expunged in order to define situation. In view of the strategic significance of demonstrating the existential impact of the situation of original sin, it is at first glance surprising to observe that Schoonenberg seems to eschew rather than welcome the opportunity to do so. In the three instances that he deals with the question, he immediately admits the reality of free self-determination as a factor that coexists with that of being situated but does not proceed to indicate in what way the former is integrally linked with the latter. Two of these instances will be examined.[62]

---

58   See ch. I, sec. A, 3, c above.
59   See ch. III, sec. C, 1, b above.
60   See ch. I, sec. A, 3 above.
61   See ch. I, sec. A, 1 above.
62   A third instance, found in *Man and Sin,* 181, is essentially similar to *MS,* II, 930.

In response to the objection that the reality of original sin cannot be understood simply as situation because a situation becomes one's own only through inner appropriation, Schoonenberg grants that the basis for this objection is well taken but does not consider that to be a ground for reassessing the situational interpretation of original sin. Instead, he responds by pointing out that appropriation belongs to the category of *personal* decision. Appropriation, says Schoonenberg, represents an *active* response, a response which presupposes the *passive* element of *being*-situated.[63] The same holds true for original sin: "Everyone's original sin requires appropriation in order to become *his* original sin, but this appropriation is already personal sin."[64] Here Schoonenberg has relegated the element of appropriation to its own unique "realm,"[65] that of personal sin. Similarly, he assigns the reality of original sin to an equally unique "realm," that of being situated by sin: "Original sin, precisely as distinct from and opposed to personal sin, is the element of passively being situated that is presupposed by its affirmation (or its refusal in the acceptance of justifying grace)."[66]

The same process of approach and withdrawal from the point where man's being situated and his central free decision touch is evident when Schoonenberg considers another, though similar, objection. He has just stated that original sin represents "ein existentiales, und nicht nur existentielles Situiert-Sein." Whereas the latter proceeds simultaneously from both the external situation and an inner choice of position, the situation as *Existential* "kommt als solches nur aus der äusseren Situation, es ist reines Situiert-*Sein* und Situiert-*Werden,* das jeder Selbstsituierung vorausgeht."[67] It is at this point that Schoonenberg anticipates the objection that such situatedness never exists "rein für sich, weil der Mensch auch in seinem Anfang, nie nur passives Dasein, sondern immer auch persönliche Existenz ist."[68] As in the previous instance, Schoonenberg again concedes that the point is well taken but still considers the objection to be of little import because it merely reveals that original sin is "immer nur ein Moment an der ganzen Existenz des Menschen, das gilt auch schon für das Kind, das am Anfang des Lebens steht; das andere Moment ist seine eigene, teilweise sündige, teilweise erlöste Stellungnahme."[69]

63 *TvTh*, IV, 74.
64 *Ibid.*; cf. *ThPQ*, CXVII, 122.
65 In this and the following instances the term "realm" has been placed in quotation marks in order to indicate that it is being used not in a spatial but in an ontic sense.
66 *TvTh*, IV, 74.
67 *MS*, II, 930.
68 *Ibid.* See also *Ex Auditu Verbi,* 263.
69 *MS*, II, 930.

In both instances, Schoonenberg's reply is remarkable despite the fact that it is a consistent restatement of the coexistence of freedom and situation.[70] Indeed, his reply is remarkable precisely because, in response to a suggestion of a concrete *coalescence,* Schoonenberg does not move beyond a restatement of the *coexistence* of self-determination and being situated as elements purified by abstraction. By immediately consigning being situated and free appropriation to their unique and opposite "realms," as Schoonenberg does in the first instance considered, an opportunity to demonstrate the factual interaction between man's being situated in original sin and his perpetual self-situating is lost. Even after admitting, in the second instance, that original sin in fact never exists "rein für sich," Schoonenberg does not, as might be expected, proceed to analyze the concrete inner nexus at the only *locus* where original sin in fact has its being and exerts its influence, namely, in man's central act of free self-determination. At the very moment that one expects a close-up of the juncture where situation and freedom meet, it fades from view because our conceptual apparatus is being focussed once more on two distinct realities in their uniqueness.

Although this withdrawal from the point at which being situated and free self-determination touch tangentially is surprising in view of the critical significance of precisely this point for the existential meaning of the situation of original sin, this withdrawal is understandable in view of the type of categories that have been employed. Schoonenberg's proclivity for immediately withdrawing even the potentially mediating category "appropriation" from the point of contact is driven by the polar tension with which the dominant categories have been charged. Situation is to freedom as passive element to active element,[71] as "passives Dasein" to "persönliche Existenz," as "Situiert-Werden" to "Selbst-Situierung."[72] Whereas being situated as such proceeds exclusively from the "äusseren Situation" and becomes man's interior determination,[73] man's freedom means "nicht von aussen bestimmt sein, sondern von innen her sich selbst bestimmen."[74] This juxtapositioning discloses not merely distinct, but *diametrically opposite* categories. This becomes explicit when at one point Schoonenberg speaks of original sin and personal sin in terms of polar opposition: Original sin "geht . . . jeder eigenen Entscheidung und selbstgewälten Haltung des Subjekts voraus oder besser: sie

---

70 See ch. I, sec. A,3 above.
71 *TvTh,* IV, 74-75; *MS,* II, 930.
72 *MS,* II, 930.
73 *MS,* II, 930; cf. 890-91. See also *Man and Sin,* 105.
74 Schoonenberg, *Theologie der Sünde: Ein theologischer Versuch* (Einsiedeln: Benziger, 1966), 123. Cf. *Man and Sin,* 105.

ist dieser, bei aller Gleichzeitigkeit, polar entgegengesetzt, weil sie eben nicht der eigenen Entscheidung des Subjekts entspringt."[75]

To point out this polar opposition is not to suggest that simultaneously maintaining the opposites entails a contradiction. From the presentation of the various forms of the structural coexistence of freedom and situation[76] it should have become abundantly clear that both can be maintained without inner contradiction. A problem arises only when one enquires beyond the notion of coexistence. The moment one asks concerning the inner connection that was held in prospect, a problem erupts: In what sense can the personal sins of one generation be intrinsically connected to those of the next by a reality described by diametrically opposite categories? To facilitate analysis, that question can be narrowed down to the problem as to the inner connection between the free act of personal sin and the situational *Existential* of original sin.

Perhaps that problem as stated is insoluble due to the fact that a static reality (inner connection) is sought to join dynamic phenomena. The entire problem may be set up less statically by using the category "appropriation" as mediating device and by viewing the phenomenon of being situated as a passive, and that of self-determination as an active dynamics. As we have seen, Schoonenberg speaks of situatedness as a "Daseinsweise" and of its correlate as "persönliche Existenz."[77] In line with this terminology, the correlates may be distinguished by designating them as a mode of being and as a mode of existence, respectively. Now if the idea of appropriation is pushed to its limits in order to probe the point of connection between being situated and self-determination, the problem is this: how can the personal mode of existence appropriate the opposite mode of being without destroying either itself or its opposite? Insofar as being-situated is indeed taken over by self-situating, the former loses its unique, original structure: the passive — if truly appropriated by the active — is no more. The two modes of reality can coexist and even be encapsulated within one being;[78] the polar opposites can touch at midpoint; the midpoint can even be traversed, but only on the condition of transformation, a *metabasis eis allo genos*. But in that case, any *inner* connection seems to vanish at the midpoint.[79]

75 *Theologie der Sünde,* 222; cf. *Man and Sin,* 198.
76 See ch. I, sec. A, 3 above.
77 *MS,* II, 930.
78 See ch. I, sec. A, 2, b above.
79 Cf. *Thought,* XLV (1970), 97-98 where Betty says of Schoonenberg's understanding of original sin as situation, "There is no explicit reference to the future free-will choice, no connection between the mature personal response of the adult by which situation is interiorized and the situation of the child."

The problem as to the inner connection between being-situated and self-determination need not mean that the situation of original sin has little or no impact upon man's central free decision. The centrifugal force unleashed by ontologically opposite poles makes a struggle inevitable, and the additional negative moral qualification of being situated *by sin* cannot but intensify that struggle. The problems encountered in the endeavor to find that inner connection do demonstrate that the ultimate effect of being-situated by sin is to a significant degree limited and determined by the existential, free act of self-determination. That means that the ultimate consequences of original sin, reinterpreted as situation, cannot properly be assessed without incorporating the critical factor of man's central freedom in that assessment.

2. Inevitable *Nachvollzug* and Free Appropriation

Although the notion of an inevitable effect of being-situated upon man's free decision has already been elaborated in the discussion of the general framework of the situation theory as it was articulated by Schoonenberg,[80] the bearing of this notion on the problem of assessing the radicality and effect of the situation of original sin can be explicated more readily in terms of Weger's idea of "Nachvollzug."[81]

Although Weger sometimes uses the concept *Nachvollzug* as an equivalent of the concept "free appropriation,"[82] the former usually has a different connotation. In distinction from the notion of the free appropriation of a situation, the notion of *Nachvollzug* usually designates the inevitability with which a specific situation becomes the content of and an inextricable part of free decision. A specific situation is "taken over" even when that situation is *not* made one's own by free appropriation.[83] Even the rejection of one's situation has that situation as its content.[84] In this sense, Weger points out, man cannot dissociate himself from the *Existential* of his concrete situation.[85]

Like Schoonenberg, Weger emphasizes this inextricable situatedness of every free decision in order to indicate the depth dimension or interiority of man's being situated by sin. This situation makes its impact and has its effect

---

80 Ch. I, sec. A, 3 above.
81 For the various terms used by Weger, see ch. I, n. 201 above.
82 *Theologie der Erbsünde*, 120.
83 *Ibid.*, 119-20, 135.
84 This is an articulation of Weger's intention in terms of Schoonenberg's formulation (see ch. I, sec. A, 3, a above).
85 *Theologie der Erbsünde*, 119, 150, 153.

even *before* (ontically) man's free *re-action.*[86] By virtue of this depth impact of being-situated, Weger suggests, original sin, conceived of as situation, has grave repercussions on personal sin. He says, for example, that in the situation of original sin man is inextricably directed towards personal sin.[87] At the same time Weger emphasizes that being situated by sin does not itself determine a response of personal sin.[88] This effect is precluded not only because of God's continued offer of grace[89] but also because man remains free.[90] It is in keeping with these counter-phenomena to the determinative effect of being situated by sin that Weger speaks of man's freedom as involving *also* the *Nachvollzug* of his situation.[91] Similarly, he speaks of *Nachvollzug* as being an *element* or *aspect* of man's free decision.[92]

Whatever Weger may mean by positing that being situated by sin involves an inextricable directedness to personal sin, in view of the *dual* factors of inevitable *Nachvollzug* and free appropriation that directedness cannot mean that personal sin is in any way inevitable due to the situation of original sin. Nor is such directedness to personal sin substantiated by Weger's appeal to his thesis that in the free act of personal sin man becomes what he already is by virtue of being situated by (original) sin.[93] This recourse to the continuity postulate examined earlier is of no avail in this context due to the problematic but essential discontinuity between the situational "is" and the "is" that consists of and results from free "becoming." By virtue of that discontinuity one cannot conclude that man will *become* a personal sinner from the fact that he *is* situated by (original) sin.

Rahner also speaks of man's ratification or appropriation of his situational *Existential.*[94] "Adam's" sin, Rahner points out, determines the "Freiheits*situation"* of all men, but not freedom itself.[95] In his central act of freedom man appropriates a particular *Existential.* Thus, in personal sin, man ratifies the situational *Existential* of original sin, making its content the

---

86 *Ibid.*, 116, 120-21, 145, 150, 166. This concern to point out an influence of the situation *before* man's personal reaction represents the situational antidote to the Pelagian imitation theory (see *ibid.*, esp. 67, 121, 145).
87 *Ibid.*, 142. Weger adds the important qualification, "except for the grace of Jesus Christ." This qualification will be examined thoroughly in the next chapter.
88 *Ibid.*, 119, 150. Cf. Rahner, *Exkurs*, 204.
89 *Ibid.*, 142, 150.
90 *Ibid.*, 119.
91 *Ibid.*, 141.
92 *Ibid.*, 142, 149.
93 *Ibid.*, 141, 166.
94 *SM*, I, 1110, 1114; *SM*e IV, 330-31, 332; *Schriften*, IX, 272; *Exkurs*, 192.
95 *Exkurs*, 219-20.

meaning and freely chosen ground of his existence.[96] Rahner analyzes the inner process involved in the existential appropriation of a situational *Existential* outside the context of his discussion of original sin. As we have seen, due to the polar opposition between the situational *Existential* and existential self-determination and due to their inextricable relatedness, self-realization always entails man's (ontological) self-alienation.[97] Insofar as the situational *Existential* retains its character of determinate situatedness even *in* the act of self-determination, that free act cannot make being situated its own. For that reason self-realization and self-alienation are inextricable correlates of the human situational condition. As will become evident in the following section, in Rahner's view, too, being situated by sin intensifies the ontological tension that is given with this human condition.

C. SITUATIONAL CONCUPISCENCE AND INTEGRATING FREE ACT

The full gravity of the situation of original sin becomes manifest only when the factor of concupiscence is taken into consideration. The precise influence of this factor in a *sinful* situation is not readily established, however, since both Schoonenberg and Rahner[98] view concupiscence as a natural phenomenon that is modified by the presence of sin.[99] Hence, if the full effect of being situated by *sin* is to be clarified by the notion of concupiscence, it must first be understood as a natural phenomenon.

1. Natural Lack of *Integritas* and Personal Integration

Both Schoonenberg and Rahner view concupiscence as a natural[100] phenomenon, a reality that is given with man's spiritual-physical constitu-

---

96 *SM*, I, 1114; *SM*e, IV, 332; *Schriften*, IX, 271.

97 See ch. I, sec. B, 2, b, iii above,

98 Weger deals with the subject of concupiscence very briefly, mainly in an attempt to distinguish the essence from the results of the situation of original sin (*Theologie der Erbsünde*, 154-57).

99 This conception represents a historical-situational reinterpretation of Aquinas' view of concupiscence (compare Introduction, sec. A,7 above to especially Rahner, *Schriften*, VIII, 660-61).

100 In this context the term "natural" unavoidably vacillates between its theological and its philosophical sense (see ch.II, n.2 above), depending upon whether concupiscence is seen as belonging to man as nature apart from *grace* ("nature" in its theological sense), or whether concupiscence is viewed as a specific given of man's nature in distinction from man's *freedom* ("nature" in its philosophical sense). In which sense the term "natural" is being used in a particular instance can usually be determined by observing

tion.[101] As we have seen, that duality does not entail a dichotomy between man's higher, spiritual powers and his lower, sensual drives. Rather, it involves a tension and polarity between that which the whole man is as nature and what he becomes as person, i.e., by free self-determination. This discrepancy between (natural) essence and (personal) existence is not simply an expression of finitude, but derives its peculiar character and intensity from the fact that human nature is embodied materially.[102] By virtue of his corporeality, and thus his participation in material reality, man is *by nature* subject to a plurality of drives that require integration *by personal freedom*.[103] Whether these drives are sensual-biotic[104] or whether they take on psychic or even spiritual form,[105] they are expressions of concupiscence in its broad sense by virtue of their *spontaneity*; they constitute phenomena with a dynamics of their own, apart from human freedom.[106] Schoonenberg sums up this aspect of concupiscence succinctly when he says, "by his nature man is for himself a chaotic *datum* in need of integration through love."[107] These spontaneous drives are expressions of concupiscence in its strictest sense by virtue of their *recalcitrance:* these drives offer resistance to man's free acts, whether they be evil *or good*.[108] In comparison to the flexibility of freedom, these spontaneous drives constitute a retarding force. As a result a person can never be wholly "his own man," but is always dependant upon the determinate structures and processes of his material nature.

Although the integration or channeling of this multiplicity of spontaneous, relatively autonomous drives is to be accomplished by man's free act,[109] even apart from sin *integritas* would not have been a *datum* of man's

whether grace or freedom functions as the counterpart of nature. See *Schriften*, I, 406, where Rahner explicitly makes the transition from the philosophical to the theological meaning of "nature" in the context of his discussion of concupiscence.

101 Schoonenberg, *Geloof*, IV, 235-36, cf. 61-62; *Man and Sin*, 79, cf. 32-33. Rahner, *Schriften*, I, 394-96, 400, 403-405; VIII, 660-62; *Exkurs*, 207, 213-14.

102 See ch. I, secs. A, 2, b; B, 1; and B, 2, b above. See esp. Rahner, *Schriften*, I, 394-96, 400; *SM*, I, 1112-13; *SM*e, IV, 332; *Exkurs*, 213. Schoonenberg, *Geloof*, IV, 58-59 n. 2, 235; *Man and Sin*, 32-33, 79.

103 Rahner, *Schriften*, I, 383-84. Schoonenberg, *Geloof*, IV, 235; *Man and Sin*, 79.

104 Rahner, *Schriften*, I, 395; *Exkurs*, 207, 213. Schoonenberg, *Geloof*, IV, 61-62, 235-36; *Man and Sin*, 32-33, 79, 184.

105 Rahner, *Schriften*, I, 383-84, 388-90. Schoonenberg, *Geloof*, IV, 61; *Man and Sin*, 33, 79, 184.

106 Rahner, *Schriften*, I, 390-91, 396, 400-405. Cf. Schoonenberg, *Man and Sin*, 33-34; *Geloof*, IV, 58, n. 2, 61-63.

107 *Man and Sin*, 79; *Geloof*, IV, 236.

108 Rahner, *Schriften*, I, 396

109 Rahner, *Schriften*, I, 391-400. Schoonenberg, *Man and Sin*, 32-34, 182, 184-85; *Geloof*, IV, 61-62, 235-36.

nature but a personal *task*.[110] That task was to be accomplished through the process of human history. Indeed, according to Rahner, human, i.e., spatiotemporal history would be impossible without this *natural* concupiscence, for without the resistance of man's material nature total integration could have been accomplished in an *instant*.[111] Without the retarding effect of his own material nature, man could have attained his goal in "no time." A gradual integration process through space and time would have been unthinkable.[112] History as linear process and gradual progress is possible because even the central free act by which man appropriates his nature does not simply transform his nature into person, for nature retains its own spontaneous dynamics by virtue of the principle of materiality. That natural dynamics can – to a greater or lesser extent – be directed by the free act, but offers renewed resistance to a subsequent free act.[113] In view of the retarding force of man's nature, Rahner repeatedly defines human freedom as the *tendency* towards self-determination and towards total control over the entire breadth of man's reality.[114] The *status integritatis* of primordial man is seen by both Rahner and Schoonenberg, not as a state, but as a dynamic possibility.[115] "Paradise" is not a condition of pristine harmony, but an eschatological goal.[116] Pre-fall integrity is the experience of being positively directed to that goal – not without resistance, but without the added resistance introduced by sin.

The possibility of total integration through a gradual process of history, though accomplished in and through the free acts of man, is not itself a "natural"possibility.[117] Given simply the integrating force of freedom and the disintegrating forces of nature, the attainment of total integration is by

---

110 Rahner, *Schriften*, I, 403-404; *Exkurs*, 213-16. Schoonenberg, *Man and Sin*, 79; *Geloof*, IV, 236.

111 As in the case of Angels (see the references to Rahner's comments on this subject: Ch. I, n. 228 above).

112 Rahner, *Exkurs*, 213-14. Cf. ch. I, sec. B, 2, b, introductory paragraphs and i above.

113 See Rahner, *Schriften*, I, 397-400, 404-405; *Exkurs*, 213-14. See also the discussion of the relation of man's *option fondamentale* to its temporalization and materialization (ch. I, sec. B, 2, b, i above).

114 *Schriften*, I, 392-95, 396n, 404.

115 Rahner, *Schriften*, I, 402-405; *Exkurs*, 214-16. Schoonenberg, *Man and Sin*, 79; *Geloof*, IV, 235-36.

116 Rahner, *Schriften*, I, 405; *Exkurs*, 209. Schoonenberg, *Man and Sin*, 194: "Paradise lies not at the beginning but at the end . . . ." See also Schoonenberg's essay, "Natuur en zondeval," *TvTh*, II (1962), 173-201, esp. 191-93 where the idea of paradise as an evolving reality is formulated in terms of death and immortality.

117 The term is here used in its theological sense.

no means assured; in and by itself human history is inherently tragic.[118] The possibility of gradual integration and the dynamic directedness to total integration is a gift of *grace*.[119] Grace is the divine unifying force that enables freedom to attain its ultimate goal: integral unity in love.[120] As we have seen, however, grace itself is not a static given but the dynamic upward force of salvation history, a process borne by God's free decision to communicate His inner being to man and, through him, to the entire and wholly integrated world.[121] Thus, both by virtue of the resistance of man's material nature and by virtue of the process-character of grace in salvation history, the gift of *integritas* unfolds dynamically in history.

2. Concupiscence in a Sinful Situation

It goes without saying that sin, being primarily a wrongly directed free act that goes counter to unifying grace, profoundly disrupts the process of integration.[122] It is not the effect of the "first" *act* of personal sin upon natural concupiscence that is of direct relevance, but the effect of the *situation* of sin-affected-concupiscence upon man's free acts. Without the disruption of sin, each successive generation would have found itself within an increasingly integrated situation. The integration of man's material nature and historical situation achieved by one generation would have been handed on situationally, so that the next generation could have continued the integration process where the previous generation had left off. The entrance of sin into the world changed all that. Man is no longer situated by a degree of historical integration nor even by a degree of primordial natural disintegration. Rather, postlapsarian man finds himself situated by the *added dis*integration that is due to man's resistance to grace.[123] Presently, man experiences his freedom within a situation that cannot adequately be integrated by grace-borne free decisions.[124] Each free decision encounters the additional

---

118 See Rahner, *Schriften*, V, 130-31, 174.
119 Rahner, *Schriften*, I, 387, 402-403, 406; VIII, 660-66; Schoonenberg, *Man and Sin*, 182, 184.
120 Schoonenberg, *Man and Sin*, 185, 189. Rahner, *Exkurs*, 212 n; *SM*, I, 1113; *SM*e, IV, 332.
121 Ch. II, sec. C, 1 above.
122 See Schoonenberg, *Geloof*, IV, 236. Rahner, *Exkurs*, 213-14.
123 See Rahner, *SM*, I, 1113, *SM*e, IV, 332.
124 Rahner, *Exkurs*, 215; cf. *SM*, I, 1115 (*SM*e, IV, 333): "Das 'Paradies' ist kein innerweltlich erreichbares Ziel mehr; die Utopie, es herzustellen, müsste als selbst schuldbare Hybris das Gegenteil bewirken." If "paradise" may plausbily be interpreted as com-

retarding force of situationally embodied sinful decisions and thus of situationally fixed disintegration.[125] Moreover, insofar as the situational absence of grace hampers the love required for integration, the situation of original sin brings with it the inability to attain the degree of integration that ought to have been attained at a particular point in history.[126]

By taking the phenomenon of concupiscence into consideration, the gravity of being situated by sin is underscored. Original sin is then seen to be not purely a state of privation, but a situation that includes a specific kind of active force. The spontaneous drives of human nature, misdirected by sin, attain a certain situational momentum that becomes the historical *Existential* of postlapsarian freedom. Morally positive decisions are buffeted by the counter-momentum of these misdirected natural drives that have obtained situational autonomy and thus historical power.[127] The impossibility of bringing love to full expression is, therefore, not due solely to a moral-religious vacuum, the situational absence of grace, but also to the counter-force of situationally embodied misdirected drives. Because of this negative natural-historical dynamics, the situation of original sin can be said to bring with it the temptation to person sin,[128] or at least a greater proximity of evil.[129]

* * *

To this point, the consequences of original sin as situation have been examined in terms of the phenomena freedom, situatedness and grace. A severe restriction was placed upon the action-radius of grace, however. In accordance with the definition of original sin as the *spatiotemporal lack* of grace, the *presence* of grace was confined within the *transcendental* dimension. That restriction of grace to a transcendental dynamic, assuming as it does a totally negative spatiotemporal situation, made it possible to assess the

---

prising *Heil* and *integritas*, the difficulty of understanding this statement lies in the fact that Rahner often contends that paradise in this sense is not "innerweltlich erreichbar" *even apart from sin*. Rahner's precise view on this subject is very difficult to determine (cf. *Schriften*, V,130-31, 174; VI, 59-76, 77-88; VIII, 660-66, 586-90, 593-609; see also ch. II, C, 3 above).

125 See Rahner, *Schriften*, VIII, 665-66.
126 See Schoonenberg, *Geloof*, IV, 236, 239-40.
127 As an example of a typically historical power, Schoonenberg often mentions colonialism (see, e.g., *Man and Sin*, 105, 118). Such a phenomenon may be (partially) ascribed to some natural drive, a drive that has been untamed or misdirected; but once it receives situational expression, colonialism is not simply a natural drive nor simply a phenomenon dependent on a personal decision, but a typically *historical* power.
128 Weger, *Theologie der Erbsünde*, 157.
129 Schoonenberg, *Man and Sin*, 122.

maximum possible effect that can plausibly be ascribed to original sin interpreted as situation. Its *actual* effect, however, comes into view only when the continuing presence of grace is regarded not merely as a transcendental dynamic, but as a transcendental dynamic that — despite original sin — finds concrete spatiotemporal expression. Only when man is viewed as standing in the dual situation of the *spatiotemporal presence* and *privation* of grace does the actual effect of original sin become manifest.

CHAPTER V PRIVATION OF GRACE –
UNIVERSAL SITUATION?

The subject of the universality of original sin does not involve a merely quantitative question concerning the extent of this negative situation. Rather, what seems to be a mere question of statistics involves comprehensive value judgements. Moreover, the validity of these general value judgements determines whether the peculiar *quality* of original sin as situational *Existential* can be maintained as a reality to which each human being is subject.

As to the comprehensive question, by its very scope the issue as to the universality of original sin forces the serious interpreter of this doctrine to come to a concrete assessment of "the world" – its meaning, its direction, its relation to salvation, to the coming of Christ. The situationalists' general perspective on these embracive yet decisive issues has been set forth previously in terms of their views of the relation grace-nature, and more concretely in terms of their conception of salvation history.[1] That presentation needs to be elaborated, however, in terms of the situationalists' attempt to integrate the interpretation of original sin as a universal, situational privation of grace within that general perspective.

These general questions converge in the very specific question concerning the concrete situation – inside or outside the realm of empirical Christianity – of an individual human being. He represents, as it were, a test case concerning the nature of original sin interpreted as situation. Precisely in such an individual case, the question as to the universality of original sin becomes the crystallization point of the question concerning the concrete significance and kernel meaning of original sin interpreted as the *situational privation of grace*. It will be recalled that the situation of original sin was said to constitute an *Existential*.[2] The situation of original sin, therefore, must be such that the privation of grace represents man's *initial, encompassing* situation. This *kind* of situation can be categorically maintained only if the

1 See ch. II, sec. C above.
2 See ch. III, sec. A above.

situational privation of grace can be said to be universal in *extent*. However, such universality is seriously threatened from two directions.

A. SOURCES OF THE PROBLEM

1. Evolution, Polygenesis, Situational Nexus

In the traditional view, the maintenance of the universality of original sin is relatively simple: all men descend from Adam who, when he sinned, lost holiness and justice, not only for himself, but also for all his progeny.[3] Universality is safeguarded in this conception by *monogenesis*, by a relatively *proximate* and *definite origin* and by a *unity of* (human) *nature* constituted by realistic inclusion or genetic derivation, or both.[4] In the view of the situationalists this stable framework, within which the universality of original sin is securely nestled, is basically undermined.

The situationalists locate the evolutionary origin of man in a remote and elusive past about which nothing is known historically.[5] To further complicate matters, all accept the possibility or probability of the polygenetic origin of mankind.[6] Lastly, they minimize the function of nature in the transmission of original sin.[7] With the beginning of man's history vanishing in

---

3   See Introduction, sec. A, 8.
4   Cf. *DS*, 3897 (*Humani Generis*).
5   Schoonenberg, see sec. B, 1, a below. Rahner, see sec. B, 2, b below. Weger, *Theologie der Erbsünde*, 48-55, 80-90.
6   Schoonenberg, *TvTh*, IV, 69; *Bijdragen*, XXIV, 382-86, *MS*, II, 936-38, *Man and Sin*, 187-191. Rahner, *Exkurs*, 176-85. Weger, *Theologie der Erbsünde*, 42-47. The encyclical *Humani Generis* plays an extremely interesting role in the present discussion regarding polygenism. Regarding this theory the encyclical declares that "it does not appear how such views can be reconciled with the doctrine of original sin..." (*DS*, 3897). Whereas in the encyclical this apparent irreconcilability constitutes the basis for declaring that polygenism is not an open question (in distinction from the question of the evolution of the human body [*DS*, 3896-97]), all the theologians under consideration reopen the question of polygenesis by placing the accent on the fact that, to the magisterium, it is in no way *apparent (nequaquam appareat)* how original sin and polygenesis are reconcilable. They argue that if this reconcilability can – contrary to appearances – be demonstrated, polygenesis *is* an open question (Schoonenberg, *Geloof*, IV, 197-98; *Man and Sin*, 188. Rahner, *Exkurs*, 181. Cf. Weger, *Theologie der Erbsünde*, 53). Rahner formulates this interpretation of *Humani Generis* nicely by stating that it does not posit the irreconcilability of original sin and polygenesis but that it denies the *perspecuity* of such reconcilability (*Schriften*, I, 261). Rahner rightly points out that the encyclical did not intend to leave the door to polygenism *open* but neither, he in effect contends, did it *lock* that door (ibid.).
7   Schoonenberg, *Man and Sin*, 185-87; *Geloof*, IV, 183-91. Rahner, *Exkurs*, 194, 196-200, 203. Weger, *Theologie der Erbsünde*, 34-42, 65-70, 109-21.

the sheer remoteness, and disintegrating in the plurality of his origin, how can original sin be imagined as a universal situation? And even if something could be *postulated* about a first sin, how can its effect conceivably be inescapable for all men if its transmission depends upon the fluctuating nexus of man's historical situation? The collapse of the traditional framework appears to threaten not merely the universality but the very reality of original sin. The situational reinterpretation is in part an attempt to meet this challenge.[8] The problem of the universality of original sin is compounded by a factor that is closely related to the substitution of a situational for a natural nexus.

2. The Situational Presence of Grace

As if the problem concerning the universality of original sin were not rendered sufficiently formidable from the viewpoint of man's origin, the problem is even more pressing from the viewpoint of the *situational* present. As was noted, this source of difficulty is closely related to the relativization of a natural interhuman nexus. In the traditional conception original sin can be said to be the initial condition of every human being despite the presence of grace, because the lack of holiness and justice was considered to be, so to speak, "congenital" – original sin is passed on *generatione* or *propagatione*. Original sin can therefore be said to be strictly universal, for it is present, not only from the origin of *mankind,* but also at the origin of *each individual.* Hence no one can come into being without contracting original sin. Once this natural nexus is relativized, however, in favor of the historical nexus of situation, this reality tends to usurp the role of medium for original sin *and for grace.* Not only the privation, but also the presence of grace must be viewed concretely and, therefore, situationally. If grace finds concrete, situational expression, original sin as situational *Existential* is correspondingly suspended, not only for the existent group but, more importantly, also for anyone *born into* that situation. A brief resumé of the situationalists' view of the universal situation of grace and its positive situational expressions will illustrate the magnitude of this problem.

As has been noted, the situationalists speak of a universal situation of salvation.[9] *This* universal presence of grace as such need not contradict a uni-

---

8 Schoonenberg, for example, considers the theories of evolution and polygenism to have the function of a catalyst of reinterpretation (see Introduction, sec. B, 3 above) and Rahner says that the theological critique of traditional teachings on origins has its *external occasion* in the findings of paleontology (*Exkurs*, 210). Cf. Weger, *Theologie der Erbsünde,* 48.

9 See ch. II, secs. B, 3 and C, 3 above.

versal situational privation of grace because the universal salvific situation is constituted by God's *offer* of salvation.[10] Although this offer, as *interior Existential*, is the situation of every man, it constitutes his *transcendental* situation in distinction from his spatiotemporal situation.[11] As (formal) horizon within which man's acts are realized, the transcendental situation by no means guarantees a *positive expression* of grace in the spatiotemporal situation. On that basis the situationalists can consistently maintain the coexistence of this universal situation of salvation and a universal situation involving the privation of grace – as long as the transcendental and the spatiotemporal situation are viewed *in mutual abstraction*. However, when man responds positively to his salvific transcendental situation, this presence of grace *does* come to expression in his spatiotemporal situation. At *that* point the strict universality of original sin, defined as the situational privation of grace, is suspended.[12]

If the positive expressions of grace in concrete situations outside the immediate action-radius of the Church represented merely hypothetical possibilities, which are contemplated as being real only in exceptional instances, these could safely be disregarded as being largely irrelevant to the universality of original sin.[13] Such concrete realization of grace, however, is not regarded as being a hypothetical possibility or a sporadic phenomenon. Rather, the situationalists regard the concrete realization of grace to be widespread. This scope of grace is given with their affirmation of the primacy of the situation of salvation, the sovereignty and creative power of grace, and the unity of man.

The situationalists ascribe a certain primacy[14] and preponderance to

10 See ch. II, sec. B, 3 above.
11 See ch. III, sec. A; and ch. II, secs. C, 2 and 3 above.
12 Cf. Schrofner's observation, occasioned by Weger's *Theologie der Erbsünde:* "Wenn demnach die Geschichte nicht nur Sünde, sondern auch Heil vermittelt, dann scheint eine Bedrohung der Universalität der Erbsünde nicht mehr ausgeschlossen. Es wäre ja vorstellbar, das zumindest in der Zeit nach Christus und zumindest in einem begrenzten Bereich die Unheilsvermittlung durch das vermittelte Heil neutralisiert oder gar überboten würde . . ." (*ZKTh,* XCIII [1971], 204).

13 The traditional acknowledgement of the possibility of salvation (by virtue of a *votum ecclesiae* or *baptismi*) for people who have no direct relationship to the empirical Church left the generally negative view of those outside the Church intact; see Berkouwer's analysis of the shift in the interpretation of the traditional adage *extra ecclesiam nulla salus, Vatikaans Concilie,* 230-52; *The Vatican Council,* 188-204; cf. idem, *Nabetrachting op het Concilie* (Kampen: Kok, 1968), 16-30; see also Rahner, *Schriften,* II, 47-48 and Schoonenberg, "Heilsgeschichte und Dialog," *ThPQ,* CXV (1967), 132.

14 Schoonenberg, *SM,* IV, 778; cf. *Geloof,* I, 38.

the universal situation of salvation. Rahner speaks of sin in general as being salvifically encompassed by grace[15] and of original sin in particular as constituting a dialectical element within *the* efficacious divine will to salvation.[16] Similarly, Weger says that the history of perdition ("Unheilsgeschichte") is healingly surrounded by salvation history.[17] On that basis he can maintain that the (universal) situation of original sin in no way affects the supernatural *Existential* by virtue of which salvation remains possible for all men.[18]

Even this preponderance of the situation of grace in comparison to the situation of original sin need not pose a problem for maintaining the universality of the latter if realized salvation were regarded as a phenomenon restricted within the inner recesses of man or attained only at the end of human life. None of the situationalists, however, reduce salvation to such an ethereal or terminal phenomenon. That reduction would contradict the sovereignty of the gracious Creator by locking the power of His grace within man's inner life and outside the concrete daily life of His creation. Moreover, such a reduction of salvation would contradict the unity of man as historically mediated being. Given that unity, man cannot even experience his transcendental *Existential* of grace except via his concrete spatiotemporal medium.[19] Both because of the creative sovereignty of God's grace and because of the unity of His creature, salvation is realized concretely.[20] Whenever man responds positively to his transcendental dynamic, grace inevitably comes to expression in spatiotemporal situations.[21]

The sovereignty of a gracious Creator, the primacy of the situation of salvation and the unity of man combine to make the situational realization of grace likely. Although all the situationalists confess ignorance as to the precise extent of such expressions of grace,[22] it is clear that they do not regard the positive response to grace outside the realm of empirical Christianity to be a sporadic occurrence. Schoonenberg ascribes the genuine love that is found on a large scale in humanity to the power of grace.[23] Rahner is a fervent

15   *Schriften*, V, 215 ("umfangen" und "eingefangen"); also *SM*, I, 1106; *SM*e, IV, 329. See *Schriften*, VIII, 343-44 for the philosophical and theological basis for this positive view.
16   *Schriften*, IX, 270-71; cf. *SM*,I, 1109, 1114; *SM*e, IV, 330, 333. Similarly, Weger, *Theologie der Erbsünde*, 108.
17   Weger, *Theologie der Erbsünde*, 137; cf. 150.
18   *Ibid.*, 125-26; 151.
19   See ch. I, secs. B, 1 and B, 2, b; and ch. II, sec. C, 2 above.
20   Weger, *Theologie der Erbsünde*, 131. Rahner, *Schriften*, V, 146.
21   Weger,*Theologie der Erbsünde*, 132-33, 139. Rahner, *Schriften*, II, 84-88.
22   Rahner, *Schriften*, V, 144; X, 533-34. Weger, *Theologie der Erbsünde*, 139-40. Schoonenberg, *Man and Sin*, 196.
23   *Geloof*, IV, 224; cf. *Man and Sin*, 72 and *ThPQ*, CXV, 132-38.

exponent of *Heilsoptimismus*, an optimism regarding the concrete and actual salvation of man also outside the pale of empirical Christianity.[24] Such salvation, in his view, is realized, not merely in anonymous *Christians*, but concretely in anonymous *Christianity*, i.e., in the grace of Christ that comes to expression in the interhuman, historical forms of man's existence;[25] grace is objectified in situational and institutional manifestations.[26]

It is clear that the situationalists' view of the widespread situational realization of grace is wholly in accord with their general philosophical-theological framework: man as situated freedom, as mediated transcendence, is internally directed to the bestowal of supernatural grace, taken up in the dynamics of salvation history.[27] The only question is whether this general framework and its implications for the situational realization of grace leaves room for a doctrine of original sin as the initial lack of grace precisely from man's spatiotemporal situation. In the face of this widespread realization of grace, how and in what sense can original sin be maintained as the universal privation of grace from man's initial situation?

B. PROPOSED SOLUTIONS

In view of the fact that the universality of original sin becomes problematical for all three situational reinterpretations, it comes as somewhat of a surprise that Rahner does not deal with this problem directly and that Weger does not deal with it as a problem that plagues his own theory.[28] Rahner's failure to deal with this problem directly may well be due to the fact that his retention of a definitive fall at the beginning of human history appears to safeguard the universality of original sin adequately. Moreover, the theories that appear to compromise the universality of original sin most directly, especially those concerning anonymous Christianity, are dealt with

---

24 *Schriften*, V, 144-47.

25 See *Schriften*, VI, 546, where Rahner speaks expressly of anonymous *Christianity*, by which he means the historical expressions of Christian grace in "heathen" religions. Such expressions may include being baptized into anonymous Christianity (*ibid.*; cf. *Schriften*, V, 146-54; VIII, 370). See also *Schriften*, IX, 499-500, where Rahner rightly maintains that if one accepts the reality of anonymous Christians one must also accept that of anonymous Christianity (cf. *Schriften*, X, 532).

26 Weger frequently uses the term *Erscheinung* as a designation of this historical mediation of grace (see Weger, *Theologie der Erbsünde*, 121-37 where this term occurs on almost every page). Cf. Rahner's use of this term (*Schriften*, II, 127, 128; IV, 296; the term appears in quotation marks in each case).

27 See "Part I" above.

28 Weger does discuss the question of universality as a problem affecting other reinterpretations of original sin (*Theologie der Erbsünde*, 23-38).

outside the context of his discussion of original sin. Weger's omission can perhaps be ascribed to his deference to Rahner's theory of origins.[29] His circumvention of the problem of universality is nonetheless remarkable because it stands out in bold relief within his reinterpretation due to two factors. In the first place, he materially integrates Rahner's theory regarding anonymous Christianity within the discussion of original sin.[30] In the second place, at the outset of his study Weger declares universality to be an indispensable element of the doctrine of original sin.[31] Nevertheless, within his own reinterpretation Weger returns to the universality of original sin only to posit — despite all the evidence to the contrary — that the basic elements of this doctrine, including that of universality, have been verified.[32]

Of the situationalists, only Schoonenberg acknowledges that the extent of original sin represents a serious problem for the situational reinterpretation of this doctrine. This exception is both felicitous and infelicitous. His *lone* recognition of the problem is unfortunate in that it erroneously suggests that the universality problem is peculiar to his reinterpretation of original sin. His awareness of the problem is, of course, fortunate in that it leads him to a protracted and revealing struggle,[33] one that will hopefully lead us to the core of the situational reinterpretation. In any case, his direct confrontation with the present problem and his earnest search for its solution serves us well as a focal point for the essential issues that remain relatively dormant in Rahner's and Weger's discussions. After Schoonenberg's extensive and tenacious grappling with the problem of universality has been traced, Rahner's enviable solution by means of the remarkable retention of a definitive fall within a polygenetic origin will be examined.[34]

1. The Sin of the World and a "Second" Fall

Schoonenberg attempts to replace the entire doctrine of original sin as

---

29 *Ibid.*, 161. Here he refers to Rahner's *Exkurs* for an explanation of the way in which the universality of original sin may be safeguarded from the beginning.
30 *Ibid.*, 121-37.
31 *Ibid.*, 23-28.
32 *Ibid.*, 161.
33 In retrospect, Schoonenberg says of the element of the universality of original sin that this is the issue with which he wrestled most ("Feit en gebeuren: Eenvoudige hermeneutische beschouwingen bij enkele in discussie staande vragen," *TvTh*, VIII [1968], 36; "Ereignis und Geschehen: Einfache hermeneutische Überlegungen zu einigen gegenwärtig diskutierten Fragen," *ZKTh*, XC [1968], 16).
34 Although specific conceptions of human origins will come into view in the following sections, it must be kept in mind that these conceptions are treated only in terms of their repercussions upon the question of the universality of original sin.

traditionally conceived with a complex which he designates as the history of sin or, using a Johannine phrase, as the sin of the world.[35] This complex, as we shall see, is constituted both by the sinful acts stretching through history and by the historical situations created by those acts. In itself the idea of the sin of the world need not entail that *one* of the acts occurring within it constitutes a definitive fall. For some time Schoonenberg did consider the idea of a "second" fall as a hypothetical possibility but later abandoned it. Because of its peculiar status within the whole of Schoonenberg's conception and because it reflects more problems that it resolves, the second-fall hypothesis will be given separate treatment. First, Schoonenberg's general view of the sin of the world will be presented.

a. *"The Fall" — a History of Falling*

Even apart from the fact that Schoonenberg accepts polygenism as a viable option, his evolutionary view of human development[36] itself explains the increasing minimization of the historical significance of the first human acts. Taking the idea of an evolutionary development wholly seriously in its repercussions for theology, Schoonenberg views the first human acts as being relatively insignificant for the overall sweep of history. Rather than attributing a special importance to these acts, he views them as mere beginnings of human freedom, the stature of which may be assumed to be commensurate with what he calls the inconceivably primitive stature of early man.[37] If to this diminution of beginnings one adds the staggering protraction of the intervening time-span, the first human act is reduced to a vanishing point on the threshold of human development. Accordingly, Schoonenberg considers the more proximate acts to have proportionally greater historical weight than those at the dawn of human development, for the former overshadow, if not obscure, the latter.[38] The only uniqueness of the first act is numerical — it opens a series.[39]

---

35   For Schoonenberg's derivation of this designation from John, see *Man and Sin*, 101; *Bijdragen*, XXIV, 351; *MS*, II, 888.
36   See ch. II, sec. C, 1 above.
37   *Ex Auditu Verbi*, 267; cf. *TvTh*, II, 199; *TvTh*, IV, 70; *Man and Sin*, 177, 183; *Geloof*, IV, 8; *Gods wordende wereld*, 56; *God's World in the Making*, 70.
38   Schoonenberg, "Einige Bemerkungen zur gegenwärtigen Diskussion über die Erbsünde," *IDO-C*, 68-4 (January 28, 1968), 15; "Some Remarks on the Present Discussion of Original Sin," *IDO-Ce*, 68-4 (January 28, 1968), 14.
39   *Ibid.* Cf. *TvTh*, II, 199; *ThPQ*, CXVII, 122; *Ex Auditu Verbi*, 267-68. Schoonenberg gradually severs the doctrine of original sin from a unique beginning, proceeding step by step with extreme caution (cf. *Geloof*, I, 177-88 and IV, 191-98 to *TvTh*, II,

The diminution of the first sinful act is of great importance for the thoroughness of the situational reinterpretation of original sin. Whether the idea of the sin of the world is to supplant or merely to supplement the traditional conception of original sin depends, in Schoonenberg's view, upon whether or not a unique effect must be attributed to "Adam's" sin.[40] Schoonenberg himself makes an attempt at total renovation by radically attenuating the first act.[41]

When the significance of the beginnings of human development approaches the vanishing point, the center of gravity shifts decidedly towards the future. We have seen this to be the case in Schoonenberg's view of salvation history as ascent.[42] Remarkably, a similar shift is reflected in his view of the history of sin.

i. *The history of sin as descent*

From his delineation of the grand process of salvation history as ascent, one might conclude that Schoonenberg harbors an uncomplicated optimism concerning man's historical development, so that this dynamic *process* necessarily entails *progress.* Schoonenberg does not nurture such naive optimism with respect to this process, however, precisely because the name of that process is *history.* Historical development has as its distinguishing feature freedom,[43] so that Schoonenberg's conception of history precludes any *automatic* development towards perfection, a process in which all evil would represent merely a necessary by-product subservient to the overall good of evolution.[44] He conceives of man's ascent, not as a programmed journey to

173-201). Even when he himself is satisfied that a unique beginning need not be maintained he introduces this position merely as a hypothesis worthy of serious consideration (see *Man and Sin,* 179-80, 191; *Bijdragen,* XXIV, 377, 386; *MS,* II, 933, 938).

40   *Ex Auditu Verbi,* 267-68. Cf. *Bijdragen,* XXIV, 375-88; *Man and Sin,* 177-91; *MS,* II, 932-38; *IDO-C,68-4,* 15; *IDO-Ce,68-4,* 14.

41   The reinterpretation of the *dona praeternaturalia* (immortality, special [intuitive] knowledge, impassibility, immunity from concupiscence) traditionally attributed to Adam plays a pivotal role in Schoonenberg's gradual minimization of the beginning of human history (see especially *TvTh,* II, 173-201 as well as the other references mentioned in n. 39 above).

42   See ch. II, sec. C, 1 above.

43   *Man and Sin,* 194.

44   See ch II, n. 133 above. Accordingly, Schoonenberg consistently opposes the tendency of reducing original sin to an aspect of natural evolution (*Bijdragen,* XXIV, 349) and warns against the danger of an evolutionistic interpretation "des erbsündlichen Daseins" (*MS,* II, 931). See also *WuW,* XXI, 557; *Man and Sin,* 42-47. Bakker calls attention to the fact that precisely during the time that he was deeply influenced by Teilhard de Chardin, Schoonenberg published prolifically on the subject of *sin,* particularly original sin (*TvTh,* XI, 366).

bliss but as a perilous venture of freedom.

The recognition of man's freedom in itself need not, of course, temper an optimistic view of history. Man's freedom could be emphasized merely to warn against *possible* failure, to point out the *risk* of falling, falling into an abyss that *borders* on the pathway to perfection. Despite Schoonenberg's view of salvation history as involving an ascent, however, he conceives of "the fall" not merely as a past reality, nor merely as a future possibility, but as an ongoing actuality.

> In this upward progression sin plays a role. . . . Here the word "history" must be emphasized. Salvation does not grow in the manner of infrahuman life; it has to be freely accepted and may therefore also be rejected. Therefore, there is no "evolution of grace," but a history of salvation *and* perdition. [45]

Viewing the history of sin as a continuing, intensifying reality, Schoonenberg can say that both salvation and doom grow *apace*.[46]

The optimism that does survive in the face of the counterforce of sin is the qualified optimism of hope. "Optimism in the good course of nature," says Schoonenberg, "may not be prolonged in a straight line, it must cross the harsh reality of our sinful world before becoming hope of salvation."[47] That hope is embodied in love; love is realized by faith; and faith is directed to the unmerited favor of God's grace.[48] Accordingly, the deepest ground of Schoonenberg's optimism comes into view when he says, "The ultimate basis of our hope is God's salvific will."[49] On that foundation, the idea of salvation history as ascent survives as the dominant theme – yet without squelching the discordant note of sin. For that reason Schoonenberg states that he needs *two* sentences to outline his "evolutionary picture of the world":

> The whole evolution of creation is crowned by a historical ascent of mankind, crowned in its turn by Christ's presence, which keeps growing too towards his manifestation in the parousia, the beginning of "God all and in all." That ascent is crossed by a similar ascent of sin, but God brings about the triumph of the ascent in Christ. [50]

Within that compound picture of the world and its historical development, the idea of a fall is not lost from sight but incisively modified. Schoonenberg does not wish to reduce the fall to an intra-personal event by inter-

---

45 *Man and Sin*, 195 emphasis added.
46 *Ibid.*, 195.
47 *Ibid.*, 47.
48 *God's World in the Making*, 82-83; *Gods wordende wereld*, 63-64.
49 *God's World in the Making*, 83; *Gods wordende wereld*, 64.
50 *Man and Sin*, 194.

preting "Adam" simply as "Everyman," a symbol of the existential act of sin.[51] When Schoonenberg says, therefore, that he does not wish to abolish, but to multiply "Adam,"[52] he is not proposing an ahistorical actualization of "Adam." On the contrary, Schoonenberg speaks elsewhere of the legitimacy of a relative *historicization* of Adam.[53] This means that the idea of the fall must be allowed neither to vanish behind the mysterious natural bond that was traditionally thought to link each individual to Adam,[54] nor to evaporate in the rarified air of an existential event. Rather, the fall must be taken up in man's element, the palpable stream of history, specifically, the polluted stream of the history of sin.[55] Having undergone the metamorphosis of Schoonenberg's conception of history, therefore, the historic fall becomes a history of falling.[56]

ii. *Contours of the history of sin*

The phases of the history of sin correspond, as counterforce, to the ascending phases of the history of salvation that were described earlier,[57] for sin is the refusal to become positively involved in the history of salvation.[58] In the heathen religions this refusal took form especially in the usurpation entailed in idol worship, an expression of man's desire to become as God. In Israel this resistance to salvation history took form especially in the rejection of the prophets, a sin that foreshadows the rejection of Christ.[59] Since all the phases of the universal history of salvation are taken up in an ascent to Christ, all resistance to grace before Christ's appearance, also the sin outside Israel, represents a resistance to Christ, namely, "a refusal to take part in the ascension towards him...."[60] In a very real sense, therefore, all sins previous

---

51 *Geloof,* IV, 100-103, 158; *Man and Sin,* 126; *ThPQ,* CXVII, 121-122.
52 *WuW,* XXI, 584.
53 *Ex Auditu Verbi,* 267.
54 *Man and Sin,* 98; *MS,* II, 886.
55 *Man and Sin,* 178-79; *Bijdragen,* XXIV, 375-76; *MS,* II, 930-33.
56 Schoonenberg speaks of "Sündenfall als Geschichte" (*WuW,* XXI, 585) and of the fall as constituting "a gradual history," (*Bijdragen,* XXIV, 372; cf. *Man and Sin,* 174) and a "history of sin" (*Bijdragen,* XXIV, 385). Given that meaning of the term history, Schoonenberg rightly says that he maintains a "historical fall" (*TvTh,* IV, 69).
57 See ch. II, sec. C, 1 above. For the idea of the history of sin as an organic process of decline Schoonenberg appeals to those Scripture passages that speak of the resistance to Christ as being a completion and fulfillment of sins committed in the past (*Man and Sin,* 107-108; *MS,* II, 891-92).
58 *SM,* IV, 769.
59 *Man and Sin,* 108; *MS,* II, 892; *Bijdragen,* XXIV, 357-58.
60 *Man and Sin,* 107; *Bijdragen,* XXIV, 356.

to Christ's coming, according to Schoonenberg, "may be considered as an ascending, or better a descending, progression towards the killing of Christ."[61]

Since the appearance of Christ represents a critical midpoint and high point in the history of salvation, rebellion against his personal presence cannot but mark a corresponding lowpoint in the history of sin:

> The Mediator and source of God's grace has been exiled from our human existence on earth; he has been killed, which is the most complete and final rejection and exclusion which we human beings can inflict upon somebody. It follows necessarily that we have lost grace in a manner which is complete and final from our point of view, that we have turned into a "world lying in evil" (I Jn 5: 19).[62]

Although Schoonenberg attaches a unique significance to the act of Christ's rejection, he depicts this event as a high point, not as the end point of the history of sin. Sin constitutes an even higher degree of opposition to Christ after His ascension than before. Being glorified by His Spirit, Christ "wishes to assume us in himself."[63] Consequently, all willful squandering of grace now entails, "consciously or unconsciously, a refusal to be in him."[64] Moreover, because of the close relationship between Christ and the Spirit since the resurrection and ascension, resistance to grace in the present epoch reaches new anti-*Christ*ian heights as resistance to the *Spirit*. Continued resistance despite the light of the Spirit is thereby uncovered as perfidious darkness. Schoonenberg therefore views "the sin against the Holy Spirit" as "sin in its deepest malice."[65] Thus sin goes its appalling way through history, until in the end "the 'mystery of godlessness' fully develops in the revelation of 'the godless,' who will be destroyed by Christ in the Parousia (2 Th 2:7f.) and who is therefore rightly called 'the Antichrist.' "[66]

iii. *Sin-of-the-world, a "history" of "sin"*

Because the second-fall hypothesis, to be discussed momentarily, involves an attempt to establish the precise material correlation between the two constituents of the sin of the world (sinful act and sinful situation), a description of the formal aspect of that correlation suffices at this point to clarify the idea of the sin of the world. That description involves little more

---

61 *Man and Sin,* 108; *MS,* II, 982; *Bijdragen,* XXIV, 357.
62 *Man and Sin,* 110-11; *MS,* II, 894; *Bijdragen,* XXIV, 359.
63 *Man and Sin,* 24; *MS,* II, 852.
64 *Ibid.*
65 *Man and Sin,* 11.
66 *Ibid.,* 107. See also *Bijdragen,* XXIV, 356; *MS,* II, 852; *Man and Sin,* 24.

than an elaboration of what was said regarding the relation of freedom and situation.[67]

One can understand Schoonenberg's intention embodied in the expression, the sin of the world, or its equivalent, the history of sin, by observing either Schoonenberg's preference for the singular form of the word sin in both expressions or his use of the word history in the latter. As has been noted, Schoonenberg defines history as the interlinkage of free decision and situation.[68] Transposed to the present context, this means that although the temporally successive sinful acts represent a constitutive element of the history of sin,[69] in and of themselves these acts cannot constitute the sin of the world or the history of sin. That history is not simply the aggregate of a temporal *series* of sins, but a unified, situational *concatenation* of sins. It is the other constituent of the sin of the world, situation, that incorporates historical sins into a history of sin.[70] For Schoonenberg, the Johannine phrase, the sin of the world, becomes a *terminus technicus* designed to capture the history of sin as a unified whole.

b. *The Second-fall Hypothesis*

Although Schoonenberg dispenses with a definitive fall at the beginning of human history, he does not immediately abandon the idea of a definitive fall as such. This is not surprising in view of the problem of conceiving of original sin concretely as a universal situation. If this problem represented merely a quantitative question, however, the search for a definitive fall at a point far beyond the beginnings of human history would have been invested with less urgency. It would have involved the endeavor of demonstrating formal agreement merely concerning the *extent* of original sin between the Church doctrine and its situational reinterpretation. As has been noted, there are reasons more intrinsic to the situational reinterpretation itself that render the universality of original sin a problem that clamors for a solution.

Original sin has been reinterpreted as a negative, situational *Existential*, i.e., a prepersonal situation, a situation that is antecedent to every personal decision.[71] This priority constitutes an indispensable dimension of original sin defined as situational *Existential*. To be sure, that priority is in the first place

---

67 See ch. I, sec. A, 3 above.
68 See *ibid.*
69 *Man and Sin*, 98-111; *MS*, II, 886-94; *Bijdragen*, XXIV, 350-359.
70 *Man and Sin*, 103-105, 112; *MS*, II, 888, 891; *Bijdragen*, XXIV, 353-55, 359.
71 See ch. I, sec. A, 3, c; ch. III, secs. C, 1, b and C, 2, b, i and ii; and ch. IV, sec. B above.

of an *ontological* nature: as inextricable element in every free decision, being-situated has priority in the sense that it is the inescapable given presupposed by that decision. Nevertheless, as *inextricable* element and *inescapable* given, a situational *Existential* of necessity also has *temporal* priority with respect to every decision of an individual. Accordingly, it is abundantly clear from Schoonenberg's descriptions that in identifying original sin as a situational *Existential* such temporal priority is essential: the situational privation must obtain at the moment of birth.[72] If the privation of grace is not the child's initial concrete situation, original sin may certainly be real as situation, but it is not real as the *Existential* of that child. Conversely, that child will certainly experience a situational *Existential*, but that *Existential* is not original sin. Thus the seemingly purely quantitative question as to the universality of original sin in fact entails a critical qualitative issue that can be expressed in a pair of corollaries. *Formally*, the interpretation of original sin as the historical *Existential* of every human being is at stake. *Materially*, the identification of a situational *Existential* with original sin — defined as the privation of grace — is at stake. Sensing the challenge presented by this issue, Schoonenberg faces it squarely.

It is in answer to the nettlesome problem of maintaining original sin as a universal situation that Schoonenberg entertained the hypothesis that the definitive fall took place in and by the rejection and crucifixion of Christ.[73] Although in his publications he never presented the idea of the "second" fall[74] as being more than a hypothesis,[75] for Schoonenberg himself it never-

---

72 See ch. I sec. A, b and c above. Although Rahner does not deal with the case of an infant directly and, for that reason, does not speak explicitly of a temporal priority, it is clear from his understanding of *Existential* that this reality by its very nature precedes the existence of individuals (see ch. I, n. 163 above).

73 Greshake points out that Schoonenberg's theory is in fact a repristination of Pelagius' position that the universality of sin did not become real until the crucifixion of Christ (*Gnade als konkrete Freiheit*, 99, n. 31).

74 Schoonenberg refers to Romano Guardini's description of the rejection and crucifixion of Christ as "the second fall," but registers his misgivings about the aptness of the modifier, "second." Schoonenberg considers it more accurate to speak of this event as a "final ratification of the fall" (*Man and Sin*, 121; *Bijdragen*, XXIV, 366) or as a "summit" of the history of sin (*Man and Sin*, 107-108; *Bijdragen*, XXIV, 356;cf. *MS*, II, 892, 938; *TvTh*, II, 199-200; *TvTh*, IV, 75). Although this objection is well taken since from Schoonenberg's viewpoint there is no *first*, definitive fall upon which a *second* fall follows, for the sake of convenience the term "second-fall" will be retained in the following analysis. Moreover, in retrospect this designation proves to be a remarkably apt historical description of Schoonenberg's conception because the second-fall hypothesis becomes manifest as being an exact, updated replica of the "first fall."

75 See *Man and Sin*, 196 where he refers to this hypothesis as being "the most hypothetical element of the whole work" (cf. *MS*, II, 938; *TvTh*, IV, 75).

theless represented a working hypothesis to which he personally attached considerable significance.[76] As working hypothesis the idea of the second fall — if it may be personified for a moment — enjoyed a brief, but eventful career. First introduced inconspicuously in an epilogue, the second-fall hypothesis soon gained in prominence, even constituting an integral part of a thoroughgoing reinterpretation of the doctrine of original sin. Soon thereafter, however, it suffered the fate of sudden demise and, ultimately, dismissal for being problematical and even superfluous — an ignominy only partially mitigated by a final word of appreciation.[77]

Despite its hypothetical status, its problematic nature and its ephemeral existence, the second-fall hypothesis is more than a mere curiosity. It is of inestimable value in uncovering several facets of the situational reinterpretation of original sin, facets that transcend the mere question of the extent of original sin. The second-fall hypothesis provides us with a rare opportunity of observing (hopefully, feeling from within) the powerful dynamics and tensions that converge in the process of reinterpretation. This tenuous hypothesis may even put us on the track that leads to the kernel meaning and ultimate ground of the situational reinterpretation of original sin.

---

76 Aside from the integral function which this hypothesis fulfilled as the key underpinning for the comprehensive situational reinterpretation of the doctrine of original sin, it is noteworthy that in a discussion Schoonenberg is reported to have said, "For me the ultimate reason for original sin is the fact that Christ himself was banished from this life by man" (*Jaarboek 1963-64*, 86; a discussion following the essay by H. A. M. Fiolet, "De Erfzonde als Verbondsmysterie," *ibid.*, 53-85).

77 The history of the second fall hypothesis may be outlined as follows:

Ascending prominence:

    1960: mentioned in passing (*AvT*, XLVIII, 147).

    1962: introduced in an epilogue (*Geloof*, IV, 275-76) and incorporated into a definition of original sin (*TvTh*, II, 200).

    1963: given a central and integral role (*Bijdragen*, XXIV; reflected in *Man and Sin* and *MS*, II).

Declining prominence:

    1964: accentuation of its hypothetical character (*TvTh*, IV, 75; reflected in *Man and Sin*, 196 [epilogue], *MS*, II, 938 [last page of essay]).

    1966: proposed subordination to the general history of sin (*WuW*, XXI, 590; cf. *MS*, II, 938).

    1968: attempted subordination to the general history of sin (*MS*d, VIII, 72-73, 123-24).

Demise:

    1968: abandoned (*ZKTh*, XC, 16; *TvTh*, VIII, 37; *IDO-C, 68-4*, 15-16; *IDO-C*e, *68-4*, 14: "*for the most part* I have rejected it" [emphasis added]).

i. *Its intended function*

As was implicit in the description of the history of sin,[78] if an equivalent of Adam's fall is to be found at a later stage of the process of historical development, it must be sought at the point of Christ's rejection and crucifixion. As Schoonenberg points out, the history of salvation reaches an apex in the grace embodied in the person of Jesus. He is the Way, the Truth, the Life. He is the mediator and *source* of grace.[79] Consequently the banishment of the source and fullness of grace by an irrevocable act of murder could not but usher in a definitive and inescapable situation devoid of grace. That act atrociously transforms the zenith of the history of salvation into the nadir of the history of sin.[80] "In the Gospel of John," says Schoonenberg, "it seems that through the rejection of Christ God's world first becomes a world-lying-in-evil."[81] Although God's sovereign and creative grace transforms the cross into a sign of salvation,[82] the universal situation of doom is not thereby abolished.[83]

The idea of a definitive fall at the midpoint of salvation history appears to be a welcome and functional supplement to the situational reinterpretation of original sin. More than that, it may even supply a foundation for the reality of original sin as the situational privation of grace. In introducing the second-fall hypothesis, Schoonenberg is driven by the awareness that without a definitive fall there is no reason for precluding a history of positive responses to grace that create a situation of grace rather than one of original sin, the privation of grace: "For if the fall should not occur in a single, special sin which obtains significance for each human being by way of heredity, if the fall is instead realized through a long history [of sin], then it is possible that Christ's redemption would, in a history of faith, hope and love, permeate a certain milieu in such a way that within it human beings would start their existence in an openness for the life of grace; that is, they would start their existence without original sin, in a state of 'immaculate conception.'"[84] These grace-filled, sinless enclaves in human history, however small or few,

---

78 See sec. B, 1, a, ii above.
79 Man and Sin, 120-23; *MS*, II, 896; *Bijdragen*, XXIV, 366-68.
80 *Man and Sin*, 108; *MS*, II, 892; *Bijdragen*, XXIV, 357.
81 *TvTh*, IV, 75; cf. *Man and Sin*, 110-11; *Bijdragen*, XXIV, 359. See also sec. B, 1, a, ii above.
82 *Ibid*., Cf. *Man and Sin*, 120-21, 190; *MS*, II, 897-98; *Bijdragen*, XXIV, 366-67, 385-86.
83 *Geloof*, IV, 276; *Bijdragen*, XXIV, 384-85. Cf. *Man and Sin*, 120-21, 190; *MS*, II, 897-98.
84 *Man and Sin*, 189; *Bijdragen*, XXIV, 384-85.

represent a direct negation of the "grace-less" world that was said to constitute the situation of original sin.[85] That negation of original sin as the situational *Existential* of every human being must be precluded.

If original sin is to be strictly universal, i.e., the initial situational *Existential* of gracelessness of every human being, Schoonenberg argues, its cause must be an irreversible act, an act of which the effects cannot be undone by positive responses to grace.[86] The rejection of Christ by crucifixion seems to meet precisely this requirement: as an act of *murder,* it is from man's point of view irreversible; as the murder of *the source* of grace within the world, it plunges that world into a situation of total gracelessness.[87] The second-fall hypothesis is of great import for Schoonenberg because it enables him to by-pass the *subjective ambiguity* that inheres in historical acts and in the resultant situation by localizing the cause of the situation of doom in "an *objective fact* which stays real even in the absence of all guilt . . . ."[88] In this way the second-fall hypothesis explains both the essence of original sin, namely, the privation of grace as well as the precise structure of original sin, namely, an inescapable (historical) *Existential,* the initial situation of each human being.[89]

Because the second-fall explains the incisive nature, the categorical negativity and the strict universality of original sin as situation, this hypothesis also serves to render the universal necessity of a radical and unique remedy plausible. When Schoonenberg speaks of the irreversible situation that is brought about by the rejection of Christ, he usually qualifies this by stating that it cannot be reversed from *within* this world,[90] from within the dynamics of general salvation history. The world no longer contains a "source of grace," an "earthly mediator" of grace.[91] Because the chain of personal-situational communication of grace has been disastrously disrupted by the rejection of the fullness of grace, a radically different medium of grace has become necessary. That medium is the sacrament, specifically the sacrament of (infant) baptism.[92]

Schoonenberg starkly contrasts the new with the original medium of

---

85   See ch. III, nn. 1 and 2 above.
86   *Man and Sin,* 120-21, 189-90; *MS,* II, 896-97; *Bijdragen,* XXIV, 366-67, 385-86.
87   *Ibid.*
88   *Man and Sin,* 196 emphasis added; see also n. 130 below.
89   *Bijdragen,* XXIV, 365-66; *MS,* II, 896-97 ("Die Gnadenlosigkeit ist zu einer 'existentialen' Situation geworden"). Cf. *Man and Sin,* 120.
90   *Man and Sin,* 110, 121, 196, 197; *MS,* II, 896-97; *Bijdragen,* XXIV, 359, 366.
91   *Man and Sin,* 121; *MS,* II, 897; *Bijdragen,* XXIV, 366.
92   *Geloof,* IV, 187-88; *MS,* II, 897-98, 938; *Bijdragen,* XXIV, 367-68, 386; *Man and Sin,* 121-22, 190-91.

grace. Originally, grace was to be mediated personally, charismatically. Now grace is first mediated *institutionally,* i.e., by a medium whose reliability is *not* dependent on the precarious element of personal commitment.[93] Instead of the original *ex opere operantis* or – to underscore the personal element – *ex communione sese communicantis* mediation of grace, the institutionalized sacrament functions *ex opere operato.*[94] This does not mean that the institutional medium simply supplants the personal communication of grace. Rather, the institutional-sacramental medium of grace represents an indestructible, reliable bridgehead of grace.[95] That institutional emergency measure is meant to mobilize the force of personal love and thus reactivate the interpersonal communication of grace.[96] Accordingly, the institutional medium of grace may be seen as the inverse counterpart of the situation of original sin. Whereas original sin is a situation of gracelessness that arises from and inclines to sin,[97] the Church and its sacraments represent an institutional agency of "grace-fullness" that arises from and inclines to personal love.[98]

In this way the second-fall hypothesis is not a negation of the presence of grace in the world. Rather, insofar as this hypothesis explains the reality of an *irreversible* situation of original sin which is the initial *Existential* of each human being, it explains the necessity of a *peculiar remedy* – *in re* or *in voto* – for all men.[99]

ii. *Its intrinsic inadequacy and general incongruity*

The second-fall hypothesis seems to be an ideal component of the situational reinterpretation of original sin, for it appears to explain the universality and categoriality of original sin as situational *Existential* as well as the necessity of a novel, institutional medium of grace. Contrary to appearances, however, the seond-fall hypothesis fails to explain any of these. Moreover, this hypothesis represents an incongruent element within the general frame-

93 *Geloof,* IV, 187-88; *Man and Sin,* 121, 190-91; *Bijdragen,* XXIV, 367.
94 *Geloof,* IV, 187-88.
95 *God of mens,* 26: "The uniqueness of the symbolic sacramental act lies in the fact that the Church as eschatological, i.e., definitive communion of salvation in Christ, a communion that cannot again be eliminated from the world by our sins, stands totally behind, expresses herself in, and guarantees this sign. In this way the precariousness that adheres to the minister's involvement in the sacrament due to our sinfulness is transcended."
96 *Geloof,* IV, 188; *Man and Sin,* 190.
97 See ch. III, sec. C, 1, b above.
98 It arises from Christ's love and is directed to Christian love (see *Geloof,* IV, 188; *Man and Sin,* 121, 190).
99 *Bijdragen,* XXIV,386; cf. *Geloof,* IV, 163; *TvTh,* II, 199.

work of Schoonenberg's reinterpretation.

That the second-fall hypothesis fails to serve the purpose for which it was designed can readily be demonstrated. Let us assume that the banishment of Christ from this world by an act of murder indeed leaves behind a world devoid of grace, necessitating a new and unique emergency measure if grace is to penetrate this world once more. In this situation, the sacramental-institutional medium would reopen the personal communication of grace. But then, wherever people continue to respond positively to this initial sacramental breakthrough, this emergency measure — by its own efficacy — is obviated for the following generation.

Even assuming the reality of the second fall, the categorical negativity of the resultant situation and the necessity of the sacramental mediation of grace in *that* situation, a new situation is quite conceivable in which *baptized* believing parents or an entire community of baptized believers surround a child so thoroughly with their (sacramentally infused) love that the situation of original sin, though existent and real, cannot be said to be *this child's interior* determination, its concrete situational *Existential*. In the most concrete manner imaginable, that child finds itself in a situation of "original salvation."[100] In this instance original sin becomes literally the child's *Um-Welt*, a complex of *circum*-stances just beyond its immediate situational *Existential*.[101] Probably temporarily, but nevertheless effectively, the universality of original sin has been suspended — despite the assumed reality and effect of a second fall.[102]

The second-fall hypothesis, therefore, can at most explain only a temporary universality of original sin. Whenever the dynamic power of salvation history, resurgent by virtue of a new initiative of grace, penetrates and permeates a specific period and milieu anew, another pre-fall situation obtains once more — until the "third" fall. That brings us to the general incongruity of the second-fall hypothesis.

The second-fall hypothesis is foreign to the historical framework within

---

100 *Man and Sin*, 198.
101 Cf. Schoonenberg's objection to the idea of situation as "Umwelt," ch. I, sec. A, 3 (introductory paragraphs).
102 It is not surprising, therefore, that Betty, though relying on the work in which the second-fall hypothesis is meant to secure the strict universality of original sin, namely *Man and Sin*, nonetheless raises the question whether a child in a community of saints would not escape original sin altogether (*Thought*, XLV, 99). He goes on to suggest that "this is a consideration which Schoonenberg does not seem to have taken into account" (ibid.). Ironically, the fact of the matter is that because Schoonenberg did take into account precisely this consideration (*Man and Sin*, 189-90; see sec. B, 1, b, i above) he introduced the second-fall hypothesis and gave it a central place in this work.

which Schoonenberg reinterprets original sin. That framework consists of a view of history as an evolutionary process in the sense that the heart of history, salvation history, is viewed as an ascending development.[103] Within that conception, a definitive fall at the beginning of history is, of course, out of the question — but so is a definitive fall anywhere within the process of history.[104] Every "fall," or rather, low-point within the development of salvation history is in principle superable by the dynamics of grace. Within that view of history, the idea of a definitive fall cannot be salvaged by shifting its occurrence from the beginning to the midpoint of history. The only "time" that is left for a definitive fall is the end of time. Just as in the case of "paradise,"[105] so too in the case of the "fall" the center of gravity shifts inexorably towards the eschaton.[106] Indeed, even while Schoonenberg is still exploring the possibilities of the second-fall hypothesis, the forward thrust of his conception of history makes itself felt. In the very book in which the second-fall hypothesis plays a central role, Schoonenberg makes statements that reveal the idea of a definitive fall within history to be incompatible with the idea of salvation history as ongoing ascent. Significantly, this decisive and consistent shift towards the future comes to light in an epilogue in which Schoonenberg attempts to integrate his conception of sin and salvation as historical processes even more fully with an evolutionary picture of the world:

> Both salvation and doom grow apace, and only God knows to what extent they are at work, realized in each man. At any rate they grow towards the final outcome in which an eternal fixation in sin is a frightening possibility, and a universe of love is our beckoning hope.[107]

103   See ch. II, sec. C, 1 above.

104   From this viewpoint it is probably more accurate to speak of the history of sin as a counterforce that accompanies salvation history rather than to contrast the two as descent and ascent.

105   *Man and Sin,* 194: "Paradise lies not at the beginning, but at the end, so that sin and Redemption, too, should be measured in their deepest meaning against that fulfillment."

106   Betty levels this perceptive criticism at the second-fall hypothesis: "Logically, the inner coherence of the theory would seem to call for an ongoing 'fall' rather than the concrete historical 'fall' located in the act of the crucifixion. There is no intrinsic reason for Schoonenberg to place the 'fall' in the event of the murder of Jesus. It would be more in line with the whole of his theory to see the 'fall' as a constant process of the rejection of the person of Christ throughout history, one manifestation of which was the concrete rejection of the historical Jesus" (*Thought,* XLV, 99).

107   *Man and Sin,* 196. See also the statement cited in n. 105 above. Cf. Teilhard de Chardin's view (as expounded by Schmitz-Moormann): "Die Sünde als Ablehnung des von Gott gnadenhaft angebotenen Heils wächst durch die Geschichte hindurch, um in der Ablehnung des geschichtlichen Erlösers ihren vorläufigen, und in der Ablehnung des

That statement eloquently and accurately sums up the (only) way in which the idea of a definitive fall is compatible with Schoonenberg's mature conception of history. But what are the repercussions of this shift for the universality of original sin? A definitive fall at the end of history seems to have relevance for the present only as a *frightening possibility*. In any case, for the present time the universality of original sin does not seem real, for we live before a (possible) definitive fall. In that sense we live in a *pre*lapsarian situation. In that interim epoch a degree of situational privation of grace is quite conceivable. The question to be asked, however, is whether each man can be said to be subject to original sin, i.e., the situational privation of grace, a privation that constitutes the historical *Existential*, the initial situation of each human being.

iii. *Its abandonment and the lingering problem*

After functioning prominently as working hypothesis, the identification of the rejection of Christ as the definitive fall was reluctantly abandoned.[108] It is unfortunate that this takes place after the situational reinterpretation of original sin was completed, for that edifice was erected by falling back — at critical points — upon the second-fall hypothesis to explain the reality of original sin as situational *Existential* and as initial privation of grace.[109] Hence, the question arises how, despite its intrinsic inadequacy, the second-fall hypothesis *in fact* functioned in Schoonenberg's situational reconstruction of the doctrine of original sin. Did it function as scaffold or as key underpinning?[110]

Although the second-fall hypothesis is intrinsically inadequate for either function, evidence of a weak scaffold need not have any repercussions once the building is completed. For Schoonenberg, however, the second-fall hypothesis did function as underpinning upon which the reality of original sin as situational *Existential* and as situational privation of grace rests.[111] The collapse of this faulty underpinning could be calamitous. In any case a thorough inspection of the edifice resting on this support would seem to be in order.

in der Parusie die Erlösung vollendenden Christus ihren endgültigen Höhepunkt zu erreichen" (Schmitz-Moormann, *Die Erbsünde*, 118).

108 See n. 77 above. Even in abandoning the idea of a second fall, Schoonenberg states that it "has something attractive about it" (*TvTh*, VIII, 37; *ZKTh*, XC, 16).

109 See sec. B, 1, b, i above.

110 Stenzel characterizes Schoonenberg's second-fall hypothesis variously as a "Stützannahme" and as a "Hilfskonstruktion" (*ThuPh*, XLVI, 560).

111 This is implicitly corroborated by Stenzel's judgement (see n. 135 below).

From Schoonenberg's point of view, however, this inspection is not necessary because he is convinced that an underpinning such as the second-fall hypothesis is superfluous. That conviction enables Schoonenberg to relinquish this hypothesis rather casually. Despite its service, therefore, as temporary underpinning for the situational reconstruction of original sin, the removal of this support does not appear to send so much as a tremor through the building. This feat can be accomplished only if another and more substantial underpinning is uncovered.

When Schoonenberg definitively discards the second-fall hypothesis, he suggests that a single source of the situation of original sin is not required to safeguard its universality.[112] He then states as his present, equally hypothetical view that every sin that has occurred creates the situation into which each human being enters at birth. From this fact Schoonenberg concludes that there is no man who does not exist in a situation which has been co-determined by all the sins of the past.[113] As such, Schoonenberg's statement regarding man's situation is accurate — but not complete. To be complete, it is necessary to take into account the significant fact that man's concrete situation is *also* determined by every act of love in the past.[114]

Although the co-determination of the general world-situation by sin is undeniable, the suggestion that this affirmation adequately safeguards the universality of the situation of original sin is erroneous — as Schoonenberg himself pointed out in an article written six years earlier. There he searched for a way to account for the universality of original sin as situation without falling back upon Adam's sin. He then asked, "Is it perhaps simply the multitude of personal sins that is responsible for this inescapability?"[115] At that time, however, Schoonenberg found that answer wanting for the following reason: "It is difficult to conceive that an inescapability *for each* would result."[116] To safeguard this universality, Schoonenberg then advocated the second-fall hypothesis.[117] Schoonenberg's present solution, therefore,

---

112   *TvTh*, VIII, 37; *ZKTh*, XC, 16. Cf. *WuW*, XXI, 590; *MS*, II, 938.
113   *TvTh*, VIII, 37; *ZKTh*, XC, 16.
114   By using the term *co*determination Schoonenberg may have wished to acknowledge the fact that man's concrete situation is not exclusively determined by sin. He may also have chosen this term to leave room for the traditional conception of a primordial fall, so that man's situation may be viewed as being codetermined by a primordial fall *and* the intervening history of sin.
115   *TvTh*, II, 199.
116   *Ibid.* (similarly, *TvTh*, IV, 78; *Man and Sin*, 189). As is evident from the immediate context, the phrase underlined by Schoonenberg has reference to Trent's *omnibus inest* (*DS*, 1513).
117   *TvTh*, II, 199-200.

represents a remarkable reversal of position. Whereas he originally rejected the general history-of-sin as a solution in favor of the second-fall hypothesis, he later rejects the second-fall hypothesis in favor of the history-of-sin.

After Schoonenberg relinquished the second-fall hypothesis, it is not surprising that he should reconsider an answer proposed but by-passed at an earlier stage. It is surprising that in doing so Schoonenberg does not suggest a remedy for the inadequacy which he saw so clearly earlier; for "to conceive that an inescapability *for each* would result" remains as difficult as when Schoonenberg first perceived this problem. Although Schoonenberg now suggests that the general history-of-sin does result in a strictly universal situation of original sin,[118] elsewhere it becomes clear that, confronted by the inadequacy and the problematic nature of the second-fall hypothesis, he tacitly abandons the strict universality of original sin.[119]

Schoonenberg's tacit abandonment of the strict universality of original sin becomes evident upon comparison of his essay in *Mysterium Salutis* in the German version of 1967 and in the Dutch version of 1968. In the German edition,[120] the second-fall hypothesis still plays an integral role in rendering the categorically negative situation of original sin plausible.[121] Having explained the specific character of a situational *Existential* and the general notion of a situation in which man is deprived of grace,[122] Schoonenberg approaches the critical point at which these must converge by postulating the possibility of a "gnadenlose Situation...die 'existential' ist, die all unseren freien Entscheidungen vorausgeht und sie umfasst."[123] He then asks whether a situation of that kind and with that content is also *real* and takes the decisive step by answering affirmatively on the basis of the fall embodied in the rejection of Christ.[124] The Dutch version is identical to the German up

---

118   Although in the Dutch and the German texts Schoonenberg uses the ambiguous term general (*algemeen, allgemein*), his circumscription of the situation indicates that he intends to maintain its strict universality (*TvTh*, VIII, 37: "each human being"; Mary is said to be the only one escaping this situation). This intention is wholly in keeping with the purpose for which Schoonenberg designed the second-fall hypothesis: the maintenance of a strictly universal – in explicit distinction from a merely general – situation (*TvTh*, II, 199; *Man and Sin*, 190).

119   That Schoonenberg himself senses this problem may be evidenced by the fact that he characterizes also this latest answer as the most dubious element of his theory (*IDO-C*, 68-4, 16; *IDO-Ce*, 68-4, 14).

120   This text is substantially equivalent to the relevant sections in *Man and Sin* and in his essay in *Bijdragen*, XXIV.

121   The imminent rejection of the second-fall hypothesis has occasioned a revision of only the last page of this essay (*MS*, II, 938).

122   *MS*, II, 894-96; see *Man and Sin*, 111-20; *Bijdragen*, XXIV, 359-65.

123   *MS*, II, 896; *Man and Sin*, 120; *Bijdragen*, XXIV, 366.

124   *Ibid.*

to and including the postulated possibility of a situational *Existential* of gracelessness. Then the question that followed in the German version is deleted and replaced by this extremely significant statement: "Such a situation is . . . real *in the same measure as the absence of moral values and norms* (an absence preceding our decisions) *is real.*"[125] The crucial question that now faces Schoonenberg, of course, is whether this absence of moral values is indeed real.

Reflecting the imminent abandonment of the second-fall hypothesis,[126] Schoonenberg at first attempts to answer the "reality" question without appealing to the act of Christ's rejection:

> If we leave the doctrine of original[127] sin out of consideration at this point, we would probably look for another significant act of sin and end up at the rejection of Christ. Yet, the answer is more simple: *Every* sin situates everyone for evil.[128]

Schoonenberg proceeds by (rightly) complicating this seemingly simple answer when he states that insofar as human acts are good, grace is communicated and, insofar as they are evil, grace is not communicated to fellowman.[129] Here the *ambiguity* of man's situation — an ambiguity masked by the second-fall hypothesis[130] — begins to emerge. Nevertheless, Schoonenberg goes on to conclude that every sin contributes to the *graceless* situation *into which every* human being is born.[131] That the general history-of-sin

---

125 *Mysterium Salutis: Dogmatiek in heilshistorisch perspectief,* trans. Otto Krops and Theodoor de Meijer (Hilversum: Uitgeverij Paul Brand, 1968), VIII, 72-73, emphasis added.

126 See n. 77 above.

127 Schoonenberg probably has in mind specifically the traditional primordial fall (see *TvTh,* II, 199; *TvTh,* IV, 75; *Man and Sin,* 189-90; in each of these instances Schoonenberg similarly prescinds from a traditional option but specifically mentions Adam's sin).

128 *MS*d, VIII, 74.

129 *Ibid.*

130 As we have seen (sec. B, 1, b, i above), the attractiveness of the second-fall hypothesis, by contrast, lies precisely in the fact that it appeared to open a route that safely bypasses the nettlesome realm of a multitude of various subjective decisions and the correspondingly ambiguous situation(s). Accordingly, Schoonenberg points out that the second-fall hypothesis explains the universality of original sin, not primarily in terms of "the subject of the sinful decision . . ., but in terms of the 'object': the Mediator Jesus Christ, God's grace-in-person who departed from our earthly interhuman existence" (*Bijdragen,* XXIV, 386; similarly, *TvTh,* IV, 78; *Man and Sin,* 196). In other words, even though *subjectively* the situation at the time of Christ's crucifixion was entirely ambiguous (followers, as well as doubters, unbelievers and enemies of Christ), *objectively* the situation appears to be wholly unambiguous: Christ's banishment by murder was literally a "mortal sin" that causes the loss of this grace-in-person for *all* (cf. *TvTh,* IV, 76, 78; *Man and Sin,* 196; *Geloof,* IV, 275).

131 *MS*d, VIII, 74.

does not warrant this conclusion, however, is evidenced in the very next paragraph where Schoonenberg acknowledges once again that the degree of situational privation of grace is commensurate with the heinousness (and prevalence) of the sins that combine to create a concrete situation.[132]

At this stage Schoonenberg's momentous acknowledgement of the ambiguity of each concrete situation fails to clash overtly with his simultaneous maintenance of original sin as unambiguous situational *Existential* of gracelessness because the second-fall hypothesis is still in place, fulfilling its tenuous but critical function as key underpinning of Schoonenberg's theory. In the same paragraph, therefore, he can fall back upon this hypothesis once more to explain the universality and radicality of the situation of original sin: "By Christ's crucifixion, therefore, the *world* has from man's point of view become *graceless in the most radical way that is possible.*"[133] Nevertheless, Schoonenberg concludes this essay by suggesting that such a universal situational *Existential* is adequately explained by the general-history-of-sin.[134]

Schoonenberg's contention that the general history-of-sin is sufficient ground for maintaining the strict universality of original sin as situational *Existential* is demonstrated to be untenable by his own description of the resultant situation.[135] He describes that universality by stating that by virtue of man's situational *Existential* each man is destined to encounter sin *at some time and in some way.*[136] This description reveals that the crucial goal which Schoonenberg originally set for his situational reinterpretation of original sin remains elusive. This predicament becomes manifest when one notes the discrepancy between Schoonenberg's present description of the situation of original sin and the original intention of his reinterpretation.

If original sin is truly a situational *Existential,* it cannot but be encountered at the moment of birth, for an *Existential* — also a historical

---

132 *Ibid.* Cf. *Man and Sin,* 119-20.
133 *MS*d, VIII, 74 emphasis added.
134 *Ibid.,* 123-24.
135 Stenzel puts it well when he says that the weakness inherent in Schoonenberg's theory that *calls for* the second-fall hypothesis remains after that hypothesis is discarded: "Nun hat er, gut beraten, diese Hilfskonstruktion inzwischen zurückgenommen, ohne allerdings die nach ihr rufende Schwäche seines Systems anderweitig abzudecken. Es will doch sehr scheinen, dass hier nicht nur auf eine jederzeit entbehrliche Illustrierung verzichtet worden ist" (*ThuPh,* XLVI, 560).
136 *MS,* II, 938: "Vielleicht ist es aber gar nicht notwendig, eine einzige Sünde unter vielen zu suchen, die die Allgemeinheit des ersündlichen Situiert-Seins verursacht, da jeder Mensch existential situiert ist, der Sünde irgendwann und irgendwie in seinem Leben zu begegnen." Cf. *WuW,* XXI, 590: "auf irgendeine weise."

Existential — by its very nature[137] and as applied in the situation theory[138] is not a reality that one comes upon in some way at a later point in life. The present difficulty, therefore, does not lie in conceiving of historical situatedness as being man's *Existential* nor in conceiving of (original) sin as being *a* factor of such situatedness. The difficulty lies in conceiving of *original sin* as being man's situational *Existential* — if it be granted, as Schoonenberg understandably does,[139] that man is destined to encounter this reality *at some time* and *in some way*. From its inception, however, the situation theory was designed to demonstrate that sin does not encounter man merely at some time and in some way, but at a very specific time, at birth, and in a very specific way, as situational *Existential.* If that crucial intention has not become clear from Schoonenberg's use of the model of the child,[140] from his delimitation of situation as *Existential*,[141] from his anti-Pelagian polemic[142] and from his argumentation in support of the second-fall hypothesis,[143] it becomes manifest in a relatively late statement which reaffirms the temporal and structural criteria that apply to the situation of original sin:

> In my view the situaion of sin is not a situation in the sense of being mere "Umwelt." Rather, it is a being-situated of man himself. Just as in the classic teaching, original sin is not something that befalls man after a certain time, but a situation that is his own from the moment of birth, a situation that precedes all his free decisions, encompasses and conditions them. This being-situated in original sin is an *Existential* of man.[144]

The critical discrepancy between this original intention and the ultimate result of Schoonenberg's situational reinterpretation of original sin will become even more evident in the following chapter. First, Rahner's apparent avoidance of Schoonenberg's problem by the expedient of maintaining a definitive, primordial fall will be examined.

2. Definitive Fall within Polygenetic Origin

a. *Its Foundational Function*

For almost fifteen years Rahner maintained the theory of the

---

137 See ch. I, n. 163 above.
138 See the references in nn. 140-44 below.
139 "Understandably" — i.e., in view of the impossibility of maintaining the strict universality of original sin. Cf. Stenzel, *ThuPh*, XLVI, 560.
140 See ch. I, sec. A, 3, b above.
141 See ch. I, sec. A, 3, c above.
142 See ibid.
143 See esp. sec. B, 1, b, i above.
144 *IDO-C, 68-4,* 14. Cf. *IDO-C*e, *68-4,* 13.

monogenetic origin of mankind.[145] Although the maintenance of this theory was doubtless inspired by theological motives,[146] it was accomplished by philosophical means, namely, by what he designates as the metaphysical argument, an application of Occam's razor to the problem of origins.[147] Of late, Rahner has relinquished this position and has accepted the theory of polygenesis as being a viable option.[148] The remarkable aspect of this change of position on the question of origins is that, theologically, very little changes.

The basic similarity of theological position is rooted in the fact that Rahner continues to maintain a unique and unified original group of human beings despite their possibly varied pedigree. The acts of that original group are viewed, as in the traditional conception, as having a definitive influence on all future generations. This formal resemblance to the traditional framework rests on Rahner's conception of the unity of mankind, on the one hand, and on his conception of the unique significance of beginnings, on the other.

Rahner contends that, despite its polygenetic origin, the first human group constitutes a physical-historical unity.[149] This primordial group constitutes an integral whole by virtue of several factors. Rahner mentions the following: 1) the unity of its physical and biotic habitat, 2) the unity of its ancestral animal population, 3) the unity of concrete human-personal intercommunication (a constitutive element of man's physical-*historical* unity) and 4) the radicalized unity that is given with man's directedness towards a supernatural goal and towards Christ.[150] Far from atomizing man into disparate individuals, Rahner argues, the theory of polygenesis is rooted in a realization that man cannot live as an individual. He is dependent for survival upon an intimate unity with a coexistent group. It is *monogenism* that views man as being an individual in origin, incorporated into a group only conceptually. The theory of *polygenism*, by contrast, views man as originally being a concretely unified group.[151] Accordingly, in a surprising turn of the

---

145 See his extensive essay, "Theologisches zum Monogenismus," *Schriften*, I, 253-322 (first published in 1954).
146 See *Schriften*, I, 253-311, esp. 305-11.
147 *Ibid.*, 311-22.
148 See his article on evolution and original sin published in *Concilium*, 1967 (English edition vol. XXVI, 25-33; German edition vol. III, 459-65; Dutch edition vol. III/6 57-69);*Exkurs* (an expanded version of his article in *Concilium*); *Sacramentum Mundi, sub voce* "Monogenism."
149 *Exkurs*, 196-99 ("leibhaftig geschichtliche Einheit"). By positing that this single original group constitutes the origin of all mankind, Rahner rejects the theory of a polyphyletic origin of mankind (see *Exkurs*, 197-98).
150 *Exkurs*, 197; cf. 196, n. 24.
151 *Ibid.*, 198.

traditional argument, Rahner contends that polygenism is more appropriate to the doctrine of original sin that monogenism.[152]

Given this unified original group, the first sin can be viewed as having been perpetrated by one or a few members of this group or by the entire group as a totality.[153] In either case, the entire group would cease to function as intended, i.e., as the medium of grace for the generations that descend from the original group. For even if only one or two of this group were involved in the first sin, the entire group would be situationally affected.[154] Whatever the precise constitution of the "Adamite subject," therefore, the first sin creates a determinative situation, an *Existential* of gracelessness for all successive generations.[155]

Although the original unity of mankind ensures a *universal* effect of the first sin, the *permanence* that Rahner attributes to that effect is based on his view on the unique significance of the beginning of history. As has been noted earlier, Rahner does not consider the first act that occurs in human history to be merely the first within a homogeneous series.[156] Unlike Schoonenberg, Rahner contends that the first act – despite its remoteness and obscurity – is of critical importance for all subsequent history. He speaks, therefore, of the origin as being the law and controlling power under which the subsequent phases of history develop.[157] In fact, it is precisely because the origin is as such irrecoverable and hence irrevocable that it has perpetual effect.[158] The origin exercises its power as an elusive, remote, yet impinging force. The beginning is "behind," yet present.[159]

The unity of mankind and the unique function of the original human group clarify Rahner's ascription of an irrevocable and universal effect to the first sinful act, however its precise scope, content or subject is to be conceived. By virtue of this conception of beginnings, Rahner speaks of original sin as belonging to an insuperable beginning[160] and as an irreversible, permanent constituent of all history.[161] The situational privation of grace, therefore, represents a negative *Existential* that is not negated by the opposite

---

152 *Ibid.*
153 *Ibid.*, 199-205.
154 *Ibid.*, 204.
155 *Ibid.*, 204-205.
156 See ch. I, sec. B, 2, b, i above.
157 *Exkurs*, 193-94, 209-10; *Schriften*, IX, 265-66.
158 *Exkurs*, 193-94; *Schriften*, IX, 266; *SM*, I, 1115; *SM*e, IV, 333.
159 *Exkurs*, 193-94; *Schriften*, IX, 265-66.
160 *Schriften*, IX, 266.
161 *SM*, I, 1115; *SM*e, IV, 333.

Existential, the presence of grace in Christ, because the former roots in a definitive fall in the beginning. Thus man is situated by a protological and an eschatological *Existential,* by the irreversible beginning that includes the first sin and by the irreversible eschaton manifest in Christ.[162] The grace that should have been man's immediate situational *Existential* from the beginning via physical-historical descent[163] is now present only via Christ as manifestation of the *eschaton*.[164] By retaining a definitive *primordial* fall, therefore, Rahner maintains original sin as an inescapable situation.

Rahner's concept of a definitive primordial fall provides the background that elucidates his somewhat cryptic, indirect criticism of Schoonenberg's minimization of beginnings and its consequences.[165] Although Rahner considers the conception of "the sin of the world" as such to be a potentially fruitful one, he objects to the attendant absorption of a unique beginning into a homogeneous series of sins.[166] The objection stands even when the sin of the world includes – as it does in Schoonenberg's conception – the situational consequences of these sins.[167] In Rahner's view, the idea of the sin of the world may supplement but cannot supplant the unique impact of the *original* sin, because the latter is the unique beginning of the former.[168]

Interestingly, like Schoonenberg's defense of the second-fall hypothesis, Rahner's maintenance of a definitive primordial fall reflects concern for safeguarding, not merely the extent of sin, but also the specific character

---

162 *Schriften,* IX, 271; *SM,* I, 1113-14; *SM*e, IV, 332-33.

163 The apparent contradiction between "immediate" and "via" is resolved when one takes the term immediate as a temporal designation. This is a likely interpretation of Rahner's use of this seemingly contradictory combination: "Die Herkünftigkeit *sollte* aber ... die *unmittelbare Vermittlung* der (vorexistentiellen, also existentialen) Heiligkeit des Menschen sein ..." (*Exkurs,* 188, emphasis – except of "sollte" – added).

164 *SM,* I, 1113-14; *SM*e, IV, 332-33.

165 Although Rahner never mentions Schoonenberg's name in the following references, it is safe to assume that he does have Schoonenberg in mind. This may be concluded from the fact that Rahner combines his criticism of the conception "the sin of the world" with a warning against the minimization of the first sin. That Schoonenberg is indeed intended by Rahner is indirectly corroborated by the fact that Vorgrimler (a close associate of Rahner), in an essay that intends to be no more than a popularization of Rahner's conception of original sin, levels the same criticism of "the sin of the world" directly at Schoonenberg's view (Herbert Vorgrimler, "Die Erbsünde in der katholischen Glaubenslehre," *Unheilslast und Erbschuld der Menschheit: Das Problem der Erbsünde,* Rudolf Schmid, Eugen Ruckstuhl, Herbert Vorgrimler [Luzern: Rex-Verlag, 1969], 139-41; for the relation of this essay to Rahner's thought, see Vorgrimler's comments on p. 115).

166 *SM,* I, 1115-16; cf. *SM*e, IV, 333.

167 *Exkurs,* 192-93, 194.

168 *SM* I, 1115-16; *SM*e, IV, 333. Cf. *Exkurs,* 192-93.

of the situation of original sin. Without a unique beginning of original sin, Rahner contends, it is impossible to maintain the essential distinction between *imitatione* and *generatione*, a distinction that must be maintained even when the hereditary propagation of original sin is stripped of all sensual-biotic connotations.[169] In view of Schoonenberg's concerted effort to retain the anti-Pelagian thrust of *generatione* with the aid of the concept *Existential*,[170] and in view of Rahner's general familiarity with and specific employment of this concept, Rahner's criticism of a position such as that of Schoonenberg may be formulated as follows: although the idea of a situational *Existential* is indeed a legitimate equivalent of the deepest intention of *generatione*, such an *Existential* can be maintained only on the basis of a unique origin within which a definitive fall takes place.[171]

b. *Its Etiological Anchorage*

Rahner's retention of a definitive fall appears to invest his position with a profound advantage over that of Schoonenberg. Nevertheless, aside from philosophical difficulties that possibly plague his theory of origins as applied to original sin,[172] Rahner's seemingly solid basis for original sin as situational *Existential*, the primordial fall, is undermined by the same force that ultimately eroded Schoonenberg's second-fall hypothesis, namely, the *situational presence* of grace, the coexistence of two opposite *Existentialia*.[173] The difficulty that originates from this source for Rahner's retention of a definitive fall can be clarified by considering his application of the etiological method[174] to the doctrine of original sin.

Although the primordial fall represents the *ontic ground* of the universal situational *Existential* of original sin, the *noetic ground* of that fall is the universality of original sin. This inescapable circle is given with Rahner's conviction that no source of information exists that provides "direct" knowledge of the beginning and a definitive fall.[175] Therefore, only an indirect route remains open. The entire reality of original sin, including a definitive fall, is

169   *Exkurs*, 192-94, 202.
170   See ch. I, sec. A, 3, c above.
171   Cf. *Exkurs*, 194.
172   See Rahner's characterization of the origin as the "Setzung," and of history as "das Gesetzte" which takes place within and under the transcendental law ("Gesetz") and horizon (*Schriften*, IX, 265-66; *Exkurs*, 193-94, 209-10).
173   See sec. A, 2 above.
174   For Rahner's conception of etiology as such, see *LThK*, I, 1011-12; VIII, 835-37; *Hominisation*, 35-41; *MS*, II, 417-20.
175   *Exkurs*, 208; *Schriften*, IX, 261.

derived by etiological retrospection from the *present experience* of reality, specifically, from the experience of the presence and absence of grace.[176] The definitive fall is derived from the fact that every man experiences the privation of grace as his situational *Existential*. From the fact that no one receives grace simply as a member of the human race, i.e., via his physical-historical descent, and from the fact that grace ought to have been received in this way, Rahner concludes that this absence of grace *must have been* caused by guilt,[177] else a privation of grace counter to God's will is impossible.[178] Since the situational privation of grace is not the fault of those who incur it as *Existential*, this privation *must have been* caused by previous generations. Finally, since this privation is an inescapable, universal *Existential*, it *must have been* caused by a fall at the beginning of human history.[179] By following and accentuating the various steps in the process of etiological retrospection, it becomes clear that in Rahner's conception the primordial fall is, as he himself puts it, a postulate derived from man's *present situation*.[180]

Rahner's retention of a definitive primordial fall *as such* in no way represents an advantage over Schoonenberg's position. That primordial fall, though ontic basis for the universality of original sin as situational *Existential*, stands or falls with the solidity of its noetic basis, its etiological point of departure in the present, namely, *the universality of original sin as situational Existential*. If the present situation provides no solid base for etiological retrospection, a definitive primordial fall is as problematical for Rahner as it is for Schoonenberg. In the following chapter an attempt will be made to uncover the concrete, historical ground in the present situation that constitutes the noetic base from which the reality of original sin as situational *Existential* is derived — with or without the postulate of a primordial fall.

---

176 *Exkurs,* 193, 200, 208; *MS,* II, 418-19; *LThK,* VIII, 835.
177 *Exkurs,* 188-89; *Schriften,* IX, 267-69.
178 *Exkurs,* 189; *Schriften,* IX, 269.
179 *Exkurs,* 189; *SM,* I, 1111-12; *SMe,* IV, 331.
180 *SM,* III, 597 (*sub voce* "Monogenismus").

CHAPTER VI   *THE SACRAMENTAL CHURCH*
AS GROUND OF REINTERPRETATION

The preceding chapter gives rise to the question: What constitutes the deepest ground upon which the reinterpretation of original sin as the situational privation of grace rests. Because the traditional Adamic framework — primordial fall, monogenism, natural-biotic means of transmission — has collapsed, there appears to be no basis for the categorical and universal statement that the initial situation (*Existential*) of each human being consists of the privation of grace. Moreover, the situationalists' thesis regarding the universal *presence* of grace renders the question concerning the ground for positing a universal *privation* of grace even more acute. In view of the universal presence of what may be called anonymous grace (transcendental situation) and the phenomenon of anonymous Christianity (spatio-temporal situation), on what ground can the situationalists assert so unhesitatingly that the privation of grace is the situational *Existential* of every human being?

We will attempt to answer that question by exploring and testing the following hypothesis: in predicating a universal situational lack of grace, the situationalists ground themselves upon and proceed from the unquestioned axiom that the sacramental Church is the unique and necessary agent of sanctifying grace. Formally this procedure from the Church and its sacraments closely parallels that of the post-Tridentine theologians who determined the nature of original sin by analyzing the nature of its sacramental remedy.[1] Materially, however, a significant difference emerges. For these post-Tridentine theologians the *reality* of original sin was assured by the traditional Adamic framework; only the *nature* of this reality was determined by the ingenious recourse to the sacramental remedy. Although the situationalists, as theologians of the Church, may proceed from the conviction of the reality of original sin, the collapse of the Adamic framework combined

---

1   See Introduction, sec. A, 9 above.

with the introduction of the theological framework of anonymous grace appears to remove the ground from beneath that conviction. The very *reality* of original sin as universal initial situation is called into question. Due to a shift in historical and theological horizons, the conception of the sacramental Church functions not simply as the criterion by which the nature of a firmly grounded reality is determined but as the axiom upon which an otherwise imperilled doctrine rests. The presence and necessity of a unique remedy in effect becomes the basis for assuming the reality of a unique and universal malady.

That the sacramental Church in fact functions as the ground for postulating the reality of original sin as the initial situation of each human being becomes evident in various ways in the writings of Schoonenberg, Weger and Rahner. Of these, Schoonenberg has written on the subject most extensively and over the longest period of time and, specifically, has struggled most intensively with the problem of the reality of original sin as universal, perpetual situation. For that reason the peculiar relationship of the situational reinterpretation of original sin to the sacramental Church is most readily demonstrated by the progression of his thought. We will begin, therefore, by examining the gradual shift in Schoonenberg's position on this issue.

A. THE SACRAMENTAL BASIS

1. Schoonenberg

The question concerning the reality of original sin emerges at the very outset of Schoonenberg's "theological reflection on original sin."[2] For that reason he begins with what he calls an extremely commonplace yet necessary remark: "Original sin in us [i.e., *peccatum originale originatum*] is a reality."[3] As becomes clear from what follows, the *necessity* of thus positing the existence of original sin derives from the fact that this reality appears to be jeopardized by the situation of grace in which every human being is said to stand by virtue of the coming of Christ. This situation of grace appears to negate the universal privation of grace that, according to Schoonenberg, constitutes original sin. To avert this apparent negation, Schoonenberg begins by firmly positing the reality of original sin.

---

2   The subsection above which this title appears, *Geloof,* IV, 142-200, represents an early stage of the development of Schoonenberg's reinterpretation of original sin.
3   *Geloof,* IV, 143.

As an initial argument for this assertion, he points to the fact that for every human being redemption is not merely *preventative* — as it was for the Virgin Mary — but also *restorative*, i.e., a rescue from an existent condition of sin.[4] In itself this reference to the restorative aspect of salvation does not render the existence of original sin plausible. Since the reality of original sin is called into question precisely by the universal *situation of grace* in Jesus Christ, the question remains why that grace should entail the *rescue* of each and every human being from a *situational privation of grace*. In other words, precisely because of the *situational* effect of restorative grace the question concerning the existence of original sin as universal situation remains unanswered.

At this point in his reflection, however, Schoonenberg shelves the troublesome question regarding the reality of original sin in a surprising way. After repeating that original sin in us is not something hypothetical (as it was for Mary), something that would exist were it not for salvation in Jesus Christ, Schoonenberg asserts,

> Before baptism, original sin is a reality in each of us; it happens to be God's mystery that He wished not merely to safeguard each of us against but also to rescue us out of an existent condition of sin; that He kept all imprisoned in sin to have mercy on all (Ro 11:32).[5]

This appeal to God's mysterious will, however, does not establish the reality of original sin, for that reality is rendered dubious precisely by the situational realization of God's graceful wish in Jesus Christ.[6] Moreover, an appeal to God's inscrutable will to support a paradoxical concurrence of the situational presence and privation of grace constitutes a reversion to a theological positivism ("it happens to be God's mystery that He wished") that is wholly inimical to Schoonenberg's conception of theology in general[7] and to the purpose of his reinterpretation of original sin in particular.[8] Accordingly, this recourse to God's mysterious will — though it remains a remarkable side step — is best understood as a temporary resting point in Schoonenberg's thinking,

---

4 *Ibid.*
5 *Ibid.,* 144.
6 Schoonenberg's reference to Ro 11:32 is therefore not wholly appropriate. Paul is speaking here of before and after Christ as redemptive historical epochs. Schoonenberg applies the idea of captivity to the epoch "after Christ" and to an individual's condition *before baptism.*
7 See Bakker, *TvTh,* XI, 353-63. For a formal statement expressing Schoonenberg's view of the relationship theologian-magisterium, see *Man and Sin,* 157-58.
8 For example, Schoonenberg frequently rejects an isolated appeal to the idea that the doctrine of original sin is a *"mystery"* (see *Geloof,* IV, 155-57; *Ex Auditu Verbi,* 269-70; *WuW,* XXII, 740-41; *NM,* XIX, 198-99).

a postulate which will be stripped of its arbitrary mysteriousness by his further reflection on the counterpart to the restorative function of God's grace, namely, the reality of original sin as situation.

The direction which this reflection on the reality of original sin will take is implied in Schoonenberg's statement that original sin is a reality in each of us *before baptism*. Thereby the question concerning the reality of original sin, is narrowed down to the question concerning the precise function of God's restorative grace in baptism. This approach is in keeping with Schoonenberg's view of the historical development of the doctrine of original sin. He frequently points out that the doctrine of original sin was formulated by the Church in order to proclaim the necessity of baptism.[9] The established practice of baptizing *all* (including infants) "in the forgiveness of sins" raised the question as to the *necessity* of this practice. The Church answered that it was necessary because of original sin. The crucial question at this point is whether in formulating the doctrine of original sin the Church rightly saw original sin as an existent reality that justifies the necessity of infant baptism or whether the doctrine of original sin represents a mistaken rationalization for an established practice. In the early stages of his reinterpretation of original sin, Schoonenberg clearly judges the former to be the case and therefore proceeds from the assumption that via the sacrament of baptism one can arrive at the reality of original sin.

The decisive function of the sacrament of baptism in Schoonenberg's reinterpretation becomes manifest once again when, elsewhere, he considers the possibility that for a given individual original sin may not be real because his concrete and immediate situation is one of grace.[10] At this point, Schoonenberg reflects upon the teaching of the Church that (due to original sin) baptism is necessary even for the children of baptized parents.[11] The question which he now faces is whether that teaching can be maintained if original sin is viewed as a concrete situation, which in the instance which Schoonenberg envisages appears not to exist. Or to phrase the question differently, can the thrust of the situational reinterpretation that appears to render doubtful that a given individual is subject to the *malady* described by ecclesiastical doctrine be parried by proceeding from the *remedy* prescribed by that doctrine?

In attempting to solve the problem he has posed, Schoonenberg indeed

---

9 See *Geloof,* IV, 134, 139-40, 142, 188, 197, 200; *Man and Sin,* 124, 140-41; *WuW,* XXI, 589, 590, 591; *Ex Auditu Verbi,* 270n; *TvTh,* IV, 77.
10 *TvTh,* II, 199.
11 *DS,* 1514 (see Introduction, sec. A, 8, d above).

proceeds from the remedy prescribed by the Church. This procedure becomes manifest in a formulation that constitutes a (probably unintentional) methodological statement: "In faith we cannot think of original sin in another way than as the initial situation of each and everyone, now and in the future, so that the sacrament of baptism (in reality or desire) is and remains necessary in order to be liberated from that situation."[12] In effect this statement represents an application of the traditional adage *fides quarens intellectum*. When in a given instance reflection on reality leads to results that clash with the faith of the Church expressed in the doctrine of original sin, that faith becomes the starting point for thinking about reality once more: *in faith* we cannot *think* of original sin in another way than is demanded by the peculiar remedy prescribed by the Church.

The same procedure is in evidence when in this context Schoonenberg answers his own question whether it is not thinkable that redemption should become so dominant that children would begin their existence untouched by original sin — something that is quite conceivable within the situational reinterpretation. He answers, "According to the teaching of the Church just presented, this does not seem thinkable."[13] Just as with the earlier appeal to the mysterious will of God, so the present appeal to the teaching of the Church cannot represent an end-point but simply another (slightly more proximate) starting point of theological reflection. Accordingly, Schoonenberg proceeds by attempting to render plausible by theological reflection the teaching regarding baptism that entails the unthinkableness of the suspension of original sin. In the course of that reflection, he introduces the second-fall hypothesis discussed in the previous chapter:[14] because Christ was banished from our earthly existence it is, as he thought at that time, *in fact unthinkable* that original sin should not be real in a specific person.

The procedure thus far is entirely in accord with that of the post-Tridentine theologians mentioned earlier, except that it is not the nature of original sin but its reality that is at stake. The second-fall hypothesis appeared to demonstrate the reality of original sin as situation, as an *Existential* interior to every human being. As has been shown in the previous chapter, however, this hypothesis is wholly inadequate for its intended purpose and is later discarded by Schoonenberg. That raises the intriguing question whether faith-reflection is now brought to a halt, replaced by simple assent to the Church's teaching that original sin is a reality in each and every human being.

12 *TvTh*, II, 199.
13 *Ibid*.
14 Ch. V, sec. B, 1, b above.

Even at this point, however, Schoonenberg does not allow theological reflection to be destroyed by such theological positivism, for he suggests that the general "history of sin" gives sufficient ground for positing that original sin is a reality in each human being.[15] Nevertheless, this suggested final answer does not represent the final step in the development of Schoonenberg's thought on the subject; for, as indicated by that development, this answer too is inadequate. Consequently, the question as to whether Schoonenberg's reflection on the present problem does finally end in theological positivism (the Church happens to teach...) looms once more.

As we shall see presently, even in this final step Schoonenberg avoids destroying theological reflection — but in a strikingly different manner. He no longer proceeds from the teaching of the Church regarding the sacrament as starting point in order to arrive at an explanation (the second-fall hypothesis) that renders that teaching plausible. Rather, in this final step he proceeds from his reflection upon man's concrete situation; he then goes on to emphasize a meaning of the sacrament that is quite different from the teaching of the Church that functioned as his initial starting point. More specifically, formerly he worked from the Church's teaching regarding the sacramental remedy and from that standpoint attempted to maintain the strict universality of original sin by means of a novel hypothesis. Now he works from man's concrete situation and on that basis begins to deemphasize the remedial function of the sacrament of baptism.

Manifesting the tenuousness of the notion that the privation of grace is an initial situational *Existential* interior to every human being, Schoonenberg increasingly emphasizes functions of baptismal grace that do not relate to the recipient's immediate situation. Especially in his later writings on the subject of original sin, he begins to underscore the preventative and confirmative functions of the sacrament of baptism. This sacrament is necessary, Schoonenberg points out, not merely as a remedy for a *present condition of sin* but also as an antidote against *future sin* and as a seal and crown upon one's *present situation of grace*.[16] In itself the preventative and confirmative functions of baptism plausibly explain the necessity, or at least the meaning-

---

15. See ch. V, sec. B, 1, b, iii above.
16. *Man and Sin*, 197; *WuW*, XXI, 590; *MS*, II, 938; *Ex Auditu Verbi*, 270n.; "Gedanken über die Kindertaufe," *ThPQ*, CXIV (1966), 231, 237; and "Theologische Fragen zur Kindertaufe," *Christsein ohne Entscheidung oder soll die Kirche Kinder taufen?* ed. Walter Kasper (Mainz: Matthias-Grünewald-Verlag, 1970), 112, 118-19. Cf. "Sünde — Sakrament — Jugendalter: einige theologische Bemerkungen," *Einübung des Glaubens*, ed. Günter Stachel and Alois Zenner (Würzburg: Echter-Verlag, 1965), 104. Schoonenberg mentions also that incorporation into the Church is one of the meanings

fulness,[17] of this sacrament. This emphasis is remarkable — and symptomatic of a basic problem — only because it occurs in the context of the doctrine of *original* sin. In the teaching of the Church, it is precisely this context that renders any emphasis upon the function of baptism as an antidote to *future* sin or as a confirmation of present salvation superfluous.[18] Convinced that sin has insinuated itself into human history in a deeper way than can be expressed by the example-imitation phenomenon, the Church teaches that original sin is passed on *generatione*. In that context the sacrament of baptism is said to be necessary even for the children born of baptized parents.[19] As was pointed out in the previous chapter,[20] Schoonenberg's elaboration of the situation theory cannot be understood except as an attempt to do justice to the depth dimension of sin that is reflected in the teaching that the grace bestowed in baptism is necessary in order to effect deliverance from an existent condition of sin.[21] The shift in emphasis from the remedial and restorative to the preventative and confirmative function of baptism is therefore a significant shift away from the initial starting point of Schoonenberg's reinterpretation, which was anchored in precisely the opposite emphasis, namely, that grace is not merely preventative but also restorative.[22] Similarly, in the early stages of his reinterpretation of original sin, Schoonenberg saw the sacrament of baptism not so much as the crown of realized salvation but as the initial institutional breakthrough of salvation.[23]

The final step in the development of Schoonenberg's thought appears

---

and functions of baptism. We can leave this meaning out of consideration because, as Schoonenberg's own explication of the significance of incorporation show, incorporation involves either confirmation or restoration (see, *NM,* XIX, 205; *Einübung des Glaubens,* 108; *Christsein ohne Entscheidung,* 118-19.

17   It is significant that Weger himself points out that he proceeds from the fact that the baptism of children is not merely meaningful and good but also *necessary* for salvation (*Theologie der Erbsünde,* 168). Cf. n. 19 below.

18   See *DS,* 223-24, 231, 780, 794, 1314, 1514-15, 1524, 1618, 1671-72.

19   *DS,* 1514. In a recent essay, Schoonenberg contends that this canon teaches the meaningfulness and legitimacy, but not the necessity of infant baptism (*Christsein ohne Entscheidung,* 117, n. 18). The expansion of the second canon of the Council of Carthage by the Council of Trent, however, underscores precisely the *necessity* of this sacrament (see Introduction, sec. A, 8, d above; in emphasizing the necessity, in distinction from the meaningfulness, of the baptism of children, Weger refers to this fourth canon of the Council of Trent [see n. 17 above]).

20   Ch. V, sec. B, 1, b, iii above.

21   See also the citations annotated as nn. 5 and 12 above. Cf. *TvTh,* II, 200; *Man and Sin,* 124.

22   See the citation annotated as n. 5 above.

23   See *Geloof,* IV, 188; *Man and Sin,* 121, 124, 190; *TvTh,* II, 200; *NM,* XIX, 205; and ch. V, sec. B, 1, b, i above.

to have invalidated our working hypothesis that the deepest ground upon which the situational reinterpretation of original sin rests is the axiomatic acceptance of the necessity of the sacramental Church as unique medium of grace. For in this final stage Schoonenberg begins to disconnect his situational reinterpretation of original sin from the notion of the necessity of baptismal restoration. In fact, the situational reinterpretation of man's concrete situation begins to take a seemingly independent position vis-à-vis the function which the Church ascribes to baptism. Nevertheless our working hypothesis retains its heuristic significance for two reasons. First, the shift in emphasis away from the restorative function and towards the preventative and confirmative functions of baptism reveals how difficult it is to maintain – in terms of the situationalists' overall framework – that original sin is an initial situational *Existential* interior to *every* human being. In other words, to the extent that Schoonenberg abandons his original anchorage in the ecclesiastical groundwork, to that same extent he casts the reality of original sin as concrete initial situation of every human being into doubt.[24] Secondly, not the link to the sacramental Church as such but the traditional link with the restorative function of baptism is severed. Thus the interpretation of the human situation as entailing a qualified privation of grace retains its link with the axiom concerning the sacramental Church. That link lies in the notion of the sacrament as crown and seal of salvation.[25] The significance of *this* link for the reintepretation of original sin becomes manifest especially in Weger's and Rahner's thought.

2. Weger

Weger's reinterpretation of original sin as a situational privation of grace depends upon the conviction that the sacramental Church represents the supreme medium of grace. This becomes evident especially at the point where the reality of original sin as situation is least evident, namely, in the

---

24 That the reality of original sin as situation is indeed called into question by the later development of Schoonenberg's thought is confirmed by his recent statement that the doctrine of original sin "is in a certain sense the elaboration of a *futuribile*: it expresses what the world *would* be *if* God were not redemptively and healingly present and if this redemption of God had not attained its apex in Jesus Christ" (Letter, April 5, 1974). This statement strikingly negates a statement that served as Schoonenberg's initial starting point: "Something hypothetical (a *futuribile* in scholastic terminology), something that *would* exist were it not for redemption . . ., that is by no means what original sin is in us" (*Geloof*, IV, 144; see also the beginning of the present section on Schoonenberg).

25 For Schoonenberg's conception of the Church as superlative mediator of grace, see ch. V, n. 95 above.

case of a child born of believing parents. Weger acknowledges that this child is situated by grace, so that this constitutes the child's *Existential*.[26] The question arises how original sin — the privation of grace — can be said to be a situational reality for this child. In attempting to answer this question, Weger rigorously applies his method of determining the reality of original sin by negating the present (rather than a postulated primeval) order of grace.[27]

This procedure is not as simple as it at first glance appears, for in the present order, according to Weger, grace is communicated to fellowman wherever a Christian acts in love.[28] A negation of *this* order of grace, however, would bring original sin into view as a largely hypothetical situation in the case being considered. The *concrete* reality of original sin, therefore, cannot be determined by negating simply the general order of grace but only by negating the specific, ecclesiastical order of bestowing grace. What is the present order of grace for the child? It is the sacrament of baptism administered by the Church.[29] Hence the reality of original sin for the child of baptized believing parents, says Weger, can be determined only by analyzing that which is bestowed upon it in baptism.[30]

What is the uniqueness of the ecclesiastical bestowal of grace in baptism? Weger posits that baptism takes away *every* lack of grace.[31] This means that the *ecclesiastical* sacrament is conceived of as a medium which supplies that which the *"everyday* sacrament" of Christian love can never supply,[32] namely, the wholly reliable, of itself wholly effective communication of grace.[33] In the official, ecclesiastical sacraments, grace is bestowed unfailingly, i.e., independently of the holiness of the personal agent; it is communicated *ex opere operato*.[34] There alone grace is manifest in its eschatological irrevocability and fullness.[35]

Having thus determined the uniqueness of the ecclesiastical communication of grace, the reality of original sin in the child can, according to Weger, be readily determined: it is the absence of *that* grace which is given in

---

26 Weger, *Theologie der Erbsünde*, 171-72, 173.
27 *Ibid.*, 167; see also ch. III, n. 134 above.
28 *Ibid.*, 130-31.
29 *Theologie der Erbsünde*, 167-68 (with the assumption that this sacrament is necessary [*ibid.*, 168]).
30 *Ibid.*, 167-68.
31 *Ibid.*, 169.
32 *Ibid.*, 130; cf. 173.
33 *Ibid.*, 129, 131.
34 *Ibid.*, 129.
35 *Ibid.*, 173; cf. 169.

baptism.[36] "As long as the child is not baptized, it belongs to the *sinful world*, [i.e.] does not belong to the *holy Church* and thus does not possess the offer of the *ecclesiastical*-historical mediation of the grace of Jesus Christ and is in this sense subject to original sin."[37] In other words, despite the universal presence of grace (transcendental situation) and despite the widespread presence of anonymous Christianity as well as of explicit personal Christianity (spatiotemporal situation), it is possible to make a categorical and universal judgement concerning original sin conceived of as a situational piivation of grace. This is possible on the basis of the reality and assumed necessity of the sacramental Church: of every human being it can be said that in his initial situation he is deprived of the infallible, eschatological, irrevocable, untainted grace that is bestowed by the institutional Church.[38] No one is naturally *born (generatione)* within such an institution; one must be supernaturally *reborn (regeneratione)* via the sacrament to receive this ecclesiastical summit of grace. That is the initial lack that can be predicated of every human being. The sense in which the privation of this ecclesiastical apex of grace can legitimately be called "original sin" will be considered after we have examined the relationship of Rahner's reinterpretation of original sin to the idea of the sacramental Church.

3. Rahner

The dependence of the situational reinterpretation of original sin upon the idea of the sacramental Church is less explicit in Rahner's expositions than in those of Schoonenberg and Weger. This is partly due to the fact that Rahner's notion of a primordial fall appears to represent a self-sufficient ground for positing a universal privation of grace.[39] Consequently, neither the possibility of polygenesis nor the reality of anonymous Christianity

---

36 *Ibid.*, 171.
37 *Ibid.*, 172, emphasis added.
38 Weger says, for example that in the Church human history is (conditionally) *only* salvation history, whereas outside the Church human history is a mixture of *Heilsgeschichte and Unheilsgeschichte (Ibid.,* 136; cf. 141, 158-59; see also p. 139, where Weger says that outside of Christianity, the rejection of God's grace is objectified *also institutionally*). Although Weger acknowledges that sin insinuates itself also into the institution of the Christian Church, he immediately adds that this is true only within certain limits (*ibid.,* 172). Those limits are entailed in the fact that the *essence* of this institution is holy (*ibid.*) because it possesses the Holy Spirit incessantly (ibid., 171; cf. 129). Elsewhere Weger delineates these limits by stating that objectified guilt is found also in the Church as institution, namely, where it is not assured of the grace of infallibility (*ibid.,* 143).
39 See ch. V, sec. B, 2 above.

appears to jeopardize the reality of original sin as universal situation. For that reason, Rahner does not need to fall back — at least not overtly — upon the assumed necessity of the sacramental-ecclesiastical remedy to posit the reality of an original and universal malady. However, since his theory of a primordial fall does not represent a primary and independent datum but a secondary postulate derived from an assessment of man's *present* situation,[40] his conception of original sin as situational *Existential* is factually and implicitly dependent upon the idea of the sacramental Church. This dependence can be demonstrated by examining Rahner's assessment of man's present situation.

What characterizes man's present situation in Rahner's view? Ambivalence. On the one hand, there is the reality of salvation history, explicit in Christianity, implicit yet concrete in anonymous Christianity.[41] On the other hand, man's negative responses to grace render the human situation ambivalent. As Rahner recognizes, however, such ambivalence in itself does not constitute original sin.[42] For that one needs a larger theological framework. For Rahner this framework consists of the reality of sanctifying grace, a divine quality bestowed upon man as his *Existential*.[43] Original sin, in Rahner's view, is the initial lack of this quality from man's concrete situation. Yet Rahner's affirmation of the universal possibility of the concrete situational realization of grace appears to invalidate the negative judgement entailed in his conception of original sin. What then is the grace that every human being is said to lack initially? That can best be clarified by considering his view of the sacramental Church.

Despite the fact that anonymous Christians and even anonymous Christian communities and institutions can arise everywhere without any contact with empirical Christianity,[44] there is one thing that all of these anonymous expressions of the grace of Jesus Christ lack, namely, the unique way in which grace is realized and communicated in the Catholic Church.[45] What is the uniqueness of this medium of grace? Perhaps that question can best be answered by what appears to be a tautology: the uniqueness of this institutional medium of grace is constituted by its institutional embodiment of all the instrinsic qualities of grace. Since grace involves the communication of God's own being, it may be assumed to be absolutely pure, holy, reliable

40   See ch. V, sec. B, 2, b above.
41   See ch. II, sec. C, 2 and 3; and ch. V, sec. A, 2 above.
42   See *SM*, I, 1115-16 and his implicit criticism of Schoonenberg discussed in ch. V, sec. B, 2, a above.
43   See ch. III, C, 2, b above.
44   See n. 41 above.
45   See, e.g., *Schriften*, VIII, 344.

and effective. These divine qualities become historically manifest, first in the *person* of Christ,[46] then, by extension, in the institution of the Church.[47] Accordingly, the Catholic Church is in its core the historical yet wholly unambiguous embodiment of the eschatological (i.e., irreversible and efficacious) appearance of grace.[48] The Church is not a representative substitute for an absent Christ but an institutional *presentation* of Christ.[49]

This view of the uniqueness of the Church does not entail a simplistic objectification of the Church as institute.[50] On the contrary, recognizing that the Church is not an end in itself, Rahner frequently attenuates this aspect to a bare minimum.[51] Nevertheless, it is precisely this bare minimum that constitutes the *sine qua non* of the uniqueness of the Church and the absoluteness of Christianity.[52] The uniqueness of overt Christians does not consist in their personal commitment or subjective condition, nor simply in the faithfulness of God in which they trust; for the former may be and the latter is just as real in non-Christian religions. Rather, the uniqueness of explicit Christians is grounded in their link with the *official institution* which by its very nature (conferred by grace) cannot be destroyed and cannot fail.[53] Even when this Church is called sinful and even when this sinfulness is said to affect the Church itself, also institutionally,[54] the *essential* holiness of that historical, visible Church is not thereby negated. The holiness of the Church is assured because this institution is grounded in holiness, not in sinfulness.[55] Whereas holiness is the essential ground of the Church, sin is a

46 See ch. II, sec. C, 3 above.
47 See ibid., esp. n. 197. See also *Schriften*, II, 83.
48 See *Schriften*, IV, 297-98; VI, 312-13, 342, 343; VIII, 339-41, 365, 520-21. See also ch. II, sec. C, 3 above.
49 *Schriften*, IV, 303; X, 386. See *Schriften*, VI, 315 for an ecclesiological use of the christological formulations "unmixed and unseparated." See also *Schriften*, II, 83 where Rahner speaks of the "God-man" quality of the Church (cf. II, 80).
50 Rahner objects to a *false hypostatization* of the essence of the Church (*Schriften*, VI, 342).
51 See *Schriften*, X, 398-99. See also his recent book *Strukturwandel der Kirche als Aufgabe und Chance* (Freiburg: Herder, 1972). Although the Church as institution is viewed as the "end" in the sense that it represents the consummation of grace, the coming-to-itself of grace in this perfect medium (see *Schriften*, IV, 347; V, 155; VIII, 341, 347; see also ch. II, sec. C, 3 above), the Church can also be viewed as the beginning of grace in the sense that the *institutional* mediation of grace is meant to lead to the *personal* realization of grace (see *Schriften*, II, 115-41; X, 405-29; "Überlegungen zum *personalen Vollzug* des sakramentalen Geschehens," emphasis added).
52 See *Schriften*, V, 142; VIII, 365-73.
53 *Schriften*, IV, 339; VIII, 520-22; see also VI, 312, 341-43. Cf. ch. II, n. 210 above. Schoonenberg describes the Church in a similar way (see ch. V, n. 95 above).
54 See *Schriften*, VI, 308-10, 336.
55 *Ibid.*, 312, 342.

reality which, though cleaving to the Church, exists as an (accidental) contradiction of the essence of the Church.[56] In fact, this essence of the Church is an institutional antidote that continually and effectively counteracts the sin that besets the Church.[57] The paradigm of this effective and indestructible institutionalized communication of grace is the sacramental *opus operatum*, for there that which is tangibly symbolized is effectively and irrevocably realized.[58] In fact, by virtue of its unfailing efficacy the Church itself is, as Rahner calls it, the "arch-sacrament." "*Opus operatum . . .* is the absolute self-realization of the Church in its own essence as arch-sacrament."[59] Precisely as sacramental institution the Church is the extension of the incarnate Christ.[60] Compared to the Church as "arch-sacrament," therefore, all extraecclesiastical realizations of grace are qualified as quasi-sacramental[61] and as ambivalent manifestations of grace.[62]

Against this ecclesiological background, the peculiar relation of Rahner's conception of the Church to his reinterpretation of original sin can be clarified. The Church is essentially holy and a uniquely efficacious medium of that holiness. The primary given from which original sin is derived is *sanctifying* grace: the essentially (ontologically) holy God communicates his own nature to man so that this divine holiness becomes an ontological quality, an immediate *Existential*, of man.[63] Now, using as criterion the perfect match of medium (irrevocable efficacy) and content (God's nature) that is embodied in the sacramental Church, one can say that all men initially lack the essential quality of holiness *as mediated by this unique institution*. This basic assumption regarding the Church as quintessential medium of grace is in evidence when Rahner remarks that the primal interhuman nexus – our collective and individual origin – no longer functions as a *sacrament*.[64] In maintaining a universal lack of grace, Rahner surveys man's present situation from the sacramental Church as institutionalized peak of grace. The (assumed) necessity of this summit for the full realization of salvation provides

---

56   *Ibid.*, 313: "Die Sünde bleibt Wirklichkeit an ihr, die ihrem Wesen widerspricht; ihre Heiligkeit aber ist Offenbarung ihres Wesensgrundes."
57   *Ibid.*, 339.
58   *Ibid.*, IV, 339-40; X; 384-86.
59   *Ibid.*, IV, 340. For Rahner's conception of the Church as *Ursakrament*, see *Kirche und Sakramente* ("Quaestiones Disputatae," 10; Freiburg: Herder, 1960), 11-45; cf. *Schriften*, IV, 337-45; X, 384-86, 424-27.
60   See *Schriften*, III, 295-96; IV, 337-38; VIII, 340; IX, 252; X, 384-86.
61   *Ibid.*, II, 84-94, 135-36.
62   *Ibid.*, V, 117, 143, 152.
63   See ch. III, sec. C, 2, b above.
64   *Schriften*, IX, 267, cf. 268.

the basis both for positing a universal privation of grace and for postulating a primordial fall to explain such privation.

The reinterpretation of original sin as a situation in which every human being is initially deprived of grace, it has been argued, finds its ground in the axiom that the sacramental Church is the only perfect manifestation and medium of supernatural grace and is necessary for the full realization of salvation. This ecclesiological axiom involves not merely a matter of theological method but has important implications for the *relevance* of the reinterpreted doctrine.

B. THE SACRAMENTAL MEDIUM AS PROBLEMATIC MESSAGE

Before posing the question concerning the relevance of the situational reinterpretation of original sin in the light of its relation to a specific conception of the Church, it may be well to place this reinterpretation within its larger context.

The horizon within which man exists is grace. This transcendental *Existential* is man's fundamental situation which (as horizon) is unaffected by sin. Wherever man is true to his conscience and is motivated by love, grace is realized in man's concrete (spatiotemporal) situation. The only perfect realization and mediation of grace takes place in the context of the sacramental Church. To the degree that human decisions are immoral, a negative element is introduced within the horizon of grace. Insofar as this negative element entails a universal privation of grace, it represents original sin in the post-Tridentine, Thomistic sense. The situational objectifications of misdirected and disintegrated natural powers that accompany this privation of grace may be called man's concupiscent situation.[65]

Within this larger context, it is very difficult to indicate the relevance of intepreting the negative element, the privation of grace, as a situational *Existential*. This difficulty becomes manifest when one imagines trying to explain to an (adult) catechumen this interpretation of his concrete situation. Assuming that he can be convinced that the fulfillment of his life is to be sought in the possession of sanctifying grace (a critical step), he must in addition be brought to accept that in some way every one is initially deprived of this grace. Since he has been told that grace is the horizon of his existence, he would naturally assume that the degree of privation of grace that exists can be counteracted by joining hands with Christians and men of good will in order to create situations that embody grace. To the extent that this com-

---

65   See ch. IV, sec. C above.

munal endeavor fails, a degree of privation would remain, but he would ascribe this privation of grace to personal sin.[66]

The theologian informs him, however, that it is impossible to banish the situational privation of grace even in a single instance because this privation constitutes an abiding initial *Existential*, i.e., an ineradicable element in the situational structure of human existence. If he should then ask how one knows that this is so, the theologian would point (implicitly or explicitly) to the existence of the Church as the unique, necessary and perfect sacramental remedy for this privation of grace. Even if the catechumen were willing to grant that the Church is the only perfect mediation of grace and to accept the corollary thesis regarding the universal privation of this mode and measure of grace, the problem of relevance remains. He will find it difficult, if not impossible, to see the sacramental Church as the necessary *remedy* for *original sin as situation*; for this ecclesiastical medium of grace as such does not change the situation of original sin, which is said to be an abiding *Existential*. How then can the ecclesiastical medium of grace be said to be a remedy for the situational privation of grace? Does that medium of grace, instead of changing the situation, pluck a person out of the situational privation of grace? But that is impossible, for if the situational privation of grace is truly an *Existential*, it is an interior determinant of man. To leave it behind would be to leave this world.

The problem of the relevance of the situational reinterpretation of original sin consists in the fact that its *positive* message for man's situation is that the sacramental Church represents the perfect medium of grace. That message is highly problematic, however, because the framework that once rendered this medium plausible as being the remedy for a universal malady has collapsed. For the ecclesiastical medium to be a *remedy* for the *situational* privation of grace, the Church would have to become "world" or the "world" would have to become Church. In a pluralistic and differentiated society neither is possible. Consequently, in relation to the human situation the ecclesiastical medium of grace becomes a *donum* – if not simply a *factum* – *superadditum*. Accordingly, the situational reinterpretation of original sin – given its new cosmological and theological horizons – takes on the appearance of a mere rationalization for the unquestioned assumption of the necessity of this institutional *donum*. Rahner's understanding of the relevance

---

66 He could also point to man's powerlessness vis-à-vis his "concupiscent situation," but this can be left out of consideration because only the relevance of the essence of original sin as the privation of grace is being examined at this point. For the existential relevance of man's concupiscent situation, see ch. IV, sec. C above.

of the doctrine of original sin as a teaching that entails the rejection of the attempt to realize "paradise" on earth as Utopian[67] may, therefore, well be countered by a rejection of the foundational axiom regarding the perfect and necessary realization of sanctifying grace on earth in the Church. For to the contemporary addressee of the situational reinterpretation of original sin this axiom may well seem equally Utopian.

Possible misgivings by contemporary man regarding the concrete relevance of the situational reinterpretation of original sin may not, of course, be taken as the final criterion of the success or failure of this reinterpretation. Nevertheless, since concern for concrete relevance for modern man is one of the major impulses for the situational reinterpretation of original sin and since the foregoing misgivings arise out of the situationalists' own frame of reference, such objections cannot be dismissed out of hand. The problem of the relevance of the situational understanding of original sin is worthy of careful examination, moreover, because that relevance is hampered most deeply by a remnant of the nature-grace dualism that the situationalists overtly reject.[68] Despite their attempt to integrate nature and grace, however, the old dualism becomes manifest in a cultural-institutional form: sanctifying grace, though ubiquitous, can be realized perfectly and fully only in the official acts of the institutional Church. All non-ecclesiastical or unofficial ecclesiastical institutions, structures and situations can embody grace only imperfectly and partially.

In view of the problems that have come into view in this and the previous chapters, the question must be asked whether both the content and the relevance of the doctrine of original sin might not be better served by a more radical reinterpretation. That possibility can readily be examined by considering the reinterpretation of original sin in terms of personal sin.

---

67 On the basis of the doctrine of original sin, Rahner calls the attempt to realize "paradise" Utopian and an expression of culpable hubris. The doctrine of original sin, he says, is a warning that the task of producing a concrete historical manifestation of the presence of grace is a duty that cannot be completed within this world (*SM*, I, 1115; *SM*e, IV, 333).

68 See ch. II above.

PART III

ORIGINAL SIN
AS
PERSONAL SIN

CHAPTER VII   *ORIGINAL SIN AS THE UNIVERSALITY*
OF ACTUAL SINS: A. VANNESTE

A. THE DYNAMICS OF RADICAL REINTERPRETATION

1. Radical Reinterpretation

With a measure of justification, Vanneste presents his treatment of the doctrine of original sin[1] as a *radical* reinterpretation and demythologization,[2] and as a thorough, *ab ovo*[3] renovation of the doctrine. His approach to the doctrine of original sin is radical not merely because it involves the rejection of its traditional framework — historical Adam, primordial fall, monogenesis, biological unity of mankind — but especially because it also involves the rejec-

---

[1] Vanneste deals with the doctrine of original sin systematically in the following studies: "De theologie van de erfzonde," *CollBG*, XII (1966), 289-312;

French version: "La théologie du péché originel," *Revue du Clergé Africain*, XXII (1967), 492-513.

English condensation: "Toward a Theology of Original Sin," *ThD*, XV (1967), 209-14.

"Is de erfzonde een historische zonde?" *CollBG*, XIV (1968), 289-321;

French version: "Le péché originel est-il un péché historique? *Message et Mission. Recueil Commémoratif du Xe Anniversaire de la Faculté Théologie* ("Publications de l'Université de Kinshasa, 23"; Louvain: Nauwelaerts, 1968), 129-54.

Het dogma van de erfzonde: Zinloze mythe of openbaring van een grondstruktuur van het menselijk bestaan? ("Woord en Beleving," Series II, No. 9; Tielt: Lannoo, 1969); cited hereafter as *Dogma;*

French translation: *Le dogme du péché originel* ("Recherches africaines de théologie. Travaux de la Faculté de Théologie de Kinshasa, Université Nationale du Zaïre"; Louvain: Nauwelaerts, 1971).

"De erfzonde: Repliek op vragen en moeilijkheden," *Bijdragen*, XXXIII (1972), 152-75.
"Le dogme de l'immaculée conception et l'évolution actuelle de la théologie du péché originel," *EphM*, XXIII (1973), 77-93.

[2] See *Dogma*, 14, 85, 173, 182, 192; *Bijdragen*, XXXIII, 160, 163; *EphM*, XXIII, 79.

[3] *Dogma*, 13-14.

tion of all the primary givens which remain central for the situationalists. Generally, but also basically, Vanneste diverges from the situational approach to original sin by resolutely repudiating all attempts to understand original sin as some kind of pre-personal sinfulness.[4] *Ipso facto* all the notions that play a central role in the situational reinterpretation – original sin as situational *Existential*, as privation of sanctifying grace, as analogical sin – are deliberately jettisoned.[5] This radical reinterpretation of the doctrine of original sin obviates the recondite but fundamental situationalist distinctions between, e.g., transcendental and spatiotemporal situation, existential situation and situational *Existential,* personal sin and analogous sinfulness, sanctifying and forgiving grace. The theology of original sin is delivered of such complexities in one clean sweep.

This radical departure from both the traditional and contemporary mainstream of the Roman Catholic approach to the doctrine of original sin promises a welcome rejuvenation of this teaching. Moreover, Vanneste's characterization of the history of the theology of original sin as "a concatenation of confusion, ambiguities and unsolved difficulties,"[6] his disqualification of other contemporary reinterpretations as unsatisfactory, irresolute and insufficiently radical,[7] and his conviction that he has found a satisfactory solution to the basic questions posed by the doctrine of original sin[8] charge the air with even more intense expectation. Most important from the viewpoint of this study, Vanneste's interpretation of the doctrine of original sin presents a striking alternative to the situational reinterpretation.

2. The Anthropological Mainspring and the
   Soteriological Basis of Reinterpretation

Despite his radical rejection of the situational reinterpretation of original sin, Vanneste holds one central motif in common with the situationalists, namely, the emphasis on personal responsibility and, specifically, indivi-

---

[4] *Dogma,* 83; *Bijdragen,* XXXIII, 154, 168, 169. See also his vehement rejection of Rahner's definition of the minimum of the Catholic doctrine of original sin (*Bijdragen,* XXXIII, 154, n. 13).

[5] Contra situation (as *Existential*), see: *Dogma,* 12, 82-83, 183-86; *CollBG,* XII, 289; *Bijdragen,* XXXIII, 169. Contra privation of grace, see: *Dogma,* 122-25. Contra analogical sin, see: *Dogma,* 149, 189.

[6] *Dogma,* 13. Elsewhere Vanneste says that, whatever different theories and modes of representation were occasioned by the Christian doctrine of original sin, in its deepest core this doctrine has remained marvelously homogeneous (*Dogma,* 17).

[7] See *Dogma,* 11, 182, 191-92. Cf. *Bijdragen,* XXXIII, 162.

[8] *Dogma,* 14 including n. 8.

dual freedom. As has been indicated, this idea of freedom is an indispensable presupposition of the situational framework, a primary given which, contrary to Vanneste's suggestion,[9] is never negated by the idea of situation.[10] Vanneste's agreement with the situationalists extends even farther in that he acknowledges the reality of man's situational solidarity.[11] Nonetheless, a decisive parting of ways does occur rather quickly because Vanneste considers the notion of situation in its polarity to personal freedom to be *theologically* irrelevant. In contrast to the situationalists, therefore, for whom the idea of freedom functions as *negative* criterion for establishing the *situational* reality of original sin,[12] in Vanneste's reinterpretation the idea of freedom functions as *positive* criterion for establishing the *personal* nature of original sin.[13] Vanneste's reinterpretation of the doctrine of original sin must be viewed as a passionate defense of man's responsibility based on an appeal to the idea of individual freedom.[14]

A mainspring cannot, of course, function in midair; the anthropological mainspring of Vanneste's reinterpretation finds its theological anchorage in the teaching that all men need the saving grace that has appeared in Jesus Christ. As we shall see, this teaching functions as the soteriological basis of Vanneste's reinterpretation of the doctrine of original sin.

B. THE REDUCTION OF ORIGINAL SIN TO
   THE UNIVERSALITY OF ACTUAL SINS

Impelled by the anthropological mainspring of reinterpretation[15] and guided by the soteriological basis of the doctrine,[16] Vanneste applies a rigorous process of reduction to the doctrine of original sin. He contends that this doctrine has nothing to do with theories regarding evolution,[17] polygenesis[18]

---

9 *Dogma*, 186; *Bijdragen*, XXXIII, 169; *CollBG*, XIV, 318.
10 See ch. I, sec. A, 3 and B, 2 above; and ch. IV, sec. B above.
11 *Dogma*, 12, 83, 185; *CollBG*, XIV, 317; *Bijdragen*, XXXIII, 169.
12 See ch. I, sec. A, 3 (introductory paragraphs).
13 *Dogma*, 12, 183, 185; in each instance, Vanneste defends the personal nature of original sin explicitly against the situational interpretation of the doctrine.
14 See, e.g., *Dogma*, 83.
15 Indicated by "A" following the references in nn. 17-21 below.
16 Indicated by "Th" following the references in nn. 17-21 below. See also *CollBG*, XIV, 294n where Vanneste speaks of this doctrine as being a "typically Christian *theologoumenon*" (cf. *CollBG*, XII, 310).
17 *Dogma*, 12 (Th), 190 (A); *CollBG*, XII, 308 (Th); *ThD*, XV, 213 (Th); *CollBG*, XIV, 320 (Th & A).
18 *Dogma*, 139, 182-83 (A).

or heredity,[19] nor with the findings of psychology[20] or sociology.[21] Moreover, original sin cannot be something prepersonal,[22] a condition of a small child,[23] an inherited stain.[24] Because *sin*, according to Vanneste, consists of nothing other than the voluntary free acts of the individual,[25] *original sin*, too, can consist of nothing other than actual sins.[26] More precisely, Vanneste presents his reinterpretation as involving the reduction of the doctrine of original sin to the universality of actual sins.[27] This, in his view, constitutes the indispensable kernel wrapped in the outdated, mythological husk of the traditional teaching. Vanneste applies this winnowing process in an extremely radical and novel way, discovering more husk than would a theologian employing a less stringent principle of demythologization.

1. The Demythologization of Original Sin as
   Condition (*Peccatum Originale Originatum*)

Vanneste chooses the second canon of the Council of Carthage (418) as basic text for his reinterpretation, a canon which he considers to be the most important ecclesiastical text in the entire history of the doctrine of original sin.[28] As we have seen, this canon, appealing to the *in quo* rendering of Ro 5:12, teaches that infants contract original sin from Adam by generation and that they therefore need the regeneration conferred in baptism, which is truly administered "in the remission of sins."[29] Appealing to the central intention of Augustine's teaching on original sin,[30] Vanneste thoroughly demythologizes this canon in the light of its anti-Pelagian thrust.[31] Against Pelagius, Augustine held that all men need Christ's redeeming grace because all men are sinners.[32] In Augustine's thought, therefore, the doctrine of original sin — as Vanneste points out — functions as an indispensable implication of the uni-

---

19 *Dogma*, 82.
20 *Dogma*, 73-74 (Th); *CollBG*, XII (Th).
21 *Dogma*, 82-83 (A), 184-85 (A), 188-89 (A).
22 See n. 4 above.
23 *Dogma*, 76-77, 82.
24 *Dogma*, 139, 162; *Bijdragen*, XXXIII, 154.
25 *Dogma*, 74-75, 83, 189. Vanneste declares that on this score he is in full agreement with Pelagius (*Dogma*, 74-75, 83; *CollBG*, XIV, 293, 304).
26 *Dogma*, 189; *Bijdragen*, XXXIII, 169.
27 *Dogma*, 79; *Bijdragen* XXXIII, 157; *EphM*, XXIII, 79, 84.
28 *CollBG*, XII, 291; *ThD*, XV, 209; *CollBG*, XIV, 290; *Dogma*, 54.
29 Introduction, sec. A, 5 above.
30 *Dogma*, 65; cf. 56, 67. See also *Bijdragen*, XXXIII, 160, 168, 172.
31 *Dogma*, 50, 55-56; cf. 67.
32 *Dogma*, 65-66.

versal necessity of redemption in Jesus Christ.[33] To deny that infants are born in sin is to deny that Christ came to save children as well as adults.[34] In similar fashion, Augustine argued that if Pelagius' idea of the basic soundness of human nature (*bonum naturae*) were correct, the healing grace of Jesus Christ would be superfluous.[35]

On the basis of this analysis of the intention of the doctrine of original sin, Vanneste concludes that its kernel is the teaching that all men are (actual) sinners. The novelty of Vanneste's demythologization of this teaching of the magisterium lies in the fact that he treats not merely the fall of a historical Adam (*peccatum originale originans*)[36] but also the subjection of children to original sin (*peccatum originale originatum*) as a myth. Vanneste removes also the latter as husk, while at the same time attempting to maintain the universality of actual sins as kernel. In so doing, he at one point qualifies the explicit teaching of the Council of Carthage that *infants* are born in a *condition of original sin* as the *form* of this doctrine, and goes on to say that its (implicit) *content* – its deeper meaning, its basic intention – is the teaching that all *adults* are *actual sinners*.[37] A greater contrast between form and content can hardly be imagined.

How is it possible to argue that a document which explicitly speaks of the sinful condition of infants in fact intends to teach the universality of the actual sins of adults? Vanneste argues his case by subjecting a basic presupposition of the second canon of the Council of Carthage to a critical examination. The "radical question" must be posed, he asserts, as to whether the theologian can say anything meaningful about infants.[38] Vanneste answers this question negatively. Theology "has adults in view, i.e., those who are actually capable of a conscious and free choice vis-à-vis God."[39] This restricted scope of theology, Vanneste holds, is an implication of the fact that religion (presumably the object of theology) "is nothing other than freely loving God – or turning away from Him."[40] Since religious categories have

---

33 *Dogma*, 65-67, 164, 173.
34 *Dogma*, 66.
35 *Dogma*, 67.
36 For a critical discussion of this aspect of Vanneste's demythologization of original sin, see Rudolf Haubst, "Was bleibt von der 'Erbsünde'? Zur aktuellen Diskussion um 'Ursünde' und 'allgemeine Sündigkeit' bzw. 'Mitsündigkeit,' " *TThZ*, LXXXIII (1974), 214-31.
37 *Bijdragen*, XXXIII, 154-55, 159-60; cf. 172.
38 *Dogma*, 71.
39 *Dogma*, 72.
40 *Dogma*, 72; cf. 191.

exclusive reference to the experience of adults, theology can at most extrapolate from such categories and in this way make affirmations regarding small children "which would be correct if they were adults."[41] Strictly speaking, however, the theologian can say nothing meaningful about the religious condition of infants themselves;[42] they exist in a "pre-theological stage."[43] Though granting that both in everyday life and in theology small children are spontaneously treated as small adults or as human beings in-the-making, he insists that in principle theology should maintain silence with respect to these children.[44]

Despite this clear delineation of the limits of theology, Vanneste immediately proceeds to transgress these limits. Moreover, he justifies going beyond these limits by contending that it is advisable and even necessary to speak of original sin in terms of small children. It is advisable to continue speaking of original sin in terms of infants, says Vanneste, because to date it has always been spoken of in that way, a custom which indicates that in the context of this doctrine people spontaneously speak of small children.[45] In view of the fact that Vanneste has judged the custom of applying the category "sin" to small children to be an essentially erroneous practice, its customariness can hardly serve as a ground for recommending its perpetuation. It is not surprising, therefore, to find that he proceeds to argue the necessity of continuing this practice on theological grounds. Theology must continue to speak of children, he contends, because in that way it can say

---

41 *Dogma*, 72.

42 *Bijdragen*, XXXIII, 160-62; *Dogma*, 73-74.

43 *Bijdragen*, XXXIII, 161. Cf. *Dogma*, 122.

44 *Dogma*, 73. On the whole, Vanneste's position with respect to the small child remains rather ambiguous. Besides urging caution due to the limitation of theology, as he does in the passages cited or referred to thus far, he also expresses his doubt about the genuine humanity of the small child. He says, e.g., that a child is "not an ordinary human," (*Dogma*, 84), "a human being in a somewhat special meaning of the word" (*Dogma*, 186), "an extremely peculiar being" (*Dogma*, 168) and "not yet human like the other human beings" (*CollBG*, XIV, 299); accordingly, he speaks of the child as a being that is yet to become human (see below, esp. n. 58). Elsewhere, Vanneste posits as his personal conviction that the child is indeed human (*Bijdragen*, XXXIII, 162; cf. *Dogma*, 186). In accordance with this conviction, the continued doubt expressed regarding the status of the small child is ascribed to a limitation of our knowledge of the child (*Dogma*, 73, 116, 168; *CollBG*, XII, 302, 311; *ThD*, XV, 212; *CollBG*, XIV, 304). Hence he often leaves the status of the child in doubt by using formulations such as "insofar as the child is a human being" (*Dogma*, 75, 78, 85, 122; *CollBG*, XII, 302, 303; *ThD*, XV, 212; *CollBG*, XIV, 316, 318, n. 55), and "if the newly born infant is human" (*Dogma*, 81) or "if the child is viewed [or treated] as a human being" (*Dogma*, 78; *CollBG*, XII, 303).

45 *Dogma*, 74-75.

something regarding *adults*.⁴⁶ "The small child becomes something like a borderline case, a testcase," by means of which the universality of sin is driven to its extreme.⁴⁷ In saying that a child is "born in sin" one is not really saying anything about the present condition of that child itself but by means of the mythical symbol⁴⁸ of the sinful infant one is in fact making a categorical statement regarding all adults.⁴⁹ To say "that children are born in a state of original sin means that all men are sinners – absolutely all men – from the first moment that they are [adult] human beings, not because their nature is evil, but because they themselves have chosen to be sinners."⁵⁰

Although the full implication of Vanneste's use of the symbol of the sinful infant requires critical examination,⁵¹ at this point it suffices to note that his demythologization of the relevant ecclesiastical text is based on the assumption that, at least from the viewpoint of theology, a time-lag exists between birth and (individual) hominization. In other words, a lag is assumed to exist between the moment one enters this world and the time when one begins to exist and act as an authentic (adult) human being. Accordingly, when Vanneste expresses his understanding of original sin, he never speaks of man as sinner from the moment of birth; that is an expression which for him holds truth only as mythological symbol. Instead, he consistently speaks of man as sinner from the first moment he "becomes a human being,"⁵² "exists as human being,"⁵³ "acts as human being"⁵⁴ or "as adult."⁵⁵ Or he says that there has never been a moment in one's "personal history" when one was not a sinner.⁵⁶ Whether true to fact or not,⁵⁷ *theologically* the small child is viewed as a creature that is not yet (fully) human, but which will become authentically human at the moment of its first free and conscious act.⁵⁸

---

46 *Dogma*, 75.
47 *Ibid.*
48 See *Bijdragen*, XXXIII, 160, 162, 172.
49 *Bijdragen*, XXXIII, 160: "By eliminating the small children as real term [i.e., in contrast to the small child as symbol or myth], we have indeed carried out a far-reaching demythologization.... Strictly speaking the dogmatician can say nothing about such children; what he says about them has meaning solely insofar as it affirms something of value regarding the adults." Cf. *CollBG*, XII, 306. See also *Dogma*, 75, 81, 87.
50 *Dogma*, 77.
51 See sec. C, 2, b below.
52 *Dogma*, 192; cf. 77, 173; *CollBG*, XIV, 316.
53 *Dogma*, 99; *CollBG*, XIV, 321; cf. 302.
54 *Dogma*, 15, 79; *CollBG*, XIV, 316; *Bijdragen*, XXXIII, 155.
55 *Dogma*, 74.
56 *Dogma*, 78; cf. 81.
57 See n. 44 above.
58 Accordingly, Vanneste refers to the small child or children as a "virtual human

In Vanneste's view therefore an ecclesiastical statement regarding the sinful condition of the small child means that *insofar as* that child is or is regarded to be an (adult) human being, it is or must be regarded to be a sinner.[59] The small child must be regarded as a sinner because the first conscious and free choice of every human being is a religiously negative choice.[60] That choice is made at the point at which one begins to exist and act as an authentic (adult) human being.[61] In the same sense that a child can be called a "virtual human being," therefore, it can be called a "virtual sinner."[62] The small child can be called a virtual sinner by virtue of the certainty that he will become an actual sinner in his first free act.[63] The doctrine of original sin, couched by the magisterium in terms of infants subject to original sin, means nothing other or more than the absolute universality of actual sins.

At this point it becomes evident that in Vanneste's view the scriptural "Adam" and the ecclesiastical "sinful infant" play essentially the same role. The myth or symbol of Adam gives expression to the fact that the first free and conscious act of every human being (from the moment of the hominization of the species) is a sinful one.[64] The doctrine that all children are born in (original) sin represents simply a multiplication of the Adamic myth, for it intends to teach that the first choice of *every* human being (at the moment of individual hominization) is a sinful one: "from the moment of their awakening to conscious life they will become like Adam; they will reject the grace which God offers them."[65] Vanneste's radical demythologization, therefore, consists in the recognition that both the story of Adam and the teaching regarding sinful infants are myths.[66] One can and perhaps ought to do without them; but one may and perhaps should use them, provided their mythical character is constantly taken into account.[67] In either case, all that

being" (*Dogma*, 82n), as "not yet genuine human beings in the full sense of the word" (*CollBG*, XIV, 298) and as "about to become a human being" (*CollBG*, XIV, 299). It is clear that the criterion of genuine humanness is the adult, specifically, his free and conscious acts (see *CollBG*, XIV, 292, 298, 304; *Dogma*, 79).

59 See the "insofar as" statements referred to in n. 44 above.
60 *Dogma*, 74, 77, 78, 79, 81.
61 *CollBG*, XIV, 292, 299, 304.
62 *Dogma*, 82n. Cf. *CollBG*, XIV, 299-300, 301-302.
63 *Dogma*, 162-63.
64 *Dogma*, 23, 85; cf. 12, 14, 183.
65 *EphM*, XXIII, 79. Cf. *CollBG*, XIV, 305: "A child is, therefore, born as sinner because it will be a sinner on the very day that it is a human being like us. On that day it will freely transgress God's law. We are certain of this, with an absolute certainty. For each human being that comes into the world is a virtual sinner. His first act will consist in committing sin *as Adam has done*" (emphasis added).
66 See *Bijdragen*, XXXIII, 159, 160, 162, 172.
67 *Dogma*, 58, 74, 76-77, 84, 85, 141-42; *EphM*, XXIII, 79; *CollBG*, XIV, 298.

one in fact affirms is the strict universality of actual (adult) sins.

The radicality of Vanneste's understanding of original sin becomes even more clearly manifest upon comparison to the situational reinterpretation of this doctrine. Though displaying varying degrees of scepticism regarding the reality of the *peccatum originale originans* (the sin of Adam), the situationalists do not question the reality of the *peccatum originale originatum* (original-sin-in-us). They reinterpret it as a prepersonal situational *Existential* interior to man. Vanneste's reinterpretation, as he himself comes to acknowledge, entails the negation, not only of the *peccatum originale originans*. but also of the *peccatum originale originatum*.[68] This negative conclusion is the consistent result of the viewpoint that the only sin that exists is the free actual sin of the individual. A term such as "original sin" is needed only as an expression of the *absolute universality* of actual sins. Indeed, a more radically demythologizing reinterpretation of the doctrine of original sin hardly seems possible.

To this point the mainspring, method and principal results of Vanneste's demythologization of the doctrine of original sin have been examined. The remainder of this expository section will be devoted to an examination of the way in which this reduction of the doctrine of original sin includes the rejection of the notion of an enslaved will.

2. Weakened Free Will contra Enslaved (Free) Will

As we have seen, Vanneste contends that the deepest intention of Augustine's doctrine of original sin is safeguarded by the affirmation of the strict universality of actual sins. Vanneste himself points out, however, that in his anti-Pelagian polemic Augustine did more than affirm the strict universality of sins: he also mounted a frontal attack on the Pelagian view of the *bonum naturae*.[69] This further attack upon the Pelagian position is not surprising, since for the Pelagians the *bonum naturae* provided the morally neutral ground which man could fall back upon in the attempt to live a sinless life.[70] One might say, therefore, that from Augustine's viewpoint the Pelagian denial of the strict universality of sin was merely a symptom; it was the affirmation of the *bonum naturae* that represented the disease. It is very

68 In his book, Vanneste merely raises the question whether his reinterpretation does not amount to saying "that original sin does *not* exist, that a child is in fact *not* born in sin? " (*Dogma,* 84). In later publications, Vanneste grants that this is indeed the case (*Bijdragen,* XXXIII, 154, 162; *EphM*, XXIII, 79).

69 See Introduction, sec. A, 4 above.

70 See Introduction, sec. A, 3 above and *Dogma,* 50-51.

interesting to notice that Vanneste agrees with Augustine regarding the *extent* of sin but — in effect — comes to the defense of the *bonum naturae* in order to limit the *radicality* of sin. This intriguing position will be examined in the first place for the purpose of demonstrating the radicality of Vanneste's reduction of original sin to the strict universality of the voluntary sins committed by individuals, and in the second place in order to bring into focus the framework within which he places the question as to the effect of sin.

Within Vanneste's reinterpretation of original sin, the idea of the *bonum naturae* makes itself felt especially in his discussion of concupiscence. In this context Vanneste opposes the association of original sin with radical concupiscence, the latter understood as an inescapable inclination to evil, as enslavement in sin. In opposing this notion of concupiscence, Vanneste makes a distinction between first and second concupiscence.[71] "First concupiscence" has reference to the spontaneous inclinations to good and to evil which are part of man's nature as moral being.[72] It may be called natural concupiscence. "Second concupiscence" has reference to a reality brought about by sin, a reality which, though always linked with human nature, is not a necessary part of man's metaphysical nature.[73] It may therefore be designated as sinful concupiscence.

On the basis of this distinction between natural and sinful concupiscence, Vanneste opposes the association of original sin with *radical* concupiscence. Only natural concupiscence to evil can be called radical, says Vanneste, in the sense that it "drives man inescapably to evil, if it is not overcome by the natural concupiscence to the good (aided by grace)."[74] Sin, by contrast, has not radically changed human nature. Therefore, Vanneste concludes, sinful concupiscence, in the nature of the case, "cannot be called a radical concupiscence. Human nature has merely deteriorated, *in deterius mutata.*"[75]

In the same way, Vanneste opposes Luther's identification of original sin with radical concupiscence, which is the source of daily sins.[76] Luther, according to Vanneste, denies man's ability freely to choose the good by appealing to the fact that man's nature is injured and corrupted by sin.

71 *Dogma*, 101, 130.
72 *Dogma*, 101. Vanneste's conception of "first concupiscence" is similar to Schoonenberg's and Rahner's conception of man's natural lack of integrity (see ch. IV, sec. C above).
73 *Dogma*, 101.
74 *Ibid.*
75 *Ibid.*
76 *Dogma*, 129-31

Luther's mistake, in Vanneste's opinion, lies in his identification of sinful concupiscence with a radical, invincible (natural) concupiscence. This error, Vanneste contends once more, can best be refuted by determining the precise meaning of the traditional theme of the corruption of human nature as it comes to expression in the Augustinian idea of *natura in deterius mutata*.[77] In other words, the *corruption* of human nature can be understood only as the *deterioration* of human nature, not as its enslavement in sin.

The force of the distinction between first and second concupiscence becomes even more clearly manifest in the way in which Vanneste opposes the idea of a radically evil nature. Drawn to its extreme conclusion, such an idea is unthinkable, he argues, because the deterioration of nature due to sin always represents a *second* element within the history of human nature. This second element always *presupposes* a *first* element which, to a greater or lesser degree, remains in force. Or, again, putting this relationship in terms of metaphysics, Vanneste says that evil cannot exist in itself but can only subsist in the good.[78]

The notion of human nature deteriorated by sin also constitutes the viewpoint from which Vanneste considers and sharply opposes Augustine's notion of man's enslavement in sin. As we have noted earlier, Vanneste places a great deal of emphasis on the fact that the Council of Orange amended an Augustinian thesis by deleting the notion that man's will is enslaved and his freedom lost and by substituting the notion that man's will is weakened.[79] In that context, Vanneste expresses his regret of the fact that in speaking of the possibilities retained by the will of man in sin, Augustine frequently "falls into" the theme of the slavery of sin.[80] Vanneste clearly considers the idea of bondage to be an unfortunate abberation. The theme of the injured human will, he says, "is connected with that of the corruption and the general deterioration of human nature, not with that of the slavery of sin."[81]

Vanneste's opposition to the understanding of original sin in terms of radical concupiscence or enslavement provides the background necessary for an examination of his assessment of the gravity of sin. As this opposition reveals, Vanneste places the question as to the effect of sin within the framework of a metaphysical concept of human nature: man's *essence*. Because this essence allows of only a certain degree of deterioration, the effect of sin is

---

77 *Dogma,* 130; cf. 147 including n. 41.
78 *Dogma,* 147.
79 See Introduction, sec. A, 5 above.
80 *Dogma,* 97.
81 *Ibid.*

rigorously circumscribed. Given this framework, it is not surprising to find that Vanneste attempts to determine the effect of sin in typically Semi-Pelagian fashion by eliminating two extremes: that sin either changes nothing in man or totally transforms man.[82] Despite this clear rejection of these two extremes, Vanneste's own position between these boundaries is not readily determined. We will proceed by simply presenting, first Vanneste's descriptions of the deterioration of human nature and then his assessment of the capacities that are retained by man-in-sin.

In opposition to Pelagius, Vanneste holds that sin does not leave human nature unaffected. He remains rather vague, however, concerning the nature and degree of the deterioration of human nature. Man is conscious of the fact that after sin "he is no longer what he used to be,"[83] "that something in him is broken, that some residue of evil clings to his soul."[84] Man feels that "something in him is injured and that his human capacities have lost some of their previous purity."[85] More specifically, all men are injured, says Vanneste, "especially in their highest and noblest capacities: their intellect and their will."[86] More specifically still, he says that man's will is weakened and that the concupiscence that dwells in him is no longer neutral; the natural equilibrium between the spontaneous inclinations to good and to evil is disrupted in favor of evil.[87]

In contrast to these descriptions of the damage inflicted by sin, Vanneste's assessment of the capacities that remain in man after sin is far more clear. Although after sin man is aware of something having been injured within him, he is at the same time conscious of remaining man and thus of not being wholly bound to his sinful act.[88] However hardened in sin man may be, the self-directedness entailed in his *amor sui* is not his ultimate and deepest characteristic.[89] On the contrary, "even the greatest sinner remains man and therefore bears in himself a radical openness for God's grace."[90]

---

82 *Dogma*, 98. That Vanneste expressly adopts a Semi-Pelagian position is evidenced by the identity that exists between Vanneste's characterization of the Semi-Pelagian position (*Dogma*, 92) and his description of his own approach presented above. See also his defense of a Semi-Pelagian interpretation of the Council of Orange (Introduction, sec. A, 5 above).
83 *Dogma*, 107.
84 *Dogma*, 98.
85 *Dogma*, 99.
86 *Ibid.*
87 *Dogma*, 102; cf. 151-52.
88 *Dogma*, 98-99.
89 *Dogma*, 147.
90 *Dogma*, 147-48.

Despite its injury, the *essence* of human nature remains untouched by sin.[91] However deeply evil may be rooted in man, we must continue to believe, urges Vanneste, in the fundamental goodness of man.[92] Man's retention of his essence has momentous implications for his remaining capacities. Because man's structure remains the same, "he is capable, even after sin, of loving God above all — be it with greater difficulty; for to be capable of loving God above all happens to be precisely that which constitutes the religious essence of man."[93]

In emphasizing man's fundamental goodness and man's retained capacity for the ultimate good, Vanneste does not intend to defend the notion of an autonomous goodness and power of nature. On the contrary, he considers Pelagius' appeal to goodness of nature apart from Christ to be a serious error, for the ultimate goodness of creation exists only in its relation to Jesus Christ.[94] In Vanneste's view, all "natural" goodness is ultimately "Christian" goodness.[95] Accordingly, after having posited man's retained capability of loving God above all, he adds that man can do nothing that is good without the aid of grace.[96] The necessity of grace which is thus affirmed, however, is attributed not to sin but to man's "creaturely," "metaphysical" dependence on God,[97] or, as he puts it elsewhere, to "man's ontological need of the grace of Christ."[98]

Once Vanneste's affirmation of this metaphysical necessity of grace is taken into consideration, the precise significance of his emphasis upon the capability of man in sin comes into focus. In speaking of the capabilities that remain after sin by virtue of man's religious essence and the (indispensable) aid of "original" grace, he wishes to negate the thesis that sin disrupts man's religious-ontological structure so basically as to make a *radical renewal by saving grace mandatory*. Vanneste expressly rejects the notion that "an 'historical' disturbance in our natural powers brought about by sin could render man wholly incapable of that which he is by nature called to do."[99] For that reason he distinguishes between man's *radical inability* to do the good

---

91 *Dogma*, 107.
92 *Dogma*, 148; cf. 178.
93 *Dogma*, 99-100; cf. 79 where Vanneste speaks of the metaphysical goodness that is essential for man.
94 *Dogma*, 164-66; cf. 53-54, n. 11.
95 *Bijdragen*, XXXIII, 159. Cf. *Dogma*, 79 where Vanneste qualifies the metaphysical goodness which is essential for man as being (in the eyes of the theologian) a *supernatural* goodness.
96 *Dogma*, 100.
97 *Ibid*.
98 *CollBG*, XIV, 292.
99 *Dogma*, 100.

due to his metaphysical dependence on God, on the one hand, and the *special difficulty* of doing the good which man experiences due to his frequent sins and loss of integrity, on the other.[100] Correspondingly, he warns against the frequent confusion (to which, he feels, Augustine at times falls prey) "between the *absolute necessity* of grace which is due to our general creaturely situation and the *second necessity* of grace which is due to the fact that all of us have a sinful history behind us; this makes it *more difficult* for us to love God because our free will is *injured.*"[101] Because man is not radically corrupted by sin, Vanneste explains elsewhere, God's healing (second) grace does not need to remedy a radical impossibility.[102]

Vanneste's difficulty with the notion of an *enslaved free* will and its concomitant radical moral-religious inability is entirely understandable given the framework within which he places the problem of the effect of sin. That framework, as we have seen, consists of an ontological or metaphysical conception of human nature. From that viewpoint, the idea of enslavement in sin and of radical moral-religious incapacity apart from *saving* grace can mean nothing other than the metaphysical annihilation, the ontic destruction of man's essence. From the perspective of that ontological framework, an appeal to the fact that man remains man is indeed the conclusive refutation of the opposite position. Furthermore, given that framework, the only viable alternative to the idea of an enslaved will must be formulated in terms of an injury of human nature which, as Vanneste says, does not touch the essence of that nature:[103] a measure of deterioration of human nature, a degree of attenuation of man's natural powers, a relative weakening of the free will and a correspondingly increased difficulty of doing the good. It is the exclusiveness of this ontological approach to the question of the *radicality* of sin that determines the answer to that question and that simultaneously marks the incisive divergence of views that lies just beneath the surface of the agreement between Augustine and Vanneste regarding the *extent* of sin.

As we have seen, Augustine, too, maintains the reality of man's free choice.[104] When he teaches that apart from the saving grace of Jesus Christ man is incapable of virtue, however, and speaks of the *bondage* of the free will, he places man's free choice within a different perspective. In determining the effect of sin, Augustine is able to speak of a radical change of human

100 *Ibid.*
101 *Dogma,* 188 emphasis of "absolute necessity" and "second necessity" added.
102 *Dogma,* 99n.
103 *Dogma,* 107.
104 See introduction, sec. A, 4 above.

"nature" because he does not view man first of all in terms of his *metaphysical structure* from which can be deduced man's essence as (single) indestructible root of certain inalienable capacities. Rather, in speaking of man's enslavement in sin, Augustine views man in terms of his *transcendental-religious direction,* concluding that there are *two* roots of human existence: man's love of self rooted in Adam and man's love of God rooted in Christ.[105] From that viewpoint, the effect of sin becomes manifest as being truly radical, i.e., affecting the very *radix* of human existence; and that radicality is by no means limited but rather *accentuated* by Augustine's recognition of man's retention of free will. For Vanneste, by contrast, the appeal to man's inalienable metaphysical nature – specifically, to man's (weakened) free will – entails the rejection of the idea of the enslavement of the human will and the radical effect of evil. In attempting to assess the effect of sin, Vanneste gives precedence to a metaphysical over an historical (religious) conception of human nature.[106] Whether this approach is compatible with Augustine's deepest intention – to which Vanneste wishes to remain true – is an important question in the context of the reinterpretation of original sin.

Insofar as Vanneste expressly wishes to speak of human nature historically, he does so exclusively in terms of man's individual free acts. This gives rise to the problem as to what is meant when Vanneste says that man is subject to concupiscence, that his nature injured and his will weakened *"after sin."* In the context of the traditional doctrine of original sin such a statement has reference to all mankind, for Adam's fall was conceived of as affecting human nature generically. In Vanneste's view, however, human nature is, as will become evident in the following section, the nature of each individual; moreover, "after sin" means after the sins of the individual.[107] This means that all the descriptions of man's deteriorated nature do not apply at the point of his first free decision. Consequently, the loss of integrity which Vanneste affirms can, at most, have reference to a certain irrecovera-

---

105 See *ibid.*
106 It must be noted that the question at issue is not whether or not a metaphysical framework is employed but whether in attempting to assess the radicality of sin a metaphysical conception of human nature is allowed to predominate over a religious conception of human nature. In this regard it is interesting to observe that Augustine, as Vanneste himself points out, frequently employs the theme of deterioration, but mainly with reference to human nature in general. In the domain of freedom – the *essence* of human nature, one might say – Augustine speaks almost exclusively in terms of man's servitude due to sin (see Introduction, n. 186 above). Vanneste, by contrast, deliberately extends the idea of deterioration to the domain of the free will in order to *exclude* the notion of slavery.
107 See *Dogma,* 98-99, 100, 102.

bleness of one's *individual* beginnings, to the impossibility of return to the beginning of one's *personal* history. The general force of this loss of integrity depends upon Vanneste's maintenance of the strict universality of free, actual sins — a subject to which we now turn.

C. THE CONTINGENCY AND THE ABSOLUTE UNIVERSALITY OF ACTUAL SINS

1. The Problem

As we have seen, Vanneste has radically reduced the doctrine of original sin to the affirmation of the absolute universality of actual sins. With respect to the question, therefore, of why no one escapes sin even though in principle this is possible, Vanneste declines to go beyond the answer which Augustine gives at one point: man does not *want* to.[108] Accordingly, understanding sin exclusively in terms of free individual acts, Vanneste rejects the idea of enslavement in sin and chooses as his ground the idea of the fundamental goodness of man — specifically, the supreme good of human nature: the (weakened) free will.[109] The intriguing question then arises how Vanneste, standing on essentially Pelagian ground,[110] can affirm what Pelagius on that same ground denied: the strict universality of actual sins.[111] Can Vanneste avoid Pelagius' conclusion without leaving Pelagius' ground, without going — as Augustine did — beneath or beyond the actual sins committed by individual free will?

The question thus posed in historical terms can be elaborated as a

---

108 *Dogma,* 68-69, 80-82; *CollBG,* XIV, 294-300; *EphM,* XXIII, 82-85; *Bijdragen,* XXXIII, 155-56. Augustine himself does go beyond this answer by leaving room for the further question, *why* man does not want to, to which he responds cryptically by saying "that's a long story" (*Dogma,* 69; *CollBG,* XIV, 295). Moreover, Augustine adds still another question, namely, whether a man could have or can still exist who is without sin. Augustine answers this question negatively in terms of his doctrine of original sin (*Dogma,* 80; *CollBG,* XIV, 297; *EphM,* XXIII, 85).

109 In addition to the material presented in the previous section, see also *Dogma,* 94, 186; *CollBG,* XII, 310; *ThD,* XV, 213.

110 As we have seen, Vanneste significantly modifies the notion of the goodness of nature by speaking of its deterioration and specifically of the weakening or injury of man's will and by qualifying the goodness of nature as a "Christian" goodness. With respect to the question as to the extent of sin, however, it can be said that Vanneste stands on essentially Pelagian ground because the idea of a weakened will cannot and does not function as ground of the universality of sin and the idea of a "Christian" goodness of nature, as we shall see, renders the universality of sin even less likely than it was from Pelagius' understanding of the *bonum naturae.*

111 See Introduction, sec. A. 3 above.

systematic problem. When the doctrine of original sin is rigorously reduced to the universality of actual sins, the ground of this universality is the free wills of all the individuals that comprise "humanity." By virtue of that ground, however, the universality of actual sins is jeopardized, for the free act of an individual is by its very nature contingent,[112] i.e., wholly unpredictable as to direction. Consequently, the extent of actual sins must always remain an *open* question. But the doctrine of original sin, interpreted as the absolute universality of actual sins, entails, as Vanneste says, the absolute certainty that every human being is and will be a sinner from the moment of his first free act.[113] In other words, Vanneste's reinterpretation of original sin is rooted in but at the same time appears to negate the contingent openness of free acts.

The problem emerging from the contingency entailed in the mainspring of Vanneste's reinterpretation becomes even more clearly manifest when the soteriological basis of his reinterpretation is taken into account. As we have seen, Vanneste considers the doctrine of original sin to be an implication of the teaching that all men need the saving grace of Jesus Christ.[114] When at one point Vanneste formulates the doctrine of original sin explicitly as an implication of this soteriological basis, the universality of actual sins seems to become even more improbable:

> Original sin is every newly born child's need to be redeemed and saved through Christ because – and insofar as – that child has already virtually refused the grace of God and must, therefore, repent and turn to Christ. In other words, viewed from the standpoint of the newly born infant, original sin consists in the fact that the child is a virtual sinner and will become a factual sinner the day that it begins its conscious life, the day that it becomes a genuine human being – *unless, of course, its first human act would be an act of faith in Christ.*[115]

---

112 We use this term only as a terse designation of the directional openness of the free act. This is the sense in which Vanneste too uses the term (*CollBG*, XIV, 301; *Bijdragen*, XXXIII, 156).

113 At times Vanneste speaks explicitly in terms of such absolute certainty (*Dogma*, 79, 162; *CollBG*, XIV, 305 [cited in n.65 above]). This certainty is *implicit* in Vanneste's understanding of the notion "virtual sinner" (see sec. B, 1, esp. n. 65 above) as well as in his use of the concept law (to be discussed in this section). He qualifies this certainty as a "historical" certainty in contrast to a "principial" or "metaphysical" certainty. By this he means that the certainty regarding the universality is not rooted in the notion of a metaphysical necessity of sinning and that this certainty leaves room for the possibility that God should make an exception to the universality of sin, as he did in the case of Mary (*Dogma*, 79, 162-64; *CollBG*, XIV, 305, 307). From *that* point of view this certainty is *not* absolute (*Bijdragen*, XXXIII, 157).

114 See sec. B, 1 above.

115 *CollBG*, XIV, 292 original emphasis (of "because – and insofar . . . and turn to Christ") deleted; present emphasis added.

Here the seemingly indispensable condition for maintaining the radical contingency of sin, i.e., its rootedness in the free act of the individual, emerges in the form of a crucial "unless."

The reality of that "unless" becomes even more problematic when one takes into account Vanneste's thesis that all "natural" goodness (including the capacity for free decisions) is not an autonomous, but a "Christian" goodness.[116] The bearing of this thesis upon the present problem becomes evident when Vanneste points to a "third possibility," a possibility which Augustine overlooked in his polemic with Pelagius. Beyond the dilemma of either denying the necessity of Christ's saving grace by viewing man as by nature capable of being righteous (Pelagius) or affirming the necessity of this grace by viewing all men as sinners (Augustine), Vanneste points to a third way: infants could be righteous "precisely by virtue of the grace which they have already received from Christ."[117] Describing this oversight as a weak point in Augustine's system,[118] Vanneste suggests that it would have been better if Augustine "had underscored more clearly the fact that man needs the grace of Christ in any case, that even one who does not commit sin can love God only by virtue of Christ's grace."[119] At this point the soteriological floor under Vanneste's reinterpretation of original sin — all men need Christ, therefore all men are sinners — seems to collapse, for here Vanneste is not speaking simply of a prelapsarian possibility of sinlessness due to God's original grace, as he does elsewhere,[120] but of a postlapsarian possibility of sinlessness due to saving grace. That Vanneste is indeed speaking of such an historical possibility becomes apparent when he substantiates his "third possibility" by appealing to the dogma of the immaculate conception of Mary. The *significance* of this dogma, according to Vanneste, lies precisely in the fact

> that it affirms very clearly that it is not mandatory to be a sinner to need the grace of Christ. On the contrary; if, thanks to a miracle of divine election, someone is safeguarded from sin throughout his life, he proves all the more to be empowered by God's grace in Jesus Christ. In his case it is even more true that Christ died on the cross for him.[121]

Although Vanneste arrives at the meaning of this dogma by appealing to the

---

116 See sec. B, 2 above.
117 *Bijdragen*, XXXIII, 158.
118 This weakness, according to Vanneste, "was not without consequences for the subsequent development of theology" (*ibid.*).
119 *Ibid.*
120 See sec. B, 2 above.
121 *Bijdragen*, XXXIII, 159.

potentia Dei absoluta ("thanks to a miracle of divine election"),[122] as substantiation of a "third possibility" beyond the dilemma posed by Augustine and Pelagius the significance of this dogma must point to a concrete historical possibility, a possibility within the *potentia Dei ordinata*.[123]

By virtue of several facets of Vanneste's thought, the possibility of exceptions (the "unless") to the universality of actual sins seems real, posing a threat not only to an aspect but to the very substance of his reinterpretation of original sin. In an attempt to determine the existential meaning of this doctrine as reinterpreted by Vanneste, the remainder of this chapter is devoted to an examination of the way in which he excludes these seemingly possible exceptions.

2. Beyond the Self-Imposed Boundary of "History"

By virtue of both Vanneste's conception of the reality of (original) sin and his view of the nature of theological reflection, "history" – which he understands in terms of the free acts of human individuals[124] – constitutes the realm within which his reinterpretation of original sin must take place. Vanneste places *the reality of original sin* within the bounds of this conception of history generally by attempting to reinterpret this doctrine in terms of actual sin, and specifically by advocating the notion of a "historical" (contra "metaphysical") universality of actual sins,[125] by rejecting the Augustinian idea of the enslavement of the human will,[126] and by refusing to go beyond the will of the individual as ground for the universality of sin.[127] *Theological reflection upon* the reality of original sin is placed within the same boundary by virtue of Vanneste's contention that theological statements have meaning only with reference to the free acts of adults.[128] Thus both the field of enquiry and the enquiry of that field enclose his reinterpretation of original

---

122 Elsewhere Vanneste says that "faith teaches that all men are sinners – unless God disposes otherwise in this matter" (*CollBG*, XIV, 305; cf. 307). See also *Dogma*, 163 where Vanneste speaks of God's "right and power to see to it that an exception be made" to a historical law.

123 Accordingly, Herbert Haag challenges the legitimacy of Vanneste's key (soteriological) argument: all men need the grace of Jesus Christ; therefore, all men are sinners ("The Original Sin Discussion, 1966-71," *JESt*, X (1973), 276-77; *ThQ*, CL (1970), 456).

124 See, e.g., *CollBG*, XIV, 293, 301, 304; *Dogma*, 79. *EphM*, XXIII, 79, 84.

125 *Dogma*, 79, 164; *CollBG*, XIV, 301; *EphM*, XXIII, 83, 84, 87.

126 See sec. B, 2 above.

127 See *ibid*. Vanneste later underscores this point by saying, "For the free action of man there is no other explanation than this free action" (*Bijdragen*, XXXIII, 156, n. 19; cf. *Dogma*, 83).

128 See sec. B, 1 above.

sin within the self-imposed boundary of his conception of history.

Interestingly, to maintain the strict universality of actual sins — in Vanneste's view, the *substance* of the doctrine of original sin — he often goes beyond his selfimposed boundary of history and appeals to "realities" other than that of freely committed actuals sins. This appeal may indicate that in order to avoid Pelagius' conclusions regarding the extent of sin Vanneste is driven to search for grounds other than that on which he stands together with Pelagius, the free will of the individual. In any case, this tendency of transcending his self-imposed boundary has important implications for the existential meaning of the doctrine of original sin as reinterpreted by Vanneste.

a. *Mythological Transcendence*

Despite Vanneste's emphatic denial that any sin other than free, actual sin exists,[129] he at times suggests that original sin is a unique kind of sin. He says, for example, that when a child is said to be born in sin, the word sin has a special meaning. It has reference to a reality *sui generis*.[130] Elsewhere, Vanneste again suggests that original sin is a unique kind of sin when he states that the original sin to which the child is subject "must not be added to its actual sins as if it were, for example, the first in the series of personal sins."[131] Fortunately, in this context Vanneste begins to specify the *genus* of original sin when he says that it

> lies, as it were, at the source of the series and, in a certain sense, represents the whole series. Original sin is, as it were, the source — the *fomes* — which, from the first moment of our lives, virtually contains all our actual sins.[132]

These are exceedingly weighty passages if they are indeed meant as pointers to original sin as a reality *sui generis*, a reality that constitutes the source of actual sins. Before attempting to determine the precise import of these statements, we will examine a number of passages which are even more striking. In these Vanneste deals with original sin in terms of a "law of sin," specifically, the law of the universality of sin.

At one point, Vanneste speaks of the law of the universality of sin as a law to which there are no exceptions.[133] In this instance, the term "law" appears to refer simply to the *fact* that all men commit actual sins — a general

---

129 See sec. B, introductory paragraph above.
130 *Dogma*, 80.
131 *Dogma*, 82.
132 *Dogma*, 81-82.
133 *Dogma*, 77.

"rule,"[134] a matter of statistics. In a second instance, however, this minimal, statistical interpretation appears to be controverted when Vanneste hypostatizes the law by saying, "If the infant is a human being, he cannot escape the general law *which wills* that all men are sinners and wills that they are such historically."[135] The purely statistical interpretation of this law is explicitly excluded in a third passage. In the immediate context of this passage Vanneste asserts that by affirming that infants are sinners one drives the universality of sin to its limit. "One affirms emphatically," he continues, "that truly no man ever existed who was without sin. The *de facto* universality of sin among adults becomes, in a certain sense, a universality *de jure* qualifying all mankind."[136] In a parallel passage, Vanneste explicates the term *de jure* by saying, "this universality obtains the power of law."[137] Both the passages describing original sin as a reality *sui generis* that lies at the *source* of actual sins and those describing original sin in terms of a *law* of the universality of sin (a law that has the *power* to will that all men be sinners) give rise to the question as to the nature of this source and of this law. Is there, after all, a reality deeper than actual sins, namely, their source? Is there a reality transcending actual sins, namely, their law?

Although designations such as "source" and "law" appear to break through Vanneste's self-imposed boundaries of reinterpretation, each of the passages considered contains qualifications that reinforce those boundaries once more. Nevertheless, these qualifications do not nullify but in fact reveal the real import of designations such as "law" and "source."

Vanneste's specification of the unique nature of original sin in terms of "source" loses much of its precision due to important qualifications. It cannot have escaped anyone's notice that in the passage quoted he says that original sin is *as it were* the source, and lies *as it were* at the source of actual sins, and represents *in a certain sense* the whole series of actual sins. And similar qualifications appear elsewhere: original is *something like* an arch-sin, *something like* a source of ordinary sins.[138] Unfortunately, Vanneste does not specify in what sense the term "source" applies to the reality of original sin.

In the passages dealing with original sin in terms of law, modifiers

---

134 See *Dogma*, 163 where Vanneste uses the term "historical rule" synonymously with the term "historical law."

135 *Dogma*, 81 emphasis added. The same idea is expressed when Vanneste speaks of original sin as that which causes the child to stand at the point of becoming a sinner (*CollBG*, XIV, 299, literally: "that which makes that the child stands at the point of . . .").

136 *Dogma*, 79.

137 *CollBG*, XIV, 301.

138 *Dogma*, 102.

occur that do not merely qualify but even negate the very notion of law as employed by Vanneste. In personifying the law, for example, Vanneste has said not only that this law *wills* that all men be sinners but also that this law wills that all be sinners *historically*. This latter qualification negates the very possibility of a law that impinges upon man and wills that he be a sinner, for to be a sinner *historically* means for Vanneste to be a sinner *freely*.[139] And the free act, says Vanneste, allows of no other explanation than that free act.[140] A law that "wills" man to be a sinner freely means nothing other than that *man wills* to be a sinner freely.[141] In other words, no such law exists. Within Vanneste's reinterpretation, sin manifests itself, not only morally and religiously, but also *ontically* as "law-lessness." Vanneste's use of the term "law," therefore, appears to be merely a *way of speaking* about the *fact* that all men commit actual sins from the moment that they act freely.

In keeping with his conception of history and with his use of the term "myth," Vanneste's appeal to notions such as law and source may be regarded as involving the mythological transcendence of the boundaries of history. That gives rise to the question why the notions that constitute the springboard for such transcendence manage to survive his radical programme of demythologization. Why does he retain notions that are wholly inimical to his basic thesis regarding the nature of sin? What is the *theological* function of such notions within Vanneste's reinterpretation of original sin as the universality of actual sins? We will search for an answer to these questions by interpreting the notions of "law" and "source" in terms of his own frame of reference.

b. *Theological Transcendence*

Although it remains true that Vanneste's understanding of sin as a historical reality precludes the notion of a unique sin which constitutes the source of actual sins and the notion of a law of the universality of sin, conversely – and paradoxically – it is equally true that it is precisely his understanding of sin as a contingent historical reality that makes him grasp for the notion of law and source to maintain his understanding of original sin. From *within* history, as conceived of by Vanneste, it is impossible to maintain the absolute universality of actual sins. By invoking notions such as law, however, he transcends the openness intrinsic to free acts. From that transcendental position, he can then predict the direction of those acts, as is

---

139 See nn. 124-25 above.
140 *Bijdragen*, XXXIII, 156, n. 19.
141 See *Dogma*, 79.

done in the affirmation of the absolute certainty that every human being sins from the very beginning of his human existence.[142] Within Vanneste's explicit frame of reference, source and law are not themselves existent realities. The only reality to which they can refer is the transcendental theological position from which the absolute universality of actual sins is asserted. By thus applying the method and principle of Vanneste's own process of demythologization to his employment of the notions source and law, one discovers that he has gone beyond the boundaries of history that he has imposed upon his reinterpretation of original sin.[143] The transcendence of these boundaries can also be demonstrated in other ways, however.

That Vanneste stands on the verge of going beyond the bounds of history comes to expression in the curious way in which he speaks of the universality of sin. He says, for example, that the doctrine of original sin entails the necessity of thinking the universality of sin "through to the end,"[144] of carrying "this universality to its limit,"[145] and of rendering it into an *"absolute* universality."[146] Similarly, he contends at one point that the message of the second and third chapters of Genesis is adequately summarized in the single affirmation of the universality of sin — on the condition, however, that one realizes full well *all* that such universality entails: that it is a truly universal universality."[147] Upon reading these statements, one wonders how it is possible and why it is necessary to speak of something more than simple universality. Can something be more universal than universal? Is universality not its own "limit," so that expressions such as "carrying universality to its limit" are rendered superfluous and phrases such as "absolute universality" tautological? Whatever the intrinsic merits of these expressions may be, they obliquely indicate that in his reinterpretation of original sin Vanneste is on the verge of moving beyond the boundary he has set.

That precarious position on the boundary is thrown into bold relief by

---

142 See n. 113 above.

143 In precisely the same way as we have used Vanneste's method of demythologizations to understand the real function of notions such as source and law, Vanneste himself criticizes Schoonenberg's appeal to the Biblical notion of "the power of sin." This appeal, says Vanneste, is not entirely *ad rem;* "for the question is in what way a notion such as this is usable within the framework of a critical theology. Certainly, the Bible sometimes speaks of Sin (with a capital letter), but does this involve more than a kind of personification and generalization of the evil that dwells in each human being?" (*Dogma,* 186).

144 *Dogma,* 79, 85; *CollBG,* XIV, 304.

145 *Dogma,* 79.

146 *Ibid.*

147 *CollBG,* XIV, 301.

Vanneste's description of the threshold position of the doctrine of original sin:

> Original sin does not stand outside of human history. It belongs to that history; or rather, it stands as it were on the threshold, at the boundary of history. It gives expression to an historical aspect of man as he stands at the point where he begins his [personal] history – a sinful history as human history has always been.[148]

That Vanneste himself stands on the boundary of history in making such a judgement becomes manifest in the certainty that is expressed in the idea that man is a "virtual sinner":

> Original sin consists simply in the fact that each human being is a sinner from the first moment of his existence as man. This means, therefore, that he is born as a virtual sinner *of whom we are certain that he will become an actual sinner* – and that in his very first act.[149]

By formulating the idea of original sin explicitly or implicitly in terms of the infant as virtual sinner, Vanneste has moved to the place where he *must* stand if he is to maintain his understanding of this doctrine: on the boundary of human history, at the inception of man's personal history, at the point where a human being executes his first free act. There Vanneste must stand in order to be able to exclude that which – precisely at that point – seems preeminently possible: a positive act.

Although it is true that Vanneste *must* stand on this boundary to express his understanding of original sin as the absolute universality of actual sins, it is equally true that by virtue of his understanding of the scope of theology and of the reality of original sin he cannot stand at this point. Theologically meaningful statements, Vanneste has said, refer exclusively to the free acts of adult human beings.[150] The radicality of this restriction comes to clear expression in his statement, "When we assert, 'original sin does not exist,' we do so because in our view small children do not exist; we mean, do not exist as beings about which anything meaningful can be said in dogmatics."[151] Although it is true that in speaking of an infant as virtual sinner Vanneste is referring *proleptically* to the adult, he *is in fact* speaking about and interpreting the future of *this* (and every) *infant*. Moreover, insofar as he speaks of the future act of a given infant, this act no longer bears the character of free act,[152] for – as the emergence of the critical

---

148 *Ibid.*, 292.
149 *Dogma*, 162. Cf. *CollBG*, XIV, 305 (cited in n. 65 above).
150 See sec. B, 1 above.
151 *Bijdragen*, XXXIII, 162.
152 It is not surprising, therefore, that Haag asks, "Does it not border on fatalism to assume with such certainty that the first human act of every person is a sin [*Dogma*,] 162)?" (*JESt*, X (1973), 277; *ThQ*, CL, 456). Vanneste rejects this criticism without entering into the problem inherent in his absolute certainty (*Bijdragen*, XXXIII, 156).

"unless" demonstrates[153] — one must *await* the occurance of such an act before its direction can be determined.[154] Vanneste's boundary position is problematical, not only by virtue of his rigorous delimitation of the scope of theology, but also by virtue of a similar delimitation of the reality of original sin.[155] In keeping with this delimitation of his field of enquiry, Vanneste has said that the doctrine of original sin does not stand outside of history but within history; or more precisely, it stands "as it were" at the boundary of history. In order to speak of the infant as a virtual sinner in the way Vanneste does, however, one can no longer stand within but must stand *outside* of history; i.e., one must place himself outside the actual series of free acts to predict their direction with certainty.

The transcendental position entailed in Vanneste's reinterpretation of original sin, it has been argued, means that he is standing in the midst of a realm which he has himself declared to be off-limits — a theological no-man's-land. This transcendental position would not necessarily be of substantial significance if it only involved going beyond *methodological* boundaries, boundaries set by one's view of the nature and limits of theology; for any subject matter being investigated is fortunately always far richer than methodological delimitations would seem to indicate. More serious, however, is the fact that Vanneste has set his boundary by insisting that the subject matter itself consists of nothing other than free actual sins. A transgression of *that* boundary has grave repercussions for the existential meaning of the doctrine that is being reinterpreted.

c. *Implications for the Existential Meaning of the Doctrine*

By maintaining the absolute universality of actual sins, Vanneste stands at a point that lies beyond the boundary of his own conception of history. The question that remains to be considered in this: what is the existential meaning of thus maintaining the strict universality of actual sins; what function can this understanding of original sin have in the Christian life? For Vanneste the intended meaning of the affirmation of the universality of sin is the confession that as actual sinner every human being needs the saving grace of Jesus Christ.[156] One must ask, therefore, in what way the existential

---

153 See sec. C, 1 above.
154 As Vanneste himself acknowledges at one point, a historical universality cannot be ascertained except *a posteriori* (*EphM*, XXIII, 87).
155 See sec. B, 1 and C, 2 (introductory paragraphs) above.
156 See sec. B, 1 above.

meaning of that confession is affected by the doctrine of original sin as reinterpreted by Vanneste.

Vanneste says at one point that although the doctrine of original sin is in line with general human experience and with that which can be known by the human mind through its natural capacities, it is only in the Bible and the doctrine of the Church that "the breadth and the length, the height and the depth" of human sinfulness is fully revealed.[157] As to the depth of sin, the difficulty one faces here is that Vanneste's stringent delimitation of the reality of sin appears to provide no window through which the depth dimension of sin can come into view. As a result, the doctrine of original sin can serve only to elucidate the *breadth* dimension of sin. Even this dimension, however, becomes a purely quantitative one.[158] By reducing the doctrine of original sin to the absolute universality of actual sins, Vanneste also reduces its entire significance to a quantitative issue, namely, whether some or all are actual sinners.[159] When that issue is decided in favor of the "all," the question as to the existential significance of that affirmation becomes acute.[160]

The problem of the function of this doctrine in the life of the Christian comes to clear expression when Vanneste restates the meaning of original sin as follows: "That all men are born in original sin means that all are sinners from the first moment that they are man because *it happens to be a historical fact* that all men sin."[161] Strangely enough, in this affirmation of the pure (historical) *facticity of sin,* the doctrine of original sin takes on fatalistic overtones not unlike those that resound in the diametrically opposite affirmation of the *metaphysical necessity of sinning* – a necessity which Vanneste explicitly rejects in this very context.[162] This affirmation of the historical facticity of sin renders the existential meaning of Vanneste's understanding of original sin highly problematic, as becomes abundantly clear when one imagines a

---

157 *Dogma,* 106.

158 In contrast to, e.g., Schoonenberg's view which is explicitly directed against such quantification (see ch. I, sec. A, 1 above) and which represents an attempt to uncover a unique, *qualitative* breadth- (as well as depth-) dimension: being-situated as *Existential* (see ch. I, sec. A, 3, c; and ch. III, sec. C, 1, b [esp. n. 68] above).

159 See, e.g., *CollBG,* XIV, 294n.; *Dogma,* 174-75; cf. 77; *Bijdragen,* XXXIII, 167; cf. 155, 172.

160 H. M. Kuitert poses a similar question, namely, whether and how a Christian can "confess" the sinfulness and corruption of others without being Pharisaical ("Erfzonde," *Altijd bereid tot verantwoording,* A. J. Besselaar, *et. al.* [2d ed. rev.; Aalten: de Graafschap, 1966], 113).

161 *Dogma,* 163 emphasis added. In the next sentence this "fact" is referred to as an "historical law."

162 *Ibid.* See Haag's use of the term "fatalism" with reference to Vanneste's reinterpretation (n. 152 above).

Christian making the following personal confession: "I am a sinner from the moment of birth because it happens to be a historical fact that all men sin," or (to avoid the suggestion of a causal connection between "all" and "I") "I happen to be a sinner." Whatever way one may wish to translate the affirmation of the pure facticity of sin into a personal statement, the fatalistic resignation expressed in the phrase "it happens to be" seems to be incompatible with any *meaningful personal* confession of sin. But if the affirmation of the absolute universality of sin as a historical law[163] does not lend itself to personal appropriation, what then is the existential meaning of this understanding of original sin?

That question returns forcefully when Vanneste speaks of the authentic Catholic doctrine as involving the paradox of the absolute universality and the historical contingency of sin.[164] The problem of the existential meaning of Vanneste's interpretation of original sin becomes manifest when he explicitly elaborates the paradox of this doctrine by stating that sin belongs to "the *factual* basic structure of human existence, even though it remains true that (with the aid of grace) man could avoid this [sin] at any moment."[165] In the statement that sin belongs to the basic structure of human existence,[166] a surprising formal similarity comes to light between Vanneste's and the situationalists' understanding of original sin. The latter interpret original sin as a situation which, as *Existential*, represents a basic interior structure of man's being.[167] For the situationalists, however, the interpretation of original sin as sinful situation has no reference to the *specific direction of the free decision* of any individual within that situation. For Vanneste, by contrast, the term "sin" has exclusive reference to the free acts of individuals.[168] To say then that sin belongs to the structure of human

---

163 See n. 161 above.
164 *Bijdragen*, XXXIII, 156. For Vanneste's use of the notion paradox, see also *Dogma*, 71, 79; *CollBG*, XIV, 296; *Bijdragen*, XXXIII, 168; *EphM*, XXIII, 84; and the following note.
165 *Bijdragen*, XXXIII, 159. In a footnote Vanneste suggests what he calls an "even more paradoxical" formulation, namely, that sin belongs to the factual basic structure of human existence (not although, but) "*precisely because* he is capable of avoiding sin at every moment" (*ibid.*, n. 30).
166 That this understanding of original sin in terms of a basic structure of human existence is not merely an afterthought is evidenced by the subtitle of his original book on the subject: *Het dogma van de erfzonde: Zinloze mythe of openbaring van een grondstructuur van het menselijke bestaan?* ("The doctrine of original sin: meaningless myth or revelation of a basic structure of human existence?")
167 See ch. I, n. 144 and n. 163 above.
168 See sec. B (introductory paragraph) above.

existence is to interpret man's *free decisions* as a negative situation. This represents yet another way of stating not merely that man sins but that it happens to be an historical fact that all men sin, that no one "can" escape[169] the law of the universality of sin. By contending that sin belongs to the basic *structure* of human existence, Vanneste seems to have negated freedom, the core of human existence. He avoids that negation, however, by in effect maintaining the paradox that sin remains a structure of human *existence,* that sin remains a *free act*. By virtue of that paradox, the mainspring of reinterpretation – though strained to the breaking point – continues to function through to the end.

Although or precisely because freedom is not negated, the question remains: How can the paradox introduced by the doctrine of original sin as understood by Vanneste be rendered existentially meaningful? If it is true that one is a sinner by virtue of his individual free decision, is it necessary or legitimate to go beyond the bounds of this contingent historical act and – ascending to a transcendental theological position – affirm that sin is absolutely universal, part of the basic structure of human existence, inescapable-though-escapable?[170] Or should the question concerning existential significance be considered inappropriate and must the doctrine of original sin as reinterpreted by Vanneste be regarded exclusively as a *theologoumenon,* "classified information," a higher knowledge not meant to be assimilated as a Christian *confession* into the depth of everyday existence. Such theological elitism, however, goes contrary to the very purpose of Vanneste's reinterpretation; this means that the question as to the existential meaning of his understanding of the doctrine of original sin retains its urgency.

* * *

In anticipation of the following chapter, it may be helpful to present a tentative analysis of a basic weakness that inheres in Vanneste's position. The major problems – converging in the problem of existential meaning – encountered in Vanneste's reinterpretation of original sin arise due to the fact that the concrete responsibility of man is defended by means of the abstract idea of free individual acts. That idea leads to the reduction of the doctrine of

---

169 See sec. C, 2, a above.
170 Although Vanneste objects to the idea that sin is "metaphysically" inescapable (*Dogma,* 71, 164, 175) and says that ("metaphysically") man can avoid sin at any moment, (see above, quotation annotated as n. 165), he does speak of a "historical inescapability of sin (*Dogma,* 71, 81), which in Vanneste's terms means a "free inescapability."

original sin to a paradoxical *theologoumenon* regarding the absolute universality of actual sin. In other words, Vanneste's quantification of the meaning of the doctrine of original sin arises from his atomization of history, i.e., the dissolution of history into myriads of individual personal histories.[171] In the context of the doctrine of original sin, the only unity which he recognizes consists in the fact that all men stand in the same religious situation vis-à-vis God.[172] Although Vanneste acknowledges the reality of a certain interpersonal solidarity, *theologically* this is considered to be irrelevant.[173] As a result, in reinterpreting original sin, he *treats* the individual as a *monad*. Moreover, this atomization of history does not stop short of the individual; even the individual dissolves in a myriad of free acts. Vanneste does not ask what constitutes the unity of the (sinful) history of an individual. Even when Vanneste seems to be approaching a point of integration (in speaking of original sin as "source"), it becomes clear that he thinks of "sinful man" only in terms of a "series" of actual sins. The only question he poses is whether original sin stands within or outside that series.[174] He answers that question by stating that original sin stands outside that series or stands, as it were, at its source. But he elaborates this answer as follows: from the first moment of his existence man needs the grace of Jesus Christ because already at that point man "stands at the threshold of committing *an uncountable series of sins.*"[175]

It is truly regrettable that despite its promising starting point in man's responsibility before God and in the central confession of the meaning of Christ's coming, Vanneste's reinterpretation of the doctrine of original sin has fallen prey to the atomization of history and the concomitant quantification of the meaning of this doctrine. In view of this atomization and quantification, it is fortunate that within Roman Catholic theology another attempt has been made to reinterpret the doctrine of original sin in terms of personal sin, namely, by Urs Baumann. His reinterpretation of original sin is especially

---

171 J. H. Walgrave criticizes Vanneste for his individualistic approach to original sin and says, "His [Vanneste's] 'history' appears to be merely the sum of billions of [little] individual 'histories' ['historietjes,' a Dutch diminutive]" *Kultuurleven,* XXXVII (1970), 411. Cf. F. J. A. de Grijs' assessment: "History is the aggregate of all personal histories – personality being conceived of as individuality, historicity as the structure of the histories of men, universality as including each and everyone" (*Bijdragen,* XXXI (1971), 207).
172 See *CollBG,* XII, 308; *ThD,* XV, 213; *CollBG,* XIV, 302.
173 See sec. A, 2 above.
174 See sec. C, 2, a above.
175 *CollBG,* XIV, 299, emphasis added.

significant for the present study because while he proceeds from a central starting point similar to that of Vanneste, he attempts to overcome, among other things, what we have called the atomization of the individual which plagues Vanneste's reinterpretation.

*CHAPTER VIII   ORIGINAL SIN AS THE DEPTH DIMENSION
OF PERSONAL SIN: U. BAUMANN*

> The most exciting contribution to this topic so far is the dissertation presented to the Tübingen Catholic Theology Faculty by U. Baumann, *Erbsünde?* ... He presents a fundamental discussion of the exegetical and dogmatic questions from the past and present. In addition, as the result of his own reflection, he presents for discussion an understanding of original sin which decisively abandons the path followed by Catholic theology up to the present.[1]

This assessment by Herbert Haag concisely summarizes Baumann's unique contribution to the current Catholic discussion of the doctrine of original sin. In comparison to the positions analyzed to this point, his contribution is unique despite the many similarities it shows with the basic anthropological insights of the situationalists[2] as well as with Vanneste's interpretation of original sin. The boundary that separates both Vanneste's and Baumann's positions from that of the situationalists is to be found in their common opposition to the understanding of original sin as a prepersonal, analogical sinfulness. Instead both attempt to understand this doctrine in terms of personal sin. Baumann distinguishes himself from Vanneste, however, in that for Baumann the heart of the doctrine of original sin concerns primarily not the question of the *extent* (universality) but the *depth* of personal sin.[3]

Baumann's interpretation marks a decisive break with the mainstream of Catholic theological tradition in which original sin is understood as constituting a prepersonal privation of grace. This break is underscored by the great affinity which Baumann displays for the understanding of original sin as *Ursünde* by prominent Protestant theologians in approximately the first half

---

1   Haag, JESt, X, 281-82.
2   Especially with respect to the idea of person, but also with respect to its counterpart, the idea of situation (see, e.g., Baumann, *Erbsünde*, 279-80). The concept situation, however, is not considered to be appropriate as central category for reinterpreting original sin.
3   It is characteristic of Baumann's reinterpretation that he deals with the universality of sin only as one (of three) *aspects of the depth dimension* of sin (see sec. C, 2 below).

of this century.[4] Baumann's position appears as a mere break, however, only when the ultimate results of his reinterpretation of original sin are isolated from the path leading to those results. From the perspective of that pathway itself it is more accurate to say that Baumann decisively *departs from* than to say that he simply *abandons* the traditional path. For standing on the traditional path, Baumann attempts to point out a more passable, direct and congenial route leading to a common goal. He attempts to transform the Catholic tradition *from within* by indicating that the traditional doctrine of original sin, negatively and positively, calls for such transformation. It is precisely as a transformation from within Catholic doctrine and theology that Baumann's reinterpretation represents a unique Catholic-ecumenical contribution to the current discussion of the doctrine of original sin.

A. DOMINANT MOTIFS: SOLA GRATIA AND PERSONAL RESPONSIBILITY

In his reinterpretation, Baumann proceeds from the idea that the central thrust of the doctrine of original sin is its affirmation of the principle called into question by Pelagius,[5] *sola gratia*.[6] Indeed, Baumann maintains that "the *ultimate* and *only* meaning" of this doctrine is "the unconditional validity of the *sola gratia* [quality] of God's saving acts."[7] "God's never-failing favor and grace, this is the proper message and intention of the doctrine."[8]

Although *sola gratia* is the essential content of the doctrine of original sin, this doctrine is not a simple assertion but a very specific articulation of man's need of God's grace. That need is articulated in terms of a deep and dreadful truth concerning man and his world. On that basis Baumann can say on the one hand that the doctrine of original sin has its *only* meaning in the

---

4 See *Erbsünde*, 251-52, 267. Baumann's sympathy for the understanding of original sin by these Protestant theologians is reflected both in the headings under which he deals with contemporary Catholic and Protestant views, and in the remarkable difference in the length of these sections: "Zum Status quo der katholischen 'Erbsünden'-Debatte" (*ibid.*, 91-108), and "Die Ursünde in der evangelischen Theologie der Gegenwart" (*ibid.*, 109-181). In effect, Baumann attempts to break through the Catholic "status quo" regarding "Erbsünde" by means of the Protestant conception of "Ursünde." (For an explanation of his preference for the latter term, see *ibid.*, 18-19; see also n. 99 below.)

5. *Erbsünde*, 41.

6 For other contexts in which he analyzes the doctrine of original sin in terms of the *sola gratia* principle, see *ibid.*, 28, 41, 43 (re Augustine); *ibid.*, 46 (re Lutheran creeds); *ibid.*, 75 (re Trent); *ibid.*, 79 (re Protestant and Catholic views of concupiscence); *ibid.*, 222, 244 (re Paul); *ibid.*, 265 (re the Catholic doctrine).

7 *Ibid.*, 265.

8 *Ibid.*, 16.

sola gratia principle, and on the other hand that this doctrine intends *nothing other* than the clarification of *one* truth: man's knowledge of himself as accountably guilty before God.[9] In other words, the *sola gratia* principle and the reality of human guilt are not two disparate truths, nor is the latter *simply* a logical deduction from the former. Rather, the depth of grace *reveals* the abyss of sin.[10] In that interrelationship, the doctrine of original sin gives expression to what Baumann calls "the deepest mystery of the Christian message of salvation: Man has broken so radically with God that, even if he should want to, he cannot find his way back on his own – except by accepting God's judgement, confessing his guilt and throwing himself on the divine mercy which has been revealed in Jesus Christ."[11] That statement adumbrates Baumann's conception of the way in which the doctrine of original sin articulates the *sola gratia* principle.

It has already become evident that the notion of guilt plays a central role in Baumann's reinterpretation of original sin. The notion of guilt singles out the *personal* character of sin: man is *responsible* for his fallenness. Given the reality of man's apostasy, Baumann can argue that the idea of guilt must be maintained precisely in order to salvage man's person: "If we relinquish [the notion of] guilt, man loses his status as person, for in the latter his responsibility is grounded."[12] Baumann's entire reinterpretation of original sin revolves around the triad guilt-person-responsibility – with the notion "person" functioning as central axis.[13]

Both the theological motif (*sola gratia*) and the anthropological motif (personal responsibility) will be set into relief in the course of Baumann's critique of the traditional Catholic approach to sin and even more clearly, of course, in the elaboration of his own view.

B. CONTEXT AND FUNCTION OF THE TRADITIONAL DOCTRINE

Baumann's assessment of the traditional doctrine of original sin presupposes that this teaching is properly understood only in its relation to a certain conception of actual sin. Accordingly, he deals at some length with the specific view of actual sin which he considers to be the context within which the traditional doctrine of original sin functioned.

9 *Ibid.*
10 See *ibid.*, 260 (and sec. C, 2, a below).
11 *Ibid.*, 16.
12 *Ibid.*, 17.
13 See *ibid.*, 187: the central concepts of person-oriented thought are "Personalität-Entscheidung (Verantwortung) – Geschichte."

1. Context: Moralism and Actualism

The Catholic tradition, Baumann contends, is plagued by a moralistic view of man and sin.[14] Its dominant trait is legalism.[15] Since the conception of man and sin and the conception of God are interdependent, according to Baumann,[16] his description of a legalistic view of God will be considered first.

If one insists upon a moralistic approach to man, "God" is perverted by being assigned the role of "a harsh administrator of justice who watches with inexorable rigor over the observance of His law."[17] For this God the dreadful Latin proverb, "Let justice be done even if the world be destroyed," holds true.[18] In this way "God's personal will, His Spirit – of which it is said that it blows where it wills (Jn 3:8)– is domesticized as an immutable *ius divinum* (divine law)",[19] an abstract eternal code which takes into account only the cold facticity of a particular breach of law.[20] When the moral aspect is absolutized in this way, the phenomenon of law is inserted *between* God and man, distorting man's understanding not only of God but also of himself and of sin.[21]

Within a moralistic context sin is viewed almost exclusively in terms of a particular violation of God's command.[22] This fixation of the idea of sin entails the violation of man as person.[23] Human activity is judged in terms of objective *law*, not in terms of *person*.[24] The personal summons of man by God having been replaced by an absolute, universally valid codification of God's will, the human *person* is subsumed *under* an *objective norm* of moral law.[25] Not personal relationship but an ironclad code becomes decisive for determining man's moral-religious status.[26] Man is viewed as being called to a pilgrimage progressing towards moral perfection, a process that is, of course, marred by daily failures and shortcomings.[27] "Holy is he who, on the basis of

14 He sees this approach to man reflected especially in the fifth canon of the Tridentine decree on original sin (see *ibid.*, 76-79; cf. 23, 82).
15 *Ibid.*, 268.
16 *Ibid.*, 270.
17 *Ibid.*
18 *Ibid.*
19 *Ibid.*, 269.
20 *Ibid.*, 270.
21 *Ibid.*, 269.
22 *Ibid.*, 268.
23 *Ibid.*, 269.
24 *Ibid.*
25 *Ibid.*
26 *Ibid.*, 270.
27 *Ibid.*, 268.

good fortune, favorable disposition and the gift of an iron will, attains to moral 'virtuosity' and does even more than that which the norm of the moral law prescribes."[28] As for "the weary and heavy laden who do not have at their disposal the strength and the talent for such holy acts" and therefore continually fail, for them the only course that remains open is the way of "penitent contrition which leads to naked fear regarding one's salvation or to paralyzing scruples or to an audacious fideism that is fed by the confidence that one can always count on the forgiveness dispensed via the sacrament of penance...."[29] In this way, the human person is sacrificed to the stringent demands of moral laws. The inappropriateness of this moralistic approach to man and sin is manifest most clearly, says Baumann, in the fact that it entails an objective-static, rather than a personal-dynamic approach.[30]

The other traits which Baumann singles out as being characteristic of moralism are implicit in the description of legalism just given. A brief explication of these other facets, therefore, suffices.

Beside legalism, one of the most obvious traits of moralism is a rather superficial empiricism. Man is viewed only in terms of the surface expressions or objectifications of his deeds.[31] This empiricism is understandable, of course, for only in this way is it possible to determine the moral weight of man's acts on the scale of law.[32] In a moralistic approach to human life, the extremely complex and often ambiguous relationship between man's objective, empirical behavior and his innermost being is overlooked in favor of the simplicity of a phenomenological consideration of exterior expressions.[33] In other words, the manifestations of human activity are no longer seen as *manifestations of* a deeper lying central act but as the very *substance* of human life. Accordingly, the moral aspect is no longer seen as an aspect of sin but as the essence of sin.[34]

A third characteristic of the moralistic conception of sin is atomism. Precisely because the empirical manifestations are assessed without being related to a central stance, man in effect falls apart into the countless fragments of isolated acts.[35] It is this atomism that Baumann has in view when he juxtaposes the terms *"actualism"* and "moralism," as he frequently

---

28 *Ibid.,* 271.
29 *Ibid.*
30 *Ibid.,* 269: "sachlich-statisch statt dynamisch-personal."
31 *Ibid.,* 268; cf. 259.
32 *Ibid.,* 260.
33 *Ibid.,* 270; cf. 268.
34 See *ibid.,* 260, 272.
35 *Ibid.,* 268; cf. 23.

does.³⁶ As we shall discover, Baumann is not opposed to focussing on the human *act,* but rather to obscuring the *central act* of man by observing primarily the plurality of single acts as they emerge at the surface of life. The unifying threads of life are allowed to break and man dissolves into countless disparate acts devoid of inner coherence.³⁷ Baumann acknowledges that a moralistic approach need not be wholly oblivious to the unity of man. He contends, however, that this unity has usually been sought primarily in man's metaphysical-ontological nature, which as such does not play an integral role in the moral-religious assessment of man's activity.³⁸

Fortunately, this moralistic conception of sin has been complemented traditionally by a more profound notion of sin: original sin. Inasmuch as the traditional doctrine of original sin entails the attempt to provide an empirical explanation of man's fallenness, however, it too is untenable.

2. Function

The traditional doctrine has functioned in two ways, according to Baumann: as empirical explanation of the universality of sin and as necessary counterweight to moralism. Baumann's assessment of this dual function is indicative of both the discontinuity and the continuity between his own reinterpretation and the traditional doctrine.

a. *Empirical Explanation*

Grappling directly with the traditional doctrine as well as with most of its Catholic reinterpretations, Baumann elaborates a "critique of the empirical principle."³⁹ What does he understand by this principle? It is his designation of any attempt to provide an objective, empirical ground for man's sinful condition.⁴⁰ Baumann distinguishes three major forms of this principle, the historical, the evolutionary and the sociological.

The historical form of the empirical principle is embodied in the traditional doctrine of original sin. According to this doctrine, the universal fallenness of man — and thus also every person's guilt — is grounded, on the one hand, in a historical Adam and, on the other, in a biotic-historical link between Adam and his posterity.⁴¹ The historical form of the empirical

---

36 See *ibid.,* 268-69.
37 *Ibid.,* 268.
38 *Ibid.,* 271.
39 *Ibid.,* 235.
40 *Ibid.,* 243; cf. 186-87, 235-36, 244, 263.
41 *Ibid.,* 182-83.

principle can also function in a far less prominent way. It continues to be operative even in the minimal form that comes to expression in those contemporary reinterpretations that have recourse — however vaguely — to a first man or first men — however remote — as a ground for the universality of sin.[42]

The evolutionary and sociological explanations of man's sinfulness are distinctively contemporary forms of the empirical principle. The evolutionary model involves the attempt to explain or render plausible the universal sinfulness of man by appealing to the evolutionary process in which man is taken up.[43] Given the process of evolution, any particular stage of development is imperfect, attended by disharmony, conflict, weakness and suffering. This relative imperfection is viewed as posing a threat to man's moral-religious innocence,[44] or even as making sin statistically inescapable.[45]

The sociological model is the third way of applying the empirical principle. Though often combined with the historical or the evolutionary forms just mentioned, this principle in its sociological form has as its characteristic feature the attempt to ground universal sinfulness in the social-situational interwovenness of mankind.[46] As Baumann points out, it is especially under the influence of Schoonenberg that the social dimension of sin becomes the pivot of the doctrine of original sin.[47]

Although Baumann appreciates, as we shall see, one role that the empirical principle has played historically, he finds the principle itself unacceptable for several reasons. The obvious occasion for reconsidering this principle is the untenability of its historical form. The foundations of this traditional form of the empirical principle have crumbled,[48] necessitating a belated "farewell to [the historical] Adam,"[49] as well as to the idea of a biotic-historical unity of mankind.[50] However important and irreversible the undermining of the historical form of the empirical principle may be, in Baumann's view this assault represents merely an external challenge to one of

---

42 See *ibid.*, 183, 241.
43 Baumann refers, e.g., to the theories of A. Hulsbosch, Z. Alszeghy – M. Flick, P. Teilhard de Chardin, and K. Schmitz-Moormann (*ibid.*, 185, 245-46).
44 *Ibid.*, 184-85 (A. Hulsbosch).
45 *Ibid.*, 185 (Teilhard).
46 *Ibid.*, 186.
47 *Ibid.*
48 *Ibid.*, 84-85.
49 *Ibid.*, 236.
50 *Ibid.*, 243.

the forms of that principle. What is needed is an intrinsic critique of the principle as such.[51]

Within this intrinsic critique a philosophical-anthropological and a theological aspect can be distinguished. From the anthropological viewpoint, Baumann objects to the empirical principle for the same reason that he opposes the empiricism entailed in a moralistic view of actual sin: this principle represents an attempt to assess man's moral-religious state not in terms of the personal core of his being but in terms of external, empirical realities that impinge upon him.[52] The traditional doctrine of original sin, for instance, zeroes in on a historical personage of the hoary past to explain the sinfulness of mankind in the present. A decisive effect of this person's sinful act upon all of mankind is so dubious, however, that the notion of the biotic-historical inheritance of his sin is required to indicate the effect of this external factor for the inner, existential condition of his posterity vis-à-vis God.[53] In an updated manner, the evolutionary and sociological models of the empirical principle similarly approach the question of man-in-sin as if his inner condition were explainable in terms of external phenomena.[54] Specifically in opposition to the situational approach to original sin, Baumann maintains that the human situation is not simply one of doom (the privation of grace) but also one of grace[55] and that "the social, like the moral, [aspect] is merely the surface of the authentic, invisible, incomprehensible event."[56] The deepest core of man, says Baumann, the human person (the "I") is not susceptible to objectification because it is a (unique) relationship, not a specimen of a genus.[57] Hence neither man's situatedness nor his position on the scale of evolutionary development provides an empirical index of his sinfulness.[58]

Closely interwoven with this anthropological criticism is Baumann's theological criticism of the empirical principle. Baumann frequently contrasts the scientific, empirical to the theological, trans-empiric approach to man.[59] Whereas the former involves the attempt to *describe* man in the light of the empirical findings of paleontology, biology, psychology, sociology or histo-

---

51 See *ibid.*, 245, 248, 277-78.
52 *Ibid.*, 245, 246, 247; cf. 187.
53 *Ibid.*, 238; cf. 86, 240.
54 *Ibid.*, 184-86, 245-48.
55 *Ibid.*, 247, 279.
56 *Ibid.*, 247.
57 *Ibid.*, 186, 246.
58 *Ibid.*, 246-47.
59 See *ibid.*, 58, 245, 272, 281.

riography, theology attempts to *interpret* and *understand* man, in the light of faith, in his relationship to God.[60] Since sin involves precisely this central relationship to God, it allows of neither an evolutionary nor a sociological evaluation or explanation.[61] The basic incomprehensibility and groundlessness of sin may not be circumvented by having recourse to original sin as an empirical principle.[62] Any attempt to do so entails the transformation of sin into an innocuous normal state of affairs.[63]

Both from the anthropological viewpoint of man's freedom and responsibility, and from the theological viewpoint of the unique (perverted) God-relationship, then, Baumann designates sin as a *trans-empiric* phenomenon.[64] Accordingly, he considers the *empirical* principle itself to be the thorn in the flesh of the theology of original sin, a thorn that must be extracted as quickly and as radically as possible.[65] The most pressing need for this operation, however, has not yet been mentioned. That need becomes manifest in Baumann's assessment of the positive role that the doctrine of original sin has played.

b. *Counterweight to Moralism*

The historical role that the doctrine of original sin has played is twofold: positively, the maintenance of man's complete dependence on God's grace in Jesus Christ, and, negatively, the rejection of a Pelagian view of man in sin.[66] Because of this function of the traditional doctrine, Baumann

---

60 *Ibid.*, 281; cf. 58, 244, 245, 246, 282. By reserving the task of *interpreting* and *understanding* man for theology while relegating the task of merely *describing* man to other academic disciplines, Baumann places a theological monopoly on hermeneutics. This monopolization involves a systematic and historical problem in view of the fact that Dilthey who introduced the distinction between interpretive understanding and explanatory description into the discussion of hermeneutics saw the former as the task of the *humanities* (especially the historical disciplines) and the latter as the task of the natural sciences; see Wilhelm Dilthey, *Gesammelte Schriften*, V, 242-54; VII, 84-86, 118-20, 141-42 (Stuttgart: Teubner, 1957 and 1958).

61 *Erbsünde*, 245-46, 248.
62 See *ibid.*, 248.
63 *Ibid.*
64 See *ibid.*, 181, where Baumann distinguishes four approaches to original sin and characterizes the three that he rejects as the "historical-*empirical*," "evolutionary-*empirical*" and "sociological-*empirical*" models, while characterizing the approach he adopts as the "existential-*transempirical*" model (emphasis added). He borrows the term "transempirical" from Ernst Kinder (see *ibid.* 118-20). Although Baumann has some reservations regarding this term (*ibid.*, 273-74), it accurately indicates the difference between his approach and any approach in which an appeal is made to empirical data.
65 *Ibid.* 248.
66 See sec. A above.

describes the empirical principle embodied in that doctrine as being the "necessary evil of a onesidedly act-oriented conception of sin."[67] Why it must be considered an *evil* even in its positive function will become clear after the *necessity* of this evil has been articulated by Baumann.

The empirical principle is a *necessary* evil, a mixed *blessing,* insofar as it functions as a counterweight to the onesidedly act-oriented conception of sin that is characteristic of moralism.[68] This principle counterbalances moralism in a rather paradoxical fashion. Although this principle represents an attempt to explain the sinfulness of mankind in terms of empirical phenomena, this attempt at the same time *disturbs* its counterpart, the moralistic conception of actual sin. Whereas this moralistic approach to sin appears to make it possible to calculate and weigh the moral-religious state of each human being on the basis of his external deeds, the empirical principle thwarts the calculations of the moralist and upsets the scales of moralism. By pointing to a *common* sinfulness of mankind that lies beneath isolated sinful deeds, the traditional doctrine of original sin introduces an indeterminate factor into the moralistic equation.[69] This "foreign" factor makes it impossible to determine the specific gravity of freedom and sin objectively or even to restrict these phenomena to the realm of morality.[70] In this way, the empirical principle embodied in the traditional doctrine offsets the moralistic approach to man and tends to transpose the reality of sin to a deeper dimension that can be understood only by faith.[71] Thus the doctrine of original sin has played a historically significant role as a check on Pelagian optimism.[72]

Although Baumann appreciates the *counterbalancing* role of the empirical principle positively, he regrets the fact that it has functioned as a *mere* counterbalance. This principle did not directly combat the moralistic approach to man but merely offset it, held it in check. As Baumann puts it, the ecclesiastical doctrine of original sin meant the defeat of *Pelagius* but not of the *cause* of his error.[73] *Pelagianism* was not decisively defeated. In other words, insofar as the empirical principle merely *counterbalances,* it does not challenge but in fact leaves room for moralism.[74]

67 *Erbsünde,* 248.
68 *Ibid.,* 248, 256, 261 ("Kontrapunktierung des aktualistisch-moralistischen Horizonts").
69 See *ibid.* 249, 251.
70 *Ibid.,* 251.
71 *Ibid.,* 250-51.
72 *Ibid.,* 251; cf. 249, 256.
73 *Ibid.,* 249.
74 *Ibid.,* 278. Cf. *ibid.,* 256, where the same point is made implicitly and where moralism is closely associated with the "virus of Pelagianism."

Baumann's criticism of the empirical principle goes even further. He not only judges it to be an inadequate and inappropriate counterbalance to an existent error but also suggests that this principle — or rather, the approach which it represents — is the presupposition that made "Pelagius' erroneous optimism" possible.[75] Because Adam, the anchorage point of the empirical principle, was viewed by both parties of the controversy as an historical person, he was enclosed in the remote *past*. As a result, the message of the Biblical Adam for the *present* was not heard in its *immediacy*, but only as filtered through the medium of the empirical principle embodied in the doctrine of original sin.[76] Given the historical-empirical view of Adam, "it indeed takes a doctrine of original sin to demonstrate that that which is said regarding *'ādām* also concerns us."[77]

In criticizing the doctrine of original sin as a counterweight that merely establishes an equilibrium with moralism, Baumann's deepest reason for rejecting the empirical principle comes to light, namely, his concern to *unmask* and *combat* the underlying moralistic-actualistic conception of sin.[78]

Baumann's ambivalent assessment of the doctrine of original sin that comes to expression in his designation of the empirical principle as a "mixed blessing" is more subtly and precisely mirrored in his tortuous formulation of the positive function of the traditional doctrine: This teaching "has saved — or at least, *conserved* — but even so *saved* the notion of *sola gratia* for us."[79] This statement is significant in that it not only expresses his ambivalence with respect to the tradition but also points to the theological task which he has set for himself. Baumann does not consider himself acquitted of that task through a simple handing on of the notion *sola gratia* in the conserved state in which he finds it. Rather, he wishes to work out the intention of the

---

75 *Ibid.*, 238.
76 See *ibid.*, 238. It is striking that Schoonenberg similarly faults the traditional understanding of original sin for allowing a chasm to separate "Adam" and us. Equally striking — and indicative of the diametrical opposition between the situational and the personal interpretation of original sin — is the different remedy which each prescribes to overcome the diagnosed problem: Schoonenberg attempts to *fill* the chasm with the *history*-of-sin (see *Man and Sin*, 98, 178-79; *MS*, II, 886, 932-33; cf. ch. V, sec. B, 1, a, i above), i.e., with the aid of what Baumann would call the empirical principle; Baumann himself attempts to *jump* that chasm by means of the *'ādām-Geschichte*, i.e., with the aid of what might be called the existential principle (see sec. C, 1 below). It is significant that Schoonenberg explicitly opposes a solution such as Baumann's both as it concerns "Adam" and the fall (see ch. V, sec. B, 1, a, i above) and as it concerns original-sin-in-us (see ch. III, sec. C, 1,b above).
77 *Erbsünde*, 238.
78 See *ibid.*, 277-78.
79 *Ibid.*, 249, emphasis added.

ecclesiastical doctrine more consistently and more appropriately than could be done at the time of its genesis. For Baumann that possibility is created by the existential view of man. He is convinced that "at present there is no better approach than the existential method for understanding original sin."[80] He uses this tool to unmask the superficiality of moralism and to reveal the depth of sin.

C. THE DEPTH DIMENSION OF SIN

Before considering Baumann's thetic elaboration of original sin as depth-dimension, we will summarize his approach to the basic biblical material adduced in favor of his view.

1. Biblical Foundation

In Baumann's study the negative subheading *"Farewell to Adam"* in the section, "Critique of the Empirical Principle "[81] is seemingly contradicted by the positive subheading "The *Presence* of *'ādām*" appearing in the section "Personal Deepening and its Biblical Legitimization."[82] But as the contrasts both between the respective section titles and between the respective subheadings indicate, "Adam's" sudden reappearance is made possibly by his metamorphosis from the empirical-historical "Adam" into a personal-biblical *'ādām*. Baumann accomplishes this transformation by replacing the empirical principle with what might be called an existential-personal principle. The significance of this new principle of interpretation is made abundantly clear by Baumann's explication of his subheading "The Presence of *'ādām*":

> This is the basic axiom of the existential view: what Scripture says regarding man immediately concerns myself; I myself am Adam. The surrender of the Adam-*Historie* does not signify the scratching of an Old Testament text, but rather leads to the knowledge: the time of the Bible is my time, the present.[83]

---

80 *Ibid.,* 267. As in this instance, Baumann usually uses the adjective or adverb "existential" in describing the theological method or approach which he advocates (see, e.g., *ibid.,* 191, 193, 249, 251, 252, 253, 254, 257, 268, 269, 274, 278, 282, 283, 286). When he speaks of man's concrete existence itself, he always uses the adjective "existentiell" (see *ibid..,* 191, 193, 251, 254, 259, 260, 268, 271, 272, 274, 281, 282, 283). For a description of the significance of the distinction *existentiell-existential* generally, see ch. I, n. 143 above. In the presentation and analysis of Baumann's views, we will use the English term "existential" for both German terms, indicating which German term is used only where this is of interest.
81 *Erbsünde,* 236.
82 *Ibid.,* 252.
83 *Ibid.,* ("existentiale Sicht").

Baumann considers this surrender of the Adam-*Historie* in favor of the *'ādām-Geschichte*[84] to be justified by the early chapters of Genesis and by the fifth chapter of Romans.

The early chapters of Genesis were not intended as reports about an historical state of affairs in the past,[85] but were aimed at the contemporary historical situation of Israel, their (actual or imminent) apostasy.[86] The didactic poem concerning *'ādām* is intended to be a mirror "in which Israel must behold and is forced to admit to its distorted visage."[87] *'ādām* does not denote "a man" (Adam) but "man" in the generic sense, and then not as abstract concept but as designation of man in his concreteness, in the first instance, Israelitic man.[88] Accordingly, the poem of man's fall into sin unveils a type of sin in which every other sin has its roots: "Unbelief and distrust with respect to God's genuine intentions with man."[89]

Similarly, Paul, though giving a central place to "Adam" as *initiator* of sin, does not intend to write *Historie*, a report about a man of the primordial past, but to speak of the *many* who through their own fault have become *like* "Adam" (Ro 5:12).[90] For Paul, "the historical counterpart to Christ is not Adam,[91] but the many."[92] Like the author of the Old Testament story of the fall, Paul has the concrete world in view "in which the people of his time and of every time *resemble* one another *in the Adamic type of their existence* in the same way that one egg resembles another."[93] From the *hēmarton* of Ro 5:12 — especially in view of its parallel in Ro 3:23 — it is evident, Baumann contends, that

> Paul thinks unconditionally historically [*geschichtlich*]. That means: salvation history is a decision-event [*Entscheidungsgeschehen*]. *Hē hamartia*, the power of sin, is a *present* power ("because all have sinned") and by no means the power of Adam's sin.[94]

The attempt to go beyond this present (*geschichtliche*) power to a historical author of sin in the primordial past is illegitimate.[95]

---

84 See *ibid.*, 238.
85 *Ibid.*, 201, 209.
86 *Ibid.*, 236-38, 252; see also *ibid.*, 200-12.
87 *Ibid.*, 252.
88 *Ibid.*, 204-205.
89 *Ibid.*, 237.
90 *Ibid.*, 239.
91 For that reason, Baumann points out, the historicity of Adam cannot be deduced from the historicity of Christ (*ibid.*, 239).
92 *Ibid.*, 239.
93 *Ibid.*,
94 *Ibid.* Cf. *ibid.*, 221-22, 262.
95 *Ibid.*, 239.

Against the background of Baumann's conception of the biblical notion of history, his criticism of the traditional historicization of Adam as a process that involves a serious "reduction"[96] and "truncation"[97] of the real meaning of "Adam" becomes understandable. By means of an existential-personal approach, Baumann wishes to reverse the traditional historicization of Adam that buries him in the past of *Historie* and loses sight of his presence as "lebendige Geschichte."[98]

2. Threefold Expression

Baumann's own view of original sin[99] can almost be deduced from his criticism of the traditional approach to actual and original sin and from his approach to the biblical material. The following brief exposition of his articulation of the three aspects of the depth dimension of sin serves to bring his understanding of original sin into full view.[100]

a. *Radicality*[101]

"The first proposition of an existential conception of sin must read: Sin is *sin of the person*. It stems from the heart, the core, the center of the person."[102] Radicality, Baumann points out, "means the rootage, the coherence of all sinful activity in man's person."[103]

Only when this radicality of sin is taken into account is it possible to

---

96 *Ibid.*, 238.
97 *Ibid.*, 240.
98 See *ibid.*, 238.
99 In the following, the term "original sin" is used as a translation of the German "Ursünde" which Baumann prefers as a faithful translation of the Latin *peccatum originale* (see *ibid.*, 18-19).
100 As Baumann points out, these three aspects have been elaborated especially in recent Protestant theology (*ibid.*, 254, n. 13)
101 Baumann deals first with the totality and then with the radicality of sin. We have chosen to present these two aspects in the reverse order because the concept radicality is more directly and explicitly related to the embracive category, "depth dimension." In other words, radicality is the radix from which the other aspects, totality and universality, flow. Especially the first two aspects are so closely interrelated, however, that either order is appropriate. The interwovenness of the first two aspects is reflected by the fact that Baumann opens the "radicality" section by stating, "Die totale Sicht der Sünde wirkt sich aus in der Radikalität der Sünde" (*ibid.*, 259), while he opens the "totality" section by stating that sin stems from the heart, the core, the center of man (*ibid.*, 254), a statement giving expression to the radicality of sin.
102 *Ibid.*, 254. This passage occurs in Baumann's treatment of the *totality* of sin (see previous note).
103 *Ibid.*, 259.

break through the moralistic conception of sin and arrive at the depth of sin. "The seat of sin is decision." In that decision "not merely something is decided: a transgression of a command, an affront to one's fellowman, an omission of the help on which one's neighbor depends; rather, in this decision I myself am decided."[104] From the viewpoint of the radicality of man's decision, the weighing and calculating of the precise gravity of individual empirical deeds is rendered meaningless. For despite the great variety of actual sins, wherever the fall comes to light in concrete deeds they become manifest as being identical: a turning-away from the source of life.[105] In sin in its proper sense there is no 'more or less'; vis-à-vis God there is only 'yes' or 'no,' faith or defiance."[106] Because sin entails the transgression of the critical boundary between "yes" and "no," the ascertainment of precisely how, how far and where *this* boundary has been transgressed is meaningless."[107] "The meaning of an act is not determined by its moral manifestation but rather by the basic existential direction of man from which it [that act] stems."[108] Ethical reality is indeed a part of sin, in Baumann's view, but merely as a limited *aspect*. As autonomous, egocentric stance of man sin comes to expression *also* in the moral realm. But, says Baumann, "to understand sin theologically is to understand it *existentially*, as personal relationship and reality."[109]

The radicality of sin, Baumann holds, is clearly taught by Scripture. It is taught, not only in Ro 5, but is generally manifest in Paul's predominant use of the singular form of the term "sin" and in his development of the idea of enslavement in sin.[110] The unmasking of the identical guilt of all men – the radical perversion and godlessness that becomes concrete and virulent in all sinful acts – is a basic theme of the letter to the Romans.[111] Similarly, the story of the fall implicitly teaches the radicality of sin:

> Without the insight into the relativity of the ethical realm – that is, its convergent rootage in the identical depth of guilt . . . – God's conduct in the story of the fall creates a downright grotesque impression. Why does God inflict such dreadful punishment? . . . Viewed from the purely moral aspect, God appears as a cunning, devilish torturer who seems to relish awaiting the first occasion for crushing his

---

104 *Ibid.*: "Nach unserer Auffassung entscheidet sich dort nicht nur irgend *etwas* . . . , sondern ich selbst stehe in dieser Entscheidung in Entscheidung."
105 *Ibid.*, 259.
106 *Ibid.* Cf. *ibid.*, 260.
107 *Ibid.*, 259.
108 *Ibid.*
109 *Ibid.*, 272, emphasis added.
110 *Ibid.*, 260.
111 *Ibid.*

creature. Only when one discerns the *abyss* between God and his creatures that is *uncovered* by the eating of the fruit do the consequences and the background of this deed become perspicuous and does God remain the good and merciful Creator.[112]

This exposition of the story of the fall in terms of the radicality of sin serves well as a concise summary of Baumann's entire reinterpretation of "original sin." Indeed, the other two aspects of the depth dimension are in effect elaborations of his perception of the radicality of sin.

b. *Totality*

Whereas the radicality aspect has central and direct reference to the depth dimension, the totality aspect has reference to the breadth dimension of sin, i.e., its total, encompassing impact upon the individual. Anything that affects the radix of existence must also affect the *whole* of existence.

The idea of the totality of sin, Baumann points out, comes to expression especially in the biblical notion of death. In the early chapters of Genesis death is depicted not as a partial reality, a reality affecting only the body and leaving the immortal soul unscathed but as an event "which befalls man in his totality, in all his powers and all his activity...."[113] In the fall, man put himself, his totality, that which constitutes his very humanness at stake — and lost; he forfeited *his life*.[114] "Were it not for the fact that God's faithfulness and mercy is greater [than man's sin] he would have reached the end of all his possibilities. He would have been dead."[115] Although the accent of Scripture lies on *new life*, says Baumann, this is properly understood only as that new beginning that has been recreated through the crisis of judgement and death.[116]

Two implications which Baumann draws from the idea of the totality of sin deserve closer scrutiny. The one concerns the notion of freedom, the other the notion of beginnings.

In the course of his work on the subject of original sin, Baumann comments incidentally on the problematic nature of a Pelagian conception of freedom. With reference to that conception he speaks of "absolute ethical freedom,"[117] an "optimistic concept of freedom"[118] and a "onesidedly

---

112 *Ibid.*
113 *Ibid.*, 255.
114 *Ibid.*
115 *Ibid.*
116 *Ibid.*
117 *Ibid.*, 41.
118 *Ibid.*, 249.

moralistic concept of freedom."[119] Moreover, he suggests that in the anti-Pelagian polemic, it would have been sufficient for Augustine to have demonstrated the "anti-Christian" nature of this "individualistic-monadic freedom-ideal."[120] This is a highly intriguing suggestion, especially in view of the fact that Baumann gives the concept of freedom a central place in his thought. He maintains that freedom constitutes the "decisive focal point" of human existence,[121] that "only my own [free] act is totally and radically decisive for myself and my future"[122] and, even more pointedly, that the cause of sin is one's irreducible free act.[123] Upon reading these affirmations of the centrality, radicality and totality of freedom, the question arises how Baumann considers it possible to subject the Pelagian conception of freedom to a radical critique.

That question is answered in terms of the idea of the totality of sin:

> The totality of sin means the totality of being sinful [Sünderseins]. That is, the sinner is incapable of placing himself outside of his sin, for he is sinner with his total existence, in all that *he* is because through his act he has imprisoned himself. "He who sins is a slave of sin" (Jn 8:34).[124]

It is in this sense and only in this sense, Baumann adds, that the reformational thesis that man has lost his proper free will, the *liberum arbitrium* can be understood.[125] Baumann explains that this thesis does not mean that man cannot act freely, but that such freedom exists only with respect to "the realm of *iustitia civilis,* not in the area of the personal God-relationship."[126] In other words, with respect to the question of man's freedom, the totality of sin must be understood in connection with the specific *relational nature* of sin, i.e., its relatedness to God and one's fellowman.[127] Sin is a radical and therefore total perversion of that relation, an autonomous self-liberation that is in fact a fatal *Umorientierung* of the whole of human existence away from God, the source of life.[128] When sin is so understood, it is impossible to maintain that at this deepest level man is free. Sin is so total that it embraces freedom, encloses it *within* that totality. In a hamartiology thus oriented to

---

119 *Ibid.*
120 *Ibid.*
121 *Ibid.,* 282.
122 *Ibid.,* 266; cf. 282.
123 *Ibid.,* 258, a statement by G. Hasenhüttl which Baumann uses to express his own view.
124 *Ibid.,* 255.
125 *Ibid.*
126 *Ibid.*
127 *Ibid.,* 191, 259, 271, 280, 282-83.
128 *Ibid.,* 255.

the personal core of human existence, Baumann contends, the virus of Pelagianism can no longer do any harm.[129]

The second implication which Baumann derives from the notion of the totality of sin is the "repudiation of the ascertainment of the empirical beginning of sin in man."[130] This stricture applies in the first place to the beginning of sin in the individual. Just as the totality of sin makes it impossible to step outside of sin in order to arrive at freedom as a neutral capacity, so this same totality makes it impossible to arrive at a beginning as neutral starting point. Both the road that leads via structural abstraction to untainted freedom and the road that leads via temporal-historical retrogression to pristine beginnings are blocked by the sheer massiveness of sin. In view of the fact that it is the whole man that is illuminated by the searchlight of revelation, says Baumann, "it becomes illusory to isolate individual deeds from a man's life."[131] Hence it is impossible to return to an isolated first act where sin "began" and "before which" sin did "not yet" totally affect one's existence.

The elusiveness of the beginning of sin in an individual is adumbrated, Baumann contends, by both Scripture and Catholic theological-ecclesiastic tradition. The impossibility of establishing a beginning of sin is the essential purport of the prevalent Catholic interpretation of original sin in terms of a "prepersonal condition of sin" constituting a "culpable privation of grace."[132] Since these descriptions intend to point to the fact that man is somehow sinful even before his first concrete and tangible sinful act, they represent an attempt to express in some way the depth dimension of sin, the "perversion" of man's basic existential stance before God.[133] Similarly the Bible knows of no *pre*-sinful state.[134] It is the intention of Gn 2-3 to indicate "how matters stand between God and man: 'the imagination of man's heart is evil from his youth' (Gn 8:21).[135]

Baumann considers the beginning of sin to be unascertainable, not only in the life of the individual, but also in the history of mankind. The Bible, he says, knows of no beginning of sin, no "original state" and no "pre-sinful" people.[136] This is the meaning of Gn 2-3 (in the light of Gn 8:21) and of Ro

129 *Ibid.*
130 *Ibid.,* 257.
131 *Ibid.*
132 *Ibid.,* 258.
133 *Ibid.,* 259.
134 *Ibid.,* 257 citing Herbert Haag; see also *ibid.,* 106-107.
135 *Ibid.,* 257.
136 *Ibid.*

5:12-21 where Paul contrasts exclusively "the *old*, Adamic men and the *new*, wholly different, obedient men. Before the old aeon there is no third aeon in the sense of a golden age. There is only the old aeon and the new aeon that begins with Jesus Christ."[137]

Why and in what way does Baumann consider the beginning of sin to be inaccessible? Is it inaccessible because the beginning *no longer* exists, so that there is no present ground for retrogression? Or is the beginning of sin inaccessible because a temporal beginning of sin, a beginning of sin within history *never occurred*? With respect to the inaccessibility of sin in the life of the individual, Baumann accentuates especially the former reason. He says, for example, that because God's Word has as its object the *whole* man in the all-embracive horizon of his existence and the *whole* of history as they are in reality, "the beginning of sin in [individual] men and in [communal] history is to be spoken of not psychologically but existentially."[138] The "psychological" approach to the beginning of sin has reference to the attempt to *separate* an empirical *first* act of sin – "the beginning" – from the *total* sinfulness of existence and of history. Within existential thought, Baumann contends, such historicization of beginnings is totally incomprehensible.[139] One must speak of the beginning existentially,[140] he maintains, because "there is no *experience* of the historical beginning; there is only the experience of having-begun, the [*unfolding*] *expression* of the beginning yielded by the process of becoming-conscious-in-decision."[141]

Unfortunately, despite the fact that in the passage just discussed Baumann initially refers to the beginnings of sin both in individuals and in the history of mankind,[142] he proceeds to elaborate his objections to a *non-*existential approach to beginnings primarily in terms of individuals. This restriction is attested to by the narrow characterization of the non-existential approach as a "psychological" approach. Fortunately, his views regarding the beginning of sin in the history of *mankind* need not be gleaned exclusively from the passage in which he advocates a non-psychological, existential approach.

137 *Ibid.,* emphasis added
138 *Ibid.,* 283: "Vom Anfang der Sünde im Menschen und in der Geschichte ist nicht psychologisch, sondern existential zu reden . . . ." A little later Baumann uses the other term: "Vom Anfang ist also *existentiell* zu reden" (*ibid.,* emphasis added).
139 *Ibid.,* 283 ("existentiale Denken").
140 *Ibid.* (here: "existentiell"; see n. 138 above).
141 *Ibid:* Es gibt keine *Erfahrung* des historischen Anfangs, es gibt nur die Erfahrung des Angefangen-Habens, die im Bewusstwerden-in-der-Entscheidung sich ergebende *Auslegung* des Anfangs."
142 *Ibid.,* 283 (see n. 138 above).

As is clear from statements considered earlier, Baumann is convinced that the Bible knows of no pre-sinful situation or time. The "before" of a good creation is not a *temporal* qualification of a past epoch but a *directional* qualification of present reality, namely, the reality of a right God-man relationship that originates in the Creator and impinges continuously upon His creature.[143] In other words, the anteriority of the good creation does not consist in a temporal primordial condition but in a dynamic relationship that perpetually conditions temporal reality. The priority of God as the good Creator, His priority with respect to His creature, this is the content of the "good creation." He is always the one who creates "wholeness," (*Heil*), the one who is *more* faithful than man.[144] "God's ever new, merciful beginning with man is the great theme of the biblical message regarding origins ...."[145] Correspondingly, the story of Adam is not the story of the dramatic fall of a first man, but the model, the mirror-image of Israel's (and of every) breach-of-covenant.[146] Sin is so total, so far-reaching that it cannot be said to have *a* (historical) *beginning* but to have been present (existentially) *"from-the-beginning."*[147] Scripture, Baumann adds, simply proceeds from sin as a *Faktum* which has no further ground – except in the responsibility of man.[148] It is especially out of concern for this personal responsibility that Baumann declares the realm of beginnings principially off-limits: "To look for an original state or for the fall in 'prehistorical' facts... is to minimize the scope of our own apostasy [*Abfall*] that *we*, by our own responsibility, have brought about and to withdraw the cause of our sin into inaccessible realms, which *au fond* in no way concern us."[149] In summary, to speak of the beginning of sin existentially is to approach that beginning not as *Historie* but as *Geschichte*, as the continuing event of God-defiance that began and begins with man.

c. *Universality*

The universality of sin is in turn closely related to the totality of sin, for both aspects have reference to the extent of sin. The difference between them is one of scope. The idea of *totality* has reference to the embraciveness

---

143 *Ibid.,* 188 (in a summary of the approach to original sin in Protestant theology; this approach is adopted by Baumann [see *ibid.,* 240-43]).
144 *Ibid.,* 242.
145 *Ibid.*
146 *Ibid.* See also sec. C, 1 above.
147 *Ibid.,* 257; cf. 187, 208, 211, 223, 236.
148 *Ibid.,* 257.
149 *Ibid.,* 86.

of sin primarily as it concerns the *individual* – mankind coming into view only insofar as the idea of totality affects the question of the beginning of sin. Within the perspective of the *universality* of sin, the notion of embraciveness has a broader scope: "the generality or the universal facticity of sin."[150] "If the scriptural Word of God is aimed immediately at *each man* himself, this also means that it concerns *all men.*"[151]

The uniqueness of Baumann's conception of the universality of sin in comparison to the situationalist conception lies not merely in the fact that he treats this unity as an *aspect of* the personal *depth dimension* of sin and, accordingly, proceeds from the individual to the universal ("each," therefore, "all"), but especially in the fact that he stresses the *theological* nature of the unity of mankind.[152] He points out several theological points of unity. Because there is only *one God* and *one revelation* for all men, because the Bible portrays *God's* history with man, because Israel understands itself as salvation for the world and as a sign of God for all nations, because *Jesus* is the *only* Savior for all men, because there is only *one Church* for all – *therefore* mankind is one.[153] Elaborating the christological focal point of the unity of mankind, Baumann states that it is in Christ that the unity in creation and in sin is perceived in a retrospectiveness that breaks through the boundaries of individuality. In this way, "the zenith of personalness is revealed: man stands before God *as individual for the whole,* and *the whole* stands *in individuals* before God."[154]

Baumann grants that the Catholic doctrine of original sin indeed represents an expression of the dependence of all men upon *Jesus Christ* and thus approximates a theological notion of unity. He considers it a weakness, however, that the traditional doctrine attempts to ground this dependence in a typically *non-theological* manner, namely, by means of the empirical principle.[155] Though conceding that this unity may secondarily be one of a biotic or social nature, Baumann stresses that for the Christian proclamation

---

150 *Ibid.,* 262.
151 *Ibid.,* emphasis added.
152 Baumann remarks that those Catholic theologians who have attempted to formulate the unity of mankind in a new way have done so in terms of *Personalität* (i.e., in anthropological terms), rather than grounding this unity *theologically* (ibid., 263).
153 *Ibid.,* 262.
154 *Ibid.,* 263. emphasis added. The original reads: "In Christus wird die Einheit in Schöpfung und Sünde auch in ihrer die geschichtlichen Grenzen des Individuums sprengenden Retrospektivität erkannt. In ihr offenbart sich der Zenit menschlichen Personseins: dass der Mensch als einzelner wie das Ganze vor Gott steht und dass das Ganze im einzelnen vor Gott steht."
155 *Ibid.,* 265.

the unity of mankind represents a *faith*-demanding summons.[156] "In Scripture," he says, "solidarity in sin is of a theological not of an empirical order."[157] This unity can be understood only by faith,[158] a faith which abandons the attempt to find a ground for the *pantes hēmarton* (Ro 3:23 and 5:12) and accepts, in addition to the radical and total, also the *universal* meaninglessness of sin as a *Faktum* of Scripture.[159]

* * *

Baumann's unique contribution to the current Roman Catholic discussion of original sin consists in having grappled most directly and intensively with the central issue that gave rise to the ecclesiastical doctrine, namely, the issue concerning the assessment of the fundamental directedness of human life apart from God's saving grace in Jesus Christ. Four facets of this contribution are especially relevant within the scope of the present study. First, by means of the existential-theological approach which Baumann expressly adopts,[160] he has uncovered the depth dimension of sin in its relationship to God and to fellowman. Second, in the same way he brings the unity of an individual's countless acts into focus. Thereby he overcomes the atomization of the individual that plagues Vanneste's interpretation of original sin. Third, he has focused on the direct relationship between (original) sin and responsibility, abandoning the prevalent tendency of dissociating guilt and original sin that results in (or from) the reduction of original sin to an impersonal, fatalistic given. Fourth, he has dealt with original sin in integral relationship with the revelation of God's grace in Jesus Christ. Only by virtue of that integration can he place the confession of sin – including its depth, original sin – in the context of "the revolutionary power of Christianity."[161] In other words, Baumann's association of radical guilt with original sin does not lead to paralyzing resignation because in his view this doctrine involves the con-

---

156 *Ibid.,* 262; cf. 264, 266.
157 *Ibid.,* 263.
158 *Ibid.,* 262.
159 *Ibid.,* 262-63: "Der Glaubende vermag die radikale, totale und auch die universale Unsinnigkeit der Sünde auszuhalten. Er will gerade nicht seine Sünde begreiflich machen. Die Umschreibung der Universalität der Sünde hat vom Faktum der Schrift auszugehen, dass es den konkreten Menschen, von dem sie handelt, immer und überall nur und schon als den sündigen gibt. Die einzige legitime Begründung ist: 'weil sie alle gesündigt haben" (Ro 5:12). Cf. *ibid.,* 265.
160 *Ibid.,* 267, 278, 286; cf. 251-52, 252-53.
161 *Ibid.,* 16.

fession of *"responsible* guilt vis-à-vis God," the God who in Jesus Christ is known as the source of and summons to (new) life.[162]

To point out Baumann's unique contribution to the contemporary Roman Catholic discussion of original sin is not to suggest that his interpretation is devoid of problems. These can best be dealt with in the Epilogue where they can be placed in the context of the lingering problems and possible perspectives of both the personal and situational reinterpretations of original sin.

---

162 See *ibid.,* 16, 241-42, 258, 274, 276.

EPILOGUE *LINGERING PROBLEMS AND POSSIBLE PERSPECTIVES*

Having pursued the principal aim of this study — an in-depth analysis of two major streams within the contemporary Roman Catholic reinterpretation of original sin — in the preceding chapters, we now turn to an epilogue devoted to a summary of the central problems that have been encountered and to a search for perspectives within the situational and the personal reinterpretation of original sin.

A. ORIGINAL SIN AS PRIVATION OF GRACE

Surprisingly, one of the central problems encountered in the situational understanding of original sin is due to the fact that none of the situationalists subjects the relatively late theological development, namely, the post-Tridentine[1] definition of the essence of original sin in terms of the privation of sanctifying grace, to a critical reexamination.[2] Although in Schoonenberg's reinterpretation this explicit definition increasingly recedes into the background, its substance remains central. This is evidenced by his description of original sin in terms of "gracelessness" and in terms of a world "devoid of grace" as well as by the way in which he conceives of the problem which the second-fall hypothesis was designed to solve.[3] Rahner and, in his footsteps, Weger do not merely proceed from the definition of original sin in terms of the privation of grace; they also elaborate this conception systematically for the specific purpose of elucidating the guilt character of original sin.[4] Within the situational reinterpretation the uncritical acceptance of this post-Tridentine understanding of original sin gives rise to several problems.

In the first place, the understanding of original sin as the privation of

1 See Introduction, sec. A, 9.
2 See ch. III above.
3 See *ibid.,* sec. A and ch. V, sec. B, 1, b, i.
4 See ch. III, sec. C, 2, b, i above.

sanctifying grace renders the guilt character of original sin problematical. This becomes clear, strangely enough, precisely in Rahner's and Weger's attempt to *demonstrate* the guilt character of original sin by an elaboration of the privational definition of this doctrine.[5] According to this elaboration, original sin consists of "unholinesss" in the sense that man lacks divine holiness as an ontological quality; he is deprived of this quality in his concrete (spatiotemporal) historical situation. Divine holiness ought to have constituted a concrete situational *Existential* qualifying man's existence; original sin is the privation of this *Existential*.

This elaboration fails to clarify the guilt character of original sin, however, because the "unholiness" arrived at, though suggesting a moral-ethical qualification, is sharply dissociated from any responsible direction of life of those qualified as "unholy." This designation has no reference whatsoever to man's moral-religious stance vis-à-vis God but describes a historical relational structure (*Existential*) that impinges upon man interiorly. In order to avoid any connotation of moral-religious turpitude, the term "a-holiness" would, therefore, be more accurate than the term "unholiness" to describe the privational condition of original sin.

Those who conceive of original sin as the privation of sanctifying grace approximate a moral-religious notion of guilt by having recourse to *God's will*: as evidenced in the abiding presence of grace as *transcendental Existential* (man's horizon), God wishes that His holiness be present as *spatiotemporal Existential* (man's atmosphere) qualifying every human being. Because this holiness is not merely absent but absent contrary to a divine "ought," it involves real guilt.[6]

Since this a-holiness is viewed as man's (interior) *Existential*, however, Rahner rightly excludes every element of personal responsibility from the notion of guilt that is approximated by having recourse to a divine ought.[7] Hence, the term "Schuld" that is properly predicated of the situational privation of sanctifying grace connotes the idea of "debt" in contradistinction to that of "guilt." Although the German term allows for the former meaning, it is clear that the idea of debt not only falls short of what Rahner and Weger wish to demonstrate by their elaboration but is also problematical as a confessionally relevant notion. For this understanding of original sin would mean that a Christian is to confess – or assent to – an a-holiness as a debt for which personal responsibility neither can nor ought to be felt. Consequently,

---

5 See *ibid.*, sec. C, 2.
6 See *ibid.*, sec. C, 2, b, ii.
7 See *ibid.*, sec. C, 2, b, iii.

the "belief in" original sin takes on the character of a complaint rather than of a confession. The question then arises as to the real significance of this doctrine in the life of the Christian. That question leads us to the next problem entailed in the understanding of original sin as the privation of grace.

The second problem arising from the uncritical acceptance of the theological tradition that defines original sin as the privation of sanctifying grace is how this lack is to be concretely imagined. This problem becomes acute due to the fact that this understanding of original sin is placed within a new anthropological-theological framework. The basic element of this framework is the idea of situation. Original sin is reinterpreted in terms of situation precisely because this category is considered to be more concrete than the traditional natural-biological categories. The abandonment of these outmoded categories, however, represents a certain loss, for traditionally they made it possible to differentiate rather sharply between a defective natural-biological medium and an effective sacramental-institutional medium of grace. The category "situation" however, does not allow for such sharp differentiation. Its intended referent is the concrete historical context that impinges upon man's inner being and constitutes his situational *Existential.* The problem concerning the concrete nature of original sin as *Existential* emerges when one observes that the situationalists conceive of *grace* as being a universal situational *Existential,* in the first place as *transcendental horizon* and in the second place, in varying degrees of intensity, as concrete, *spatiotemporal atmosphere* of human activity.[8] This affirmation of the presence of grace as universal situation makes it exceedingly difficult to understand what precisely is meant by the affirmation of the privation of grace as universal situation. What concretely does every human being upon entering into this world lack? In pursuit of an answer to that question, we have defended the hyposthesis that the grace which everyone can be said to lack situationally is the ecclesiastical-sacramental manifestation of grace.[9] The unfailing, irreversible and efficacious fullness of grace that constitutes the "Church-situation" is not (yet) the "world-situation," not the situation into which man is born. That means that every human being can be said to lack a highly qualified mode of sanctifying grace: however positive an individual's milieu may be, that concrete (spatiotemporal) situation is devoid, not of sanctifying grace per se, but of that intensity and efficacy of sanctifying grace that is realized in the official sacramental Church. The confession of original sin as the situational

8 See *ibid.,* sec. A.
9 See ch. VI above.

privation of grace is, therefore, a confession of the necessity of the institutional Church as unique sacramental remedy. Overt incorporation in this Church is confessed to be necessary not for salvation itself but for the objective certainty and full manifestation of salvation.

Rendering this confession meaningful is extremely difficult because it introduces a bifurcation into the fabric of human life, a bifurcation not between the world as graceless "nature" and the Church as exclusive vessel of grace, but between the world (man's immediate historical situation) as an ambivalent mixture of privation and presence of grace, a disrupted medium of grace, and the Church as institutionally pure, unambiguous and efficacious medium of grace.

Granted that man's historical situation is ambivalent, is this ambivalence elucidated by introducing the notion of the presence and privation of "sanctifying grace"? Is man's historical situation elucidated or obscured when the light by which its assessment takes place proves to be the Church as institutional model of sanctifying grace? Does the message of the gospel ask of anyone to accept that any institution — as institution — is a pure manifestation and medium of grace? Even if this is to be answered affirmatively, the problem remains: how can the initial privation of this institutional mode of grace be plausibly construed as the situation of "original sin in us."

The Problem regarding the relevance of a certain conception of the *medium* of grace is a repercussion of the more fundamental — indeed, decisive — issue as to the *nature* of grace. The interpretation of original sin in terms of the privation of grace rests on the assumption that grace is essentially a supernatural ontic quality that elevates and perfects man.[10] Due to this assumption regarding the nature of grace, the reinterpretation of original sin as the privation of such grace continues to be plagued by remnants of a nature-grace dualism in a subtle and modified form.[11]

Certain tendencies within the situational reinterpretation of original sin disclose a perspective within which the unquestioned point of departure can be subjected to critical reexamination. This perspective is disclosed by the method of theologizing which Schoonenberg and Rahner advocate.

As we have indicated, Schoonenberg advocates a centripetal (or

---

10 This conception of grace gives rise to the question Haag poses in connection with Weger's reinterpretation: "Can one 'possess' sinfulness [the privation of grace] or grace?" Haag goes on to suggest that on this score Weger appears to be caught in the scholastic thought-forms which he has rejected elsewhere (*ThQ*, CL, 448n; cf. *JESt*, X, 270).

11 See ch. VI, sec. B above.

genetic) method of theologizing.[12] This means that in considering any aspect of the Christian faith, one must not simply proceed from later ecclesiastical or theological formulations (the centrifugal or deductive method); rather, one must return to the original, primal reality that gives rise to the later creedal and theological formulations. This original reality must function continuously as point of reference, indeed, as vital source of reinterpretation. True to that method, Schoonenberg painstakingly examines the scriptural (especially Old Testament) data that attests to solidarity in sin. However, once the idea of situation is introduced in order to capture the scriptural notion of solidarity in sin, Schoonenberg makes a methodologically abrupt transition by "filling" this situation with the notion "privation of grace."[13] At that point a post-Tridentine *theologoumenon* is allowed to dominate the data culled from Scripture; the rejected centrifugal method begins to overshadow the advocated centripetal method.

In presenting Rahner's reinterpretation of original sin, we have traced a method that is formally similar to Schoonenberg's centripetal method, namely, the "concentric" method of theologizing.[14] According to this method, any particular Christian teaching must be reduced to, i.e., constantly referred back to, the central mystery of Christianity. Applying this method to the doctrine of original sin, Rahner at one point states that the reality of grace as renewing forgiveness of and redemption from sin is the fundamental revelation of Christianity and the primary datum for the reinterpretation of the doctrine of original sin.[15] Also in Rahner's reinterpretation, however, another datum begins to play a dominant role, namely, the notion of sanctifying grace as the impartation of a divine quality of holiness, the self-communication of the divine essence to man — divinizing grace.[16] The notion of redeeming grace having been appropriately posited as the primary given for the doctrine of original *sin*, the concentric method obliges Rahner to justify the factual dominance of the notion "divinizing grace" — in itself unrelated to sin — in terms of redeeming grace. The demonstration of an intrinsic connection between redeeming and divinizing grace is especially urgent in view of the fact that it proves to be extremely difficult to indicate in what

---

12   See ch. I, sec. A, esp. n. 12 above.
13   See ch. III, sec. B, 1 above.
14   See *ibid.,* sec. C, 2, a.
15   See *ibid*.
16   See *ibid.,* sec. C, 2, b, i and ii. For an elaboration of the meaning of divinizing grace, see ch. II, sec. A, 2 above.

sense the privation of divine holiness (sanctifying or divinizing grace) can be regarded as (original) sin.[17]

To point to the centripetal or concentric method as a possible perspective within which a central problem entailed in the situationalists' understanding of original sin may be overcome is not to suggest that a more consistent application of this method would provide a ready solution. Nevertheless, this theological method does open a perspective in that it paves the way for a more radical and more critical approach to the reinterpretation of original sin. Such an approach must subject not merely the categories and thought-forms of creedal statements but *a fortiori* the assumed *theologoumenon* (original sin is the privation of sanctifying grace) to a critical reexamination.[18]

B. SITUATION

Although the notion of situation has already come into view obliquely in the examination of the definition of original sin as the privation of grace, the problematic nature of the concept "situation" deserves separate attention.

Though chosen for its concreteness, the category "situation," as it functions in the reinterpretation of original sin, is an abstraction. It will be recalled that the concept of situation that is deemed appropriate for reinterpreting original sin has reference not to the as yet undifferentiated complexity of concrete reality but to an *Existential*.[19] Situation as *Existential* designates a structure of human existence. In order to bring this structure into clear focus it must be "drawn away," abstracted, from every foreign, i.e., non-situational element. Accordingly, Schoonenberg, for example, methodically expunges every element of human activity, every personal element, every element of free shaping and forming.[20] Only by means of this rigorous expurgation is it possible to retain as residue a purely passive situated*ness*, *being*-situated — and that not as a reality external to man, his environment, his *Um-Welt*, but as an interior *Existential* that permeates and limits his freedom.

17   See ch. III, sec. C, 2, b, i and ii.
18   Haag points to the necessity of such reexamination by his assessment of Weger's justification of this understanding of original sin by appealing to the present consensus in Roman Catholic theology. This consensus, Haag contends, provides no ground for Weger's treatment of the conception of original sin in question as if it were an incontrovertible, revealed truth (*ThQ*, CL, 437-38).
19   See ch. I, n. 163 and sec. B, 2, b, ii above. Cf. ch. II, sec. B, 3 and ch. III, sec. C, 2, b (introductory paragraphs) above.
20   See ch. I, sec. A, 3 (introductory paragraphs) and c; and ch. III, sec. C, 1 above.

The same process of abstraction lies behind Rahner's and Weger's concept of a situational *Existential*. This underlying abstraction becomes manifest most clearly in Rahner's description of the interpenetration of "situation" and "freedom." Here it becomes evident that, having been obtained by abstraction, the concepts freedom (or person) and situation are regarded as mutually exclusive and opposite magnitudes, so that their interpenetration takes on the form of a clash of opposing forces: a person can find himself only through an *ontic* process of losing himself; he can come to himself only through *ontic* self-estrangement. In fact, he finds himself only *in* such self-estrangement, i.e., by "appropriating" the "otherness" of being situated.[21] Even apart from any negative moral-religious qualification, "situation" presents itself to "person" as sheer "otherness."

Within limits, abstraction is an entirely legitimate process, an indispensable aid to every academic discipline. But it is not an entirely innocuous process if one forgets, even for a moment, that one is wielding a *dissecting* knife. That knife makes it possible to obtain a clear view of the tissues, perhaps even of the cells, of human life; but at the moment that these are laid bare, *life is gone*; the dissected tissue is no longer a functioning part of a living whole. Dissection is useful only when one imagines the separated tissue as an integral part of the living organism. To drop the metaphor, the clarity of abstraction serves insight only when the abstractness of this clarity is constantly kept in mind, when the living whole is constantly kept in view. Moreover, one must realize that the living whole is not re-obtained by simply putting the dissected elements – in our case "freedom" and "situation" – back together, for such reconstruction does not yield more than the imagined interaction of abstract, mutually exclusive concepts – the dead tissues of human life. That the abstract character of the concept "situation" is not sufficiently taken into account by the situationalists becomes evident in different ways at various levels of their reinterpretation of original sin.

The abstract nature of the notion "situation" becomes apparent when one observes the situationalists' attempts to give this formal category content. As an intermediate step, Schoonenberg introduces the model of the child in a totally negative moral situation.[22] Schoonenberg indirectly testifies to the abstraction entailed in this model when he grants that such a totally negative situation cannot exist because the indispensable communal fabric of human life is lacking.[23] Nevertheless, this admission does not lead to a critical

21 See ch. I, sec. B, 2, b, iii above.
22 See *ibid.*, sec. A, 3, b.
23 See *ibid.*

relativization of the model. Rather, it finds its parallel in the attempt to establish a wholly negative initial situation of man with the aid of the second-fall hypothesis and in his description of the world as being "grace-less." Although he acknowledges that man's concrete situation is one of grace, Schoonenberg does not sufficiently bring this acknowledgement to bear on his reinterpretation of original sin in terms of "gracelessness."

The concrete situation of grace plays a more central role in Rahner's and Weger's elaboration of the doctrine of original sin. Rahner explicitly states that man is subject to *two* ("theological") *Existentialia*, namely, that of the concrete privation of grace ("Adam") and that of the concrete presence of grace (Christ).[24] Nevertheless, the abstractness of the notion situational *Existential* remains problematical. Although the formal idea that man's historical *situatedness* constitutes an *Existential* (a relational structure of existence) is plausible, that plausibility disappears when this philosophical analysis is translated "theologically" by positing that the presence of sanctifying grace is *one structure of existence* and the lack of grace (original sin) is *another structure of existence*. This difficulty can be partially alleviated by carefully differentiating between the privation and the presence of grace from the vantage point of the institutional summit of grace, the sacramental Church.[25] Even from this vantage point, however, it remains difficult to designate the privation of grace as an *Existential*. At most one could say that man's *single Existential* of historical situatedness is ambiguous – even within the pale of the Church – with respect to the reality of sanctifying grace. But that thesis can stand on its own merits, without being supported by a doctrine of original sin.

In view of the historical controversy that gave rise to the doctrine of original sin, the most astonishing abstraction that is consistently carried through by the situationalist is the abstraction of original sin from the subject's religious stance before God. Yet this is at the same time the most self-evident abstraction once one has chosen for a strictly situational reinterpretation of this doctrine. By focussing on original sin exclusively as situational *Existential*, one has, by virtue of that abstraction, methodologically turned one's back on the deepest issue in the controversy that occasioned the doctrine of original sin. Interpreting original sin strictly as situational *Existential* means that man comes into view only formally. He is viewed exclusively in terms of his free decision, the decision by which he can either appropriate or reject the situation of original sin. And thus, by

24 See ch. III, sec. A and ch. V, sec. B, 2, a above.
25 This differentiation is elaborated in ch. VI above.

implicitly or explicitly presupposing the counterpart of this situational *Existential* purely formally ("freedom"), the critical question concerning man's stance vis-à-vis God is left undecided — yet on the other hand *decided* insofar as the situational approach reflects the conviction that in his innermost being man in (the situation of) original sin is aptly characterized formally, as free being. In other words, in their reinterpretation of original sin, the situationalists are content to remain within the most fundamental abstraction, the abstraction of the reality of original sin from the central direction of man's life apart from the grace of Jesus Christ. The danger of abiding by that abstraction is that it is no longer recognized as such and presents itself as concrete reality.

This critique of the situationalists' approach to man in the doctrine of original sin does not, of course, entail the suggestion that they are oblivious to the significance of man's stance vis-à-vis God. Especially Schoonenberg recognizes the value of the Protestant emphasis upon the depth dimension of sin.[26] Moreover, in his discussion of *personal* sin, he gives expression to a profound understanding of sin as being basically a closing off of oneself from God and an enslavement of the will.[27] This recognition, however, is not brought to bear upon the reinterpretation of original sin. Indeed, from Schoonenberg's viewpoint, this depth dimension of sin *need not* be taken into account in the doctrine of original sin for two reasons: on the one hand, this doctrine is understood in terms of the privation of sanctifying grace; on the other hand, this privation is understood as situational *Existential*, a historical structure of existence that can be analyzed in total abstraction from the religious direction of those subject to that structure. Accordingly, Schoonenberg resolutely and methodically avoids the crucial point at which the "situation" of original sin meets the "free decision" of appropriation. The latter is immediately relegated to the realm of *personal* sin, a reality that need not be taken into account when dealing with the *unique* and *antipodal* reality of original sin as situational *Existential*.[28]

Although this withdrawal from the critical juncture of "free decision" and "situational *Existential*" is entirely legitimate once one has chosen for a strict situational reinterpretation of original sin, the fact that the crucial question as to the religious direction of human life apart from grace can be

---

26 See ch. III, sec. C, 1, b above.
27 See *Geloof*, IV, 14-50, 242, 245; *Man and Sin*, 1-25, 87-88. Even here, however, descriptions of freedom and its relationship to (supernatural) grace occur that attenuate the gravity of enslavement in sin.
28 See ch. IV, sec. B, 1 above.

dismissed so readily as being extraneous to the doctrine of original sin should give one pause to question the legitimacy of an exclusively situational approach. Has an abstraction — "situational *Existential*" — usurped the place of concrete reality? Has the dissecting knife of abstraction been wielded correctly, and, if so, has this dissection deepened our insight into the ground of human life, man's relationship to God? Is a dissecting knife at all appropriate at that deepest level, or is that instrument designed only for the tissues, not for the core of human life? These questions return in the attempt to grapple with the doctrine of original sin in terms of personal sin.

C. FREEDOM, FATE AND HISTORY

In the discussion of the doctrine of original sin, the idea of freedom presents itself as at once a self-evident and a problematic notion.[29] It is problematic because by its very nature the idea of freedom itself appears to allow of no positive or negative moral-religious qualification. Freedom appears to be the neutral starting point and abiding ground of human life from which all acts that are morally, religiously qualified derive. The free self-determination of the individual appears, therefore, as the *original* given of man's life. Yet according to the doctrine of *original sin*, man is said to be sinful prior to his individual free act, so that fate encroaches upon freedom.[30] At the same time, however, the idea of freedom asserts itself as a

---

29 For a profound analysis of the problem of freedom as it relates to the religious core of human life, see Berkouwer *De mens het beeld Gods* (Kampen: Kok, 1957), 346-89; *Man: The Image of God,* trans. Dirk W. Jellema (Grand Rapids: Eerdmans, 1962), 310-66.

30 The problem of fate and freedom (or responsibility) plays a prominent role in most treatises on original sin. See Baumann's survey of Protestant theology in *Erbsünde*, 109-93, the lion's share of which is treated under the heading "Verantwortung als Schicksal der Menschheit." See also Reinhold Niebuhr's treatment of the doctrine of original sin (not discussed by Baumann) in *The Nature and Destiny of Man*, Vol. I: *Human Nature* (New York: Scribners, 1964), 241-64, esp. 255-60, a section entitled, "Responsibility Despite Inevitability." In his recent study, H. Berkhof combines the ideas of fate and sin: *Christelijk geloof: Een inleiding tot de geloofsleer* (Nijkerk: Callenbach, 1973), 214-23. He distinguishes between sub-personal fate (evolutionary remnants) and supra-personal fate (historical-situational determinants) and combines both with the notions of guilt, freedom or responsibility in an extremely subtle way: he says that fate is the sub-personal background of guilt (220) that guilt and fate go "hand in hand" (221) and that sin is surrounded on all sides by fate without being absorbed by it (222). In a doctoral dissertation (written under the mentorship of Prof. H. Berkhof) J. Verburg elaborates the sub-human (natural-evolutionary) aspect of fate (*Adam: Een onderzoek naar de betekenis van de figuur van een eerste mens in het christelijk geloof* [Wageningen: Veenman, 1973]). Speaking in terms of natural science and theology, Verburg combines fate as evolutionary determinant with culpable responsibility as follows: "In view

self-evident factor, as is demonstrated by the syllogism: man is (originally) sinful; sin entails responsibility; responsibility entails freedom; hence "fallen" man remains free. But the conclusion, "man is free," appears to relativize the starting point, "man is sinful" — at least if this sinfulness is retained as *original* sin and is not reduced to a series of incidental missteps.

The status of "freedom" is crucial because it involves the question whether man stands in need merely of being coaxed — superficially by "example" or more profoundly by "situation" — to move in the right direction. Or is man's fundamental direction of life such that redirection by free self-determination is out of the question; is it so that an incisive redirection by means of the redeeming grace of Jesus Christ is necessary? That question, indirectly answered by the situational approach, reasserts itself powerfully in Vanneste's and Baumann's reinterpretation of original sin.

We have seen that, anthropologically, Vanneste proceeds from the myriad individual personal decisions that constitute human "history." Theologically, he posits the strict universality of personal sin as being the essential meaning of the doctrine of original sin. From his anthropological viewpoint there is no room for affirming such universality of personal sin, for from an *immanent* position within the realm of individual personal decisions one must maintain the contingent openness of an "either-or" situation. When — contrary to this contingency — Vanneste nonetheless maintains the strict universality of personal sin, he can do so only by forsaking the immanent position (*within* free personal decisions) and assuming a theologically *transcendent* position, i.e., a position above free personal decisions, the only position from which one can declare with absolute certainty that the first personal decision of every human being will be a sinful decision. In other words, the theologian posits an absolute "foreknowledge"[31] that his philosophical framework precludes: that which is anthropologically open

---

of the natural inclination to evil, all men will commit sin and become sinners; in view of their higher intelligence and their concomitant freedom, all men are responsible for and culpable on account of this sin. Hence reconcilliation in Christ is necessary for all without exception" (*ibid.*, 154).

By contrast, Berkouwer consistently dissociates the notion of fate from those of guilt and (original) sin (*Zonde*, I, 137-39; II, 300-302, 304, 310-11, 316-17, 318-19; *Sin*, 146-48, 520-22, 523-24, 529-32, 536-39).

31 This theological prescience is indirectly attested to by Labourdette when he asks whether Vanneste's contention that all men are virtual sinners means simply the *imputation* of one's *future* sins (M. M. Labourdette, "Anthropologie théologique et péché originel," *Revue Thomiste*, LXXXI (1973), 643-63. See also J. H. Walgrave's review in which he asks regarding the *ground* of the certainty which Vanneste posits (*Kultuurleven*, XXXVII, 411).

(free decisions) is theologically closed (sinful decisions). At this point, the problem of fate and freedom emerges: a move in the direction of freedom would jeopardize the universality of personal sins (the very nature of original sin, according to Vanneste); a move in the direction of fate ("absolute certainty") would jeopardize responsibility and thus the very notion of sin.[32]

The problem of fate and freedom is less central in Baumann's reinterpretation than in Vanneste's. This is due to two factors. In the first place, Baumann does not understand the doctrine of original sin exclusively in terms of the universality of personal sin. For him, this doctrine concerns primarily not the quantity (universality) but the quality of personal sin, namely, its depth dimension. From within the perspective of this depth dimension Baumann deals with the radicality, totality and universality of sin.[33] This concentration on the depth dimension of sin entails in principle a confessionally immanent position on the part of the theologian, i.e., from within the confessed actuality of this depth dimension, the doctrine of original sin is articulated.

In the second place, the problem of fate and freedom is held in abeyance by Baumann's implicit and explicit opposition to the idea of fate. His extensive critique of the empirical principle[34] must be understood as an implicit but nonetheless clear polemic against a fatalistic causalism that would explain (away) personal sin. Moreover, in explicit opposition to the threat of fatalism, Baumann emphasizes that the Christian message regarding sin entails precisely the liberation from the tragic view of man held by the ancients, liberation from "the stifling feeling of being at the mercy of an ineluctable fate or demonic powers."[35] In order to banish fate from the heart of a Christian confession of sin, Baumann centers original sin in the depth of man's responsibility. He does so by positing that the only cause of sin is one's own free decision, by understanding sin as a decision-event, as *Geschichte*.[36]

At that point the problem pointed out earlier emerges. If one maintains, as Baumann does, that sin is to be understood exclusively in terms of *Geschichte*, i.e., as a personal decision-event, does one not in fact proceed from the free decision of each individual as the basic given? And, if so, is it still possible to maintain that sin is so radical, total and original that it is impossible to revert to an underlying freedom? If sin in its depth is to be

32 See ch. VII, sec. C above.
33 See ch. VIII, sec. C, 2 above.
34 See *ibid.*, sec. B, 2, a above.
35 *Erbsünde,* 280; cf. 244, 276.
36 See ch. VIII, sec. C, 1 and 2, b above.

understood as decision-event, must it not be viewed as originating from and as constantly being borne by free dicision, so that *freedom* must be regarded as the radical, embracive and original given without which sin is no longer sin?

In Baumann's reinterpretation of original sin, this problem of the relationship between sin and freedom is obscured and even slips into the opposite problem of sin and fate when he posits that in Scripture sin is described as a *Faktum* behind which one cannot go,[37] as a reality that is "simply there,"[38] there from-the-beginning.[39] Although directed specifically against any recourse to an "empirical principle,"[40] Baumann's emphasis upon sin as being a groundless fact also reflects his understanding of sin as an individual decision-event beyond which no further reflection upon trans-individual relationships is possible. Or, insofar as such further reflection *is* possible, it is regarded as being either illigitimate or irrelevant. Placed within the context of Baumann's general approach, his description of sin as a fact that is simply there becomes problematical; for if this fact has the nature of a decision-event, it has as its origin the free decision of the individual and is not "simply there". This seems to warrant the conclusion that each individual instigates his own personal "fall" from his private "state of integrity." Baumann, however, cuts off all recourse to such a "beginning"[41] and instead affirms that sin is present from-the-beginning and posits fallen*ness* as *Faktum*. At that point *fact* congeals to yield *fate*. Indeed, because it manifests itself in the core of an intensified awareness of freedom, the quasi-fatalism of isolated *geschichtliche* facts is possibly even less bearable than the fatalism of the causal nexus embodied in the "empirical principle." Enclosed within the narrow limits of *Geschichte* and interpreted as radically sinful, human existence as such appears to be obliterated.

We have driven the problem emerging at the periphery of Baumann's understanding of original sin towards the center of his reinterpretation because that periphery poses a threat to the core. Moreover, as Schoonenberg pointed out[42] long before Baumann's reinterpretation and as Baumann's critics are presently pointing out,[43] an existential interpretation (with decision-event or *Geschichte* as its central category) provides too narrow a

37 *Erbsünde*, 239.
38 *Ibid.*, 246; cf. 247.
39 *Ibid.*, 257.
40 See ch. VIII, sec. B, 2, a above.
41 See *ibid.*, sec. C, 2, b.
42 See ch. III, sec. C, 1, b above.
43 See E. Schrofner, *ZKTh*, XCIII, 208; A. Stenzel, *ThuPh*, XLVI, 562-63; C. Dumont, *NRTh*, XCV, 904.

base for understanding the full implications of the Christian message of sin and salvation.

D. HISTORY, SIN AND SALVATION

Is there a way ouf of the fate-freedom problem that hovers over the doctrine of original sin? Perhaps not. Even if there is, this epilogue does not pretend to present a solution, much less *the* solution. For a "possible perspective," however, a search for a correct way *into* the problem suffices.

Even this modest search, however, proves to be immensely difficult. This difficulty is due to the fact that, as was suggested earlier, the dissecting knife of abstraction is indeed inadequate and inappropriate at the deepest level of human life. The doctrine of original sin is in essence a confession regarding that deepest level, a confession of one's original enslavement in sin and one's consequent need of radical redemption in Jesus Christ. If this understanding of the doctrine of original sin and the relativizing of abstraction at this level is correct, one must grant that many of the (natural-biological) categories in the traditional formulations of the doctrine of original sin are inadequate insofar as they represent quasi-scientific, neutral descriptions of empirical states of affairs. By the same token, however, one must constantly remain open to the very real possibility that modern categories, such as "situation," "freedom," "Geschichte," "person," insofar as they represent products of conceptual abstraction and isolation, are equally inadequate for fathoming the depth of the reality of sin and salvation. The key question with respect to the contemporary categories of reinterpretation is whether they leave the trans-individual matrix as well as the integral unity of human life intact. One cannot fail to observe that the awareness of the integral historical unity of mankind to which the scriptural view of man's solidarity in sin and salvation as well as the ecclesiastical doctrine of original sin bear witness is lacking in both the personal and in the situational reinterpretation of original sin. This conclusion appears to be unwarranted, for the situationalists attempt to capture this unity in the notion of situational *Existential*; as for the personalists, Vanneste understands this unity in terms of the similarity of the religious situation of all men[44] and Baumann formulates it in terms of an "identity of the personal essence of all men."[45] The situationalists, however, attempt to understand this unity in abstraction from the deepest level of history, the religious direction of man's life, while

---

44 See ch. VII, n. 172 above.
45 *Erbsünde*, 263.

Baumann and Vanneste divest this unity of its temporal-historical dimension, so that this unity evaporates in an "ahistorical abstractness"[46] or disintegrates in a multitude of individual acts.[47]

To obtain a proper perspective on the doctrine of original sin, it is necessary to probe beyond a conception of history that is torn by the tension between situational *Existential* and its antipode, freedom (the situationalists), or caught in the dilemma *Historie-Geschichte* (Baumann), or dissolved into countless individual acts (Vanneste). At that deeper level, history presents itself as the embracive movement of creation through time, a movement in which man is communally involved and in which he is called to live before God in righteousness and love. This integral notion of history — though necessarily circumscribed in formal terms — is not meant as an abstract concept but as a notion that has reference to the only concrete reality we know: creaturely reality — specifically, history — in its decisive relationship to God.[47b] Applied to the doctrine of original sin, this notion of history confronts us with the issue of the religious direction of human life apart from redemption in Christ. One must answer the question as to how and where one stands apart from redemption in Jesus Christ: in neutral freedom at the juncture where the negative direction of Adamic history and the positive direction effected in Christ meet; or in "freedom" that is decisively qualified by being taken up in a directedness away from God, "freedom" in need of radical *liberation* in Jesus Christ.

This question is answered in various ways in the situational and in the personal approach. The idea that in and of himself man stands at the juncture of two roads is implied in the situational approach to (original) sin and salvation. The privation of grace through Adam and the presence of grace in Christ are conceived of as two *Existentialia* interior to man; but in his innermost

---

46 In criticism of Baumann's thought Schrofner speaks of "die drohende Gefahr einer geschichtslosen Abstraktheit als Folge des existentialen Verständnisses der Erbsünde..." (*ZKTh*, XCIII, 208) and Stenzel of a "geschichtssperrige Abstraktheit" (*ThuPh*, XLVI, 563). Baumann himself is aware of this problem, as is evidenced by the section in his book entitled, "Wider subjektivistische Theozentrik und die Flucht in das Transemperische" (*Erbsünde*, 273-76; cf. *ibid.*, 268, 272). With respect to the matter of "beginnings" he concedes, "Eine bessere und verständlichere Lösung dieses Problems wird zu geben sein, wenn es gelingt, das Verhältnis von Historizität und Geschichtlichkeit befriedigend zu bestimmen." He adds, however, "Diese Unsicherheit berührt aber nicht die grundsätzliche Richtung des Gedankens" (*ibid.*, 283).

47 See ch. VII, n. 171 above.

47b M. C. Smit calls attention to the decisive significance of such a notion of history not only for the philosophy of history but also for historiography (*De verhouding van Christendom en historie,* esp. chs. IV, V and VII; see also his *Cultuur en heil*).

being man stands in freedom, in a "sittliche *Entscheidungssituation,"* a "dialectische *Freiheitssituation."*[48] The idea that, left to himself, man walks on the Adamic road is most closely approximated by Baumann. Due to the gap between individual-personal *Geschichte* and general-empirical *Historie,* however, the metaphors referring to direction through time — "walking" and "road" — are hardly appropriate, for man is viewed as *standing* at the *point* of decision-event, a point at which man in fact decides negatively. The notion of history as the integral movement of creation through time is elaborated with respect to "salvation history" by Schoonenberg and Rahner in their articulation of a grand and all-encompassing notion of cosmic-human development.[49] Unfortunately, the integral and religious nature of history is obscured 1) by the disintegrating effect of the polarity between situation and freedom, 2) by the conception of original sin as a privation of grace rather than as a misdirection of human life, and 3) by the dominance of an ontological conception of grace, so that grace is viewed primarily as an elevating power, specifically, as the motor of the "ascent" of salvation history.[50] The polarity of freedom and situation obscures the integrality, the deeper unity of history; the conception of grace (and its privation) obscures the religious nature of history and the deadly struggle between the enslaving power of sin and the radical liberation in Christ.

To avoid both the situational abstraction of original sin from the religious depth dimension, as well as the personal-existential isolation of this dimension from concrete history, an integral religious notion of history is

48 *SM,* I, 1114; cf. 1109.
49 See ch. II, sec. C, 1 above.
50 We are not suggesting that this idea of salvation history as "ascent" necessarily involves an optimistic idea of progress. As was pointed out, Schoonenberg conceives of the "history of sin" as a simultaneous movement of "descent" (see pp. 9-10 [ch. V] above). Nevertheless, the maintenance of the idea of "ascent," though avowedly based on faith in God's grace (see p. 10 [ch. V] above), represents an unwarranted transposition of an evolutionary ontology to the course of human history *coram Deo.* Within Rahner's and Schoonenberg's conception, that transposition is entirely legitimate, of course, by virtue of an ontological conception of grace. With respect to Rahner's view of salvation history, Manfred Köhnlein poses a highly significant question: "Wie kann dann die Dogmatik noch die Heilsgeschichte als eine wirkliche, ablaufende *Geschichte* beschreiben, wenn sie sofort die Konzipierung alles Geschaffenen auf Christus hin und die Gipfelung des Aufstiegs aller Wirklichkeiten in Ihm an den Anfang ihrer systematischen Betrachtungen setzt und dann erst lange hernach auf die Wirklichkeit der sündigen Welt und der entlaufenen Schöpfung eingeht, die den Zorn Gottes verdient hätte? " (*Was bringt das Sakrament? Disputation mit Karl Rahner* [Göttingen: Vandenhoeck und Ruprecht, 1971], 45). For an incisive analysis and critique of the idea of progress linked as it is in Roman Catholic thought to the notion of grace discussed above, see M. C. Smit, *De verhouding van Christendom en historie,* 106-35).

needed: *integral* in that it points to a unity beneath the polarity of *Geschichte* and *Historie,* on the one hand, or of freedom and situation, on the other; *religious* in that it points to the decisive directedness of human life toward or away from God. This notion of history makes it possible to do justice to the reality of sin as enslaving power, to the fact that the individual does not appear on the stage of history as a free subject in confrontation with evil. Rather, *Sin* presents itself as *subject.*[51] Sin, with death in its wake, "entered into the world."[52] That entry at the beginning of human history had an "embracive historical effect:"[53] death reigned "because all have sinned"[54] and "sin reigned in death."[55] Having established its historical bridgehead, sin need not re-enter history ever anew to gain access to and dominion over each subsequent individual. Accordingly, the individual cannot be summoned to "stand up and fight" from within the bastion of an as yet undirected freedom.[56] Because sin has established its enslaving dominion historically, it is effectively countered only by acts which are equally historical, the death and resurrection of Christ, which inaugurate the reign of "grace through righteousness."[57] Those redemptive acts in Christ, too, have their effect historically, in the integral and religious sense of that term: "we died *with* Christ" and through His resurrection may "walk in newness of life" as "servants of righteousness"[58] — the liberating break-through of the "new

---

51 Käsemann points out that in Ro 5:12-21 Paul does not view man primarily as the subject but as the "object," "projection," "manifestation" or "exponent" of history (Ernst Käsemann, *An die Römer* ["Handbuch zum Neuen Testament," 8a; Tübingen: Mohr, 1973], 140-45). The inadequacy of each of the terms used to express Paul's view is offset by Käsemann's statement that insofar as the concept "existence" must at all be used to interpret Paul's thought, this concept must have reference to the concretization "einer Herschaftssphäre im personalen Bereich" (*ibid.,* 141). Accordingly, Käsemann argues that although Ro 5:12d represents a shift within the overall argumentation in vss. 12-21, this shift does not involve a correction or attenuation but a deepening of the scope of doom (*Unheil*) and a manifestation of the universal enslavement of mankind to sin (*ibid.,* 139-40).
52 Ro 5:12.
53 Egon Brandenburger, *Adam und Christus: Exegetisch-religions-geschichtliche Untersuchung zu Röm. 5:12-21 (I Kor. 15)* (Neukirchen: Neukirchener Verlag, 1962), 241; cf. 245. Cf. J. M. Hasselaar, *Erfzonde en vrijheid* ('s-Gravenhage: Boekencentrum, 1953), 338: "Als historisch-bovenhistorische grootheid is de zonde een essentiële factor, die de gehele geschiedenis van individu en gemeenschap richt en bepaalt."
54 Ro 5:12; cf. vss. 14, 17.
55 Ro 5:21.
56 Cf. Käsemann (re Ro 5:12-21): "Es geht um eine alte und eine neue Welt, in denen niemand neutral steht und für ein Drittes optieren kann" (*ibid.,* 127; cf. 139-41).
57 Ro 5:21; cf. vs. 17.
58 Ro 6:1-11, 13, 16-23.

creation."[59] Only from within the history of the radical break of dying with Christ and the break-through of His resurrection can one be meaningfully summoned to "stand up and fight."[60] For through this double death and resurrection (Christ and ours) the reign of grace, life and righteousness is inaugurated. At the same time the deadly historical power of sin becomes fully manifest – most astoundingly and painfully in our strange willingness to serve this alien power.

As is implicit in the preceding description, it is impossible to do full justice to the historical power of sin without speaking of man's inner enslavement in sin. Sin exerts its deepest power in such enslavement. For that reason it is impossible to translate the biblical notion of the power of sin adequately in terms of situation[61] (especially when this situation is understood purely negatively as the privation of sanctifying grace). For this "situation" is obtained by a double abstraction: first, "freedom" is abstracted from the central direction of man's life; then, this freedom is abstracted from the structural coherence of man's stance-in-the-world. Only by way of this abstraction can the concept "situation" as pure *Existential* be obtained.

If the power of *sin* is to be articulated, a notion such as "enslaved will" appears to be indispensable. Although this notion is given a central place by other authors,[62] P. Smulders' comments on this subject are especially instructive for our purposes because they are made from within the contemporary Roman Catholic discussion of original sin with which we have been dealing. After an appreciative presentation of Schoonenberg's situation theory, Smulders introduces the notion of a deep unwillingness of the will as being essential to the doctrine of original sin. He considers the situational approach "from without," as he calls it, helpful in that it provides the possibility of rendering original sin concretely visible; nevertheless, he contends that one must go deeper to do full justice to this doctrine.[63] The doctrine of original

---

59 II Cor 5: 14-17.
60 Cf. Ro 6:12-23. See also Käsemann, 146.
61 See Schoonenberg, *Geloof,* IV, 157-58, 181-82; *Ex Auditu Verbi,* 270. Weger, *Theologie der Erbsünde,* 139, 140-42, 147-48.
62 See, e.g., Pierre Grelot, *Péché originel et rédemption; examinés à partir de l'Épître aux Romains:* essay théologique (Paris: Desclée: 1973), 106-13; and Paul Ricoeur who summarizes his discussion of the symbols of evil in terms of the "enslaved will": *Finitude et culpabilité,* Vol. II: *La symbolique du mal* (Paris: Aubier, 1960), 145-50; see also his essay, "Le 'péché originel': étude de signification,"*Le conflit des interprétations: essais d'herméneutique* [Paris: Editions du Seuil, 1969], 265-82).
63 P. Smulders, *Het visioen van Teilhard de Chardin: Poging tot theologische waardering* (5th rev. ed.; Brugge: Desclée de Brouwer, 1966), 257; *La vision de Teilhard de Chardin: Essai de réflection theologique,* trans. (from the 3d Dutch edition) Augustin

sin, he says, is an articulation of the deep roots through which evil nourishes itself.[64] The core of original sin lies deeply concealed in man's heart: "in concupiscence and, even deeper, in a turning-away from the God-given goal."[65] This *aversio* from God is said to lie in the will itself[66] or, more precisely, in the heart.[67] The deepest core of original sin, according to Smulders, is constituted by the fact that "anterior to every personal choice, embracing it and keeping it imprisoned, a kind of 'unwillingness' to love God lies deeply ensconced in man's heart."[68] This is man's enslavement[69] and his "spiritual death."[70]

It is obvious that the introduction of a notion such as a deep enslavement of the will does not solve the problem of fate and freedom. In fact, in some ways such notions render that problem even more acute. This becomes clear when Smulders characterizes this enslavement and unwillingness not only as the deepest but also as the *most mysterious* core of original sin.[71] In his view this mystery concerns the fact that sin is spontaneous and voluntary; yet it is not simply a free act but an expression of slavery;[72] it involves the coincidence of moral-religious *powerlessness* and *unwillingness*, a powerlessness that is simultaneously an unwillingness.[73] In this context the term

---

Kerkvoorde and Christian d'Armagnac (2d rev. ed.; Paris: Desclée de Brouwer, 1965), 186-87; *The Design of Teilhard de Chardin: An Essay in Theological Reflection*, trans. (from the French translation) Arthur Gibson (Westminster, Md.: Newman Press, 1967), 175. When Smulders characterizes the situational treatment of original sin as an approach "from without" and as one in which original sin is understood as being "merely an external situation" (*ibid.*), one can anticipate the accusation that Smulders has misrepresented Schoonenberg's interpretation. Given the viewpoint, however, from which Smulders assesses the situational approach, namely, the viewpoint of the will itself, the incisive criticism implied in the above characterizations holds also for Schoonenberg's reinterpretation of original sin (see ch. IV, secs. A and B, 1 above; see also n. 73 below).

64 *Visioen*, 257; *La vision*, 187; *Design*, 175.
65 *Ibid.*
66 *Visioen*, 258; *La vision*, 187; *Design* 176. Cf. Grelot, 164.
67 *Visioen*, 257-59; *La vision*, 186-88; *Design*, 175-76.
68 *Visioen*, 259; *La vision*, 188; *Design*, 176.
69 *Ibid.*
70 *Visioen*, 260, *La vision*, 189; *Design*, 176.
71 *Visioen*, 259; *La vision*, 188; *Design*, 176.
72 *Ibid.*
73 *Visioen*, 260n; *La vision*, 188, n. 57; *Design*, 294, n. 57. The divergence between Smulders' "interior" and Schoonenberg's situational understanding of enslavement (see n. 63 above) becomes manifest when Schoonenberg, commenting on Smulders' use of the term "unwillingness," states that he wishes to clarify this "unwillingness" (*on-wil*) by calling it "impotence" (*on-macht*; "Erfzonde, I," *DO-C, 63-44* [March 29, 1963], 8). This clarification is tantamount to a negation of Smulders' attempt to understand original sin in terms of a powerlessness that is at the same time an unwillingness.

"mystery" is appropriate only insofar as it points to the fact that conceptualization is not an independent source of truth regarding man's condition but is subservient to the primary givens of life as illumined by the gospel. With respect to the doctrine of original sin, these basic givens comprise, as Schoonenberg has demonstrated extensively,[74] man's historical solidarity in sin[75] and, as Smulders has pointed out, the deep-seated unwillingness of the will by which man turns away from God.

The paralyzing fatalism that threatens the basic intention of the doctrine of original sin can be withstood only by taking one's point of departure from *within* the depth dimension of sin. The historical power of sin that comes to expression in our inner solidarity and enslavement in sin does not jeopardize personal responsibility if this power is not beheld from a transcendent, spectator position but confessed from the immanent position of the actuality of personal sin.[76] In other words, the historical, trans-(not simply "supra-") personal power and personal enslavement in sin are mutually inclusive: enslavement is real within this reign of sin and, vice versa, the historical power of sin holds its sway in enslavement. This circle of death is broken not by "freedom" but by the liberating grace revealed in the death and resurrection of Jesus Christ.[77]

At this point the question arises whether expressions such as "religious direction," "power of sin," and "enslavement in sin," are introduced at the expense of the conceptual clarity attained in the situational approach and of the admirable existential simplicity of the personal approach. Indeed. If that clarity and that simplicity are used as criteria, the present search for "possible *perspectives*" is of no avail. It must be kept in mind, however, that neither conceptual clarity nor personal-existential simplicity as such provide perspective. Perspective concerns interrelationships within concrete reality

---

74 See ch. I, sec. A, 1 above.

75 For an interpretation of a specific historical situation in terms of the solidarity in sin expressed in the doctrine of original sin, see Ilse Bertinetti, *Krisis des Erbsündendogmas: Eine Untersuchung zur theologischen Gegenwartsproblematik von Gesamtschuld und ethischer Verantwortung* (Berlin: Habilitationsschrift, Theologische Fakultät der Humboldt-Universität, 1970). Regarding solidarity in guilt, see also A. J. Rasker *et al.*, *Problemen rondom de schuld* (een publicatie van het Nederlands Gesprek Centrum; Baarn: Bosch en Keuning, 1973), 42-45, 49-52, 56-58, 65-67.

76 This dominant theme of Berkouwer's penetrating study on the doctrine of original sin comes to expression in his strong emphasis on the guilt character of original sin (*De Zonde*, II, 207-25; *Sin*, 424-45). See also Smulders, 237-38.

77 Berkouwer frequently points out that it is the revelation of God's *grace* that demonstrates the irreconcilability of fate and sin (see *De Zonde*, II, 298-99, 300-302, 304, 318; *Sin*, 518, 520-22, 524, 538).

and a central — invisible — point in which this reality finds its coherence and meaning. The situationalists are rightly concerned about concreteness; but by interpreting the human condition in terms of the privation of sanctifying grace and by attempting to understand that condition situationally, as *Existential*, they abandon the central point of coherence, the religious direction of history. As a result, both perspective and potential concreteness are lost. In the personal approach a potential point of coherence is prominent but, because this point is enclosed within personal decisions (Vanneste) or decision-events (Baumann), trans-personal reality — specifically, history — is lost from view. And again, the result, though for different reasons, is the same: a loss in perspective and concreteness.

Unfortunately, this loss cannot be recovered by simply combining the potential concreteness of the situational approach with the central point of coherence of the personal approach. Such a combination is rendered impossible due to the opposite philosophical and theological approaches that are involved. True, the situational and personal approaches to original sin take place within a common philosophical-anthropological ellipse with antipodal foci, one of which can be designated as "person," "freedom," or "Geschichte," and the other as "situation," "Existential" or "Historie." The situationalists and the personalists part ways, however, by choosing opposite foci as the center of reinterpretation. Accordingly their reinterpretation of original sin takes place within mutually exclusive circles. The mutual inclusiveness and exclusiveness of the two approaches may be visualized with the aid of the following diagram:

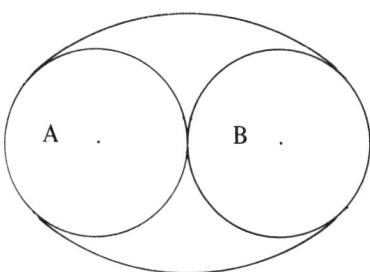

	Ellipse	=	common philosophical framework
	Foci	=	antipodal centers of reinterpretation
	Circles	=	mutually exclusive reinterpretations of original sin

Focus A	=	situational *Existential*	Focus B	=	person, freedom or *Geschichte*
Circle A	=	privation of grace	Circle B	=	universality or depth dimension of personal sin

Despite this common ellipse,[78] a synthesis of the personal and the situational interpretations cannot yield true perspective due to the philosophical polarity and the theological incompatibility depicted by the circles. A fruitful confrontation of these alternatives demands a critical discussion of the fundamental choices which underlie that theological and philosophical contrariety.

If that confrontation is to yield perspective, the question concerning the religious direction of man's historical existence and, with that, the perennial question concerning the meaning of Christ's coming must be given a central place. Real *perspective* is then possible because, though *anchored in* a central point of convergence, "religious direction" cannot be *enclosed within* that point. The comprehensive and concrete perspective disclosed from that invisible point is sketched in rough outline by Smulders. He points out that the directedness away from God that is deeply rooted in man's heart or will yields a world and a society in which pleasure, possessions, prestige and power are elevated to absolute values.[79] Not designed to carry the burden of this "absolute" weight, this overtaxed world threatens to collapse into meaninglessness, as all creatures, including one's fellow-man, are sacrificed to the salvation promised by synthetic gods.[80] A world results in which creaturely values do not serve the true well-being of creation but, like an opaque wall, close off the horizon that points to God.[81] Only the liberating redirection historically inaugurated in Jesus Christ breaks through this stifling atmosphere of death.[82] In view of the incisive, embracive and decisive significance of the "religious direction" of life, reflection at this fundamental level opens up a deeper and wider perspective for the ongoing discussion of the doctrine of original sin.

---

78 It must be kept in mind, of course, that in drawing this ellipse we have left the specific way in which a particular theologian elaborates the foci out of consideration (think, e.g., of Rahner's elaboration of the ideas of person and *Existential* in terms of his transcendental anthropology).

79 *Visioen*, 249-51; *La vision*, 181-83; *Design*, 170-71.

80 *Visioen*, 248-53; *La vision*, 181-84; *Design*, 169-73.

81 *Visioen*, 252; *La vision*, 183; *Design*, 172.

82 H. J. Heering expresses this insight concisely and profoundly: "To change evil into righteousness – that only forgiveness can accomplish. Forgiveness, not as palliation but as overpowering benevolence" (*Over het boze – als macht en als werkelijkheid* [Meppel: Boom 1974], 147).

SELECTED BIBLIOGRAPHY

For more complete bibliographies see Urs Baumann, *Erbsünde?* and Ferdinand Dexinger *et al., Ist Adam an allem schuld?*

Aanvulling bij de Nieuwe Katechismus. Op last van de Kardinalencommissie samengesteld door Ed. Dhanis en J. Visser. 2d ed. Hilversum: Paul Brand, 1969.
    Trans.: *The Supplement* (see below.)

Adam, Alfred. "Das Fortwirken des Manichäismus bei Augustin," *Zeitschrift für Kirchengeschichte,* LXIX (1958), 1-25.

——— "Der manichäische Ursprung der Lehre von der zwei Reichen bei Augustin," *Theologische Literaturzeitung,* LXXVII (1952), 385-90.

Angelius (O.F.M. Cap.). *Algemene zijnsleer.* Edited and completed by Martinianus (O.F.M. Cap.). ("Bibliotheek van Thomistische Wijsbegeerte.") Utrecht: Het Spectrum, 1947.

Aquinas, Thomas. *Summa Theologiae.* Cum Textu ex Recensione Leonina. Turin: Marrietti [1962-63].
    Trans.: Anton C. Pegis (ed.). *Basic Writings of Saint Thomas Aquinas.* 2 vols. New York: Random House, 1945.

Aurelius Augustinus: Der Lehrer der Gnade. Schriften gegen die Pelagianer/ Semipelagianer. Edited by Adalbero Kunzelman and Adolar Zumkeller. Würzburg: Augustinus-Verlag, 1955–.

Bakker, J. T. "Zonde en schuld," *Rondom het Woord,* XI (1969), 392-99.

Bakker, L. "Schoonenberg's theologie: Spiegel van onze eigen ontwikkeling?" *Tijdschrift voor Theologie,* XI (1971), 353-82.

Baumann, Urs. *Erbsünde? Ihr traditionelles Verständnis in der Krise heutiger Theologie.* ("Ökumenische Forschungen.") Freiburg: Herder, 1970.

Bavinck, H. *Gereformeerde Dogmatiek.* Vol. III. 5th ed. Kampen: Kok, 1967.

Benz, Ernst. *Schöpfungsglaube und Endzeiterwartung: Antwort auf Teilhard de Chardins Theologie der Evolution.* München: Nymphenburger, 1965.
> Trans.: *Evolution and Christian Hope: Man's Concept of the Future from the Early Fathers to Teilhard de Chardin.* Translated by Heinz G. Frank. Garden City, N.Y.: Doubleday, 1966.

Berkhof, H. *Christelijk geloof: Een inleiding tot de geloofsleer.* Nijkerk: Callenbach, 1973.

Berkouwer, G. C. *Conflict met Rome.* 3d ed. Kampen: Kok, 1955.

——— *De Heilige Schrift.* 2 vols. ("Dogmatische Studiën.") Kampen: Kok, 1966 and 1967.
> Trans.: *Holy Scripture.* ("Studies in Dogmatics.") Translated by Jack B. Rogers. Grand Rapids: Eerdmans, 1975.

——— "Identiteit of conflict? " *Philosophia Reformata,* XXI (1956), 1-43.

——— *De kerk, I: Eenheid en katholiciteit.* ("Dogmatische Studiën.") Kampen: Kok, 1970.

——— *De mens het beeld Gods.* ("Dogmatische Studiën.") Kampen: Kok, 1957.
> Trans.: *Man: The Image of God.* ("Studies in Dogmatics.") Translated by Dirk W. Jellema. Grand Rapids: Eerdmans, 1962.

——— *Nabetrachting op het Concilie.* Kampen: Kok, 1968.

——— *De sacramenten.* ("Dogmatische Studiën.") Kampen: Kok, 1954.
> Trans.: *The Sacraments.* ("Studies in Dogmatics.") Translated by Hugo Bekker. Grand Rapids: Eerdmans, 1969.

——— *Vatikaans Concilie en nieuwe theologie.* Kampen: Kok, 1964.
> Trans.: *The Second Vatican Council and the New Catholicism.* Translated by Lewis B. Smedes. Grand Rapids: Eerdmans, 1965.

——— *Verdienste of genade: Een centraal hoofdstuk uit de geschiedenis der grote controvers.* Kampen: Kok, 1958.

——— *De zonde.* Vol. I: *Oorsprong en kennis der zonde.* Vol. II: *Wezen en verbreiding der zonde.* ("Dogmatische Studiën.") Kampen, Kok, 1958 and 1960.
> Trans.: *Sin* ("Studies in Dogmatics.") Translated by Philip C. Holtrop. Grand Rapids: Eerdmans, 1971.

Bertinetti, Ilse. *Krisis des Erbsündendogmas: Eine Untersuchung zur theologischen Gegenwartsproblematik von Gesamtschuld und ethischer Verantwortung.* Unpublished Habilitationsschrift, Theologische Fakultät der Humboldt-Universität, Berlin, 1970.

Betty, Christa Campbell. "Piet Schoonenberg's Theory of Original Sin," *Thought*, XLV (1970), 83-101.

Bless, W. *Witboek over de Nieuwe Katechismus*. Utrecht: Ambo, 1969.

Boyer, Charles. *Handboek der wijsbegeerte*. Vol. I. Translated and edited by H. G. Rambonnet. 's-Hertogenbosch: Malmberg, [1947].

Brandenburger, Egon. *Adam und Christus: Exegetisch-religionsgeschichtliche Untersuchung zu Röm. 5:12-21 (I Kor. 15)*. Neukirchen: Neukirchener Verlag, 1962.

Brown, Peter. "Pelagius and His Supporters: Aims and Environment," *The Journal of Theological Studies*, XIX (1968), 93-114.

Bruna, M. and Schoonenberg, P. "Tweegesprek over het ontstaan der zondigheid," *Tijdschrift voor Theologie*, IV (1964), 54-79.

Burck, Erich (ed.). *Die Idee des Fortschritts: Neun Vorträge über Wege und Grenzen des Fortschrittsglaubens*. München: Beck, 1963.

Bury, J. B. *The Idea of Progress: An Inquiry into Its Growth and Origin*. New York, Dover Publications, 1955.

Concilium Tridentinum: Diariorum, Actorum, Epistularum, Tractatuum. Nova Collectio. Edited by Societas Goerresiana. Freiburg: Herder, 1901-63.

Conner, J. L. "Original Sin: Contemporary Approaches," *Theological Studies*, XXIX (1968), 215-40.

Daly, Gabriel. "Theological Models in the Doctrine of Original Sin," *The Heythrop Journal*, XIII (1972), 121-42.

De Grijs, F. J. A. "De erfzonde," *Bijdragen*, XXXI (1970), 114-36.

Denzinger, Henricus and Schönmetzer, Adolfus. (eds.) *Enchiridion Symbolorum: Definitionum et Declarationum de Rebus. Fidei et Morum*. 32d ed. Freiburg: Herder, 1963.
Trans.: *The Church Teaches: Documents of the Church in English Translation*. Translated by John F. Clarkson *et al*. (from Denzinger, 29th ed.) London: B. Herder, 1955.

Dexinger, Ferdinand, *et al. Ist Adam an allem schuld? Erbsünde oder Sündenverflochtenheit?* Innsbruck: Tyrolia-Verlag, 1971.

Dictionaire de Théologie Catholique. Edited by A. Vacant, E. Mangenot and E. Amann. Paris: Librairie Letouzey et Ané, 1930-50.

The Documents of Vatican II. Edited by Walter M. Abbott. London: Geoffrey Chapman, 1967.

Dunn, Mary Saint Anne. *The Unity of Man and the Doctrine of Original Sin.* Ann Arbor, Mich.: University Microfilms, 1967.

Ecclesia Docens: Pauselijke documenten voor onze tijd. [text and translation]. Hilversum: Gooi en Sticht, 1939—.

Echternach, Helmut. *Die lutherische Erbsündenlehre— als ökumenische Verheissung.* Amsterdam: Rodopi, 1973.

Eicher, Peter. *Die anthropologische Wende: Karl Rahners philosophischer Weg vom Wesen des Menschen zur personalen Existenz.* ("Dokiminion," Vol. 1.) Fribourg: Universitätsverlag, 1970.

Egan, Robert James. *New Directions in the Doctrine of Original Sin.* Ann Arbor, Mich.: University Microfilms, 1973.

Enchiridion Biblicum: Documenta Ecclesiastica Sacram Scripturam Spectantia. Auctoritate Pontificae Commissionis de Re Biblica Edita. 4th ed. Rome: Arnodo, 1961.

Fiolet, H. A. M. "De erfzonde als verbondsmysterie," *Werkgenootschap van Katholieke Theologen in Nederland, Jaarboek, 1963-64,* 53-91.

Fischer, Klaus P. *Der Mensch als Geheimnis: Die Anthropologie Karl Rahners.* ("Ökumenische Forschungen.") Freiburg: Herder, 1974.

Freundorfer, Joseph. *Erbsünde und Erbtod beim Apostel Paulus: Eine religionsgeschichtliche und exegetische Untersuchung über Römerbrief 5:12-21.* ("Neutestamentliche, Abhandlungen.") Münster: Aschendorffschen Verlagsbuchhandlung, 1927.

Gaudel, A. "Péché originel," *Dictionaire de théologie catholique,* Vol. XII, 275-606.

Geerlings, W. "Zur Frage des Nachwirkens des Manichäismus in der Theologie Augustins," *Zeitschrift für katholische Theologie,* XCIII (1971), 45-60.

Grelot, Pierre. *Péché originel et rédemption — examinés à partir de l'Epître aux Romains: Essay théologique.* Paris: Desclée, 1973.

Greshake, Gisbert. *Gnade als konkrete Freiheit: Eine Untersuchung zur Gnadenlehre des Pelagius.* Mainz: Matthias-Grünewald-Verlag, 1972.

Gross, J. *Geschichte des Erbsündendogmas: Ein Beitrag zur Geschichte des Problems vom Ursprung des Übels.* 4 vols. München: Reinhardt, 1960-72.

——— "Katholische Erbsündentheologie heute," *Zeitschrift für Religions- und Geistesgeschichte,* XXII (1970), 375-77.

——— "Ein neuer Erbsündenbegriff," *Zeitschrift für Religions- und Geistesgeschichte,* XXVI (1974), 68-74.

Grossouw, W. "Enkele gegevens omtrent de tegenwoordige situatie van de katholieke bijbelwetenschap," *Documentatie Centrum Concilie,* no. 21 (Nov. 8, 1962).

——— "Korte voorgeschiedenis van de hedendaagse katholieke bijbelwetenschap," *Documentatie Centrum Concilie,* no. 20 (Nov. 8, 1962).

Gutwenger, E. "Die Erbsünde und das Konzil von Trient," *Zeitschrift für katholische Theologie,* XCIX (1967), 433-46.

Haag, Herbert. *Biblische Schöpfungslehre und kirchliche Erbsündenlehre.* ("Stuttgarter Bibelstudien," 10). 4th ed. Stuttgart: Katholisches Bibelwerk, 1968.
Trans.: *Is Original Sin in Scripture?* Translated by Dorothy Thompson. New York: Sheed and Ward, 1969.

——— "Die hartnäckige Erbsünde: Überlegungen zu einigen Neuerscheinungen," *Theologische Quartalschrift,* CL (1970), 358-66, 436-56; CLI (1971), 70-86.

——— "The Original Sin Discussion, 1966-1971," *Journal of Ecumenical Studies,* X (1973), 259-89.

——— "Ein Verfahren der Glaubenskongregation," *Theologische Quartalschrift,* CLIII (1973), 184-92.

——— "Zur Diskussion um das Problem der 'Erbsünde,' " *Theologische Quartalschrift,* CXLIX (1969), 86-94.

Hamilton, William. "New Thinking on Original Sin," *Herders Correspondence,* IV (1967), 135-41.

Hasselaar, J. M. *Erfzonde en vrijheid.* 's-Gravenhage: Boekencentrum, 1953.

Haubst, Rudolf. "Was bleibt von der 'Erbsünde'? Zur aktuellen Diskussion um 'Ursünde' und 'allgemeine Sündigkeit' bzw. 'Mitsündigkeit.' " *Trierer theologische Zeitschrift,* LXXXIII (1974), 214-31.

Heering, H. J. *Over het boze – als macht en werkelijkheid.* Meppel: Boom, 1974.

Heidegger, Martin. *Being and Time.* Translated by John Macquarrie and Edward Robinson. New York: Harper and Row, 1962.

Herders Theologisches Taschenlexikon. 8 vols. Edited by Karl Rahner. Freiburg: Herder, 1972-73.

Jacquin, M. "A quelle date apparaît le terme 'Semipélagien'? " *Revue des Sciences Philosophiques et Théologiques,* I (1907), 506-508.

Jedin, Hubert. *Geschichte des Konzils von Trient.* Vol. II. Freiburg: Herder, 1957.

Käsemann, Ernst. *An die Römer* ("Handbuch zum Neuen Testament," 8a.) Tübingen: Mohr, 1973.

Kelly, J. N. D. *Early Christian Doctrines*. 3d ed. London: Adam and Charles Black, 1965.

Köhler, W. *Dogmengeschichte als Geschichte des christlichen Selbstbewusstseins: Von den Anfängen bis zur Reformation*. 2d ed. revised. Zürich: Niehans, 1943.

Köhnlein, Manfred. *Was bringt das Sakrament? Disputation mit Karl Rahner*. Göttingen: Vandenhoeck und Ruprecht, 1971.

Kors, J. B. *La justice primitive et le péché originel d'après S. Thomas*. ("Bibliothèque Thomiste," II.) Kain: Le Saulchoir, 1922.

Kreling, G., et al. *Genade en kerk: Studies ten dienste van het gesprek Rome-Reformatie*. Utrecht: Het Spectrum, 1953.

Krüger, Gerhard. *Freiheit und Weltverwaltung: Aufsätze zur Philosophie der Geschichte*. Freiburg: Karl Alber, 1958.

Kuitert, H. M. "Erfzonde," in *Altijd bereid tot verantwoording* (A. J. Besselaar, et al.; 2d ed. rev.; Aalten: de Graafschap, 1966), 106-13.

Labourdette, M. M. "Anthropologie théologique et péché originel," *Revue Thomiste*, LXXXI (1973), 643-63.

――― *Le péché originel et les origines de l'homme*. Paris: Alsatia, 1953.

Landgraf, A. M. *Dogmengeschichte der Frühscholastik*. 8 vols. Regensburg: Friedrich Pustet, 1952-56.

Lehman, Karl. "Theologische Portraits: Karl Rahner," in *Bilanz der Theologie im 20. Jahrhundert*. Bd. IV: *Bahnbrechende Theologen* (Edited by Herbert Vorgrimler and Robert Vander Gucht; Freiburg: Herder, 1970), 143-81.

Lengsfeld, Peter. *Adam und Christus: Die Adam-Christus Typologie im Neuen Testament und ihre Verwendung bei M. Scheeben und Karl Barth* ("Koinonia," IX.) Essen: Ludgerus Verlag, 1965.

Lexikon für Theologie und Kirche. 11 vols. Edited by J. Höfer and Karl Rahner. 2d ed. Freiburg: Herder, 1957-67.

Lexikon für Theologie und Kirche. Das Zweite Vatikanische Konzil: Konstitutionen, Dekrete und Erklärungen, lateinisch und deutsch. Edited by Herbert Vorgrimler. 3 vols. Freiburg: Herder, 1966-68.

Lohse, Bernhard. *Epochen der Dogmengeschichte*. Stuttgart: Kreuz-Verlag, 1963.

Loofs, Friedrich. *Leitfaden zum Studium der Dogmengeschichte.* Edited by Kurt Aland. 6th ed. Tübingen: Niemeyer, 1959.

Lorenz, Rudolf. "Zwölf Jahre Augustinusforschung (1959-1970)," *Theologische Rundschau*, XL (1975), 1-41.

Lukken, G. M. *Original Sin in the Roman Liturgy.* Leiden: Brill, 1973.

Lyonnet, St. "Le sens de *eph hoi* en Rom 5:12 et l'exégèse des Pères grecs," *Biblica*, XXXVI (1955), 436-56.

McCool, Gerald A. "The Philosophy of the Human Person in Karl Rahner's Theology," *Theological Studies*, XXII (1961), 537-62.

Mekkes, J. P. A. *Radix, tijd en kennen: Proeve ener critiek van de belevingssubjectiviteit.* ("Christelijk Perspectief," 17.) Amsterdam: Buijten en Schipperheijn, 1971.

Menninger, Karl. *Whatever Became of Sin?* New York: Hawthorn, 1973.

Meuleman, G. E. "Natuur en genade," in *Protestantse verkenningen na Vaticanum II* (H. Berkhof, *et al.*; 's-Gravenhage: Boekencentrum, 1967), 65-89.

Michel, M. "Le péché originel, question herméneutique," *Revue des Sciences Religieuses*, XLVIII (1974), 113-35.

Muck, Otto. *Die transzendentale Methode in der scholastischen Philosophie der Gegenwart.* Innsbruck: Felizian Rauch, 1964.
Trans.: *The Transcendental Method.* Translated by William D. Seidensticker. New York: Herder and Herder, 1968.

Mysterium Salutis: Grundriss einer heilsgeschichtlichen Dogmatik. Edited by J. Feiner and M. Löhrer. Einsiedeln: Benziger, 1965–.

Niebuhr, Reinhold. *The Nature and Destiny of Man.* Vol. I: *Human Nature.* New York: Scribners, 1964.

De nieuwe katechismus: Geloofsverkondiging voor volwassenen. In opdracht van de bisschoppen van Nederland. Hilversum: Paul Brand, 1966.
Trans.: *A New Catechism: Catholic Faith for Adults.* Translated by Kevin Smyth. London: Burns and Oates, 1967.

Patrologia Latina. Edited by J. P. Migne. Paris: Garnier Fratres et J. P. Migne Successores, 1944–.

Paul VI. "Address to Conference of Theologians Discussing Original Sin," *The Pope Speaks*, XI (1966), 229-35 (= *Acta Apostolicae Sedis*, LVIII [1966], 649-55).

——— "Credo" (*Sollemnis professio fidei*). *The Pope Speaks*, XIII (1968), 273-82 (= *Acta Apostolicae Sedis*, LX [1968], 433-45).

Peters, John A. *Metaphysics: A Systematic Survey.* Translated by Henry J. Koren. ("Duquesne Studies, Philosophical Series," 16.) Pittsburgh, Pa.: Duquesne University Press, 1963.

Polman, A. D. R. *Onze Nederlandsche Geloofsbelijdenis.* Vol. II. Franeker: Wever, n.d.

Rahner, Karl. "Anonymer und expliziter Glaube," *Stimmen der Zeit,* CXCII (1974), 147-52.

——— "Bemerkungen zum Begriff Offenbarung," in *Offenbarung und Überlieferung,* by Karl Rahner and Joseph Ratzinger ("Quaestiones Disputatae," 25; Freiburg: Herder, 1965), 11-24.

——— "Der dreifaltige Gott als transzendenter Urgrund der Heilsgeschichte," *Mysterium Salutis,* II, 317-401.

——— *Das Dynamische in der Kirche.* ("Quaestiones Disputatae," 5.) Freiburg: Herder, 1958.

——— "Erbsünde," *Sacramentum Mundi,* I, 1104-1117.

——— "Erbsünde und Evolution," *Concilium,* III (1967), 458-65.

——— "(Exkurs:) Erbsünde und Monogenismus," in *Theologie der Erbsünde,* (by Karl-Heinz Weger), 176-223.

——— "Erlösungswirklichkeit in der Schöpfungswirklichkeit," in *Sendung und Gnade: Beiträge zur Pastoraltheologie* (Innsbruck: Tyrolia-Verlag, 1959), 51-88.

——— "Die Frage nach dem Erscheinungsbild des Menschen als Quaestio disputata der Theologie," in *Um das Erscheinungsbild der ersten Menschen,* by Paul Overhage ("Quaestiones Disputatae," 7; Freiburg: Herder, 1959), 11-30.

——— *Geist in Welt: Zur Metaphysik der endlichen Erkenntnis bei Thomas von Aquin.* 2e Auflage im Auftrag des Verfassers überarbeitet und ergänzt von Johannes Baptist Metz. München: Kösel-Verlag, 1957.

——— *Gnade als Freiheit: Kleine theologische Beiträge.* Freiburg: Herder, 1968.

——— "Grundsätzliche Überlegungen zur Anthropologie und Protologie im Rahmen der Theologie," *Mysterium Salutis,* II, 406-20.

——— "Die Hominisation als theologische Frage," in *Das Problem der Hominisation,* by Paul Overhage and Karl Rahner ("Quaestiones Disputatae," 12/13; Freiburg: Herder, 1961), 13-90.

——— *Hörer des Wortes: Zur Grundlegung einer Religionsphilosophie.* Neu bearbeitet von Johannes Baptist Metz. München: Kösel-Verlag, 1963.

――― *Kirche und Sakramente.* ("Quaestiones Disputatae," 10.) Freiburg: Herder, 1960.

――― "Kirchliche und ausserkirchliche Religiosität," *Stimmen der Zeit,* XCXII (1973), 3-13.

――― "Original Sin," *Sacramentum Mundi,* IV (New York: Herder and Herder, 1969), 328-34.

――― *Schriften zur Theologie.* 11 Vols. Einsiedeln: Benziger, 1954-73.

――― *Sendung und Gnade: Beiträge zur Pastoraltheologie.* Innsbruck: Tyrolia-Verlag, 1959.

――― *Strukturwandel der Kirche als Aufgabe und Chance.* Freiburg: Herder, 1972.

――― (ed.). *Zum Problem Unfehlbarkeit: Antworten auf die Anfrage von Hans Kung.* ("Quaestiones Disputatate," 54.) Freiburg: Herder, 1971.

――― *Zur Lage der Theologie: Probleme nach dem Konzil. Karl Rahner antwortet Eberhard Simons.* ("Das Theologische Interview," 1.) Düsseldorf: Patmos-Verlag, 1969.

――― *Zur Theologie des Todes.* ("Quaestiones Disputatae," 2.) Freiburg: Herder, 1958.

Rasker, A. J., et al. *Problemen rondom de schuld.* (Een publicatie van het Nederlands Gesprek Centrum.) Baarn: Bosch en Keuning, 1973.

Reese, J. M. "Current Thinking on Original Sin," *The American Ecclesiastical Review,* CLVII (1967), 92-100.

Ricoeur, Paul. *Finitude et culpabilité.* Vol. II: *La symbolique du mal.* Paris: Aubier, 1960.

――― "Le 'Péché originel': étude de signification," *Le Conflit des interprétations: Essais d'herméneutique.* Paris: Editions du Seuil, 1969.

Robinson, James M. and Cobb, John B., Jr. (eds.) *New Frontiers in Theology: Discussions among German and American Theologians.* Vol. I: *The Later Heidegger and Theology.* New York: Harper and Row, 1963.

Rondet, Henri. *Essais sur la théologie de la grâce.* Paris: Beauchesne, 1964.

――― *Gratia Christi: Essai d'histoire du dogme et de théologie dogmatique.* ("Verbum Salutis.") Paris: Beauchesne, 1948.

――― *Le péché originel dans la tradition patristique et théologique.* Paris: Fayard, 1967.

Sacramentum Mundi: Theologisches Lexikon für die Praxis. 4 vols. Edited by Karl Rahner and A. Darlap. Freiburg: Herder, 1968-69.

Trans.: *Sacramentum Mundi: An Encyclopedia of Sacred Theology.*
New York: Herder and Herder, 1968-70.

Scheffczyk, Leo (ed.). *Der Mensch als Bild Gottes.* Darmstadt: Wissenschaftliche Buchgesellschaft, 1969.

――― "Versuche zur Neuaussprache der Erbschuld-Wahrheit," *Münchener Theologische Zeitschrift,* XVII (1966), 253-60.

Schelke, K. H. *Paulus Lehrer der Väter: Die altkirchliche Auslegung von Römer 1-11.* Düsseldorf: Patmos-Verlag, 1956.

――― *Schuld als Erbteil?* ("Theologische Meditationen," 20.) Einsiedeln: Benziger, 1968.

Schemata Constitutionum et Decretorum de quibus disceptabitur in Concilii sessionibus. Series Prima. Rome: Typis Polyglottis Vaticanis, 1962.

Schillebeeckx, E. *Theologische peilingen.* Vol. I: *Openbaring en theologie.* Bilthoven: Nelissen, 1964.

Schmaus, Michael. *Katholische Dogmatik.* Vol. II/1. 5th ed. München: Max Hueber, 1954.

Schmid, R., Ruckstuhl, E., and Vorgrimler, H. *Unheilstat und Erbschuld der Menschheit: Das Problem der Erbsünde.* Luzern: Rex, 1969.

Schmitz-Moormann, Karl. *Die Erbsünde: Überholte Vorstellung, bleibender Glaube.* Olten: Walter-Verlag, 1969.

Schoof, T. M. *Aggiornamento: De doorbraak van een nieuwe katholieke theologie.* ("Theologische Monografieën.") Baarn: Wereldvenster, 1968.
Trans.: *Breakthrough: Beginnings of the New Catholic Theology.* Translated by N. D. Smith. Dublin: Gill and Macmillan, 1970.

Schoonenberg, P. "Aantekeningen over natuur en genade," in *Katholicisme en geestelijke vrijheid: Bijdragen tot een gedachtewisseling.* (Utrecht: Het Spectrum, 1951), 13-29.

――― "Altes Testament, Neues Testament und Erbsündenlehre," *Theologisch-praktische Quartalschrift,* CXVII (1969), 115-24.

――― *Covenant and Creation.* Translated by Peter Tomlinson. London: Sheed and Ward, 1968.

――― "Einige Bemerkungen zur gegenwärtigen Diskussion über die Erbsünde," *International Documentation on the Conciliar Church,* 68-4 (January 28, 1968).
Trans.: "Some Remarks on the Present Discussion of Original Sin," *International Documentation on the Conciliar Church,* 68-4 (January 28, 1968).

——— "Erfzonde," *Documentatie Centrum Concilie,* 63-44 and -45 (March, 1963).

——— "Erfzonde als situatie," *Bijdragen,* XXII (1961), 1-30.

——— "Erfzonde en 'zonde der wereld,'" *Nederlandse Katholieke Stemmen,* LVIII (1962), 69-78.
Trans.: "Erbsünde und 'Sünde der Welt,'" *Orientierung,* XXVI (1962), 65-69.

——— "Feit en gebeuren: Eenvoudige hermeneutische beschouwingen bij enkele in discussie staande vragen," *Tijdschrift voor Theologie,* VIII (1968), 22-42.
Trans.: "Ereignis und Geschehen: Einfache hermeneutische Überlegungen zu einigen gegenwärtig diskutierten Fragen," *Zeitschrift für katholische Theologie,* XC (1968), 1-21.
"Event and Happening: Hermeneutical Reflections on Some Contemporary Disputed Questions," *Theology Digest,* XVII (1969), 196-202.

——— "Gedanken über die Kindertaufe," *Theologisch-praktische Quartalschrift,* CXIV (1969), 230-39.

——— *Het geloof van ons doopsel.* 4 vols. 's-Hertogenbosch: Malmberg, 1955-62.
Trans.: *Covenant and Creation* includes translated sections of vol. I and II.
Man and Sin is a translation and revision of vol. IV.

——— "Genade en natuurlijke Godsliefde," *Werkgenootschap van Katholieke Theologen in Nederland, Jaarboek, 1959,* 19-37.

——— "De genade en de zedelijke goede act," *Werkgenootschap van Katholieke Theologen in Nederland, Jaarboek, 1950,* 203-53.

——— "Geschichtlichkeit und Interpretation des Dogmas," in *Die Interpretation des Dogmas* (ed. P. Schoonenberg; Düsseldorf: Patmos-Verlag, 1969), 58-110.

——— "Gesprek over de erfzonde," in *Ex Auditu Verbi: Theologische opstellen aangeboden aan Prof. Dr. G. C. Berkouwer* (ed. J. T. Bakker, et. al.; Kampen: Kok, 1965), 258-71.

——— *God of mens: Een vals dilemma.* 's-Hertogenbosch: Malmberg, 1965.

——— *Gods wordende wereld: Vijf theologische essays.* ("Woord en Beleving," 15.) Tielt: Lannoo, 1962.
Trans.: *God's World in the Making.* Translated by Walter VanDe Putte. 2d ed. Dublin: Gill and Son, 1968.

——— "Heilsgeschichte und Dialog," *Theologisch-praktische Quartalschrift,* CXV (1967), 123-38.

——— "Das hermeneutische Problem," in *Die Antwort der Theologen* (Düsseldorf: Patmos-Verlag, 1968), 35-41.

——— *Hij is een God van de mensen: Twee theologische studies.* 's-Hertogenbosch: Malmberg, 1969.
Trans.: *The Christ: A Study of the God-Man Relationship in the Whole of Creation and in Jesus Christ.* Translated by Della Couling. New York: Herder and Herder, 1971.

——— "Historiciteit en interpretatie van het dogma," *Tijdschrift voor Theologie,* VIII (1968), 278-311.

——— *Man and Sin: A Theological View.* Translated by Joseph Donceel. London: Sheed and Ward, 1965.

——— Der Mensch in der Sünde," *Mysterium Salutis,* II, 845-941.

——— "Mysterium Iniquitatis: Ein Versuch über die Erbsünde," *Wort und Wahrheit,* XXI (1966), 577-91.

——— "Natuur en zondeval," *Tijdschrift voor Theologie,* II (1962), 173-201.

——— "Sünde der Welt," *Theologie der Gegenwart,* V (1962), 159-64.

——— "Sünde–Sakrament–Jugendalter: Einige theologische Bemerkungen," in *Einübung des Glaubens* (ed. Günter Stachel and Alois Zenner; Würzburg: Echter-Verlag, 1965), 97-111.

——— "Sünde und Schuld," *Sacramentum Mundi,* IV, 766-79.

——— "De tekst van de Commissie Dhanis-Fortmann-Visser over de erfzonde," in *Witboek* (ed. W. Bless), 255-73.

——— "Testcase erfzonde," *De Nieuwe Mens,* XIX (1967-68), 194-205.
Trans.: "Theologie und Lehramt: Hermeneutik am Beispiel der Erbsünde-Diskussion," *Wort und Wahrheit,* XXII (1967), 737-46.

——— Theologie als kritische Prophetie," in *Die Funktion der Theologie in Kirche und Gesellschaft: Beiträge zu einer notwendigen Diskussion* (ed. Paul Neuenzeit; München: Kösel-Verlag, 1969), 371-85.

——— *Theologie der Sünde: Ein theologischer Versuch.* Einsiedeln: Benziger, 1966.

——— "Theologie in zelfbezinning," *Annalen van het Thijmgenootschap,* XLIV (1956), 225-36.

——— "Theologische Fragen zur Kindertaufe," in *Christsein ohne Entscheidung oder soll die Kirche Kinder taufen?* (ed. Walter Kasper, Mainz: Matthias-Grünewald-Verlag, 1970), 108-28.

––– and Bruna, M. "Tweegesprek over het ontstaan der zondigheid," *Tijdschrift voor Theologie*, IV (1964), 54-79.

––– "Zonde der wereld en erfzonde," *Bijdragen*, XXIV (1963), 349-89.

––– "Zonde en verlossing als grondsituaties van het mensdom," *Annalen van het Thijmgenootschap*, XLVIII (1960), 136-51.

Schrofner, E. "Theologie der Erbsünde mit und ohne Fragezeichen," *Zeitschrift für katholische Theologie*, XCIII (1971), 200-209.

Schupp, F. "Die Geschichtsauffassung am Beginn der Tübinger Schule und in der gegenwärtigen Theologie," *Zeitschrift für katholische Theologie*, XCI (1969), 150-71.

Seybold, Michael. "Erbsünde und Sünde der Welt," *Münchener Theologische Zeitschrift*, XXVIII (1967), 56-60.

Simonis, Walter. "Heilsnotwendigkeit der Kirche und Erbsünde bei Augustinus: Eine dogmengeschichtlicher Beitrag zur Klärung zweier Fragen der gegenwärtigen theologischen Diskussion," *Theologie und Philosophie*, XLIII (1968), 481-502.

Simons, Eberhard. *Philosophie der Offenbarung: Auseinandersetzung mit Karl Rahner*. Stuttgart: Kohlhammer, 1966.

Smit, M. C. *Cultuur en heil*. Published by "de Oratorische Vereniging A.G.O.R.A. van het Studentencorps aan de Vrije Universiteit," 1959.

––– *De verhouding van Christendom en historie in de huidige roomskatholieke geschiedbeschouwing*. Kampen: Kok, 1950.

Smith, Roger W. (ed.) *Guilt, Man and Society*. Garden City, N.Y.: Doubleday, 1971.

Smulders, P. "Het Sacrament als Geloofsdaad," in *Geloof bij kenterend getij* (ed. H. Van Der Linde and H. A. M. Fiolet; Roermond: J. J. Romen en Zonen, 1967), 320-37.

––– *Het visioen van Teilhard de Chardin: Poging tot theologische waardering*. 5th ed. revised. Brugge: Desclée de Brouwer, 1966.

Trans.: *La vision de Teilhard de Chardin: Essai de réflection théologique*. Translated by Augustin Kerkvoorde and Christian d'Armagnac (from the 3d Dutch edition). 2d ed. revised. Paris: Desclée de Brouwer, 1965.

The Design of Teilhard de Chardin: An Essay in Theological Reflection. Translated by Arthur Gibson (from the above French translation). Westminster, Md.: Newman Press, 1967.

Spindeler, Alois. "Das Tridentinum und die neueren Erklärungsversuche zur Erbsündenlehre," *Münchener theologische Zeitschrift*, XIX (1968), 92-101.

Stakemeier, Eduard. *Der Kampf um Augustin auf dem Tridentinum.* Paderborn: Bonifacius-Druckerei, 1937.

Stenzel, Alois. "Zur Geschichte des Erbsündendogmas," *Scholastik,* XXXIX (1964), 407-12.

——— Review of *Theologie der Erbsünde* by Weger, and of *Erbsünde?* by Baumann, *Theologie und Philosophie,* XLVI (1971), 557-63.

Stuhlmueller, Carrol. "Repentance for Original Sin and Reconciliation in Christ," *International Catholic Review: Communio,* I (1974), 20-46.

The Supplement to A New Catechism. Ed. Dhanis and J. Visser, on behalf of the Commission of Cardinals appointed to examine *A New Catechism.* Translated by Kevin Smyth. London: Burns and Oates, 1969.

Tennant, F. R. *The Sources of the Doctrines of the Fall and Original Sin.* 2d ed. New York: Schocken Books, 1968.

Trooster, S. *Evolutie in de erfzondeleer.* Brugge: Desclée de Brouwer, 1965.

Van Bavel, T. "God absorbeert niet: De christologie van Schoonenberg," *Tijdschrift voor Theologie,* XI (1971), 383-412.

Van Der Heijden, Bert. *Karl Rahner: Darstellung und Kritik seiner Grundpositionen.* Einsiedeln: Johannes Verlag, 1973.

Vanneste, A. "Le Décret du Concile de Trente sur le péché originel," *Nouvelle Revue Théologique,* LXXXVII (1965), 688-726; LXXXVIII (1966), 581-602.

——— *Het dogma van de erfzonde: Zinloze mythe of openbaring van een grondstructuur van het menselijk bestaan?* Tielt: Lannoo, 1969.

——— "Le dogme de l'immaculée conception et l'evolution actuelle de la théologie du péché originel," *Ephemerides Mariologicae,* XXIII (1973), 77-93.

——— "De erfzonde: Repliek op vragen en moeilijkheden," *Bijdragen,* XXXIII (1972), 152-75.

——— "L'histoire du dogme du péché originel," *Ephemerides Theologicae Lovanienses,* XXXVIII (1962), 895-903.

——— "Is de erfzonde een historische zonde?" *Collationes Brugenses et Gandavenses,* XIV (1968), 289-321.

——— "La préhistoire du décret du Concile de Trente sur le péché originel," *Nouvelle Revue Théologique,* LXXXVI (1964), 355-68, 490-510.

——— "Saint Paul et la doctrine augustinienne du péché originel," in *Studiorum Paulinorum Congressus Internationalis Catholicus 1961.* Vol. II. (Rome: Pontifical Biblical Institute, 1963), 513-22.

––– "De theologie van de erfzonde," *Collationes Brugenses et Gandavenses,* XII (1966), 289-312.

Van Roo, William, J. *Grace and Original Justice According to St. Thomas.* Rome: Apud Aedes Universitatis Gregorianae, 1955.

Verburg, J. *Adam: Een onderzoek naar de betekenis van de figuur van een eerste mens in het christelijk geloof.* Wageningen: Veenman, 1973.

Vorgrimler, Herbert. "Die Erbsünde in der katholischen Glaubenslehre," in *Unheilslast und Erbschuld der Menschheit: Das Problem der Erbsünde* by Rudolf Schmid *et al.* (Luzern: Rex-Verlag, 1969), 115-44.

––– *Karl Rahner.* Tielt: Lannoo, 1962.

Walgrave, J. H. Review of *Dogma,* by Vanneste, *Kultuurleven,* XXXVII (1970), 410-11.

Weger, Karl-Heinz. *Erbsünde heute: Grundlegung und Verkündigungshilfen.* München: Bosco, 1972.

––– "Erbsündentheologie heute: Situation, Probleme, Aufgaben," *Stimmen der Zeit,* CLXXXI (1968), 289-302.

––– "Strukturwandel in der katholischen Glaubenslehre: Gedanken zur Theologie des neuen holländischen Erwachsenenkatechismus," *Stimmen der Zeit,* CLXXIX (1967), 105-15.

––– *Theologie der Erbsünde.* ("Questiones Disputatae," 44.) Freiburg: Herder, 1970.

Weier, Reinhold. "Erbsünde und Sünde der Welt: Probleme der Erbsündenlehre Piet Schoonenbergs und Teilhards de Chardin," *Trierer Theologische Zeitschrift,* LXXXII (1973), 154-71.

Weismayer, Josef. " 'Erbsünde' und Sündenverflochtenheit in der theologischen Tradition und in den lehramtlichen Aussagen," in *Ist Adam an allem schuld?* (Ferdinand Dexinger, *et al.*), 281-363.

Wentsel, B. *Natuur en genade: Een introductie in en confrontatie met de jongste ontwikkelingen in de rooms-katholieke theologie inzake dit thema.* Kampen: Kok, 1970.

Willaert, B. "Aantekeningen bij de erfzondeleer," *Collationes Brugenses et Gandavenses,* VI (1960), 498-519.

––– "De verkondiging van de erfzondeleer," *Collationes Brugenses et Gandavenses,* VII (1961), 166-81.

Williams, N. P. *The Ideas of the Fall and of Original Sin: A Historical and Critical Study.* London: Longmans, Green and Co. Ltd., 1927.

The Papal Encyclicals in Their Historical Context. Edited by Anne Fremantle. New York: The New American Library, 1956.

Yagi, Dickson Kazuo. *The Problem of Original Sin in Twentieth Century Theology.* Ann Arbor, Mich.: University Microfilms, 1972.

Zuidema, S. U. "Kontemporain situationisme," *Philosophia Reformata,* XXIII (1958), 22-30, 85-94.

    Trans.: "Contemporary Situationism in John Dewey and Martin Heidegger: A Comparison," in *Communication and Confrontation: A Philosophical Appraisal and Critique of Modern Society and Contemporary Thought* ([essays by S. U. Zuidema]; Toronto: Wedge, 1972), 190-214.